Cabbages and Kings

ALSO BY JAMES SLOAN ALLEN

The Romance of Commerce and Culture: Capitalism, Modernism, and the Chicago-Aspen Crusade for Cultural Reform

Worldly Wisdom: Great Books and the Meanings of Life

William James on Habit, Will, Truth, and the Meaning of Life (editor)

Aloha: The Surprising History of an Idea and a Culture

Life Line: A Novel of Romance and Rebirth

Dreamers, Runaways, and Mysteries: A Traveler's Tales and Essays

Cabbages and Kings
TO TALK OF MANY THINGS

Of Style and Humanism, Politics and Culture,
Literature, Laughter, and the Meaning of Life

Second Edition

James Sloan Allen

Copyright © 2022, 2023 by James Sloan Allen
All rights reserved. No part of this book may be reproduced or retransmitted in any form or by any means without the written consent of the author.

Note on Second Edition: This second edition incorporates some minor revisions and a couple of substantive additions clarifying points in the Proust essay "As Time Goes By" and in the dialogue on "The Meaning of Life."

ISBN: 978-1-7349787-2-8
E-ISBN: 978-1-7349787-3-5

Cover image based on René Magritte's 1964 painting *The Son of Man*.

Cover and interior book design by Rachel Davis Mariano.

To the life of ideas,
and to the loving memory of Elizabeth,
my wife from the origins of this book almost to its end.

Contents

Acknowledgments ix
Prefatory Note xi

I. ON STYLE & THE GOOD LIFE 1

1. Style in Art, Character, and Culture 3
2. The Arts of the Dining Room 11
3. Remembrance of Restaurants Past 21

STYLES OF HOSPITALITY 27

    4. Isn't It Romantic? 29
    5. Theater of Tranquility 35
    6. Starck's Swan Song: With a Note on Feng Shui at Felix 41
    7. Elegant Utility 47

8. *Mrs. Dalloway* and the Ethics of Civility 51
9. Nietzsche and Wilde: Cultural Rebellion and an Ethics of Style 65

II. ON THE POLITICAL LIFE 85

10. Notes on Liberalism and Conservatism with a Comment on Political Correctness and the Rights of Civility 87
11. Orwell, Mind Control, and Our Times 101
12. A Wartime Tragedy and a Teacher Who Would Not Let It Be Lost 111
13. Notes on Islam, America, and Human Rights with a Few Words on Good Soldiers in the War of Ideas 121
14. A Stranger to Power: On the Separation of Church and State 131

III. ON MODERNITY & MODERNISM	157
15. What Was Modernism?	159
16. Modernity, Modernism, and the Evil of Banality	173
17. Self-Consciousness and the Modernist Temper	199
18. More Emma than Nora: A Victorian/Marxist/Modernist Melodrama	225
19. Sigmund Freud: Bourgeois Modernist	235
20. Tolstoy's *fin de siècle* and Ours: From Decadence to Postmodernism	249
21. *Fin-de-siècle* America and the Twilight of Culture	275
IV. ON HUMANISM, CLASSICS, LAUGHTER, PROUST, & THE MEANING OF LIFE	293
22. How Humanists Have Betrayed Humanism	295
23. The Humanities and Their Discontents	301
24. The Existential Reader: Reading, Rumination, and the Classics	315
25. The Classics: Casebooks of Humanistic Education	329
26. Let 'em Laugh: *Tristram Shandy* and the Humanity of Laughter	337
27. As Time Goes By: On Reading Proust and Finding the Magic Sand	357
28. Thinking about the Meaning of Life: A Dialogue	408
Index	447

"The time has come," the Walrus said,
"To talk of many things:
Of shoes—and ships—and sealing-wax—
Of cabbages—and kings—
And why the sea is boiling hot—
And whether pigs have wings."

—Lewis Carroll,
"The Walrus and the Carpenter,"
Through the Looking-Glass

Acknowledgments

Since the essays here were written over a span of four decades, I have forgotten most of the people who lent a hand in their composition. Actually, there were not many such people, for the essays materialized mainly from my own Shandean curiosity and intermittent labors. Still, I would like to acknowledge that the short essays on restaurant design would not have materialized without the imaginative editorial leadership of Louis Postel, who sportingly invited me to contribute to his magazine, *Design Times*. Likewise, Neeru Nanda, editor of *Interiors and Lifestyles India*, invited me to contribute to that magazine and to the collection of essays based on it. Imaginative editors are a gift.

I have included in the text a special acknowledgement to my learned friend Stan Burnett for critically reading the essay on Marcel Proust, but I might also note here his patient criticism of an early draft of the meandering dialogue that concludes this volume. He and other intellectually curious friends and loved ones, among them my longstanding companion of mind and *esprit*, Tom Thompson, are the kinds of readers all authors wish to have.

Finally, this book would not have seen the light, and certainly not with the visual style it has, but for the creative and patient professionalism of Rachel Davis, who designed it, added artfulness to the illustrations, proofread it, and saw the whole thing through the press. And she made the production fun from start to finish. I owe her many debts.

Prefatory Note

As the title suggests, these essays range across a wide territory. This territory contains such diverse topics as restaurant design, the ethics of style and civility, the war of ideas between Islam and the West, a World War II Japanese detention camp, the relation of church and state, modern self-consciousness, the bourgeois Modernism of Karl Marx's daughter and of Sigmund Freud, the *fin de siècle* of the nineteenth and twentieth centuries, the humanity of laughter, and the meaning of life. But I have arranged them all into four general categories: Style and the Good Life; the Political Life; Modernity and Modernism; and Humanism, Classics, Laughter, Proust, and the Meaning of Life.

Most of the essays originally appeared in a variety of publications, including some academic journals and a couple of books, as well as *The Wall Street Journal*, *Design Times*, *The Nation*, *The New Republic*, and *The Christian Science Monitor*. I have identified those sources at the end of each entry. Others have remained unpublished until now. The length of the pieces fit their origins. Several are vignettes, others are lengthy articles or essays, and one is an extended dialogue; others still are review-essays revolving around then recently published books. Hence, the pieces vary somewhat in tone as well as in subject and length.

Although I have revised every entry to some extent from its original form, I have done as little as necessary and have not tried to weave them all tightly together or to efface all traces of their origins. That said, they do have some common themes discernible from beginning to end. In all, even though this is a collection of writings on many things, it is also a kind of rambling—I might almost say 'Shandean," in the sense of Laurence Sterne's *Tristram Shandy*, the subject of one entry—discourse on some ideas that to me outline, if not define, the humanistic way of life.

I.

ON STYLE & THE GOOD LIFE

The entries here consist of seven vignettes and two substantial essays. The first of the vignettes describes the character and importance of style in art and life. The next six all deal with style and dining. The first treats the essential purpose and some possible design features of the dining room at home. The rest look mainly at restaurants. The second tells the origins of the "restaurant" and some of its history as seen in the restaurant museum of the oldest restaurant in Paris, La Tour d'Argent. The four others, under the heading "Styles of Hospitality," briefly describe the "modern" designs and their effects of two hotels and their restaurants in New York and of two restaurants fashioned for distinct purposes by renowned figures, Philippe Starck in Hong Kong and the architect Richard Rogers in London. The two substantive essays that follow treat the idea of style more broadly and philosophically. The first explores the arts of civility as exemplified in the novel *Mrs. Dalloway* by Virginia Woolf; the second examines the principles of style as ethics in the allied writings of Friedrich Nietzsche and Oscar Wilde.

Style is a bridge between art and life.

Style in Art, Character, and Culture

Every culture has performing artists, be they ritual dancers, fireside singers, fable spinners, or professionals of the stage, screen, and concert hall. But not every performer is an artist. We all perform every time we speak or gesture or put on a suit of clothes. We might think of this as playing roles in life no less than in art—the roles of social, political, and cultural interactions. But let us not allow this idea to imply superficiality or deception or diminish the importance to us of playing our roles well. For we could say that culture depends on performance, since culture thrives on the calculated presentation of appearances that enable us to communicate more than words can convey. And a good performance, whether in the arts or in life, has powerful effects on us. It yields many kinds of pleasures and even enlightenment. It can also help us to share feelings and understandings, experience admiration and affection, and appreciate the delights of form—is that not why human beings created manners? If we ask what makes a good performance in art and life possible, what gives a person's actions, words, or any kind of appearance the power to move us so, I think we will not be wrong to say it has something to do with the distinctive quality that we know, in a much-abused word, as *style*.

By style I do not mean historical style like Classicism, Romanticism, Modernism, nor do I mean mere fad or fashion or that other modish vulgarity "lifestyle," a term coined in the sixties to denote merely how one spends one's time or money. I mean rather that near-magical touch of artful individuality that elevates almost anything one does above the routine, the commonplace, or even the respectable—it is the musician who sings or plays with the sensibility of a lover, the precision of a diamond cutter, and the verve of an acrobat; the dancer who leaps higher, soars farther, and lands right on a dime; the poet who finds the perfect word for every feeling; the friend who finds the perfect gift for every festive day and hidden wish; the gentleman whose winning manners are as warm as summer and as easy as air; the hostess who charms her guests into feeling they are themselves charming. The likes of these are not just studied performances, they are performances with style.

Yet there is more to style than well-wrought appearances. For there must be something within the performer, some attributes of character, that make style possible. And when we look for these attributes, I think we discover that they are two, bound together. These are imagination and will or discipline. For only when we have the imagination to envision artful forms of individuality, such as beauty, charm, grace, elegance, and wit, and the will to impose those forms on our performance, on ourselves, do we achieve true style.

Artists might reflect more often on performance and style than most people, since they deal with them directly every day. But everyone can be an artist of personal style. Style is a bridge joining art and life, a bridge that everyone should travel, artists and non-artists alike. Unfortunately, many people seem to doubt the trip is worthwhile. Some may doubt it from ignorance of the uses of art and style in life; others may doubt it because they consider art and style to be above life. Some of these doubts remind me of a certain deliciously decadent character in an emblematic play of the 1890s who waves away the prospect of living a beautiful life beyond the confines of his castle walls with the sigh: "Live? Our servants will do that for us."

It is a good line, but it is bad philosophy. We would do better to heed the words of the peerless German poet Goethe who said not long before he died at age eighty-two: "The older I get, the more convinced I become that the purpose of life is life itself; the purpose of life is to live." And he would not mind if we added the

1. STYLE IN ART, CHARACTER, AND CULTURE

note that to live fully one must live with style. He would not mind because he often spoke of style as not only a quality of art but of mind. Just as had the influential eighteenth-century scientist and author Comte de Buffon when he memorably declared, "Style is the man himself," meaning, an artful style of expression arises from an artful style of mind. The discipline of style lets art serve life by shaping mind and character.

The philosopher Friedrich Nietzsche, much devoted to Goethe, penned probably the strongest statement on this subject ever written. "One thing is needful," Nietzsche wrote: "Giving style to one's character—a great and a rare art! It is exercised by those who see all the strengths and weaknesses of their own characters and then comprehend them in an artistic plan until everything appears as art and reason and even weakness delights the eye." For only through "the constraint of style" can a "human being attain satisfaction with himself."

These are good lines and good philosophy. For they reveal how necessary style is to the well-lived life; and they do this by pointing both to the origins of style, in imagination and will, and to its ends in the joy of living and satisfaction with oneself. Let us not deceive ourselves; without this joy and, above all, this satisfaction, we suffer, either obviously in depression and anxiety, or secretly under the masks of escape or compensating behavior often hurtful to others. But with this joy and satisfaction, we experience, as if through a gift of nature, an enlarged appetite for life, a new confidence in our will, a higher respect for achievement, a keener pleasure in the necessary performances we give, and a stronger admiration for style itself and for those who exemplify it.

With this vision of style in mind, we can see how culture itself is a celebration of style as represented by the imaginative inventions and disciplined labors of artists, by the gracious manners and ubiquitous role-playing of social life, by the success of leaders with flair, and by the pleasure and confidence aroused by good performances

I. On Style and the Good Life

of any kind. In this celebration then lies the final truth about style that I will remark. It is that style, or the want of it, can shape institutions and cultures no less than it can shape art and character.

What would we say of the place of style in American culture at large today? Does this culture encourage the marriage of imagination and will? Does it prize the constraints of artful form? Does it bring growing delight and satisfaction with ourselves? Such questions come to mind when, for example, I attend the Metropolitan Opera and see ever more of the audience dressed like the fans at Yankee Stadium in shabby jeans and running shoes; when college students choose to look like hobos in the halls of Higher Learning; when strangers address me and demand that I address them by the first name only, as though we had known each other for years; when language once reserved for the locker room casually punctuates everyday conversation, and on and on.

Now, there is much to be said for such advances in the democracy of manners—we win liberation from hidebound rules and antiquated prejudices and gain physical comfort, psychological ease, spontaneity of behavior, and a heightened feeling of human equality. But these gains come at a cost, and this cost can be very high indeed. For when, to continue the examples, we allow ourselves to wear the same clothing and use the same coarse or casual language everywhere and at all times, we not only free ourselves from old rules and prejudices, we also risk making every social and cultural experience the same. Attending the opera becomes not so very different from going to a baseball game; friends and strangers claim an equal familiarity; and the locker room and the dining room resound with a single form of speech. My point is not to reproach ease and familiarity. They are as necessary to the life of style as are restraint and formality. The point is rather to stress the relation to style of what we might call *appropriateness*. An inappropriate performance, however well-executed, whether in the theater or in life, betrays a lack of style no less than does an inept performance. Evening dress at the baseball park can be as inappropriate as shabby jeans at the

1. Style in Art, Character, and Culture

opera, even if not as flagrant—although, to be fair, I suppose one could wear black tie to the ballpark as a bold statement of style. In the making of personal style, the marriage of imagination and will should therefore be accompanied by a sense of appropriateness, which some might think of as tact. Only when we embody the discipline of style in these ways can we impede the dissolution of standards of behavior that threatens to dull our lives.

This creeping sameness is bad enough in itself, but it is not the worst consequence of dissolving all distinctions of performance in our social and cultural lives. For once we have eliminated these distinctions, we cannot avoid giving up much more, namely, all the psychological and moral strengths that those distinctions, artificial as some may be, have provided us. This means we will lose first the desire, then the willingness, and finally the very ability to rise to the kinds of experiences that demand more of us than comfort, ease, spontaneity, lackluster conformity, or careless nonconformity. That is, we lose the ability to rise to the kinds of experiences that demand the best of us, and what I have been calling style.

Such a loss is regrettable in individuals because it dims the imagination and enfeebles the will and so thwarts our lives. But in a culture this loss is tragic because it causes the public imagination and will to atrophy, the esteem for true individuality and excellence to fade, and the spirit of affirmation and joy to drain away into easy and banal self-indulgence; and then instead of being a source of collective pride and diverse pleasures, culture becomes a bleak landscape of fleeting excitements, numbing monotony, agitated boredom, restless resentments, and chronic discontent. And down that road lies the very death of culture.

It is then, for no less a reason than to prevent, or at least to retard, our travel down this road, that we should contemplate the uses of style in art, character, and culture. Having style will not, of course, protect us, individually or collectively, from inadequacies and frustrations. But one thing is certain: if we have the imagination and will to impose style on our lives and our culture, then whatever those inadequacies or frustrations we cannot fail to gain the bracing confidence, the affirming delight, and the proud satisfactions that define the well-lived life and breathe energy into culture. (For more on the principles of style, see "*Mrs. Dalloway* and the Ethics of Civility" and "Nietzsche and Wilde: Cultural Rebellion and an Ethics of Style" below.)

A version of this essay was originally presented as the commencement address at the Manhattan School of Music in 1982, and a subsequent version appeared in *The Wall Street Journal*, November 26, 1982.

Victorian dining room, c. 1850s.

The gentle arts of the dining room are a formula for savoir faire in a gracious style of life.

The Arts of the Dining Room

One form of style in life resides in the arts of the dining room. The dining room is not just a place for eating. It plays a more central role in the home than that. We could think of it as the heart of the home. It is the one place in the house that brings families and friends together around a table not only to dine but to talk. It is a place for kith and kin to spend time in genial conversation over good food and drink, for teaching and learning gracious manners and the arts of conversation, for celebrating traditions and forging social bonds, for family festivities and candlelit romance. We could say that the dining room is where nature and culture meet to nurture civilization.

The dining room may have a formal setting with a glittering chandelier, silver flatware, damask napery, gilt-edged china, and pinging crystal. Or it might have a more casual ambiance with homey furnishings and everyday tableware. It might even share its space with the kitchen in an open floor plan. Whatever its material and visual style, it has indispensable social, intellectual, and psychological roles to play. And people who do not experience those roles pay a price in a diminished life.

The dining room as we know it is a creation of modern times, if we let "modern" take us back to the Renaissance. It came into existence with the age of domesticity and privacy that, in the West, started about five centuries ago. Before that time, historians tell us, the Greeks and Romans had separate dining rooms for men and women, but these were quite public affairs. Later, in Europe, palaces and great houses had banquet halls for large gatherings of

I. On Style and the Good Life

nobles, but no specific room was set aside for more intimate dining; that took place in bedrooms, antechambers, or hallways. In lesser dwellings dining occurred in the same room as almost everything else. And dining implements for everyone, high and low, amounted to goblets, knives, spoons, clumps of bread, and hands.

With the arrival of the separate dining room came new standards of eating practices and social comportment among the privileged classes, mandating the use of more refined utensils—notably the fork—dining etiquette, and studied décor. These standards issued in an array of rules intended to lend grace and style especially to manners of the court—the very term "courtesy" derives from the proper deportment of the man of the court, the "courtier." With the invention of the printing press in the mid-fifteenth century books on these manners began to appear. A pioneer among these and a classic today, *The Book of the Courtier* (1528), by Baldassare Castiglione, prescribed a range of "courteous" behavior marked by knowing "the exact emphasis to give to various actions so that they may always be done seasonably," or appropriately, and with "grace." And he stressed that doing this required *sprezzatura*, "the art that conceals art," or performing every courteous act as if by nature with no hint of affectation. It is a very good idea with many applications. Castiglione also dwelt on the arts of conversation and the uses of laughter. And many of his prescriptions apply to dining, but he did not get down to the particulars of table manners. That remained to another of these books a few decades later, *Galateo: The Rules of Polite Behavior* (1558) by Giovanni della Casa. *Galateo* reached beyond the court and had wide influence, declaring that, first of all, "good manners and fashions" will "bring delight or at least not offend the senses, the minds and sensibilities of those with whom we live." Good manners were therefore rules for curbing coarseness and making other people feel comfortable and at ease. At the table that meant the likes of no "gruff" remarks, no noisy eating, no spitting, no putting your food on another's plate, no sniffing wine glasses, and so on. Now grace, civility, and dining went together.

2. THE ARTS OF THE DINING ROOM

By the late seventeenth century the rules of courtly etiquette had grown so elaborate, especially in France, that they and their foppish practitioners became a target of ridicule in the "comedy of manners," like Molière's *The School for Wives* (1662) and *The Misanthrope* (1666). The eighteenth century and the growing influence of the bourgeoisie brought a new wave of manuals on manners for commoners, reaffirming the theme that good manners at table and elsewhere soften social life for everyone. In this vein, the young George Washington completed a list of 110 *Rules of Civility and Decent Behaviour in Company and Conversation* based on earlier manuals and often regarded as having helped to shape his character. It included this advice on dinner conversation: "Speak not of doleful Things in a Time of Mirth or at the Table, and if others Mention them, Change if you can the Discourse." Wise advice at the dining table for sure. Near the end of that century the political philosopher Edmund Burke applied the principle to nations, asserting in his *Reflections on the Revolution in France* that "there ought to be a system of manners in every nation which a well-formed mind would be disposed to relish. To make us love our country, our country ought to be lovely." The manners of the table could facilitate that every day—as could be seen in France with the invention of the "restaurant" at about this time (see next essay).

The widening of democracy in the nineteenth century brought the bourgeois home with its prized intimacy and coziness—and sometimes hothouse atmosphere—and the proudly separate family dining room, simply or ornately designed. And books on etiquette proliferated. It would not do for a solid bourgeois, especially a woman, to seem coarse at table. Hence, for example, as one guide to etiquette for ladies advised: "Eat slowly and cut your food into small pieces before putting into your mouth. Sit easily in your chair, neither too near the table, nor too far from it, and avoid such tricks as putting your arms on the table, leaning back lazily in your chair, or playing with your knife, fork, or spoon. Never raise your voice, when speaking, any higher than is necessary" (Florence Hartley,

I. ON STYLE AND THE GOOD LIFE

The Ladies' Book of Etiquette, and Manual of Politeness, 1860). Bourgeois manuals of manners could go into a lot of detail.

In the twentieth century, modernist design would partially reverse this preference for privacy—and for fastidious etiquette. The stuffy Victorian home gave way to brighter rooms and more flexible floor plans that would in time supplant or supplement the dining room with a dining area in an open kitchen. These alterations reflect changes in family life and domesticity. Nowadays it is common for houses to have not only no separate dining room but not much of a living room either. Reverting to the premodern lower-class practice of providing a single large room for all communal activities, these rooms today are at once kitchen, dining room, living room, family room, and media center with a large television screen on the wall. There cooking, eating, talking, playing games, using phones, and watching television or movies can occur at the same time. It is a celebration of democratic informality. And such rooms can provide some very happy times indeed. (See "Elegant Utility" below.)

Even so, when informality goes that far and a family has no occasion to gather around a table to dine and converse without the distractions of television or games or phones and the like, everyone loses something important. That is not just the manners of the table; it is the very refinement of mind, sociability, and sensibility through the art of conversation, along with discriminating among levels of social performance. Children who grow up without that dining experience at home virtually every day, will likely pay for that social, psychological, and intellectual lack all their lives, whether they recognize this for what it is or not. Today, the general ignorance and disregard, if not disdain, of many young people for formal manners and for proprieties of dress and speech—look at college campuses—might not have been caused by the decline of formal dining at home, but it certainly goes with that decline.

This is not to say that the salutary arts of the dining room wholly depend on the kind of space in which dining takes place. Those arts can be practiced in an open kitchen dining area, for instance, as

2. The Arts of the Dining Room

well as in a separate dining room. The crux of the matter is a family gathering around a table to dine and converse without distractions, wherever that table might be.

Granting that the arts of the dining room can be adapted to different settings, here I will sketch some possible design features of a separate dining room because the arts of dining are easiest to perform in a room set aside for those alone—children asked to dine more formally in a space they otherwise frolic in will likely show a measure of psychological resistance to the expectation.

Creating a good dining room is itself something of an art. But an art based on common sense. The reigning principle of design should be that the dining room is a kind of theater for the performance at the table. That is why, to most readily achieve its effects, the dining room will be removed from other functions of the home. To be truly separate, it will not be visible from the entrance of the residence and will be closed off to view from the working part of the kitchen, possibly by a carefully positioned doorway or a swinging door—in an open kitchen arrangement the dining table should be at least far enough from the cooking area to lessen the interference of food preparation with dining.

The best shape for a separate dining room is a rectangle or oval, not a square, since square rooms are difficult to decorate and use, especially if they hold a capacious dining table. In size the room should not be so large that it detracts from the central drama of the table or inhibits the intimacy of dinner conversation. But it cannot be so small that diners feel cramped. At best, it will comfortably accommodate a table seating up to twelve diners, with an extension. There should be enough space on all sides for easy movement and convenient service between the table and the walls as well as any furnishings like a sideboard or cupboards. And at one end of the room, a large window looking out onto a garden or a cityscape would add a sense of space and visual interest to the room. That is all common sense, with more to come.

I. On Style and the Good Life

As to the décor surrounding the table, the visual style of the room will vary with individual tastes, formal or informal, traditional or modern, regional or eclectic, and so forth. Putting aside questions of those kinds of style, let us start with a few ideas on the general stage effects of color and lighting, which influence the theatrical atmosphere and mood more than any other element of a dining room—if tending here toward the traditional.

The color of the walls should be chosen to catch the light right and to actuate furnishings and art objects. One might select bold primary colors or even black or white, but soft, muted, neutral colors, or perhaps dark warm earth tones are usually preferable since they are unobtrusive, lending themselves to most any furnishings, reflecting light effectively, and they do not become dated. The wall might even be covered with a subtle paper pattern that contributes texture and goes with the furnishings. One might also add a dado, or wooden molding, running at chair-back height around this room. This feature enhances the formality by dividing the wall into two levels, well-suited to an upper swath of paper and protecting the wall from bumps and scratches by chairs. Of course, a modernist dining room will be more stark than this, but one should take care not to stamp such a dining room with a look one readily tires of.

If the room has windows they might not need curtains. Instead of curtains, suitable plants can give a comparable frame, while supplying the visual appeal of lush greenery and a bridge to the out of doors. If curtains are used, they should complement the walls and be light, possibly sheer; heavy fabrics are ill-suited to a dining room, encumbering the space and accumulating smells and stains.

The flooring of a dining room should also complement the colors and be practical—hardwood, marble, or some other decorative stone or tile, definitely not wall-to-wall carpeting, which is impractical where food is being served. A colorful area rug or a sumptuous "oriental" carpet will add a pertinent touch of style and warmth. It should be centered under the dining table, large enough to spread beyond the legs of the chairs but not obstruct them or get in the

2. The Arts of the Dining Room

way of diners. Such a rug is both decorative and practical, serving to enhance the flooring bordering it and also to dampen noise and hide stains.

Lighting in this domestic theater could be from wall sconces, whose soft illumination diffuses upward, and from a central chandelier styled and proportioned to suit the room as a whole and the table over which it would be centered. And any lighting scheme should be equipped with a dimmer switch to adjust the radiance to the occasion, bearing in mind that bright lights are death to a dining room, dampening the elegance of any dinner and casting an unflattering glare on people's faces, making everyone feel uncomfortable—remember the creed of that pioneer of manners, Giovanni della Casa: "good manners and fashions bring delight or at least do not offend the senses, the minds, and sensibilities." Candles on the table will shed a flattering glow when the lights are turned low, but candles alone are too dim for dining, dulling the full sensory enjoyment of the dining experience.

Further enhancing that enjoyment, a painting or two might be hung on the wall, harmonized with the room's colors and lighting. But paintings should be carefully selected for a dining room. A luscious still life of glistening fruits and colorful flowers is a natural choice—even if a cliché to some sophisticates. It brings more than an artwork to the room. For its images suggest an affection for home and hearth and for cherished objects that surround us there, as intended by the burghers of seventeenth-century Holland and Belgium whose domestic tastes launched the modern still life tradition. A still life can also remind us of sweet pleasures and happy occasions shared at table with other people, especially the still life composed of food. Hence, an appropriate still life reflects the romance of domesticity and is a valentine to dining. But whatever the type of artwork one chooses, it should elicit visual pleasure and instill serenity, rather than discomfit or challenge comprehension.

Instead of a painting, or in addition to it, one might hang a large mirror on the wall to bring in the outside view, or to reflect an artwork on the opposite wall. But mirrors must be placed above the eye level of all seated diners to prevent facial reflections—although they can be tilted somewhat to catch more of the room, as in many classy Parisian brasseries. Mirrors can do wonderful things to a room, but no one likes to catch a glimpse of themselves while they are eating. According to the precepts of *feng shui*, by the way, the dining room is the most important room of the house to hang a mirror in because that room is the figurative "vault" of the house, signifying the capacity to hold wealth; hence, mirrors increase that capacity of the house by enlarging the dining room. That's good dining room *feng shui*—as long as the mirror does not bring in displeasing sights from outside.

The colors, the lighting, the artwork, the appealing objects, and the graceful furnishings focus the eye on the table. Just as the dining room is the heart of the home, the table is the heart of the dining room. As the main attraction, the table will be centered under the chandelier and should have an extension for flexibility since a table that is ample for twelve does not agreeably seat a more intimate dinner party. It can be a rectangle to match the contours of the room or an oval, which is a more graceful form and avoids obtrusively pointed corners. It should be made of, or at any rate have a top made of, an opaque material, rather than transparent glass because glass must be covered during dining to conceal people's legs, and one does not always want to use a cover.

The style of the table settings will go with the occasion. Sometimes the table will present an elegant formal candlelit dinner with fine linen, china, silver, crystal, and a tasteful centerpiece of arranged flowers and possibly fruits, akin to the still life on the wall, albeit not so grand that it impedes the view and conversation of diners across the table. At other times the table will wear a more casual appearance, but still with style, like well-designed everyday tableware, handsome place mats, cheerful napkins, and an attractive fruit bowl in the center. However formal or informal the occasion,

2. The Arts of the Dining Room

the table should be an inviting stage for the arts of the dining room to work their magic.

That magic can be aided by good design. But the arts of the dining room ultimately depend less on the particulars of design than on people putting the dining room—or just the dining table in an open kitchen—to its highest purposes. Those purposes rise beyond the function of communal eating and even learning table manners themselves. They lift us above our everyday activities and selves to teach us the art of conversation, the graces of social civility, discrimination among appropriate types of social behavior, and help us bond with family and friends by sharing experiences, thoughts, and feelings.

Such are the gentle arts of the dining room. A formula for *savoir vivre* in a gracious and enlightened style of life. And that is why they are among the highest, most gratifying, and consequential arts of civilized life.

A previous version of this essay appeared as a chapter entitled "The Dining Room" in the book *The Best of Interiors and Lifestyle India* (Mumbai, India, 1999).

Interior of La Tour d'Argent, Paris, France.

The original purveyors of restaurants brought a lasting revolution in the style of public dining.

Remembrance of Restaurants Past

The famed Parisian restaurant La Tour d'Argent may have lost two of its three long-held Michelin stars in recent years, but it still has its renowned duckling, its 400,000-bottle wine cellar, and one of the best dining views in Paris. It also has another attraction that most visitors probably overlook. This is *Le petit Musée de la table*. Lining the walls of the restaurant's diminutive ground-level bar and spilling out into the foyer, "the little museum of the table" bursts with emblems and oddities from the history of public dining in Paris. And where better to display them? For La Tour d'Argent boasts of being the oldest restaurant in Paris.

Opened as an inn in 1582 on the Left Bank of the Seine opposite the Île Saint-Louis at the Pont de la Tournelle (and periodically reconstructed), La Tour d'Argent has hosted kings and courtiers, world leaders and sybarites ever since then. During its first decade, King Henry III, a frequent guest, reputedly popularized in France the practice of eating with a fork (a principal refinement, first adopted from Italy, in the growth of modern dining etiquette) while dining here on various "mignons" (little pieces). His successor, Henry IV, is said to have especially favored La Tour's heron pâté, and also savored its delicacy of hummingbird tongues. Le Duc de Richelieu had an entire ox served here to a party of forty. In more recent times, film stars would supplant royalty and nobles as the most illustrious and Epicurean guests—to the evident pride of La Tour's long-time owner, Claude Terrail, who took over from his father in 1947 and celebrated the restaurant and its famous patrons in his books, *Ma Tour d'Argent* (1974) and *Le roman de la Tour d'Argent* (1997).

I. ON STYLE AND THE GOOD LIFE

Actually, La Tour d'Argent and its "little museum of the table" take us back to a time when no "restaurant" by that title even existed. For when La Tour d'Argent first opened its doors as an inn, all public dining occurred in inns, taverns, and the like, as it had since antiquity (cafés and pubs purveyed mainly beverages), but not in any place called a "restaurant."

The modern "restaurant" did not show up until the eighteenth century. And the word originally named only a kind of soup, not a place for eating. *Restaurants* were simply concentrated bouillons, or consommé reductions, approaching a natural essence that promised to *restore* health to people afflicted by such maladies of the day as bouts of the vapors and weakness of the chest—Diderot's great *Encyclopedia* identified "restaurant" only as a medical term. *Restaurants* were therefore the Enlightenment's health food and the eighteenth century's nouvelle cuisine. Purveyors of these *restaurants* went largely unremarked until an enterprising Parisian named Mathurin Roze de Chantoiseau opened his *restaurant* operation in 1766. A deft and tireless self-promoter, he then published an *Almanach général* identifying commercial establishments of all kinds in Paris, including his own, proclaiming himself "the first Restaurateur" and beginning the transformation of *restaurant* from the term for a restorative broth into the label of the places that served them. Before long these *restaurants* had given their name to eateries with varied menus, shedding promises of medicinal restoration.

But the modern institutions we call "restaurants" did not descend solely from that eighteenth-century French fashion for restorative bouillons. The original purveyors of *restaurants* also brought a lasting revolution in the very style of public dining.

Historians tell us it happened like this. Traditional eating establishments had offered patrons only *table d'hôte* meals served at common tables by the "host" from communal bowls and drinking cups passed around common tables—even soup spoons were sometimes shared—adjacent to the cooking. But *restaurant* providers, known after Roze de Chantoiseau as *restaurateurs*, set a new standard. They abandoned the common trough of *table d'hôte* and began letting patrons choose from a variety of *restaurants* listed *à la carte* on what they termed a *menu*, and they enabled patrons to consume their restorative choices at separate tables with their own tableware in a setting soothing to their fragile physical constitutions and delicate sensibilities. By catering to personal needs and tastes, furnishing a measure of privacy in public, and nurturing social civilities (such as modern table manners, which had emerged in the sixteenth century with the rise of private dining rooms in residences—see "The Arts of the Dining Room" above), those *restaurant* enterprises were tipping their toques to late eighteenth-century ideals of health, individuality, and propriety. Soon enough, other dining providers caught on to the trend and started offering *restaurants* as well as more substantial fare in the public/private eating style of the new "restaurant." In the next century, an affluent and status-conscious bourgeoisie would bestow the title "restaurant" on any suitably sophisticated commercial dining establishment—i.e., offering meals *à la carte* from elaborate *menus* at individual tables. Eventually, "restaurant" became a generic term for almost any commercial eating spot—although today's fast-food outlets have a character of their own.

La Tour d'Argent joined this trend around 1780, so Claude Terrail tells us, when it began serving *à la carte*—about the time that the first "luxury restaurant" debuted in Paris, La Grande Taverne de Londres in 1782, esteemed for both its elegance and its cuisine. The "little museum of the table" does not signal this change, but it displays a rich potpourri of artifacts from not only La Tour d'Argent's long history but from some rivals, notably Paris's most eminent nineteenth-century restaurant, the Café Anglais, which fell to the wrecking ball shortly before World War I.

Here are rusty utensils centuries old, including a fork of the vintage that Henry III poked his "mignons" with. Here is crystal that touched royal lips, and porcelain that served nobles. Here are fabrics that adorned rustic wooden tables. Here are dust-encrusted bottles of champagne far too old to drink. Here are original volumes of the *Almanach des gourmands,* the early nineteenth-century pioneer of French writing on food and modern restaurants. Here are testimonial letters to La Tour d'Argent from more appreciative diners than you can count, among them Honoré de Balzac and Charles Baudelaire, numerous American presidents, and scores of entertainers. Here are souvenirs from historic dinners, like that of December 9, 1896, celebrated as *La Journée Sarah Bernhardt.* And here is the table arrangement, restored down to the place settings, linens, and menu, which on June 7, 1867, at the Café Anglais received Tsar Alexander II of Russia and his son who became Tsar Alexander III, along with Kaiser Wilhelm I of Prussia and the Prussian Chancellor Otto von Bismarck—they dined on creamed chicken soufflé, fillet of sole, scalloped turbot, glazed lobster, pressed duckling, ortolans on toast, eight great wines (mostly from the 1840s), and finished, appropriately, with a *bombe glacée.* That distinguished quartet did not leave the table hungry.

The "little museum" also owes its most peculiar possession to the two Prussians at that "Dinner of the Three Emperors." For just over three years after that dinner the armies of Wilhelm I and Bismarck laid siege to Paris during the Franco-Prussian War, cutting off food supplies to starve the Parisians out. But Gallic ingenuity rose to the assault. Parisians and their restaurant chefs swiftly learned to artfully cook anything they could find. And they did not shrink from using rodents from the streets and animals from the zoo (supplied at high cost by resourceful vendors). Feast your eyes on these *à la carte* selections for Christmas Day Dinner in 1870 at the then fashionable restaurant Voisin during those parlous, culinarily inventive days.

25 Decembre 1870

Jour 99 de la Siege
(99th Day of the Siege)

Consommé d'Elephant
(Elephant Consomme)

Le Chameau roti à l'anglais
(Roast Camel English Style)

Le civet de Kangourou
(Kangaroo Stew)

Côtés d'Ours rôties, sauce poivrade
(Rib of Bear on Toast, Poivrade Sauce)

Cuissot de Loup, sauce chevreuil
(Loin of Wolf, Deer Sauce)

Le Chat flanqué de Rats, Salade de cresson
(Cat flanked by Rats, Watercress Salad)

La Terrine d'antilope aux Truffes
(Antelope Terrine with Truffles)

Vins

Latour Blanche 1861

Mouton Rothschild 1846

We get no reviews of the dinner. But this restaurant *tour de force* must heighten our respect for those French chefs and the palettes they educated.

As to La Tour d'Argent itself, after the siege ended it returned to more conventional gourmet fare. And in 1890, under the hand of its most fabled chef, Frédéric, it inaugurated a unique tradition that continues today: identifying by number each duckling served (now well over one million) printed on a card and presented to each patron along with slices of the succulent foul.

You may go to La Tour d'Argent to be "restored" with your own numbered duckling in sophisticated surroundings where refinement fills the air and your handsomely set table affords a splendid upper-floor view of Notre Dame. But don't miss the "little museum of the table" downstairs. It may not altogether whet your appetite, but it will give you some smiles and an agreeable historical *hors d'oeuvre* before your gourmet meal in style at Paris's oldest "restaurant."

A slightly different version of this essay appeared in *France Today*, September/October, 2000. Information on the origins of the restaurant comes from Rebecca L. Spang, *The Invention of the Restaurant* (2000).

STYLES OF HOSPITALITY

Previous versions of these four short essays originally appeared in *Design Times* magazine in 1995–96.

Lobby Corridor of the Essex House Hotel, adorned with Ruhlmann Art Deco chandeliers, New York City.

The romance of its elegantly celebratory moderne style suggests not just a romantic style of design but a delightful style of life.

Isn't It Romantic?

Swirling through the revolving doors of New York's Essex House Hotel on Central Park South, you are swept into a designer's fantasy of urban romance. A fantasy in the Art Deco style. Black marble and burnished brass, polished rosewood and etched glass, deep colors and sparkling chandeliers, ornamental objects in grays and gold, striking Gatsby-esque portraits of a tuxedoed playboy and a begowned socialite, all seduce you into a love affair with the hotel's visual style and the city it once reflected so well.

It is a love affair imagined by Paris designer Pierre-Yves Rochon to recapture the glamour of the Essex House when it opened in 1931. That opening came near the heyday of Art Deco. As the name—derived from that of the spectacular Paris exhibition of *Arts Décoratifs et Industriels Modernes* in 1925—implies, this was a "decorative" art. And it applied to both commercial and domestic design.

Centered in France, where it was known as *art moderne* and was exemplified by renowned designers like Émile-Jacques Ruhlmann and René Lalique, Art Deco became an eclectic style inspired by diverse sources. These included the geometrical shapes of cubism, the bright stage colors and exoticism of Diaghilev's *Ballets Russes*, the metallic forms and finishes of machines, and, as the design evolved, sleek modernistic streamlining. It tended to exuberance, especially in its early years. And in interior design Art Deco also inclined to opulence. Banishing overstuffed Victorian clutter and the overwrought organic configurations of Art Nouveau, it wove together clean modern lines with geometric and sometimes floral or fan patterns set in rich materials like rosewood, dark mahogany, blond burled-walnut, ebony, veneers, and lacquers, often inlaid with ivory or gilt. Stretches of shiny marble would likely cover the floors along with vivid area rugs, while the walls might be in veined marble or a lush golden covering, and doors and objects could be in brushed brass, bronze, nickeled steel, or etched glass. In all, an Art Deco interior captured the eye with its sheen, colors, lyrical lines, and lustrous surfaces. A striking style of design, Art Deco also suggested a style of life: spirited, sophisticated, elegant, urban, and romantic.

Embracing this style, New York was creating the very model of the twentieth-century metropolis with slender heaven-piercing Art Deco skyscrapers adorned with *à la mode* geometric designs and other decorative highlights and lobbies with expanses of luxurious marble on floors and walls embellished by ornamental touches in brass, nickel, or chromium. The Chrysler Building, whose stunning marble-clad lobby is worth the trip to see, set the model in 1930 (complete with machine-age gargoyles and a metallic, multitiered conical dome ornamented with ascending fan-shaped figures and featuring an array of star-invoking lights at night), followed by the Empire State Building (1931) and Rockefeller Center (1933), housing those Art Deco shrines, Radio City Music Hall and the Rainbow Room—imitated in the film musical *Swing Time* (1936), where Fred Astaire and Ginger Rogers hoof it on a shiny black and white dance floor backed by a matching pair of black staircases that curve down from the entrance on each side as in the Rainbow Room.

The Essex House, a hotelier's jubilant salute to that style, immediately attracted *tout le beau monde* (at least those not wiped out by the economic Depression that struck while New York's great monuments to Art Deco were rising from the ground), who reveled there in the new urban chic of *moderne* design and danced the night away to the "Essex Hop"—all in a setting somewhat more intimate than that of another Art Deco classic that debuted in the same month, the more grandiose Waldorf Astoria hotel. But over the years, changing fashions and managements let the hotel's historic design identity slip away. Finally, some six decades after it had opened, the Essex House was brought splendidly back to the spirit of its original days with a costly renovation of the public spaces by Mr. Rochon, who had designed grand hotels and residences around the world.

The result was a celebration of *moderne*, Art Deco style and romance. No austere modernist moralism. No puritanically "honest" form. No corporate impersonality. It was boldly, unapologetically, and luxuriously decorative. Delectably visual and insouciantly festive, yet graceful and elegant. You picture Fred Astaire and Ginger Rogers gliding across the polished marble floor, and you want to dance.

Mr. Rochon selected or designed every object and feature of the restoration for both historical accuracy and stylish opulence. "I tried," he says, "to recreate the spirit of the years" around 1930. "Those who denigrate the *art moderne*/Art Deco period," he adds, betray "a failure to appreciate its style." For, at its best, he insists, Art Deco was no passing fancy but a buoyant marriage of the inventively "modern" and the rigorously "classical."

To rejuvenate this marriage at the Essex House, Rochon blended "the American interior design of the thirties" (as found, for instance, in surviving elements of the hotel's original Art Deco design, notably the magnificent engraved brass elevator doors) with "the refinement of Ruhlmann's French style," which, he says, "I admire very much." That union gave birth to a beguiling "balance of surface decoration and formal design" as well as a voluptuous sensuosity wrapped in a "quiet and balanced aspect." And it is sheer romance.

Entranced by the stylish elegance and equipoise of Rochon's Essex House lobby (bounded on both sides by tall majestic doorways and eye-catching Art Deco doors ornamented in soft brass and nickel, opening one on side into a restaurant and on the other into a ballroom), you are enticed down a central corridor that is an exquisite Art Deco gallery. Overhead hangs a row of three resplendent Ruhlmann-inspired crystal chandeliers cascading in concentric circles of sparkling glass, accentuating the perspective down the corridor, and beckoning you along the glistening marble floor. Taking you past the elevators in passages to the right and left, and beyond the opening of a charming bar offering plush leather seating and a warming fireplace, the gallery is lined with luscious rosewood walls and columns, muted wall fabrics, photographs of New York from the twenties and thirties, and cylindrical rosewood étagères discreetly displaying artful objects. The gallery leads to a revolving door opening onto Fifty-Eighth Street. But just before you reach that exit, you are lured through a pair of majestic etched glass and brass doors on one side into a memorable dining destination: the restaurant Les Célébrités.

Or, I should say, you used to be. Unfortunately, that restaurant succumbed to later management, although the doors remain. But since it fit so well into Rochon's resplendent design it warrants describing as part of the hotel's Art Deco romance.

Les Célébrités was one of New York's finest restaurants, under the guidance of chef Christian Delouvrier. It was also delicious to look at. If you like a little excess. And who doesn't, especially in a special-occasion restaurant?

After pausing for a champagne cocktail in the gemlike Art Deco sitting area, with its zebra rug and vivid red walls, you would enter the intimate main dining room, awash in plush furnishings and dark mahogany accented by the stylized grandeur of fluted black marble and gold-leaf columns. A striking mural salvaged from the famed Art Deco oceanliner of the 1930s, the *Normandie*, adorned one wall. Seating only about sixty diners, comfortable banquettes and gondola chairs encircled tables set with Christofle silver and Bernardaud china—the dinner plates and tablecloths designed by Rochon to reflect each other's patterns. Light fell softly from miniature Puiforcat table lamps and from fixtures illuminating paintings studiously positioned on the walls.

It is these paintings that were the "celebrities." Desiring the restaurant to exude both a quietly luxurious and yet festive air, Rochon and manager Wolf Walter had hit on the idea of decking the walls with artworks by movieland figures like Walter's wife, actress Elke Sommer, a respectable painter in her own right. From that idea came an array of colorful creations by those *cinéastes* that looked down all around, images that, within the sea of warm sensations, lent the restaurant a perennially gala atmosphere.

You dined well at Les Célébrités. But at the Essex House the feast belonged then and still does as much to the eyes as to the palette. And when you leave Rochon's Art Deco fantasy for the gritty streets of New York, you cannot fail to carry with you the romance of its elegantly celebratory *moderne* style. And you might well feel that this is indeed not just a beautiful style of design. It is, or was—perhaps enhanced by nostalgia—a delightful style of life.

Postscript: Since the first version of this essay appeared, the Essex House has gone through more than one refurbishment, at the sad cost of not only Les Célébrités but the charming bar off the corridor and some of Rochon's touches in the lobby. But fortunately, the spirit and essence of Rochon's splendid overall *moderne* design have been kept largely intact. The romance of Rochon's original Essex House design provided the setting for several scenes—in the public areas and Les Célébrités—of the Hollywood movie *Love Affair* (1994) with Warren Beatty and Annette Bening.

Lobby of the Four Seasons Hotel, New York City.

"A sense of theater ... with a gracious stage for socializing."

—I. M. PEI.

Theater of Tranquility

It was one of those bleak, harried, New York winter days. The sky oppressively gray, the streets depressingly sloppy, the cacophony of the city reverberating on every side. We needed peace, refreshment, and renewal, so my wife and I ducked into I. M. Pei's postmodern monument to hospitality, the Four Seasons Hotel on East Fifty-Seventh Street, which had opened in 1993.

We entered an oasis in the urban maelstrom, a realm at once dramatic and calm. Drama and calm together? Looking around to detect the makings of these contrasting effects, we found an ingenious feat of design: quietude enclosed in spectacle, intimacy surrounded by grandeur, privacy nestled in public, hominess woven through spaciousness. No easy task.

The architect and designers fashioned this surprising oasis by merging somewhat conflicting aims. I. M. Pei said he wanted a "sense of theater" in the public areas to celebrate "the luxury-hotel experience" and to restore "the grand tradition when going to a hotel was an occasion." One can't miss the theater. Pei's bold ocular-punctuated façade, ascending in set-backs fifty-two stories high (the tallest hotel in New York), and his cavernous limestone and marble foyer with tiered steps ascending gracefully twenty feet upward from the entrance toward a long concierge desk and drawing one's eyes up soaring pillars and skyward to a backlit onyx ceiling some fifty feet overhead evoke scenes of a mythical Gotham City or a pharaoh's tomb. It is a *coup* of creative postmodern architecture. And we were awed. Almost overwhelmed.

But soon another mood enfolded us, the tranquility of the interior design by Chhada, Siembieda & Partners. The challenge, said partner Jay Leff, was to "humanize" the theatricality. "We wanted to create a warm, soft, and welcoming environment that would be restful and relaxing," adds Don Siembieda. A sanctuary in the city.

To achieve this, the design team chose an understated contemporary Postmodernism with occasional nods to classic Art Deco. Unlike the sumptuous Art Deco design of the Essex House interior, here the style is subdued while nonetheless skirting austerity of form for more eclectic inventiveness—taking the cue from Pei's postmodern structure. Here grace of form, precision of detail, unity of composition, and blending of earth colors were styled for serenity. "We selected interior elements very sensitive to the architectural features," Siembieda emphasized. That meant choosing finishes, furnishing, colors, and lighting to quietly suit and yet downplay the drama of the large open spaces and to complement the honeyed hues of the French limestone that sheathes the building and runs through the grand foyer and ground floor corridors (also used in Pei's spacious Louvre entrance lobby set below his controversial glass pyramid in Paris). Forget elaborate ornamentation. Avoid vivid colors. No glittering chandeliers. Reject anything that would clash with the quietude of the style and the space. Everything had to flow together into a mellow, unassuming harmony soothing to the senses and to the soul.

Beginning in the foyer, where Pei's onyx ceiling squares and matching wall sconces emit an amber glow and set a motif the designers repeat throughout, this harmony envelops the commodious lounge areas reached by wide staircases on each side of the foyer. In one of these lounges we sipped drinks amid the soft grays of vaguely Art Deco cushioned sofas and the comforting caramel shades of leather barrel chairs, deeply grained cherrywood tables, and the Belgian mohair wall covering framed in Danish beech wood, all gently illuminated by a few discreet table lamps, recessed overhead pin

5. Theater of Tranquility

spotlights, and concealed uplights along the walls. The soft blond and muted tones of furnishings, lighting, and architectural surfaces melded into a serene whole. Modern spaces this size can be cold and daunting, but thanks to adroit design these are inviting and appealingly private—"a gracious stage for socializing," as Pei himself had desired.

Following the trail of warm limestone from the lobby lounge down one of the wide corridors that wrap the central elevator bank and lead past the registration desk toward an exit on Fifty-Eighth Street, we then ascended another stairway bringing us back toward Fifty-Seventh Street and behind the striking oculus window. Twin dining areas opened on both sides. A panorama of impeccable design touches, they continue motifs from the foyer. Onyx lights high overhead recall the foyer ceiling, as do the geometrical patterns of the inlaid cherrywood tables, the wall-side banquettes, and the maplewood floor. The motif also recurs in three custom-made scagliola panels covering one wall. Richly composed in reddish and golden tones, these panels have their own reflection in identical table place mats that add another mark of unifying artistry to the room. Everything works together like a musical score.

Tranquility as design calls little attention to itself. It must look good, but it must also gracefully lull rather than continuously stir the senses. The wonder is that this tranquility thrives in I. M. Pei's theatrical setting. You might say the interior has triumphed over the architecture. But it is not really that. Rather, the design lives up to the architecture in a sublime companionship, while also fulfilling its own more intimate purposes. That makes the Four Seasons a theater of tranquility for sure, beckoning you into its calming atmosphere on cold winter days or on hot summer afternoons. Or any time you want a salutary reprieve from the world outside in a fabulous New York setting of quietly dramatic postmodern urban design. Whereas the Essex House provides the romance of New York in the festive style of *art moderne*, the Four Seasons provides the spirit of New York in a postmodern style of theatrical tranquility.

Postscript: Since the essay first appeared, the two lobby lounges in the Four Seasons have changed much of their furniture, and one of them has become a restaurant arranged with large faux trees, but the theatrical tranquility largely persists.

Felix restaurant, Peninsula Hotel, Hong Kong.

"Work on your life, think differently—it is a stage and you are the one to give it spark."
—PHILIPPE STARCK

Starck's Swan Song

WITH A NOTE ON FENG SHUI AT FELIX

Late one night after a long ocean flight, I found myself in an otherworldly realm of weirdly slanting walls and tilting stairwells, eerily glowing floors and undulating surfaces, spooky lights and biomorphic forms. It was like a surrealist dream. But it wasn't a dream. It was Philippe Starck's dramatically designed dreamlike restaurant, Felix, occupying the twentieth floor of a thirty-story tower added in 1994 to the fabled Peninsula Hotel in Hong Kong.

I had come here because, for one thing, the Peninsula is among the grand hotels of the world and one of my favorites. Opened in 1928 on the Kowloon side of the British colony across the harbor from Hong Kong Island in the South China Sea, it was a jewel among hotels in the colonial East, and its fleet of green Rolls-Royces transported guests in distinctive Peninsula luxury—which it still does. The hotel afforded splendid views of the harbor and Victoria Peak; and its magnificent, capacious lobby with soaring columns topped by gilded neoclassic ornamentations that run across the ceiling signaled a European monarchical style. The lobby lounge soon became a destination in itself and has hosted generations of notable visitors and distinguished Hong Kong residents for the lingering ritual of afternoon tea to the strains of a string quartet.

Considering that glorious tradition, one had to wonder why the management had chosen the celebrated, globe-trotting, irrepressibly idiosyncratic Starck to design the vast restaurant in the new tower. But the hotel's principal owner, Michael Kadoorie, had no doubt. He did not wish to imitate the colonial majesty of the Peninsula's lobby or past. He wanted to crown that majesty with a tribute to the future. And Starck, he said, is a "grand visionary" who "projects the future." Consequently, Starck reported, Kadoorie "told me I had complete freedom" and that he just wanted "life, heart, and spirit." Kadoorie got that in spades.

Given free rein with a large budget, Starck made Felix (named for a longtime manager of the hotel) in every detail a complete Starck creation, and, he said, "it is one of which I am particularly proud." The project clearly suited him. "I rejected the conscious state when designing Felix," he declared, since "I always work with the subconscious because it never lies." Anyone familiar with Starck's fanciful furniture and product designs or his quirky *mis-en-scene* restaurants and hotels around the world knows what marvels Starck's subconscious can perform. And Felix is a marvel for sure. Fantastic? Yes. Whimsical? Maybe. Trite? No. One might say his work, eschewing modernist canons of aesthetic purity, is postmodern with a vengeance. For his part, he says his prolific and often amusing designs all have an earnestly playful purpose. Felix exemplifies that.

This purpose, he explains, "is to change people, to wake them up, to say 'Don't be a spectator, be an actor. Work on your life, think differently—it is a stage and you are the one to give it spark.'" Inspired by his father, a bravura aerodynamics inventor, and later nourished by the futuristic fantasies of science fiction writer Philip K. Dick (whose novel *Ubik* gave the name to Starck's Paris studio), Starck has pursued this purpose by practicing his design alchemy on everything from hotels and office buildings to furniture and household appliances, from motorcycles (a biker himself) and yachts to lemon squeezers and toothbrushes. "If a toothbrush could be this," he spiritedly says of his famous flame-like toothbrush design, "you could be something else, or your life could be something else."

I pondered this jaunty notion while taking in the sensory extravagance of Felix. Its two-story height is enhanced by panoramic views over the harbor and city and by towering mahogany columns rising from massive glass vases. A bright aluminum wall ripples (in a water effect repeated on the textured glassware and elsewhere) behind a long iridescent onyx bar lined with jellyfish-shaped stools. A pair of radiant staircases at the other end of the room spirals up inside simulated gilt champagne buckets toward two intimate bar areas affording vistas of the whole. Fanciful dining chairs at well-spaced tables bear the faces of Starck and other Felix dignitaries. Changing light effects accentuate the myriad forms and features. And, not least, its Salvador Dali-esque restrooms are themselves a *coup de théâtre*, the men's room boasting individual sculpted tubular black urinals set against floor-to-ceiling windows overlooking the city, matched in the ladies room by individual ice-cream-cone-shaped dressing tables with mirrors against windows over the harbor.

"I don't know if it beautiful or not," Starck said of Felix, striking a typically irreverent tone. "I am not interested in that." Instead, "Felix is a very sophisticated and complex cocktail that both shakes and stirs" its many ingredients, inspired by "the vibrancy of Hong Kong" and "my own logic, intuition, and craziness." Changing the metaphor, he adds: "It is a machine to produce emotions." And it does. Drifting through Starck's subconscious dreamworld, you feel amusement, elation, wonder. And, paraphrasing the designer, you might ask with a smile, "If a restaurant could be this, what could any of us be?"

Starck has also said that Felix "is my last project as an interior designer.... It is my swan song." But he must have spoken that with tongue in cheek. For his unquenchable inventiveness has continued to flourish in the design of hotels, restaurants, furnishings, and all kinds of things. Meanwhile, Starck's "swan song" lives on—even after the British "handover" of Hong Kong to the Chinese in 1997—as an exuberant expression of the designer's creative imagination and a reminder of the enchantments that imagination can yield, and of the provocative questions it can raise. After all, probably more than any other designer, Starck views himself as dealing not just in styles of design but in styles of life. As he says, "Work on your life—it is a stage and you are the one to give it spark." At Felix, you feel like doing just that.

I. ON STYLE AND THE GOOD LIFE

A NOTE ON FENG SHUI AT FELIX

In designing Felix, Philippe Starck seems not to have considered the venerable Chinese design principles known as *feng shui*. Yet he unconsciously satisfied a lot of them, according to *feng shui* Master Koon Lung, who explored Felix with me. Good *feng shui*, he explained, calls for buildings and rooms to be designed to assure the proper movement of *chi*, or energy, and the users' emotional and material well-being. In Felix, he observed, such effects come from the openness of the space and the appealing symmetry of the design, along with the many striking forms and sensations that yield pleasure, which, he remarked, all restaurants must have to keep attracting customers. Felix gains more good *feng shui*, Master Lung emphasized, from its spectacular views of Victoria Harbor and Hong Kong Island as well as from many design features evoking water—like the ripples of the textured aluminum wall and of the glassware and other objects that mirror those watery effects—symbols of energy and life, motion and money. Every house needs some images of water, the Master said, or a view of it, to assure a family's prosperity; and a restaurant can hardly survive without them because it thrives on streaming social activity and on money flowing in—like water. Master Lung's only reservations about the *feng shui* of Felix concerned the parts of the room that create confined rather than open spaces, and the location of the restrooms: they should not lie so near the entrance for that implies flushing money away. Notwithstanding Master Lung's minor reservations, Felix is an enchanting visual adventure in good *feng shui*.

Quotations from Philippe Starck come from "Starck Contrasts" in *Tribute to a Very Special Lady* published by The Peninsula Group, Hong Kong, 1994.

The River Café, London, England.

"Restaurants are part of the theater of life."
—RICHARD ROGERS

Elegant Utility

It is a story of romance, the good life, dining, and design. A graduate of Bennington College in Vermont named Ruth from Woodstock, New York goes off to Europe for educational adventure. There she meets and later marries a British architect, Richard Rogers. He then gains international renown (and rouses controversy) with his shocking "inside-out" designs for the Pompidou Centre in Paris and for Lloyd's Insurance in London, brazenly putting their pipes and mechanical systems on the exterior of the buildings. He wins further celebrity, while riling traditionalists such as Prince Charles, with his vigorous advocacy of innovative buildings that function "more like robots than temples."

Such a revolutionary modern (or postmodern) architect might seem an unlikely partner in harmonious domesticity. But that is exactly what Richard and Ruth Rogers achieved, first at home and then for the public. Dividing their time between homes in London and Tuscany, where Rogers was born, the couple would live happily, graciously, and well. And they would open an Italian restaurant (with Ruth's culinary colleague Rose Gray), near Richard's office complex on the Thames in the west London district of Hammersmith, to extend their gracious way of life to others. Named the River Café, it would become the best Italian restaurant in London, and some would say it rivaled any in Europe.

"The River Café was conceived deliberately along domestic lines," Ruth Rogers and Rose Gray write in *The Rogers and Gray Italian Country Cookbook* (1996). And the intrepid technological architect Richard Rogers would design it. But how would he do it? Sitting in the

I. On Style and the Good Life

airy restaurant, the celebrated architect described how his design philosophy and the restaurant came together.

Never mind the whims of catchy styles and fancy forms, he says. Architecture and design have more important business. That business is to serve essential "social and technical" needs. These needs start with the human hunger for community. People want to interact with each other, and society depends on their doing so. Architecture and design should facilitate this by bringing people together in inviting settings—Rogers refers admiringly to piazzas and medieval city squares, which he and his partner Renzo Piano emulated in the design of the Pompidou Centre by placing the mechanical workings on the outside to maximize open space inside and by providing a large area on the grounds for social traffic, gatherings, and entertainment. Rogers's commitment to his social philosophy of design led him to become a vocal champion of a more humanistic politics, economics, and urban planning, as well as architecture—all attuned to technological change—than he saw prevalent. That he would create a restaurant in that spirit should come as no surprise. "Restaurants," he says, "are part of the theater of life," and so they "should be part of the community around them" in a practical style that works best to do that.

True to these principles and to his and Ruth's gracious domestic way of life, he designed the restaurant to be an informal social center like an open kitchen at home, where cooking and dining would share a common multi-purpose space; and he points out that this now popular idea goes back to Frank Lloyd Wright. "The kitchen in our home is in the middle of the living room," he remarks with a smile, making dining there a welcoming familial social event where good conversation invariably goes with the good food—fulfilling the social, no less than the nutritional, purpose of a dining room (see "The Arts of the Dining Room" above). That is the quality the couple wanted in the restaurant: a casual domesticity with "American simplicity and directness," as Ruth Rogers puts it, or, in Richard's words, "an elegant utility." They succeeded.

7. Elegant Utility

An open kitchen runs the length of the rectangular room, separated from the dining area by a stainless steel counter whose polished surface matches that of the adjacent dining tables and the simple Breuer side chairs, chosen, Rogers says, for their comfortable familiarity. Tilted translucent glass panels rising behind the counter reflect the work of food preparation, and a row of tiny halogen lamps descends over and illuminates the countertop. Uplights high overhead cast a soft reflection from the curved panels of blond wood inset with metallic grillwork that roll across the ceiling from one end of the room to the other. The large luminous face of a Time Beam projecting wall clock plays across an end wall above a large freestanding, see-through wood-burning oven. Opposite the kitchen counter, floor-to-ceiling windows look out toward the Thames. Serving both "social and technical" needs, the room is both friendly and tasteful. You feel at home there, a home with a design you might not quite notice at first but that cannot fail to make your time there a domestic pleasure. And the country Italian fare served up by Ruth and Grace at once goes with the setting and cannot be beaten for its unassuming excellence.

Born of romance, the good life, and a social philosophy of design, the River Café was not designed to show off its style. Or not an aesthetic style. It was designed to bring people together like a family to dine and socialize within the "elegant utility" of a convivial modern kitchen-dining room, a true "theater of life"—and a "theater" as far removed from Philippe Starck's eye-popping Felix in Hong Kong both geographically and aesthetically as it could be. In other words, the River Café was not designed to display a style of design so much as to promote a comfortably gracious way of life.

Virginia Woolf in 1925, the year Mrs. Dalloway *was published; inset: Clarissa Dalloway, Blackstone Audio Books.*

"The Gods, who never lost a chance of hurting, thwarting and spoiling human lives, were seriously put out if, all the same, you behaved like a lady."
—CLARISSA DALLOWAY

Mrs. Dalloway and the Ethics of Civility

Life after death has been good to Virginia Woolf. A respected literary critic and an admired experimental novelist among the cognoscenti when—fearing the onset of another mental collapse of the kind that had periodically disrupted her life—she stuffed rocks in her pocket and walked into the River Ouse to drown herself in 1941 just shy of age fifty-nine, Virginia Woolf has now become what in voguish parlance is dubbed a "cultural icon." She is honored as a gifted writer who invented a modernist literary style and promoted her artistic principles with bushels of adroit reviews and programmatic essays; she is revered as a pioneering feminist who berated history's fetters on the female imagination; and she is regarded hagiographically as a diligent and revealing recorder of her own life and thoughts who penned a small library of letters (six volumes), diaries (five volumes), and several miscellaneous memoirs. Studies of her novels pour from the presses lauding the brilliance of her writing, the import of her feminism, and the genius of her sensibility—usually rooting them all in the loam of her life. These prized qualities have won canonical status for one novel, *To the Lighthouse* (1927), commonly judged her masterpiece. A favorite of literature teachers for its shimmering artistry and timely themes of female psychology, creativity, and alienation, this is the book by Virginia Woolf—besides, perhaps, the seminal feminist tract, *A Room of One's Own* (1929)—most likely to be known to anyone interested in modern fiction.

I. On Style and the Good Life

But Virginia Woolf merits more than her stature as "a founder of Modernism and an important feminist," as the *Encyclopedia of the Novel* (1998) has it, who wrote tirelessly about literature, women, and herself and excelled in one diaphanous novel. She wrote another novel that goes beyond the lapidary achievement of *To the Lighthouse* to rank among the great works of world literature. Not because it is her most artistically exquisite or ideologically correct performance—leave that badge on *To the Lighthouse*. But because in this other novel she applies her talents to the large purposes that distinguish enduring classics, and in the fluidly meditative style then new to her she does justice to those purposes. She later alluded to such purposes herself in "Women and Fiction" (1929) when she enjoined female novelists to "look beyond the personal and political relationships" that had typically curbed them and take up "the wider questions . . . of our destiny and the meaning of life." This other novel is *Mrs. Dalloway* (1925).

In fact, *Mrs. Dalloway*'s stock has been rising. The book has gained more notice since an affecting British film was made of it in 1997, with Vanessa Redgrave as the lead, and the next year an American named Michael Cunningham published his own version of *Mrs. Dalloway* in a novel called *The Hours*, which won the Pulitzer Prize and was itself made into a movie in 2002. Possibly reflecting *Mrs. Dalloway*'s widening popularity, in 2010 the editors of *Time* magazine gave *Mrs. Dalloway* a higher spot than *To the Lighthouse* in a ranking of the one hundred best English-language novels since the magazine had debuted in 1923.

But even with the rise in *Mrs. Dalloway*'s standing, readers and critics tend to treat the novel chiefly as an aesthetically adventurous excursion into the mind of a psychologically fragile, emotionally wavering, circumstantially constrained, and perhaps sexually conflicted woman who bears affinities with her creator, and who pours her energies into socializing and giving parties because she has little else to do. Of course, attracting as much notice as anything is how Virginia Woolf blends these themes in the first display of her

8. Mrs. Dalloway and the Ethics of Civility

innovative artistic style. That style reflected the psychology and aestheticism of Walter Pater that she had adopted via the artistic coterie of Bloomsbury. Like Pater, she had come to view everything that happens to us, as she said in "Modern Fiction" (c. 1919), to be "myriad impressions" from outside that spark "the flickerings of that innermost flame that flashes its messages through the brain." Surface impressions and subjective flickerings—such was Virginia Woolf's modernist psychological aestheticism. It would become known, taking a phrase from William James, as "stream of consciousness." And it would give her a lasting literary identity.

But none of this is where the greatness of *Mrs. Dalloway* lies. Far more than an iridescent stream-of-consciousness novel for readers to labor over, scholars of Modernism to scrutinize, and feminists to cull, *Mrs. Dalloway* is a capacious work of fiction occupied with many of the most common troubles and consequential achievements of human existence. And beneath the literary trappings it tells us nothing more clearly than this: outside the psychic life there exists a public world, and in that world we most fully live our lives, at once shaping ourselves and serving our civilization. That is just what Clarissa Dalloway does.

This might seem unlikely since the bare subject of *Mrs. Dalloway* comes close to what Virginia Woolf had envisioned in "Modern Fiction," depicting "an ordinary mind on an ordinary day." It tells of a day in the life of Clarissa Dalloway as she prepares for and hosts a party. She shops. She talks. She frets. She reflects on her past, and on her moods, and on what people think of her, and on what matters to her. And she sets her party in motion and guides it. Yet, as that story unfolds it contains a rich cast of characters and virtually every consequential theme of literature and life: love and death, human nature and society, manners and morals, desire and denial, joy and despair, and more.

Virginia Woolf promised nearly that while writing the book when she confided to her diary in June 1923: "in this book I have almost too many ideas. I want to give life and death, sanity and insanity;

I. On Style and the Good Life

I want to criticize the social system, and to show it at work, at its most intense." In fact, *Mrs. Dalloway* is a more substantive novel and the title character a more significant and emblematic figure than even Virginia Woolf might have imagined.

We could say *Mrs. Dalloway* shares the same sweeping subject as Sigmund Freud's *Civilization and Its Discontents* (published five years later). For both books dwell on the delicate balance of nature and culture within us, recognizing inevitable human tribulations at the hands of fate, other people, and sometimes of society, and what we must do to overcome them, and how in doing that we achieve the benefactions of civilization. *Mrs. Dalloway* illustrates that kind of triumph.

We could also say that *Mrs. Dalloway* echoes Western humanism going back to *The Iliad*. For just as Homer had wrested humane ideals and social virtues from the tragedies wrought by fate and the Trojan war, Clarissa Dalloway courageously wins her own moral victories against her own tragic sense of life. And *Mrs. Dalloway* must be said to inhabit the same moral world as the eminent nineteenth-century novels that set public interests above the gratifications of private life. For in the person of Clarissa Dalloway, Virginia Woolf created a character who rises from her personal sorrows and secret fears to serve the public world and to find joy in it. She is no less a moral figure than, say, George Eliot's secular saint, Dorothea Brooke, in *Middlemarch*. Eliot's concluding words in that book fit them both: "The growing good of the world is partly dependent on unhistoric acts, and that things are not so ill with you and me is half owing to the number who have lived faithfully a hidden life and rest in unvisited tombs." Clarissa Dalloway resolutely devotes herself through "unhistoric acts" to "the growing good of the world." If those acts seem woefully bound to the traditional role of socialite—nowadays many female students scoff at Clarissa for this, and even the otherwise sympathetic biographer and critic Phyllis Rose remarks of Clarissa that "the products of her creativity may seem comically, slender," because they are merely exhibit "the cre-

8. Mrs. Dalloway and the Ethics of Civility

ativity of everyday feminine life"—this betrays a failure to value that role. For it is a social role that someone must play if we are to have a truly civil society. Clarissa Dalloway is a heroine of the ethical life if ever there was one. And a heroine with style.

It is true, and should not be ignored, that Virginia Woolf can be hard on Clarissa Dalloway, telling us "she could not think, write, even play the piano"; she "talked oceans of nonsense: and to this day ask her what the Equator was, and she did not know." But this severe portrait is hardly fair. Clarissa Dalloway thinks about many things, if not about the Equator. And her thoughts, with the story that surrounds them, as already noted, range across the landscape of human life, disclosing bitter ironies and rueful self-deceptions alongside commonplace joys and dauntless affirmations.

Still, there is no denying that Clarissa Dalloway cares a lot about socializing and especially giving parties. This makes her a ready target for those around her—and unsympathetic readers—particularly the men, who wonder why she gives parties so often and fault her for it. Her husband, Richard, an honorable government official, says to himself, "It was a very odd thing how much Clarissa minded about her parties." Her old beau Peter Walsh, who shows up for a visit, also dismisses them. "Oh these parties, he thought. Clarissa's parties. Why does she give these parties?" How "she had frittered her time away," he goes on, "lunching, dining, giving the incessant parties."

Clarissa senses these criticisms, and they sometimes make her feel trivial, even "childish," so inferior to the men in their heady realm of politics. But Clarissa Dalloway gives parties for no trivial reason. Or perhaps, as Virginia Woolf says in "Women and Fiction" that female authors should do, Clarissa makes "serious what appears insignificant to a man, and trivial what is to him important" (Woolf is surely winking at Oscar Wilde's ironic spin on "triviality" and "seriousness" in *The Importance of Being Earnest*). Be that as it may, Clarissa Dalloway stages her parties from a consciously humanistic ethical motive.

I. On Style and the Good Life

Clarissa's ethics arise from where humanistic ethics have often arisen. Henry James pointed to this source as the "imagination of disaster," the intimation that the worst can happen to us despite our best defenses—coupled, for Clarissa, with the belief that if any gods exist they do not care. As Virginia Woolf's narrator puts it, "there was in the depths of her heart an awful fear," so she "always had the feeling that it was very, very dangerous to live even one day." But Clarissa does not believe this fear is hers alone. For, she reflects, "this late stage of the world's experience had bred in them all, all men and women, a well of tears."

This is no modish existential despair awash in pretentious cosmic alienation. It bespeaks Clarissa's tragic sense of life. And it has causes closer to home. It is in part a legacy of World War I—an explicit theme of the book through the character of shell-shocked Septimus Warren Smith, whose psychosis runs through the novel, paralleling the wavering temperament of Clarissa. But it comes even closer to Clarissa Dalloway herself. She fears the tragic brittleness of life because she feels an inherent vulnerability inside her, and because she had witnessed her own sister die in an accident: "To see your sister killed by a falling tree ... before your own eyes ... Clarissa always said, was enough to turn one bitter." Or it could unhinge the mind, as it did to Septimus Smith when he saw his closest comrade killed at his side in battle.

And yet, Clarissa does not come unhinged or become bitter. Neither does she withdraw into existential anguish or seek stroking emotional consolations. Instead she erects stiff defenses to shield her tenuous psychological autonomy, and then she becomes a gracious social being.

She despises the consolations of psychotherapy, for instance (although Virginia Woolf's husband, Leonard, would publish Freud's works at his Hogarth Press as translated by James Strachey, brother of the flamboyant Lytton, a member of the Bloomsbury Group and close friend of Virginia's), because she equates them with "conversion" to someone else's manipulative "sense of proportion," like that of the smug psychotherapist Bradshaw who tries to cure Septimus Smith, and of the domineering physician Holmes whose insistent attentions literally chase poor Smith out a window to his death. For the same reason, Clarissa also distrusts the resentful lower-class tutor, Miss Kilman, who has her own ideological and religious "conversion" to press on Clarissa's daughter Elizabeth.

Clarissa focuses her resistance to "conversion" most fervently on "love and religion." They are twin enemies—"how detestable they are," she snarls—that would "destroy . . . the privacy of the soul." She identifies religion with Miss Kilman, and it was to protect her "privacy" from love that she had forsaken the emotionally consuming Peter Walsh—with whom "everything had to be shared; everything gone into. And it was intolerable."—and had married the undemanding and undemonstrative Richard, who could not even "bring himself to say he loved her; not in so many words," and with whom she could feel "a virginity preserved though childbirth which clung to her like a sheet." She does admit to feeling a *frisson* of eroticism for her childhood friend Sally Seaton, with whom she had once shared a tender girlish kiss, and she admits to later being occasionally attracted to "the charm of a woman, not a girl." But these occasions have lasted "only for a moment," and she never experienced them with a man, keeping Clarissa's soul safe.

It is easy enough to see a mentally frangible, emotionally protective woman and closeted lesbian here, like Virginia Woolf herself. But look instead at what Virginia Woolf does with Clarissa Dalloway. She has her react to personal tragedy and her psychological vulnerability with not only inner defenses but an affirming social ethic. In the words of Peter Walsh, since Clarissa disdained religion and thought "no one was to blame, . . . possibly she said to herself, As we are a doomed race, chained to a sinking ship, . . . as the whole thing is a bad joke, let us, at any rate, do our part; mitigate the sufferings of our fellow-prisoners. . . . So she evolved this atheist's religion of doing good for the sake of goodness." This meant being "as decent as we possibly can," trying at least to "decorate the dungeon with flowers and air cushions." For she believed—to switch to a religious metaphor—"those ruffians, the Gods, shan't have it all their own way" because these "Gods, who never lost a chance of hurting, thwarting and spoiling human lives, were seriously put out if, all the same, you behaved like a lady."

To behave like a lady. That is the heart of Clarissa Dalloway's ethic. This ethic has gone largely disregarded by readers probably because it smacks of a vestigial political incorrectness, as well what the critic quoted earlier dismissed as Clarissa's "comically slender... creativity of everyday feminine life." But we should be able by now to see the blindness of these perceptions. Clarissa Dalloway sets a standard of humane will and social conscience that anyone could proudly emulate. Gender is irrelevant to it. That standard requires, for one thing, performing the social gestures that warm people's moods and soften their interactions. Clarissa Dalloway performs those gestures in part through a "network of visiting, leaving cards, being kind to people, running about with bunches of flowers, little presents." There is nothing "comically slender" in that. Without such gestures, social relations would be left to harsher needs, more selfish interests, and neglect. As the English used to say, these gestures help to *gentle* social life with pleasing grace and benign sensitivity to others. This is a style of life shaped by the morality of manners and the ethics of civility.

Under assault for decades in America by the legions of psychological authenticity, cultural equality, and social informality, this morality and ethics have been derided into hypocrisy. Young people in their uniforms of shredded jeans, rumpled backpacks, and comfy running shoes tend to think—along with the generation that bred them and the commercial culture that abets them—that they are making the world better by scorning the likes of Clarissa Dalloway's manners and glorifying an earthy naturalness, instinctive integrity, and undefiled egalitarian individualism. But, as Alexis de Tocqueville had warned that democratic manners might do, this vaunted authenticity can reduce social appearances and practices to a lazy

8. *Mrs. Dalloway* and the Ethics of Civility

sameness masquerading as individualism, and even to a bestial vulgarity sanctioning public incivility in general. Clarissa Dalloway's *gentling* social gestures are not false at all. They should remind us how valuable manners and civility can be in bringing reciprocal respect and an ennoblingly humane grace and style to social life.

Then there are Clarissa Dalloway's parties. They are the crowning act of her ethics. She says as much when silently trying "to defend herself" against Richard and Peter, who, she thinks, "criticized her very unfairly, laughed at her very unjustly, for her parties." At first she gropes. Then it strikes her. "What she liked was simply life. 'That's what I do it for,' she said, speaking aloud, to life." But then she wonders, "What did it mean to her, this thing she called life?"

It means a constellation of things. These begin, as the novel does, with the "divine vitality" of London: "the bellow and the uproar; the carriages, motor cars, omnibuses, vans, sandwich men shuffling and swinging; brass bands; barrel organs," for this "was what she loved; life; London; this moment in June." Clarissa Dalloway's London is as far from that of T. S. Eliot's in *The Waste Land* (published three years before *Mrs. Dalloway*) as is her character from that of alienated modernist antiheroes. Clarissa Dalloway loves modern urban life. And that is no small achievement for someone who feels that it is "very, very dangerous to live even one day."

But her moments of urban exuberance are not the whole answer. As Clarissa thinks more about the particular quality of "life" that her parties celebrate, she discovers that it is not so much the sheer vitality of London as it is the saving charms and benevolence of civilized social life. "Oh, it was very queer," she thinks. "Here was So-and-so in South Kensington; some one up in Bayswater; and somebody else, say, in Mayfair. And she felt quite continuously a sense of their existence; and she felt what a waste; . . . she felt if only they could be brought together; so she did it." She would bring them together—in a party.

She did this for more than social entertainment. "It was her gift," she thinks, her way to "pay back from this secret deposit of exquisite moments" what she owes to *life*. It was also her way of thwarting the Gods, of wresting from life's terrors a kind of redemption with "an offering; to combine, to create." Perhaps Virginia Woolf lets Clarissa's thoughts get a bit puffy here. But what Clarissa wants to create is in truth nothing less than the essential ingredient of civil society.

A cheerful philosophical term coined in the Scottish Enlightenment betokening innate sociability, "civil society" has nowadays become a concept for the marriage of the individual and the civic life consummated by collaborations among enlightened citizens, voluntary associations, and public institutions. We might think of civil society as an expanding web of human relations spun from threads of individual and common interests by the beneficial practices of civility. (The legal scholar and social critic Stephen L. Carter ably described this process in *Civility: Manners, Morals, and the Etiquette of Democracy* [1998].) The web of civil society at once links citizens and civilizes them. And a healthy modern democracy is often said to depend on it. Clarissa Dalloway would approve. ("Civil society" is not, by the way, the same thing as "community," that vacuous tag for purported kinships attached these days to any aggregation of people from neighbors at a barbecue to sprawling ethnic groups to the entire human populace under the oxymoron "global community.")

Clarissa Dalloway's parties spin this web by assembling far-flung Londoners (practically every character in the book shows up at her party at the end, including the prime minister, to Clarissa's gratification, in a festive setting where everyone dresses splendidly and behaves beautifully, except for the dreadful psychotherapist Bradshaw, who brings news of Septimus Smith's suicide, disgusting Clarissa at his uncivil tactlessness), where everyone's social circle invariably widens, and from which no one leaves as quite the same person who had arrived. The sociologist of role-playing, Erving Goffman, once declared that "the world, in truth, is a wedding, . . . a party . . .

where reality is being performed." He had in mind how our benign social interactions both create and fête the social world in which we live our lives and form our public selves. That is the intent of Clarissa Dalloway's parties. She brings people together to weave the web of civil society while *gentling* them as social beings.

Even Peter Walsh gets swept up in her party. For here he sees her "prancing, sparkling" with the "ease and air of a creature floating in its element" and having about her "an inexpressible dignity; an exquisite cordiality as if she wished the whole world well."

And she does wish the whole world well—to spite the Gods. Clarissa Dalloway is, as Peter Walsh has remarked (with misplaced disdain), "the perfect hostess." She does what good hostesses and hosts always do: they bring out the best in their guests and make those guests feel good about themselves as social beings. Clarissa knows this calls for a distinctly seductive charm, a subtle social performance, a special art or style. The connoisseur of Renaissance court etiquette, Baldassare Castiglione, whose *Book of the Courtier* set the standard of proper courtly behavior, or "courtesy," labeled this art *sprezzatura*. It is "the art which does not seem to be art," he said, the skill of making every action, every gesture, seem natural and spontaneous, not artificial or even deliberately artful. "She did it genuinely" muses Peter Walsh, "from a natural instinct." Clarissa Dalloway makes her "offering," her "gift to life," as a hostess who assembles people from all over London and *gentles* them with *sprezzatura*.

"Every time she gave a party," Clarissa reflects, "she had this feeling of being something not herself and that every one was unreal in one way; much more real in another. It was, she thought, partly their clothes, partly being taken out of their ordinary ways, partly the background, it was possible to say things you couldn't say anyhow else, things that needed an effort; possible to go much deeper." Parties enable us to go deeper? That contradicts our ordinary assumptions. But it is what Clarissa Dalloway wants her parties to do. Or perhaps we should say she wants them to make people go higher, elevating individuals above their isolated, instinctual everyday selves. "She made her drawing room a sort of meeting place," Peter Walsh observes. "over and over again he had seen her take some raw youth, twist him, turn him, wake him up, set him going" in the graces of civility. And he concedes that whatever else he might think of Clarissa's parties, when he attended one he would always "have an experience" of "beauty anyhow."

In her way, Clarissa Dalloway is indeed an artist. But she is no Pater-esque aesthete who savors beautiful sensations for themselves. Hers is the art of forming civil society for "the growing good of the world." This art is at once aesthetic and ethical. For it requires, along with *sprezzatura*, a certain moral will no less than imagination. Virginia Woolf even hinted at this herself twenty years before writing *Mrs. Dalloway*. "The truth is," she wrote in an unpublished diary essay of 1903, "to be successful socially one wants the courage of a hero" (quoted by Phyllis Rose in *Woman of Letters: A Life of Virginia Woolf* [1978]). Clarissa Dalloway has that heroism, as noted earlier, through her artistry of social style, whether Virginia Woolf intended it or not. We could even say that Clarissa Dalloway is the companion of Friedrich Nietzsche's strong "artists who . . . build states," for "their work is an instinctive creation and imposition of form" for the sake of civilization (see "Nietzsche and Wilde: Cultural Rebellion and an Ethics of Style" below).

And that is Clarissa Dalloway's triumph over tragedy, her thwarting of the Gods by being "a lady." Summoning "courage and endurance; a perfectly upright and stoical bearing," as she had admired others for doing, she rises above the injuries and anxieties of her inner life to become a moralist and model of the public life of civil society.

Never mind *Mrs. Dalloway*'s academic claims as a monument of literary Modernism and a foray into feminism. Set aside its sources in Virginia Woolf's biography. Do not be deceived by the touches of melodrama and sentimentality that occasionally invade the narrative. And do not be swayed by myopic readers who cannot see the forest in the book for the trees. *Mrs. Dalloway* deserves to stand high among novels about character and culture. And it is the surpassing novel—luminous, inspiriting, humane, and true—about the arts of sociability, the morality of manners, the ethics of civility.

A previous version of this essay appeared in *The Sewanee Review*, Fall, 1999, and a somewhat more detailed examination of the novel, with a biographical note on Virginia Woolf, can be found as a chapter in my book *Worldly Wisdom: Great Books and the Meanings of Life* (2008).

Friedrich Nietzsche, c. 1882; Oscar Wilde, c. 1895.

"One thing is needful: Giving style to one's character—a great and rare art."
—NIETZSCHE

"It is style that makes us believe in a thing—nothing but style."
—WILDE

Nietzsche and Wilde

CULTURAL REBELLION AND AN ETHICS OF STYLE

*O*n a late August day in the year 1900, in the "sick room" of a small villa on the outskirts of Weimar, Germany, the most incendiary thinker of the nineteenth century—or probably any other—Friedrich Nietzsche, sank into a coma and died. Attended by his sister, Elisabeth, who had cared for him during his last three years, Nietzsche had fallen on the mercies of others in January, 1889, after syphilis had rotted his brain and he had collapsed on a street of Turin, Italy, at the age of forty-four. His behavior and writings had grown increasingly eccentric in the months preceding that fateful day, culminating in a spate of erratic missives signed with such *noms de plume* as "Nietzsche Caesar," "Dionysus," and "The Crucified." From then on, nothing consequential, or even truly coherent, issued from the pen of the thinker who had proclaimed in his last published book: "I am dynamite!"

A few months after Nietzsche died, another flamboyant and emblematic figure of that era, Oscar Wilde, dejected by ostracism, beleaguered by debt, and wracked by illness, lay in an upper room of the nondescript Hotel d'Alsace (now the chic L'Hotel) on the Left Bank in Paris. "My wallpaper and I are fighting a duel to the death," he complained to visitors. "One or the other of us has to go." And there, wryly observing, "I am dying beyond my means," he did die on November 30. He was forty-six years old. Like Nietzsche, Wilde had gone silent as a writer, or nearly so, in his last years. Sent to prison for homosexual crimes at the pinnacle of his fame in May 1895, shortly after the opening in London of his hit plays *An Ideal Husband* and *The Importance of Being Earnest*. He had emerged two years later a broken man. He wrote virtually nothing thereafter except the long mournful poem *The Ballad of Reading Gaol*, which he signed with only his prison identification number: C.3.3.

Nietzsche surely knew nothing of Wilde. And, although Wilde had plenty of opportunities to know of Nietzsche, Wilde left no recorded reference to him. But Nietzsche and Wilde shared several bonds. Besides their premature and equally melancholy departures from this world at almost the same time, they were, for one thing, allies in the modernist rebellion against the prevailing conventional culture of nineteenth-century Europe. Some of their contemporaries recognized the affinity and either damned or praised Nietzsche and Wilde for being intellectually iconoclastic, morally insolent, possibly dangerous, and perhaps a little daft.

The impassioned German critic Max Nordau mercilessly flogged the pair in his pseudomedical diagnosis of late nineteenth-century European artists and thinkers, *Entartung* (1892), published in English as *Degeneration* (1895). Nordau detected symptoms of Nietzsche's and Wilde's "degeneration" in a pathological "ego-mania" that blinded them to "things as they are" and induced them to exalt themselves "above all constraints of morality." He dubbed Nietzsche the "philosopher" of this "ego-mania"—a "madman" with "flashing eyes, wild gestures, foaming at the mouth, spouting forth deafening bombast" and "demented raving[s]" against the "foundations of ethics" to serve a bestial "anthropophobia" and an "individualism . . . for which the external world is non-existent." Nordau placed Wilde frothing not far away among the "decadents and aesthetes," possessed by a "megalomaniacal contempt for men," an "ego-maniacal recklessness and hysterical longing to make a sensation," "a malevolent mania for contradiction," and a delusional "glorification of art" as "the highest of all human functions." To clinch his case for this shared pathology, Nordau quoted a series of feisty aphorisms from both authors in his chapter on Nietzsche, noting their striking similarities and concluding, "this is more than a resemblance"; it is an "identity of mental qualities" in "egomaniacal degenerates."

Nietzsche remained ignorant of Nordau's indictment, lost as he was by then in his actual derangement. But Wilde knew about Nordau's book. And in a piquant irony, he even cited Nordau's medical authority in a letter to the Home Secretary of July 2, 1896, appealing for early release from prison. "Professor Nordau," Wilde pointed out, has demonstrated the "intimate connection between madness and the literary and artistic temperament." In the light of Nordau's findings, Wilde argued, he should himself be seen as an artist suffering from a "sexual madness" ranking among "diseases to be cured," not "crimes to be punished." Wilde's appeal won no sympathy from the Home Secretary.

Not long after Wilde mailed his futile letter, another of his contemporaries, André Gide, who had met Wilde in 1891 and had fallen under his influence, along with that of Nietzsche, loosely united the two in the fictional character of Ménalque, first in *Les Nourritures terrestres* (1897) then more memorably in *L'Immoraliste* (1902). Gide gives Ménalque the "immoralism" of Wilde's impious tongue and of Nietzsche's radical ideas, and he has Ménalque convert a young man in *L'Immoraliste* with his seductively wicked ideas and phrases to match. "Regrets, remorse, repentance, are past joys seen from behind," he advises coldly. Then, spinning a fateful web of moral irony, he explains that "there is nothing more detestable" than "a man of principle" because such people "never do anything but what their principles decreed"; hence you cannot "expect any sort of sincerity from them." Adopting this contrarian code, the young man convinces himself that the "worst instincts" are the "sincerest." And, acting on this code, he pursues his own desires to the detriment and ultimate death from disease of his wife, who wanly laments that his doctrine "does away with the weak." To which he callously replies, "And so it should!" Nietzsche would have applauded. Wilde would have written the scene for laughs.

I. On Style and the Good Life

Nietzsche and Wilde were truly "immoralists" gleefully deflating what they deemed the cheap pieties, smug hypocrisies, inane opinions, and easy self-deceptions of the culture around them. But, just as they assailed these common enemies, they also extolled common virtues, and they forged these virtues into similarly affirming ethical ideals (albeit Nietzsche scorned the term "ideals" as cant of a disingenuous culture). Those ideals amounted to an aesthetic ethics, or what I will call an ethics of style. But before taking up that ethics, we must make a short excursion through the combative careers of the two authors in order to set the stage for their prescription to redeem the modern world—with style.

Ten years Wilde's senior (to the day but one), Nietzsche was born October 15, 1844, and launched his career as a cultural dissident at age twenty-seven with his first book, *The Birth of Tragedy* (1871). It earned him a measure of scholarly disdain for its cheeky tone and wild speculations on the irrationality of ancient Greek culture—speculations not welcomed by those revering the presumed rational composure of Greek classicism. But Nietzsche was acquiring contempt for academic pedantry, received ideas, and the modern confidence in rationality and progress. He pilloried these kinds of things in writings over the next few years—and he would later devote a chapter to scholars in *Thus Spoke Zarathustra*, sneering, "I have departed from the house of the scholars" because "their petty sayings and truths chill me" as they "knit the socks of the soul" (most of the Nietzsche quotations here come from translations by Walter Kaufmann).

From those irreverent beginnings, Nietzsche fervently embraced the role of intellectual outsider. And he played that role with mounting zest, especially after chucking his academic post in philology at the University of Basel in 1879. For the next ten years he let his thoughts range freely in a barrage of explosive books that defied strict consistency and left no piety, no convention, no accepted idea intact. In the last of these books, his autobiographical *Ecce Homo*,

9. Nietzsche and Wilde

he exulted, under the heading "Why I Am a Destiny," that "I am not a man, I am dynamite!" And he targeted for detonation most unrelentingly the reigning assumptions of contemporary morality, tainted as these were by the platitudes of Christianity.

Morality possesses no objective truth, Nietzsche repeatedly insists. We merely invent "a moral interpretation of phenomena" to serve our interests and often to mask our self-deceptions. And he thought the dominant "moral interpretations" of his day masked, as he elaborated in *On the Genealogy of Morals*, a "sublime self-deception." This self-deception "interprets weakness as freedom" and as goodness, and it interprets strength as evil, prompting revenge of the weak against the strong because "whoever is dissatisfied with himself is always ready to revenge himself therefore." He called this the morality of *ressentiment*, or resentment. And he imagined this morality being created in "workshops" where "weakness is being lied into something meritorious" such as "goodness of heart," "humility," "patience," and "loving one's enemies." For "the man of *ressentiment*" does not see what he is doing. He "is neither upright nor naïve nor honest with himself. His soul squints; his spirit loves hiding places, secret paths, and back doors." He lurks in dark corners, licking his wounds and awaiting his chance with "a mendaciousness that is abysmal but innocent, true-hearted, blue-eyed, and virtuous." And, Nietzsche asks, "is that not *our* fate?" Yes, he answers with venomous irony dripping from his pen, "this is how things are: modern morality has made people more good natured, more prudent, more comfortable, more mediocre, more indifferent, more Chinee, more Christian—there is no doubt that man is getting 'better' all the time."

Here was the crux of Nietzsche's moral revolution: modern morality is "a seduction, a poison, a narcotic, through which the present" lives "*at the expense of the future*," and so it must be overturned. And that means responding to the question "What is good?" by saying: "Everything that heightens the feeling of power in man, the will to power, power itself." And to the question, "What

I. ON STYLE AND THE GOOD LIFE

is bad?" we must reply: "Everything that is born of weakness" (*The Anti-Christ*). Only through these truths can we have a "man who justifies man . . . something perfect, wholly achieved, happy, mighty, triumphant, something still capable of arousing fear!" To this end, Nietzsche cries, "I welcome all signs that a more manly, a warlike age is about to begin," led by "preparatory men" to be followed by a genuinely "Higher Man"—and then the *Übermensch*, the Superior Man, the Superman.

That is the now-familiar radical Nietzsche who, as he bragged, chose to "philosophize with a hammer" and let the chips fall (preface, *Ecce Homo*). No wonder he found enthusiastic disciples among warmongers such as Gabriele D'Annunzio and Adolf Hitler, who read him only selectively, ignoring his contempt for those lusting to wield power over others, and abetted as they were by Nietzsche's pernicious, nationalistic, anti-Semitic sister Elisabeth, who published her invalid brother's complete works in a bastardized edition that skewed his ideas for her own nationalistic political purposes— and about whom Nietzsche had warned: "People like by sister must be irreconcilable enemies of my thought and my philosophy." But martial bravado aside, Nietzsche could appeal to anyone yearning to elevate culture and humanity. High-minded humanists have lauded him, among them the socialist playwright George Bernard Shaw and the culturally conservative philosopher Ortega y Gasset. Iconoclast and idealist, Nietzsche would encapsulate his moral fervor and philosophy in the ethics of style that he shared with the Irish-born Nietzsche, Oscar Wilde.

While Nietzsche was savaging European morality with his revolutionary books of the 1880s, Oscar Wilde, whose career would be as brief as Nietzsche's, was becoming a youthful celebrity in England for poking fun at much the same thing. Brashly donning the role of dandy, Wilde cut a swath through London and America with his imposing physical form flashily bedecked, his manner airily flippant, and his facile wit tossing off cleverly irreverent remarks every time he opened his mouth or set his pen to paper. From his first recorded wisecrack, when he told his college friends, "I find it harder and harder every day to live up to my blue China," on through his provocative essays, his sensational novel *The Picture of Dorian Gray* (1891), his scandalous drama *Salomé* (1893), and his outpouring of drawing-room comedies in the early 1890s, Wilde flouted Victorian pieties and flaunted his daring with Nietzschean bravado and his own panache, laughing at everything, playing with paradoxes, and behaving as though life was something of a joke and he had nothing to fear from anyone.

And just as Nietzsche had philosophized fiercely about how modern morality masked self-deception, self-interest, and resentment, Wilde blithely joked about how people use morality to these same ends—recycling many of his best lines from one setting to another and collecting a batch of them in 1894 under the deceptively sober title "Phrases and Philosophy for the Use of the Young" (this and Wilde's other important nonfictional writings can be found in *The Artist as Critic*, ed. Richard Ellmann). "Morality is simply the attitude we adopt towards people whom we personally dislike," he would say. And "wickedness is a myth invented by good people to account for the curious attractiveness of others." And again, "A man who moralizes is usually a hypocrite, and a woman who moralizes is invariably plain." All of which is to say that modern morality is a self-serving lie. Such moral self-deceptions spurred Wilde to tease that "any preoccupation with ideas of what is right or wrong conduct shows an arrested intellectual development." For that matter, he writes in the saucily probing dialogue "The Critic as Artist" (1891), "even a colour-sense is more important in the development of an individual than a sense of right and wrong."

In this bodacious Nietzschean spirit Wilde delighted in turning morality on its head, telling us that the modern idea of *good* is actually *bad*, and the modern idea of *bad* is probably *good*. Take, for instance, "Humanitarian Sympathy." This moral attitude "wars against Nature," Wilde charges, "by securing the survival of the failure." And he has Lady Bracknell, that hilarious snob in *The Importance of Being Earnest*, deride "the modern sympathy with invalids" as "morbid" because "illness of any kind is hardly a thing to be encouraged in others." Likewise, he has both Lord Henry in *The Picture of Dorian Gray* and Lord Illingworth in *A Woman of No Importance* fault "sympathy for the sufferings of the poor" as "the special vice of the age" because it denies "the joy, the beauty, the color of life." As Nietzsche had said with heavy irony, modern morality is making people "'better' all the time"—at a grave cost to the energies of life. Wilde could be speaking for Nietzsche when he has Lord Henry also warn that nowadays "for any man of culture" to accept the moral "standard of his age" would be "the grossest immorality."

Fomenting his moral revolution, Wilde, like Nietzsche, staked his claim for the very opposite of conventional *good*. We must learn to see, he writes, that "what is termed Sin is an essential element of progress." For "without it the world would stagnate" in "current notions about morality" that enshrine "monotony of type." In fact, he adds, "in its rejection" of those current notions, sin becomes "one with the higher ethics." Wilde grants "it is sad to be told that it is immoral to be consciously good" ("A Chinese Sage"), but he also thinks people should be heartened by the freedom to submit to their desires, wherever these may lead. Hence, Lord Henry's advice against self-restraint: "The only way to get rid of a temptation is to yield to it. Resist it and the soul grows sick with longing" because "every impulse that we strive to strangle broods in the mind, and poisons us" (a diagnosis that echoes Nietzsche's criticism of *ressentiment*). What is more, Wilde speculates. "If we lived long enough to see the results of our actions, it may be that those who call themselves good would be sickened with dull remorse, and those the world calls evil stirred by a noble joy." Lending the idea a lighter touch, he has Jack observe in *Earnest* that "a high moral tone can hardly be said to conduce very much to either one's health or one's happiness."

9. Nietzsche and Wilde

Giving the virtues of *evil* and the vices of *good* yet another toss, Wilde even turns hypocrisy on its head. "So many conceited people go about society pretending to be good," he has Lord Darlington crack in *Lady Windermere's Fan*, "that I think it shows a rather sweet and modest disposition to pretend to be bad." And neatly recasting the idea in *Earnest*, he has Cecily caution Algernon against "leading a double life, pretending to be wicked and being really good all the time. That would be hypocrisy." How could any moral pretensions stand up to that?

All of Wilde's social comedies play on these themes. Unmasking hypocrisies and often honoring "sin," these comedies reveal good people to be not as good as they think they are, and bad people be not as bad as others judge them. The prime target of Wilde's moral barbs was, predictably, the Victorian creed of "earnestness." This creed required taking everything very seriously, upholding a "high moral" tone, exuding sincerity, working diligently, and demanding objective truth, as well as other solemn virtues. And it gave Wilde plentiful opportunities to mock the culture of "being earnest."

He took an obvious slap at this creed by having Lord Illingworth, in *A Woman of No Importance*, loftily refuse to "take sides in anything" because that brings "sincerity, and earnestness follows shortly thereafter, and the human being becomes a bore." But, as every reader of Wilde knows, he most famously skewered earnestness in his most popular play, *The Importance of Being Earnest*, which takes its title from the word and its theme from inverting the word's meaning. Wilde told a newspaper reporter that he wrote the play to dramatize how "we should treat all trivial things very seriously, and all the serious things of life with sincere and studied triviality." And he would put that idea in the subtitle of the play: "A Trivial Comedy for Serious People." He carried out his plan with a skein of witticism and humorous plot twists that rise to a climax in a comically ironic demonstration that the "importance of being earnest" consists in nothing more than the lead character discovering that his true given name is not John (Jack), as he had thought, but *Ernest*, the prized male name in Victorian England, which renders him now a suitable husband for his previously resistant beloved. Wilde's pun on the word made the name laughable and the morality with it. But, as his subtitle had suggested, it was serious laughter.

Wilde's ridicule of earnestness went with his satirizing of claims to objective truth. And this satire brought serious laughter, too. An admirer of the Taoist thinker Chuang Tzu (the subject of "A Chinese Sage") for his goofy paradoxes on the irrationalities of existence, Wilde acutely sensed the paradoxes and ironies that pervade this topsy-turvy world where good things can be bad, and bad things good, and where things at once *are* and *are not* what they seem. He conveyed this way of looking at things in spiky epigrams revealing the "amusing paradoxes" of life, as he liked to call them, that he thought everyone should see.

"Truth is independent of the facts always, inventing or selecting them at pleasure," he writes in "The Truth of Masks." He might seem to be saying here that we should not trust appearances. But that would be too obvious, lacking in irony. So he has Lord Henry assert that "it is only shallow people who do not judge by appearances" because "the true mystery of the world is the visible, not the invisible." And in "The Decay of Lying" he says, "truth is entirely and absolutely a matter of style." Appearances might be subjective and fugitive, but they are the only truths we have. Striking a philosophical note on these notions, Wilde concludes "The Truth of Masks" with these words: "The truths of metaphysics are the truths of masks." And, just as this peppers life with actual paradoxes and ironies inhospitable to objective truth, Wilde figured it also works to the advantage of art.

Extrapolating elsewhere on these themes, Wilde tells us that "things are because we see them," and we see many of them because artists have taught us to see them, like the fogs in London that "did not exist until Art had invented them." In the same vein Wilde commended "lying for its own sake" as an act of creation in art and life, and he rued "the decay of lying" as a loss of creativity

9. Nietzsche and Wilde

in modern times. It should have come as no surprise, therefore, that when asked at his first trial for homosexual indecency if he believed everything he wrote to be true, Wild nonchalantly replied, "I rarely think that anything I write is true." A punchline but a bit of philosophy, too—and a Wildean paradoxical defense.

While Wilde sent up all kinds of earnestness—jeering at conventional morality, professing triviality, scrambling sincerity, playing with paradoxes, and denying objective truth—he also aspired, like Nietzsche, to supplant the prevailing moral follies with a "higher ethics." This was the aesthetic ethics of style that animated both of them in their cultural battles from the beginning of their careers to the end.

Nietzsche had imagined this kind of ethics at the outset of his career with his ideas on art in *The Birth of Tragedy*. Inspired by his early admiration of Wagner (which later descended into loathing of Wagner's vulgar theatricality and grotesque Germanic chauvinism), Nietzsche asserts in the preface that "art is the highest human task, the true metaphysical activity." And he had decided (as he explains in a subsequent introduction to the book of 1886) that Western culture had sprung not from moral ideas but from "Dionysian" energies and "Apollonian" restraints that together had "called art into being as a completion and consummation of existence"—before soft "Socratic ethics" took over and commenced the moral decline of the West. That is, Nietzsche had decided art preceded morality and transcends it—or, rather, art should define morality.

From there, Nietzsche had gone on in various writings to treat art as the supreme model of all higher culture. Even law and the state, he said, come from the "terrible artist's egotism" that wrests order from chaos. "Those artists of violence and organizers who build states," he wrote, are in fact the "most involuntary, unconscious artists of all" because "their work is an instinctive creation and imposition of form." The discipline of artistic form—wherever it may appear—gave Nietzsche his aesthetic ethics of style.

He rapturously describes this ethics in *The Gay Science*. "One thing is needful," he proclaims: "'Giving style' to one's character—a great and rare art." This art belongs to "those who see all the strengths and weaknesses of their own natures and then comprehend them in an artistic plan . . . here the ugly which could not be removed is hidden; there it has been reinterpreted and made sublime . . . until everything appears as art and reason and even weakness delights the eye." But it takes a "strong and domineering" character to do this, for "weak characters without power over themselves who hate the constraint of style" could never do it.

This ethics might seem merely to embellish on the oft-quoted words of the Comte de Buffon from the eighteenth century: "Style is the man himself." But it doesn't. Buffon was observing how literary style expresses an author's personality. Nietzsche was talking about style as a quality of personality itself, or rather a quality imposed by strong personalities on themselves. Arising from imaginative *individuality*, depending on clear-eyed *honesty*, animated by Dionysian *energies*, and imposed by the artistic *discipline* of Apollonian *form*, this ethics of style is an art of life—not *lifestyle*, that ubiquitous catchword of our consumer culture—as both an aesthetic ethics and an ethical aesthetics. This is an aesthetics with ethical consequences, and an ethics with aesthetic form.

But skip the slippery semantics. The point is, if we can give style to our characters, Nietzsche says, we will reap many rewards. In the first place, "this secret self-ravishment, this artist's cruelty, this delight in imposing form upon oneself as a hard, recalcitrant, suffering material" gives us satisfaction with ourselves. As Nietzsche emphasizes, "one thing is needful: that a human being attain satisfaction with himself—whether it be by this or that poetry or art." For "whoever is dissatisfied with himself is always ready to revenge himself therefore; we others will be his victims, if only by always having to stand his ugly sight."

The satisfaction that comes with "imposing form on oneself" points to two more related rewards of style: beauty and good cheer.

9. Nietzsche and Wilde

The "delight in imposing form upon oneself," Nietzsche explains, yields "an abundance of strange new beauty and affirmation, and perhaps beauty itself." And this delight brings "cheerfulness" to those "who enjoy their finest gaiety" through "constraint and perfection under a law of their own"—whereas "the sight of the ugly makes men bad and gloomy."

Strength and satisfaction, form and delight, beauty and good cheer. Style entails them all. Then comes a final reward: laughter. "Do not forget good laughter," he advises his "Higher Men" (in the exuberant chapter on "The Higher Man" in *Thus Spoke Zarathustra*). "Laughter I have declared sacred; you higher men, learn how to laugh" (words he repeated at the end of his introduction of 1886 to *The Birth of Tragedy*). Nietzsche's ethics of style was no laughing matter. But laughter goes with it. For those with the imagination and strength, as he says, to "live dangerously" and to give style to their character will "learn how to laugh" as they achieve "the greatest fruitfulness and the greatest enjoyment of existence." No ethics can promise more than that.

Whether or not Oscar Wilde was one of Nietzsche's "Higher Men," he could live dangerously, impose style on his character, and laugh with Nietzschean gaiety in the name of a "higher ethics." Although that ethics owed much to art and aesthetics, it went beyond the love of art for its own sake and the aestheticism that often sticks to Wilde.

Wilde did, of course, enjoy gibing that art and aesthetics have nothing to do with ethics. Following his mentors Théophile Gautier and Walter Pater, he would repeatedly claim that "the sphere of Art and the sphere of Ethics are absolutely distinct," and "an artist has no ethical sympathies at all" (letter of July 9, 1890). He would also contend that "all art is immoral" and that "aesthetics are higher than ethics" and "it is better to be beautiful than to be good," and "to discern the beauty of a thing is the finest point to which we can arrive." His critics accused him of not only preaching this amoral aestheticism, but of practicing it. And he gave them cause. Like Gustave von Aschenbach in Thomas Mann's *Death in Venice*—who believed beauty "indifferent to good and evil"—Wilde found beauty not just in art but in a seductive boy. Wilde's boy was the fatal brat Lord Alfred Douglas, and Wilde's attraction to him ruined Wilde in late Victorian England as surely as obsession with the beautiful youth Tadzio would destroy the fictional Aschenbach in cholera-ridden Venice.

Notwithstanding the amoral aestheticism that laces much of his flashy rhetoric, Wilde (like another of his mentors, John Ruskin) saw that art actually contains both aesthetics and ethics. "If a work of art is rich, vital, and complete," he responded to a critic of the first version of *Dorian Gray* (published in *Lippincott's Monthly Magazine*, June 20, 1890), it will exhibit both "artistic beauty" and "ethical beauty." People with "artistic instincts" will see the first, and "those to whom ethics appeal more will see its moral lesson." Exceptional people, however, will "see a work of art fully, completely perfectly" as a marriage of aesthetics and ethics (Wilde letters to the *Scots Observer* in July and August, 1890).

Wilde had in fact endorsed his own ethical notion of art, implicitly and explicitly, despite his catchy phrases to the contrary, from the time he stepped onto the public stage. A lionized expert on things beautiful while still in his twenties, he gave a lecture to silver miners in Leadville, Colorado, entitled "Ethics of Art" during his American tour of 1882 and so roused their enthusiasm for the subject that they named a new vein of ore "The Oscar." And in cities and towns across the country he presented public discourses on topics like "The Decorative Arts" and "The House Beautiful," announcing, "I want to make this artistic movement the basis for a new civilization." Later he would boast in "The Soul of Man Under Socialism" that a "revolution in house-decoration and furniture and the like" was now under way in England, bringing a widening "appreciation of beauty" in everyday life and demonstrating that "people have been to a very great extent civilized."

9. Nietzsche and Wilde

Wilde believed this "new civilization," shaped by "the ethics of art," would embody nothing so much as style. For, like Nietzsche, he thought style is the artistic form that human beings should impose on themselves and on their experience. He has Lord Henry assert that "the canons of good society are, or should be, the same as the canons of art," for "form," or style, "is absolutely essential to it." He has Gwendolyn remark in *Earnest* that "in matters of grave importance, style, not sincerity, is the vital thing." And in "The Decay of Lying" he not only insists that "the condition of all art is style," but he declares that "truth is entirely and absolutely a matter of style" and goes on to say "it is style that makes us believe in a thing—nothing but style," by which he meant that artistic form or style teaches us how to envision truth and to see the world, as it did with the fogs in London.

In "The Critic as Artist" Wilde openly applied this notion to life itself. His words again echo Nietzsche's. "Life," he writes, "is terribly deficient in form"; therefore, we have "the duty of imposing form upon chaos." For "form is everything. It is the secret of life," at once "the birth of passion" and "the death of pain." Owing to these powers of form and to our "aesthetic instinct" to use them, he assures us: "Find expression for a sorrow, and it will become dear to you. Find expression for a joy, and you intensify the ecstasy." That is to say, artistic form, or style, mitigates our pains and enhances our pleasures by presenting "all things under their conditions of beauty."

Wilde also has Lord Henry play upon this idea in describing what he calls the "tragedies of life." These tragedies disturb us most, Lord Henry says, when they arrive with an "entire lack of style" in "absolute incoherence," thereby throwing us into disarray. By contrast, "a tragedy that possesses artistic elements" troubles us less because we can appreciate its "dramatic effect." Then we can become beguiled observers rather than terrified witnesses, as the "wonder of the spectacle enthralls us." Dorian Gray exploited this idea when he turned the suicide of his fiancée, an actress whom he had spurned for giving a bad performance, into a dramatic event to be appreciated. "This thing that has happened does not affect me as it should," he says to himself. It "seems to me to be simply like a wonderful ending to a wonderful play" with "all the terrible beauty of a Greek tragedy." Style or form might not altogether spare us from tragedy, but it can make tragedy endurable, even improbably pleasing. As Nietzsche says, through the discipline of style, or "the delight of imposing form," everything "delights the eye."

Wilde judged the discipline of style, "imposing form upon chaos," to be an ethical as much as an aesthetic act. By the same token, he often tended to elevate aesthetics above ethics, as he does explicitly in the phrase, "aesthetics are higher than ethics." But Wilde also knew that dangers lie in exalting aesthetics above ethics. What is *The Picture of Dorian Gray* if not a testimony to this? Wilde himself said its story of a dashing young man who lives solely for beauty and pleasure and never seems to age while a portrait of him ages and reveals the corruption of his soul, has such an "extremely obvious moral" that "the real trouble I experienced in writing" it was managing to "subordinate" that moral "to the artistic and dramatic effect" (letter of June 27, 1890). He tried to do this by, for instance, giving that moral a characteristic twist of irony. He has Dorian Gray concede to Lord Henry that it is not enough to remain beautiful in appearance if your soul goes ugly through evil. Dorian wants his soul to be beautiful, too. So he decides to mend his amoral ways. "I want to be good," he explains, because "I can't bear the idea of my soul being hideous"—suggesting Nietzsche's observation that "the sight of the ugly makes men bad and gloomy." But Lord Henry isn't fooled. He sees that Dorian has only switched his aestheticism from body to soul, and he drolly replies: "A very charming artistic basis for ethics, Dorian! I congratulate you." Quite so. In any case, by then both Dorian's soul and his portrait have begun their inexorable descent into hideousness.

But Lord Henry and Dorian Gray got the "artistic basis for ethics" wrong. "Imposing form upon chaos," or "giving style to one's character," does not mean—even to Oscar Wilde—creating or appreciating the beauty of form for its own sake. It means achieving through the hard discipline of style the "higher ethics" of what Wilde and Nietzsche both considered the crowning goal of art and life. Nietzsche called this end the "Higher Man" (prior to the *Übermensch*). Wilde called it the "true personality of man." As he has Lord Henry put it: "The aim of life is self-development. To realize one's nature perfectly." Although Lord Henry gives this principle his own perverse uses, Wilde repeats the phrase over and over. And he makes it the central theme of his most ambitious philosophical essay, "The Soul of Man under Socialism."

"What is needed," Wilde decrees there, as if mimicking Nietzsche, "is Individualism." But this is not, Wilde insists, the misconceived individualism of capitalist acquisitiveness, then gaining ascendancy in Europe. It must be the true humanistic individualism of a cultivated personality. "*The true perfection of man lies*" he writes with emphasis, "*not in what man has, but in what man is.*" Wilde had in mind something like the Greek aristocratic idea of the excellent human being. But he figured he could best advance it in his day through a kind of socialism. Wilde's socialism was, to be sure, his own idiosyncratic invention. Geared not toward promoting socioeconomic equality but to nurturing individual personality, this socialism would free people from drudgery to cultivate themselves, above all, through art. For "art is the most intense mode of individualism that the world has ever known."

Wilde acknowledges that artists themselves might make the most of this individualism, since "it is a question whether we have ever seen the full expression of a personality except on the imaginative plane of art," for, as he says elsewhere, "It is Art and Art only that reveals us to ourselves" ("The Portrait of Mr. W. H."). But anyone with sufficient imagination and will could use art to lend style or form to their personality like an artist. "The true artist" is therefore anyone "who believes absolutely in himself because he is absolutely himself." Consequently, once socialism extends this "self-development" to everyone, Wilde promises, "it will be a marvelous thing—the true personality of man—when we see it."

Wilde proceeds to depict this "true personality" almost exactly as Nietzsche describes the strong character with style or the "Higher Man." "This personality will not worry itself about the past, nor care whether things happened or did not happen. Nor will it admit any laws but its own laws: nor any authority but its own authority. Yet it will love those who sought to intensify it," and "will help all, as a beautiful thing helps us, by being what it is," complete, "in harmony with himself . . . true, beautiful, healthy." This is indubitably a personality with style—Wilde's words could again be Nietzsche's.

Wilde's "true personality of man," like Nietzsche's strong character and "Higher Man," imbued as they are with all the virtues of style—including what Nietzsche celebrates as "the great health"—will also be cheerful and laugh. How could it be otherwise? When we learn "to live intensely, fully, perfectly," Wilde tells us, "without exercising restraint on others, or suffering it," we will not only be "saner, healthier, more civilized," but surpassingly "happy." "For it is through joy," he concludes, "that the Individualism of the future will develop itself." And then it is likely that people will learn to laugh. "Humanity takes itself too seriously," Wilde has Lord Henry complain. In fact, oppressive seriousness "is the world's original sin; . . . if the cavemen had known how to laugh, history would have been different." Presumably the "true personality of man" would have come forth earlier—laughing.

We might say that Wilde himself persistently tried to purge this "original sin" by sparking laughter from his earliest bon mot about living up to his blue China down to his quips about warring with his hotel wallpaper and dying beyond his means (disregarding his jailhouse recantations, like those in the lugubrious letter published as *De Profundis* ruing that "I treated art as the supreme reality, and life as a mere mode of fiction"). The comic lines he gave his fictional characters served the same end by spreading laughter—often "serious laughter"—across the earnest moral landscape of his day. It is tempting to think that Wilde's abundant jests sparked a laughter Nietzsche would have relished and possibly considered sacred. At least those jests displayed the exuberant good cheer of a personality with style. (For more on laughter, see "Let 'em Laugh: *Tristram Shandy* and the Humanity of Laughter" below.)

Friedrich Nietzsche and Oscar Wilde marched together in the front ranks of the modernist rebellion against conventional morality, hypocrisy, vulgarity, mediocrity, and sham, blasting the culture around them with a hail of shocking ideas, sharp aphorisms, and penetrating ironies. They also sought to change their world with an infusion of intellectual integrity, moral truth, artistic sensibility, vigorous imagination, and laughter, serious and sacred, all embodied in the strength to impose style on one's character. Then they died just three months apart as the twentieth century was dawning.

Although that modernist rebellion lies far behind us now, it left many legacies, some of which got buried by the late twentieth-century reaction of Postmodernism. But Nietzsche's and Wilde's ethics of style is one legacy that deserves to survive. For, whether or not Nietzsche and Wilde themselves entirely lived up to that ethics—and they didn't, but who entirely lives up to any ethics?—we should remember their exhortations to impose style on our characters with honesty, artistry, discipline, and good cheer, ensuring that "even weakness delights the eye." This is an ethics of style for any time.

A previous version of this essay was published in *The Sewanee Review*, Summer, 2006. Fuller examinations of Nietzsche's moral philosophy and of Wilde's *Picture of Dorian Gray* appear in my book *Worldly Wisdom: Great Books and the Meanings of Life* (2008).

II.

ON THE POLITICAL LIFE

The five essays here bear loosely, and lightly for the most part, on the political life. Four of them are quite short. The first of these deals with a central theme that distinguishes Liberals from Conservatives and includes a note on "political correctness" and the Rights of Civility. The next three are previously published items on distinctly different politically-related subjects: the political and cultural import of the central ideas in George Orwell's *1984*; the contribution made by foreign exchange students to the Western War of Ideas with Islam after they return home from America to their Islamic countries; the story of a Japanese internment camp in Utah and an inspiring teacher who would not let it be forgotten. The last entry is a longer essay on the political and judicial history of, and good reasons for, the separation of church and state in America, from the founding to the penetrating observations of Alexis de Tocqueville and on through the controversies over religion in schools and the place of religion in public life today.

John Locke (1632–1704); Edmund Burke (1729–1797).

"*Reason teaches all mankind that being all equal and independent, no one ought to harm another in his life, health, liberty, or possessions.*"
—LOCKE

"*Society requires the inclinations of men should frequently be thwarted, their will controlled, and their passions brought into subjection.*"
—BURKE

Notes on Liberalism and Conservatism
WITH A COMMENT ON POLITICAL CORRECTNESS AND THE RIGHTS OF CIVILITY

Liberals don't seem to get it. They propose what they judge to be reasonable policies for serving the American people and are taken aback when opponents recoil with wild accusations of evil motives and predictions of wretched consequences and with contrived "facts" to support their case—and when much of the population falls for the fear tactics. This happened, for example, with the Equal Rights Amendment proposed in the 1970s to insure legal equality to all Americans regardless of sex but was thwarted as a threat to the family by rabid conservatives. And such opposition all but derailed Obamacare, passed to improve access to health care for everyone but was assailed as socialism by right-wing fanatics, with wide popular success according to polls (despite the actual health care benefits people received). Liberals tend to greet such reactions with surprise and baffled head scratching, and usually with a little condescension, wondering how people can be so blind to their rational self-interest. President Obama even later confessed in his memoirs that "I think I had an unwarranted faith that if we did the right thing and implemented good policies, then people would know," and this would suffice to win them over and maybe earn their gratitude. But that's what liberals don't seem to get. To paraphrase a popular Clinton-era slogan: It's human nature, stupid. And human nature is not altogether rational.

It is not news that liberals tend to count on human beings to be rational in governing their personal and political lives. This assumption could be traced back to Aristotle. He asserted in the *Ethics* that rationality ("activity of soul in accordance with a rational principle") is the defining characteristic of human beings. And his *Ethics* led directly to his *Politics*, where he explained how rational laws can facilitate a good society. Aristotle was no egalitarian, but he was a liberal-minded humanist confident that human beings can live well, individually and collectively, through rational self-interest.

Later, John Locke parlayed a kindred, if more egalitarian, idea of human rationality into an intellectual inspiration for modern democracy. "Reason," he wrote in the *Second Treatise of Government* (1690), "teaches all mankind" that "being all equal and independent, no one ought to harm another in his life, health, liberty, or possessions," and it is the responsibility of government to uphold these *natural rights* against any who would threaten them. He added the radical assertion that people have a *right* to rebel against governments that fail in this responsibility. Thomas Jefferson echoed Locke in the Declaration of Independence, where he justified the "Right" of political rebellion against Great Britain for violating the responsibility of government to protect certain "unalienable rights" rooted in rationally "self-evident" truths. In that same year (1776), the Scot Adam Smith applied a related liberal rationalism to modern economics in *The Wealth of Nations*. There he epochally argued that capitalism benefits everyone because under the free market an "invisible hand" directs the rational economic self-interest of individuals and nations to general prosperity.

These pioneers of political and economic liberalism were optimists. They envisioned a benign future for societies freed from irrational authority and shaped by rationality at last. Another influential liberal thinker, John Stuart Mill, aspired to the same end against a social tyranny born of liberal democracy itself. Confident that reason will ultimately prevail over unreason in an open society, Mill insisted in *On Liberty* (1859) that individuals should be completely free to think and to live as they choose, even if not to everyone else's "convenience," short of doing manifest harm. For only through such unfettered individuality can the rational mind grow and individuals, societies, and humanity flourish.

I mention these historic names only to mark a few familiar phases of the liberal rationalist tradition. I do not mean to imply that this tradition has denied human irrationality. But the core liberal tradition has clearly expected reason to eclipse unreason in the conduct of an enlightened individual and political life.

Socialism arose from the same liberal ideals. Utopian thinkers imagined, and some tried to create, small societies of perfectly rational equality, prosperity, and bliss. Karl Marx carried the liberal/socialist confidence in rationality to the conclusion that a thoroughly egalitarian communist utopia would arrive once revolution has buried capitalism and liberated human nature from the oppressive perversions of individualism and has freed human beings to live truly rational human lives politically, economically, and socially. History has not been kind to socialism and especially to Marxist Communism and its conception of human nature. But so-called "social engineering" has carried on the liberal ideal of believing that all social and economic ills can be remedied by rationally arranging the conditions of life. President Obama's health care reforms reflected that aspiration.

The tradition of liberal rationalism is nothing if not optimistic about human nature and politics. The conservative tradition has been more "realistic," if not outright pessimistic. And opportunistic.

Here we could start with Plato. He feared base irrationality as much as he esteemed high-minded rationality, and he imagined an ideal state ruled by an intellectual elite trained to harness their own irrationality and to suppress that of others in order to secure the good. It was to achieve this end that Plato would, for one thing, censor art from childhood onwards lest it feed the "low elements of the mind," as he thought art has a singular tendency and power to do, subverting reason and public order. Plato was a political conservative wary of human nature who idealized a closed society of inviolable order hostile to change where philosophers who understood this would be kings—the prominent twentieth-century philosopher Karl Popper wrote an influential history of such ideas in *The Open Society and Its Enemies* (1945).

The father of modern political thought, Machiavelli, was no idealist. He gave us in *The Prince* (1532) a picture of politics as an arena of bestial struggle where rulers must cope with human beings "as they are in real truth, rather than as they are imagined." And in truth, he said, they are "ungrateful, fickle, liars, and deceivers, they shun danger and are greedy for profit," they deceive themselves no less than others, they yield to fear over love, prefer appearances to reality, and side selfishly with immoral leaders over moral ones while professing to do the opposite. Machiavelli was cynical here, perhaps—and his full political philosophy was much more liberal-minded—but his observations on human nature and politics have made *The Prince* a perennial source of political advice, and one more congenial to conservatives than to liberals.

Not that modern conservatives would likely hail Machiavelli as their mentor. That title usually goes first to Edmund Burke (some conservatives might pick the psychologically pessimistic Thomas Hobbes, although his conservatism was more ambiguous), who viewed human nature less harshly than Machiavelli but nonetheless found it prone to irrationality, or passions, requiring strong traditions and enduring institutions to constrain it. "Society requires," he wrote in *Reflections on the Revolution in France* (1790), that "the inclinations of men should frequently be thwarted, their will controlled, and their passions brought into subjection." And he assigned the role for doing that particularly to the respect for tradition and reverence for religion. He saw the French Revolution, even in its early stages, unleashing the worst by uprooting, in the name of rational, abstract "Rights of Man," everything that had long exercised such beneficial constraints. As he put it with a literary flourish, "All the decent drapery of life... necessary to cover the defects of our naked, shivering nature ... is to be rudely torn off ... by the new conquering empire of light and reason." That act, he declared, could yield only chaos, because without the bonds of tradition and authority human beings will run amok—which they did during the Reign of Terror.

Burke's reactionary French ally Joseph de Maistre went farther. Discerning little in human nature but animality and evil, he announced that "man, in general, is too wicked to be free," and he urged authoritarian politics and infallible religion as the sole measures for saving human beings from themselves. The extremity of de Maistre's politics faded with monarchy and aristocracy, but his dark view of human nature did not die.

In America the revolutionary democratic spirit gained inspiration, as noted above, from rationalist ideals of equality and natural rights. But the American political system actually took its form from some rather more conservative judgments about human nature. James Madison gets much of the credit for this. Madison, the "father of the constitution," warned in the persuasive *Federalist #10*, for instance, that "as long as the reason of man continues fallible," human beings will act from the "self-love" and "passion" that are rooted in "the nature of man." And they will form "factions" aggressively seeking to impose their own selfish interests on others. Such are the "mortal diseases," Madison lamented, "under which popular governments have everywhere perished."

You cannot change human nature, Madison concluded, but you can restrain some political consequences of irrational self-love, passion, and faction. To do this, he advocated an elaborately representative rather than a direct democracy so that the people would have to elect legislators to act for them and balance the diverse interests of many citizens. Balancing those interests would beset legislating with laborious compromises, but these would lessen the pernicious effects of self-love, passion, and faction. To further head off those effects, Madison proposed splintering political power at all levels: separating federal and state authority; splitting the federal government into three discrete branches: the legislature, the executive, and judiciary, with counterbalancing responsibilities; dividing the federal legislature into a House of Representatives representing many small congressional districts in each state according to its population, and a Senate containing but two senators for each state. Nothing less could protect democracy from itself, subject as it will always be to irrational human nature. America might be the world's oldest liberal democracy, but it owes its constitutional structure, and its political stability, to a quite conservative view of human nature.

I should also point out that the rise of the social sciences in the late nineteenth and early twentieth centuries often supported the conservative more than the liberal view of human nature, if not from a conservative political bias. Anthropology, sociology, psychology, and their fellow disciplines showed that much of human behavior has roots in non-rational, often unrecognized, needs and desires. Sigmund Freud became the emblem of these intellectual discoveries, of course, and he grew more pessimistic about human nature over time, even chiding Communists in *Civilization and Its Discontents* (1930) for thinking they could put an end to irrational human aggression, because, he said, wherever civilization goes, "this indestructible feature of human nature will follow it there." A contemporary of Freud's, the French intellectual Georges Sorel, focused directly on social/political psychology in *Reflections on Violence* (1908). People don't really act on facts and rationality in politics, he said, but on *social myths*. These are big, simple ideas and images that seize emotions and ignite political action, even though these *myths* can never be realized in fact. And he advised making the most of this truth for radical political change. Both Communist and Fascist propagandists did just that during the dark years of the twentieth century. Meanwhile, the profession of modern advertising mirrored these developments by openly appealing to feelings and desires, not rationality. As the professional advertisers' magazine *Printers' Ink* baldly put it in 1920: "The appeal to reason doesn't contain the elements that make a man want to do the thing you want him to do. . . . Emotions must be aroused."

After World War II George Orwell demonstrated in "Politics and the English Language" (1946) how political language on both the Left and Right had become infected by efforts to manipulate minds and emotions instead of telling the truth. Then he put this idea to chilling fictional effect in *1984,* a novel about nothing so much as the psychology of political control, bequeathing to us the adjective "Orwellian" for the political management of language and facts to shape how people feel and think (see essay on Orwell below). More recently, in America the political Right brazenly deployed those propaganda tactics through the mass media and Internet technologies to gain and hold power in the early twenty-first century, casting aside all respect for objective truth—and the third American president of this century gained and wielded power while shamelessly doing exactly that.

The widely publicized writings of the cognitive linguist George Lakoff (e.g., *The Political Mind,* 2008) offer telling variations on these themes. His area of science, Lakoff says, proves that the human brain is itself not simplistically rational but is pervaded by emotions, illogic, and unconscious insinuations. And he scolds liberals for largely overlooking this fact and depending on a naïve notion of human rationality (which he attributes, somewhat unfairly, to the Enlightenment). Consequently, he says, unlike conservatives, who are at home with human irrationality, liberals fail to "frame" political issues and policies with manipulative language that can shape thoughts and feelings to achieve their political ends—as the Bush administration did with Orwellian bravado during the Iraq War, a strategy taken to jaw-dropping lengths in the bizarre antics of the next Republican administration. You need not be pernicious to do this, Lakoff implies, only psychologically realistic—although nowadays right-wing media demagogues and their political acolytes perniciously exploit this realism to rouse hostility against their enemies, not unlike the orchestrated "Two-Minute Hate" episodes in *1984.*

There is, by the way, one conspicuous exception to the conservative emphasis on the irrationality of human nature. This is the conservative theory of the free market. This originated as a rationalist liberal idea, but conservatives made it their own after capitalism triumphed in the twentieth century and liberals began moving toward government regulation of the economy. Following Adam Smith, exponents of the free market have always believed it driven by rational self-interest and poised to make suitable self-corrections on its own if necessary. Then came the economic cataclysms of the Great Depression and the Great Recession of 2008–09, throwing those rationalist economic assumptions into doubt. Even the libertarian economic guru Alan Greenspan finally admitted to a "flaw" in his philosophy of rationally self-regulating markets, expressing "shocked disbelief" that so many financial managers could have taken the *irrational* risks they did. He and other conservative free-market economists had retained a faith in human rationality where financial markets are concerned that no traditional political conservative would have endorsed. When it comes to economics over the last century or so, liberals have tended to be more conservative than conservatives. Liberals don't trust "economic man" and free markets to operate altogether rationally, and so they seek institutional constraints to rein them in. But in politics, liberals remain more the rationalists and conservatives more the non-rationalists (notwithstanding neoconservative intellectuals who hauled baggage of liberal rationalism with them from the left to the right and instigated the Iraq war with ideological certitude and rationalist utopian idealism).

Many self-proclaimed political conservatives today even scorn the liberal ideal of rationality as a mere sign of intellectual elitism. And they have successfully demonized the very term Liberal as code for every perceived social, political, economic, and cultural evil they can imagine, not excluding treason. Liberals themselves have caved in to this "framing" ingenuity, now defensively defining themselves not as Liberals but as "Progressives."

10. Notes on Liberalism and Conservatism

But the fact is, true conservatives today are hard to find. That is, conservatives in the mold of Edmund Burke and Alexis de Tocqueville or even James Madison, who trusted tradition and moderation, prized stability, and warned against excessive political expectations and the overweening exercise of authority. The Republican Party can hardly be "conservative" when its members are ready to overturn all traditions and are determined to rule not govern, exercising power beyond historic restraints while refusing to cooperate with the opposition party or even to recognize the right of the Democrats to govern at all. And yet these so-called conservatives have clung fast to the venerable conservative precept that human beings are irrational. Not only that, they have exalted it.

The anti-tax, anti-government, anti-egalitarian, anti-secular, anti-abortion, anti-gay, and other anti- movements have turned the politics of the Far Right, and increasingly that of mainstream of Republicans, into a campaign of rage that feeds on dark resentments and traffics in incendiary slogans, outrageous accusations, zany conspiracy theories, and self-righteous hatreds. When fanatical right-wing demagogues in the media and politics blatantly invent and repeat factual untruths to stir fears and focus resentments and to vilify anyone who refuses to fall in line as the "enemy"; when millions of Americans consume such right-wing propaganda from radio, TV, the Internet, and social media and consider it true; when a Republican president rallies thousands with mind-bending lies and frothing denials of science and fact and winds up fomenting a delusional attack on the nation's Capitol to save his deranged presidency—I could go on and on—you know that these political "conservatives" have made human irrationality their chosen arena, a place bereft of common reason and reality, to the exclusion of practically everything else.

So why are liberals surprised at any ravings from the Right against what they try to do? It is because they still dismiss these ravings as the aberrations of some irrational individuals and groups. That dismissal may arise from the generous humanity of the liberal tradition. And one can always hope that the best, not the worst, in human nature will prevail. But if liberals are to gain sway over the forces of unreason on the Right, they had better reread and make better use of the likes of Machiavelli, Burke, Madison, Sorel, and Orwell, and other psychological realists. This might help them anticipate and head off the irrationality that is bound to come at them from so-called conservatives every day. And it could encourage them to adroitly turn human irrationality to their own reasonable ends. Liberalism could never thrive on irrationality as conservatism has done—the prevalence of right-wing hate media and the absence of an alternative on the left attests to that—but that shouldn't keep liberals from seeing and accepting irrationality for what it is: it's human nature, alas.

A COMMENT ON POLITICAL CORRECTNESS AND THE RIGHTS OF CIVILITY

The successes of the crusade for civil rights—or legal equality for all Americans irrespective of race in voting, employment, access to services, and so on—in the 1960s juiced the aspirations of liberals to create a more truly egalitarian and rationally just society. Those aspirations expanded with the rise of feminism, multiculturalism, identity politics, and "political correctness." These and related movements advocated not only legal equality for all Americans but a novel type of social equality. This was nothing less than an equality free of discriminatory behavior, and possibly attitudes, by anyone toward differences of race, sex, ethnicity, and the like. Some of this kind of behavior would in time be dubbed "microaggressions," for ways of speaking and acting that condescend, even if unconsciously, through hurtful stereotypes to those who belong to groups unlike ourselves.

Trying to change such behavior was a radical aspiration, to be sure, a manifestation of liberal rationalist idealism. When before—

it is not too such to say, in the history of the world—has a society envisioned, much less established, as a standard of behavior that all people, irrespective of body or belief, be treated with equal respect in the perceptions, words, and gestures of everyday life? Throughout most of history many groups of people have suffered from overt or subtle discrimination because of who they are—including the physically and mentally disabled, who were openly disdained and ridiculed, as in Shakespeare's plays and as they still are in many parts of the world. And this elevated idea of equality is certainly far from what the slave-holder Thomas Jefferson had in mind when he penned those familiar words in the Declaration of Independence, "all men are created equal."

It should come as no surprise that the call to alter what amount to the conscience and consciousness of Americans in these ways has stirred much discomfort. Although winning the legal equality of civil rights for those previously denied them caused a lot of trouble and cost some blood, securing the social equality for everyone of what we might call "the Rights of Civility" is bound to be more complicated. For it cannot be done by legislation. It involves hearts and minds.

No wonder conservatives have recoiled at what they judge to be an effort by liberals to impose their doctrinaire ideals of human nature and morality on America. Conservatives summon baleful images of "thought police" enforcing liberal "political correctness," and they denounce the idea of "hate crimes" that punish people for attitudes as well as actions, making those crimes worse than the same crimes without the hate. Conservatives also target the universities as a hotbed of this kind of indoctrination through their many rules governing how students must treat each other and how professors must be sensitive to the students' feelings about their identities. Accusations of a New McCarthyism and of a successor to the Chinese Cultural Revolution come readily to the conservatives' pens.

To be sure, liberals have given conservatives cause for concern. Especially in the universities. There teachers are instructed to provide students with "trigger warnings" alerting them in advance to anything in the readings or discussions that might offend their sensibilities, and students monitor teachers' lectures for "inappropriate" utterances regarding race, ethnicity, gender, sexual orientation, and whatnot. Students also turn on each other for causing slights of feelings along those lines. It is not a pretty picture. And we can lay some of the blame for it on the faulty liberal assumptions about the rationality of human nature and the malleability of human beings through good ideas and intentions. After all, it seems that the liberal ideal proposes to deny or stifle an innate human disposition to prefer our kind to others. Liberals think human beings are rational enough to see the virtues of overcoming that disposition. Another liberal folly?

Not so fast. Granted that the liberal aspiration for a just society of this kind goes beyond anything previously imagined, and that the universities are stumbling in ways to achieve it, that aspiration nonetheless sets a legitimate ideal for a truly democratic society. The "Rights of Civility" should belong to everyone. Namely, everyone deserves to be treated with civility regardless of differences among them. Civility involves a type of manners or tact that soften social relations and make people feel comfortable with each other. The manners of civility do not therefore deny the irrationality of human nature. They compensate for it, rather like James Madison sought to do with the institutions of the American republic he designed to constrain the "passions and self-interest" of human nature. Civility restrains, disciplines and elevates us above our natural selves (see "Style in Art, Character, and Culture" and "*Mrs. Dalloway* and the Ethics of Civility" above). The conservative hostility to "political correctness" thus misses the point. Instead of sanctioning in the name of "free speech" anything a person might be inclined to say, whether heated with hate or not, conservatives would do well to remember some words of their mentor Edmund Burke: "There ought to be a system of manners in every nation which a well-formed mind would be disposed to relish. To make us love our country, our country ought to be lovely." The Rights of Civility should do exactly that.

So it is that the Rights of Civility go beyond legal civil rights to shape a society that is not only legally just but kind, humane, and, well, lovely. And for all of the absurdities of liberal zealots in pushing "political correctness" to uncivil excess on campuses and elsewhere, America will come closer to being such a just society if we can learn to live by the genuine Rights of Civility for all.

George Orwell, 1940s.

"*Freedom is the freedom to say that two plus two make four.*"
—WINSTON SMITH, *1984*

Orwell, Mind Control, and Our Times

The essence of freedom, its beating heart, its *sine qua non*, is the ability of the mind to think for itself and with objectivity. No one has made this point more forcefully, unforgettably, and disturbingly than George Orwell in the novel *1984*.

Mention of that book might first summon the ominous image of Big Brother, the omnipresent eye of the totalitarian State watching citizens at all times to guarantee obedience to its edicts. But Big Brother is only the most obvious mechanism of controlling people in the world of *1984*. More consequentially, the State dominates its citizens by dehumanizing them into creatures unable to truly think. That is, it strips them of the ability to judge experience and ideas logically and factually, which is to say objectively.

Orwell gave the State, or the Party, which runs the State, numerous devices for achieving this end. Besides Big Brother, the most pervasive was the manipulation of language. Orwell gave this practice the name "Newspeak." He knew well that language and thought go together, and he had bewailed the degradation of the English language and its political consequences in his essay "Politics and the English Language" (1946). We think in language (including mathematics, receiving a nod later), and according to its expansiveness and limits. In *1984* the State creates Newspeak to confine minds within the limits of how the Party wants them to think. Hence, instead of expanding the range of language and thought, Newspeak constricts. "Newspeak is the only language in the world whose vocabulary gets smaller each year," a Party spokesman tells the central character in the book, Winston Smith. For, he continues unapologetically, "the whole aim of Newspeak, is to narrow the range of thought." In the future, he boasts, "there will *be* no thought, as we understand it now. Orthodoxy means not thinking—not needing to think."

But reducing the vocabulary was not the only device of Newspeak to restrict thought. That vocabulary would also expressly eliminate all terms hinting at nuance, subtlety, or discrimination and have only easily pronounced and emotionally charged terms defined by the Party. Whatever the Party decreed was "goodthink." And "doublethink" would mask all contradictions. Hence black could be white, war could be peace, hate could be love, lies could be truth, fiction could be fact, and so forth. And while Newspeak was tightening its reign, the term "duckspeak," which meant to mindlessly "quack like a duck," was deployed as both a term of derision for unorthodox speakers and as a mark of praise for the orthodox hewing to the Party line. In this world, sanity was insanity, for sure.

Besides Newspeak, Orwell also provided the State with mechanisms that denied "not merely the validity of experience, but the ... evidence of the senses." This amounted to repudiating "the very existence of external reality." For when the State determines all thought, truth, and perceptions of the world, there can be no objective world outside of the submissive mind. Winston Smith has a job in this system to execute one of these mechanisms. In the Ministry of Truth.

The Ministry of Truth has three thousand offices to shape "every conceivable kind of information, instruction, or entertainment, from a statute to a slogan, from a lyric poem to a biological treatise" to "satisfy the needs" of the Party. Winston works in the department there devoted to none other than rewriting history for that purpose. As a Party slogan ran, "Who controls the past controls the future; who controls the present controls the past." After all, as Winston asks himself, "if both the past and the external world exist only in the mind ... what then?" Quite so.

Actually, as that very question implies, Winston has yet to submit wholly to the rule of the Party/State. His mind is still his own. For one thing, he has memories that tell him he has seen evidence in the past of things that preceded the State's domination and what the State tells him about the past. And in other ways as well he retains a secret confidence that objective reality does exist. It *must* exist. Observing sorrowfully that in his world "the heresy of heresies was common sense," he has a moment of inner defiance. "They were wrong and he was right!" he says to himself. "The obvious, the silly, the true had got to be defended. Truisms are true, hold on to that! The solid world exists, hold on to that! Stones are hard, water is wet, objects unsupported fall toward the earth's center." And "setting forth an important axiom, he wrote: *Freedom is the freedom to say that two plus two make four. If that is granted, all else follows.*"

The depressing story of *1984* records Winston's gradual submission to the Party, the State, and Big Brother, and his ultimate acceptance that, if they say so, "2 + 2 = 5." Winston eventually abandons his belief in objectivity as the salvation of thought and freedom. The book ends with the aching lines: "He had won the victory over himself. He loved Big Brother."

Orwell wrote *1984* with the images of Nazi Germany and Stalinist Russia (the Soviet Union) vividly in his mind. But not only those. He saw telltale signs of similar, if not as totalitarian, manipulations of mind in the politics of democracies. And he saw these signs notably in language. In "Politics and the English Language" he asserted unequivocally that, "Political language . . . is designed to make lies sound truthful and murder respectable"; it is "the defense of the indefensible." And it accomplished this through abstractions that obscured concrete facts, and euphemisms that camouflaged brutality with soft words. He cites examples like the term "pacification" for the destruction of defenseless villages, and "transfer of population" for the forced removal of countless people from their homes to military camps. He could also have pointed to the American action after Pearl Harbor that "evacuated" Japanese residents from the West Coast to "relocation centers" farther inland, which in fact entailed the military uprooting thousands of peaceful

Japanese Americans from their established lives with the loss of their homes, livelihoods, and possessions and confining them in barbed-wired concentration camps for years (see "A Wartime Tragedy and a Teacher Who Would Not Let It Be Lost" below). Wartime euphemisms became commonplace during the Vietnam War, of course, where Americans pursued "pacification" by sometimes mixing brutal fact with benevolent fiction, as in: "We destroyed the village in order to save it." And after the attacks of 9/11 the American government invented the illogical but catchy and emotive phrase "war on terror" to sanction any action against perceived "terrorists," including "rendition," an abstract euphemism for seizing anyone deemed a threat to America and imprisoning them endlessly in foreign lands beyond the reach of American law. That kind of linguistic ingenuity expanded during the Iraq War when the American government became cold-bloodedly blatant about torture itself, ruthlessly submitting "enemy combatants" to it under the vaguely benign heading "alternative interrogation methods."

As Orwell foresaw, the use of abstract, politically euphemistic language to defend the indefensible would become routine in governments everywhere. And, as Orwell also knew, that practice would not only apply to acts of violence or oppression. It would be a way for a government to persuade people that it is doing good. Think of the Cold War term "free world," for instance. It implies that part of the world is free and the other not, and that the "free world" comprises countries where citizens freely choose their governments and ways of life and openly express their opinions. In fact, the term was, and still is, a distorted designation for the part of the world friendly to America, including oppressive regimes whose people are not at all free as Americans understand it. But in the service of American foreign policy that contradiction did not matter. I might note that since the passing of the Cold War the term "free world" has often yielded to the euphemistic oxymoron "world community," which generally denotes not the entire population of the earth but the parts that cooperate in the economic globalization initiated by the West to reshape the world in its image.

On the domestic front, we have grown used to abstract political euphemisms. We hire accountants advertising "tax relief," implying that taxes are an illegitimate burden from which we should be "relieved." To obscure hunger among the poor in America one administration recast "hunger" as "low food security." And it planned to end government guaranteed Social Security benefits by compelling all retirees to manage their benefits in a market-driven "ownership society." Another administration, wishing to imply a sweeping reform of the health care system and its costs, inflated what came down to a modest modification of health insurance and some health care procedures into "The Affordable Care Act." The motives behind these obscurities might not always be pernicious, but reality gets distorted nonetheless.

We should also see that, apart from manipulative euphemisms, the reliance on abstractions has itself deleterious effects on the mind. In the first place, because abstractions obscure concrete realities with elevated, vague language, they cloud perceptions and impair judgment. Take the example above: "low food security" for "hunger." Hunger has a concreteness to it rooted in a physical experience. We have all experienced hunger, and some people suffer it chronically. But has anyone ever physically experienced "low food security"? No. Just as the abstraction "alternative interrogation techniques" excuses the practice of torture, "low food security" defangs the existence of hunger. The abstractions make the reality difficult to grasp and easy to disregard.

In clouding perceptions and impairing judgment, abstractions work their second effect on the mind: they limit thought itself. Or perhaps I should say they can take the place of thought. Of course, we must often think with abstractions. But therein lies the danger. Abstractions can masquerade as thought because they are mental constructions that, in a manner of speaking, can *feel* like thought. In "Politics and the English Language" Orwell provides a minor example: The phrase, "In my opinion it is a not unjustifiable assumption that. . . ." is just an abstract way of saying, "I think that. . . ." Here the very idea of thinking has been clouded and replaced by abstract verbiage. When we needlessly rely on abstractions we let the words do our thinking for us. Unfortunately, this practice has become endemic in academia, where "thinking" and speaking in abstractions is a sign of caste, inducing students and scholars alike to spout jargon, whether they know what they are saying or not, and where every subject, especially in the humanities, must now be "theorized" lest it seem too readily comprehended to be important (see "How Humanists Betray Humanism" below).

Back to politics, the political manipulation of language through euphemism and abstraction serves two related purposes. One, as Orwell observed, is to defend the indefensible. That is where abstraction works well with euphemism: abstraction clouds perceptions while euphemism sends a politically manipulative message about reality. The other purpose is to motivate people to believe and act in certain ways. Here emotions reign, not thought.

In recent times, politics in America has been much influenced by social scientists who contend that if you want to get people to approve or oppose a policy you must "frame" it with words that reach them easily and emotionally. Get people to feel right about you and your policies and bad about the opposition. Hence, "tax relief" for avoiding taxes, "tax and spend liberals" for the Democratic party, "pro-life" for opposing the choice to have an abortion, and so on. This general idea was among the principles of Newspeak. And it reflects the understanding that human beings probably do not automatically respond to experience, and certainly not in politics, with rationality but with emotions—a fact that propagandists and advertisers have long exploited (see "Notes on Liberalism and Conservatism" above). It also reminds us that the Party in *1984* was using this characteristic of human nature against human beings, to control their minds through their emotions—as in the "Two Minute Hate," which emotionally harnesses everyone to the Party's aims by requiring them to spend two minutes shouting hatred at a large picture of the Enemy broadcast everywhere. We might also remember here Dostoevsky's Grand Inquisitor as a kind of Orwellian figure who believed that deep down people don't really want to think freely after all; they want to be taken care of physically, mentally, emotionally, spiritually. He claims the Church does that for them with "miracle, mystery, and authority," conferring invincible bliss in the bargain. In *1984* the State takes care of them, too, albeit there the freedom to think is the last freedom to go, as poor Winston discovers. (Akin to the Inquisitor, the psychologist Erich Fromm concluded from studying mass political movements of the twentieth century that much of their appeal lay in how they enabled followers to "escape from freedom.")

I might add here a seemingly innocent practice that has become common in recent decades. This is to supplant the verb "to think" with the verb "to feel." From politicians and intellectuals on down to students we hear how one "feels" rather than "thinks" that an action to be right, an opinion to be true, a fact to be accurate (as a headline in the *New York Times* some years ago announced: "Missile Issue: Both Sides Feel the Other Has Advantage"). High on the list of reasons for this practice would be this: to *think* is to support one's ideas with objective fact and logical argument, and this involves both effort and risk, whereas to *feel* is to experience a nonrational impulse that is at once free of effort, seemingly invincible to contrary fact or argument, and might "feel" more authentic than thought. The advantages of supplanting thought by feeling are clear. But when feeling takes the place of thought in this way, the ability to think objectively and critically and to logically justify one's judgments can dissolve into self-serving opinions and self-deceiving ideology.

Thinking with objectivity is the essence of freedom. Winston Smith knew that, and so did the State in *1984*. The State prevailed when it got him to yield thought to mindless submission. Nowadays, threats to that objectivity abound not only in a politics that openly plays to the emotions (as all demagogues have done) and denies or discounts facts contrary to ideology. Those threats also thrive through modern media technologies that enable ideologues and psychopaths to play to the emotions of fear and hate and to purvey factless conspiracy theories about all kinds of things. Human nature being what it is, people will always be susceptible to such appeals.

The question remains: Will the respect for objectivity, and the freedom of thought that goes with it, survive despite the arsenal of weapons arrayed against it? Or will that respect succumb to irresistible influences as it did in Winston Smith—or, perhaps, to softer blandishments like those of the Grand Inquisitor or of Aldous Huxley's *Brave New World*? As long as we can ask those questions, Orwell's *1984* will have much to teach us.

A previous version of this essay appeared under the title "Newspeak: Orwell's Most Prophetic Idea," in *The Christian Science Monitor*, April 1984.

Topaz internment camp, Utah.

"People should know about this. Topaz still has much to teach us."
—JANE BECKWITH

A Wartime Tragedy and a Teacher Who Would Not Let It Be Lost

On the arid flatlands near the small town of Delta, Utah, 140 miles southwest of Salt Lake City, the scorching summer winds whip dust through the dry brush, and winter cold freezes the ground under a blanket of snow. In this forbidding landscape lie remnants of an American tragedy: an internment camp that had housed over 8,000 people of Japanese descent, including Japanese-American citizens, behind barbed-wire fences and armed guards during much of World War II. Named for a barren nearby mountain, the camp was known as Topaz.

Like the other nine wartime "relocation centers," as they were euphemistically labeled, scattered from northeastern California to Arkansas, Topaz had come to life amidst post-Pearl Harbor fears of invasion by Japan as its military overran the western Pacific in early 1942. Suspecting that ethnic Japanese on the West Coast might aid the enemy, American officials had started rounding up leaders of Japanese communities and organizations immediately after the Pearl Harbor attack and had begun searching the homes of possible subversives. When US Attorney General Francis Biddle banned these searches for violating Fourth Amendment rights, anxious patriots urged skirting that ban by simply evacuating all residents of Japanese origin from the vulnerable West Coast—in a violation of constitutional principles if not strict protections (as duly noted by Page Smith in *Democracy on Trial: The Japanese American Evacuation and Relocation in World War II* [1995]).

II. ON THE POLITICAL LIFE

On February 19, 1942—four days before the audacious Japanese submarine shelling of an oil refinery in southern California would further enflame invasion fears—President Franklin D. Roosevelt issued Executive Order #9066 authorizing "military areas" from which "any or all persons may be excluded." That wholesale order actually targeted only one group of "persons": ethnic Japanese. The crusty general in charge of West Coast defenses, John L. DeWitt, got the point and ordered all of those "persons" to vacate the coastal region and settle elsewhere on their own, and in a hurry. When few of them left "voluntarily," having homes and businesses and no place to resettle in a country now more hostile to them than ever (anti-Japanese sentiment had long simmered in this country), DeWitt ordered forced evacuation.

Notices went out along the West Coast informing "all persons of Japanese ancestry, both alien and non-alien" (chilly terms for first-generation immigrants, *issei*, who had been denied citizenship since a law of 1924, and their American-born children, *nissei*) that they would "be evacuated" from designated areas by specified dates. The evacuees were bluntly told to "report to the Civil Patrol Station" in their area before the deadlines for "further instructions." Within about three months, the coast was cleared of nearly 120,000 people—72,000 of them American-born citizens.

The Topaz "relocation center," welcomed by many of the 1,300 Delta residents who foresaw financial gains in it for landowners and merchants, received its first internees in early September 1942. Gathered mainly from San Francisco and its environs, they had resided since the spring in a temporary "assembly center" at the Tanforan Racetrack in California while the Topaz camp materialized. Now they arrived as autumn's chill bit the desert air. Snow would fall the next month. A large sign over the door of the processing center greeted them:

WELCOME
TO TOPAZ CITY

12. A Wartime Tragedy and a Teacher Who Would Not Let It Be Lost

One of those who reached the camp soon after it opened, Miné Okubo, later wrote in an affecting memoir, *Citizen 13660* (1946) that "it was a desolate scene" where "hundreds of low black barracks ... stretched out before us in a cloud of dust." She later added in a documentary film that as they approached that "Welcome" sign "we could hear Japanese members of the Berkeley Boy Scout Band playing 'Hail, California.' We were in the middle of a desert, a band was playing, and the whole thing was bizarre."

A grid divided the one-square-mile camp into forty-two blocks enclosed within a barbed-wire fence complete with guard towers. Each block would house 200 to 250 people in twelve barracks and provide a common eating hall, a recreation center, a laundry, showers and a latrine. Families were assigned to bare single rooms equipped with metal cots for sleeping, heated by coal-burning stoves, insulated with wallboard and tar paper, and lacking running water. For three years, this was home for most of the 11,000 who were processed through here.

But the Topaz internees tried to make the best of it, despite the prison-comp conditions—dramatized by the fatal fence-line shooting of one internee by a guard in 1943. They planted gardens, organized schools, fielded athletic teams that played in the regional public-school league, published a newspaper, and built a community as best they could. Some were eventually allowed to work outside the camp, a few left for college or new lives in the East, and over a hundred young men volunteered in 1943 for American military service, including enlistees in the all-Japanese-American 442 Regimental Combat Team, which became the most decorated force of its size in American military history. But none was sorry to leave the camp when the war ended. Most returned to the San Francisco area where, although many had lost their property and previous means of livelihood, they could at least pick up pieces of their broken lives.

On October 31, 1945, just over two months after Japan surrendered, the Topaz camp closed its gates for good. The barracks were disassembled, or carted off for other uses in and around Delta, and the site was reduced to rubble to be scattered by desert winds and forgotten by a triumphant postwar America.

In time, historians would start writing critically about the "relocation" episode, and Japanese Americans would press for public recognition of the camps and seek restitution for the wartime abuses of their innocent people. In Utah, the Japanese American Citizens League commemorated the American Bicentennial in 1976 by erecting historical markers at Topaz and in Delta reminding visitors of the anti-Japanese hysteria that had given this country its own "concentration camps." In 1987, a Utah public television station produced a documentary on Topaz by Ken Verdoia featuring evocative interviews with former internees, like Miné Okubo. And in 1988, the American government finally granted reparations to all surviving internees of the camps, intending to close this melancholy chapter in American history forever.

Awareness of the camps would widen over the years with the rising consciousness of ethnic identities and racial discrimination in America. Many of the camps would become sites for tourists and remembrance, notice of the internment episode would increasingly appear in school textbooks, a theatrical musical about the camp experience entitled *Allegiance*—inspired by one of the former internees, the actor George Takei—would even play on Broadway in 2015 and then around the country. But the Topaz camp might have remained mainly a subject for historians and a waning memory for some Japanese Americans as its sparse remnants vanished altogether from the arid landscape beside the lonely and weathered historic marker placed there in 1976, had it not been for a school teacher in Delta named Jane Beckwith. She took up the Topaz story to engage her students' hearts and minds, and to keep alive this troubled local and national memory.

The daughter of Delta's former newspaper publisher—a rare liberal in this conservative rural Mormon town numbering about 3,500 people in 2010—Jane Beckwith grew up with a social conscience,

12. A Wartime Tragedy and a Teacher Who Would Not Let It Be Lost

an independent bent, and a yen to teach. In 1978 she joined the faculty of Delta High School to teach English and journalism. A tall and lean woman with a no-nonsense manner but a mischievous twinkle in her eye, she earned a reputation in the school as intellectually demanding, pedagogically unconventional, free-thinking, and a little off-beat. "I am not very organized," she would confess. But "everyone knows that in my classes you read a lot, you write a lot, and you discuss a lot." She also expected her students to apply their studies outside the classroom, and to question the world around them.

While teaching George Orwell's *1984*, for instance, she had students turn the school as much as possible into an Orwellian world, adorning the halls with Big Brother posters and staging totalitarian practices. When the school principal reprimanded her and abruptly terminated the exercise for disrupting the school's routine, she used his actions to illustrate Orwell's warning against arbitrary authority and abject submission. The students loved it. And they got lessons in political power and the shaping of minds beyond the book and the classroom.

She put this same buoyant spirit to lively use in her journalism classes. Risking controversy, she continually urged students to find substantive and provocative topics for the school newspaper rather than blathering about "next week's dance or last week's football game." Topaz would become the chief of those topics.

Although she might, as some students reported, have scared off those who heard that she was too "intellectual," she changed the lives of many others. And she did this, her many admirers agree, by pushing students beyond themselves with both persistence and understanding, as well as, perhaps, by often going against the grain of her hometown, where Mormonism set the social norms, athletics dominated the high school, and conventions died hard.

"Jane Beckwith is controversial," observed a former student, now an elementary school teacher in Delta, and "you didn't want to get on her bad side," but she "sparked in me a desire to find out things

II. On the Political Life

on my own rather than rely on others." Another former student, now a lawyer, recalled that "She knows she has enemies because she arouses a corrupting-the-youth kind of feeling by asking you to question everything, but she was part of all my eye-popping educational experiences"—and he named a daughter Jane in her honor. "It takes a rare person to go against conventional wisdom," said a current army recruiter who had loved her classes, "and parents have actually pulled students from Jane's classes. But she is incredibly inspirational." He added reflectively: "I just wonder what she gets out of it. She seems so out of place in Delta."

A professional linguist, who had received a Fulbright fellowship to Finland with Jane's encouragement long after her high school days, summed up the common view among loyalists. Fondly remembering an occasion when Jane had borrowed a miniskirt from her and had worn it to class simply to learn what it feels like and to stir curiosity, she goes on: "People say Jane is crazy and radical. And parents and teachers regularly send her letters criticizing the texts she chooses to teach or the articles she allows to be printed in the school paper. But without her influence, I doubt that I would have the interest in the outside world that has been a driving force in my life. For those of us who are not cut from the same cookie cutter, thank God there was Jane Beckwith. She has made all the difference."

When asked if students have told her she has changed their lives, Jane Beckwith replies with characteristic modesty and unsentimental candor: "Yes they have. But they tell you all kinds of things. I'd rather they just came back and talked to me later on as open-minded and interesting adults." Many of them do come back, or they communicate from a distance. And they become valued friends.

Nothing reveals Jane Beckwith's intrepid character and revelatory influence more than her Topaz project. It started in 1982. Always seeking new topics to stimulate and captivate her students, she gave her journalism class the assignment of researching and writing

12. A Wartime Tragedy and a Teacher Who Would Not Let It Be Lost

about the Topaz camp. "As an English teacher," she said, "I like stories, and complicated stories, and Topaz is one of those." At that time, Topaz was known in Delta mostly from the historical markers and in the memories of old-timers, and it was known elsewhere primarily to historians and a few Japanese Americans. Jane Beckwith thought it would be good for her students to learn more, to dig into the local past by following any leads they could find from townspeople and anyone else, and from the deserted camp site itself. The assignment lit a fire. "Students literally ran to class," she recalls, bringing artifacts they had found at the site and from people who had saved them, along with reminiscences from townspeople and others. Then the students eagerly wrote up the story for the school newspaper. And that was just the beginning.

"I learned about Topaz and the other camps along with my students," Jane says. "We studied together, sought artifacts, wrote articles, and told people what we had learned." To deepen her own understanding of the inhabitants of Topaz, she even went to teach school for a year in Hiroshima, Japan, absorbing Japanese culture and probing the Japanese perspective on World War II at first hand. Some students report that their work on Topaz has permanently affected their perceptions of America and of other cultures.

But while scores of students avidly embraced Jane Beckwith's Topaz project over the years, it did not proceed without resistance. Critical colleagues derided it as one of Jane's idiosyncratic obsessions. And some townspeople argued that Topaz should be left alone because Japan had been the enemy and Japanese Americans were interned only for their own good. With the same meanness of spirit, one high school principal ordered her to desist because he said she was too sympathetic to the wartime enemy, and her Topaz project didn't belong in the school anyway. "We simply went underground for a while," she remarked with a smile. A good teacher does not give up a good cause easily.

The television documentary on Topaz by Ken Verdoia in 1987 lent new legitimacy to Jane's project. And by 1989, she and her students had accumulated enough artifacts and information that she established a rudimentary Topaz Museum to exhibit them and to stimulate research on the camp. A few years later, the museum had grown sufficiently that it became part of the new Great Basin Museum in Delta. Here you could see household implements, clothing, artworks, photographs, toys, tools, school books, newspapers, and so on from the camp. Here you could also see a chilling poster dated May 3, 1942, summoning "all persons of Japanese ancestry" in portions of Alameda county, across the lower bay from San Francisco, to report for relocation within a week to their "Civil Control Station," bringing with them only what "can be carried by the individual or family group." And here on the grounds outside you could see an actual barrack from Topaz showing the humble space that housed a family, with its narrow metal cot-like beds, a pot-bellied stove, and other haunting vestiges of camp life that could bring tears to anyone's eyes.

But Jane Beckwith was not finished. She arranged, through an American Civil Liberties Union grant, to reprint and distribute to every school library in Utah and in the San Francisco area an early short book on Topaz, *The Price of Prejudice* (1962), by the Utah historian Leonard Arrington (whom she had previously recruited to join the Topaz Museum board). She supplied information and advice to the Clinton Administration in 2000 to preserve all of the relocation camps. She obtained a grant for the Topaz Museum from the National Trust for Historic Preservation through its "Save America's Treasures" program. And, widening her efforts, she and her fellow museum trustees launched a campaign to raise funds for an independent Topaz Museum and to purchase the camp site to protect it from an uncertain future on the open lands of a demographically growing state. In 2001 she and some of her students appeared before the Utah state legislature appealing for finances to those ends—having students testify was her idea, she says, "because they are the best proof of how Topaz can awaken people to what the camps were about, and a time and a culture unlike their own."

12. A Wartime Tragedy and a Teacher Who Would Not Let It Be Lost

Jane Beckwith's efforts paid off. In 2007 Topaz was designated a National Historic Landmark. The museum board then purchased a large part of the camp site. And in 2017 a new modern Topaz Museum opened in Delta, to considerable fanfare, including the presence of Japanese officials. It brims with all kinds of artifacts, and images of the camp collected from near and far. The president of the museum is Jane Beckwith.

Jane Beckwith's Topaz project began in the classroom. But it did not stay there. For just as she prodded her students to see the world from disparate points of view, she has used the wartime memory of Topaz to open the minds of many others to a chapter in American history that had been largely lost on the vacant, dusty lands of south-central Utah.

Visiting that place with Jane Beckwith, you are led by not only an inspiring teacher but one with an anthropologist's sharp eye. She identifies traces of the camp's grid, the layout of the barracks, the location of the mess halls, foundations of a school and hospital, the position of the fence and guard towers, and the poignant remains of a Japanese garden with a pool meticulously laid out in stones, now mostly dispersed. Here and there she detects small melancholy vestiges lying in the sand—fragments of toys, combs, and cosmetic containers. "People should know about this," she sighs. "Topaz still has much to teach us."

A previous version of this essay appeared in *Teaching Tolerance*, December, 2001.

A Muslim woman looking to the future.

Human beings possess certain attributes recognized by both West and East, if in varying measure, fundamental to what we might call humanity.

Notes on Islam, America, and Human Rights

WITH A FEW WORDS ON GOOD SOLDIERS IN THE WAR OF IDEAS

The events of September 11, 2001, seared in the minds and emotions of Americans an image of Islam hostile to the American way of life and its democratic freedoms, proud openness, economic prosperity, and cultural secularity. For many Americans, those events seemed to confirm what, a few years earlier, the political scientist Samuel P. Huntington had described as, in the title of a bestselling book, *The Clash of Civilizations* (1996). He had predicted that the future would bring increasing conflicts between the West, especially America, and the rest of the world, particularly the Islamic parts of it. For, he argued, much of the world resents the Western assumption that everyone should embrace its democratic ideals, free-market practices, and commitment to human rights as defined in the West. That assumption betrays Western arrogance, as well as ignorance of how the rest of the world has passed through history and how it lives and might choose to live. No wonder that Islam, with deep roots in tradition and a religious vision of life, sees many of its votaries recoil at what they judge to be not only Western arrogance and ignorance but the abject decadence of the West's—meaning mainly America's—boundlessly secular culture.

The differing, often conflicting, views of life between Islamic nations and the West raises the question: How should human beings deal with such differences? Should we try to understand and sanction them all? That would be a triumph of tolerance. But few people would probably accept such unequivocal tolerance as a viable response to cultural disparities. And here we meet the so-called clash between Islam and the West head on. I say so-called because to characterize the distinctions between Islam and the West as a "clash of civilizations" is inaccurate. The actual division here is not between Islam and the West but between the exponents of radical Islam and everyone else, both within Islam and outside. That puts the situation in a different light.

Moderate or mainstream Islam represents a way of life that differs from that of mainstream Christianity and Judaism and other faiths only in some tenets of religious belief, rituals, and morality. But none of these differences make for a clash of civilizations. Moderate, mainstream believers of any faith can live together under disparate cultural values and traditions, as they have done for centuries in many places. In India, for instance, the Muslim emperor Akbar the Great, who ruled the sub-continent and beyond in the late sixteenth century, openly endorsed the compatibility of Islam, Hinduism, and Christianity and had emblems of those faiths inscribed together in his palaces, establishing an ecumenical society that lasted until his great-grandson, Aurangzeb, turned against Hinduism. In modern times, ideals of commonality amidst cultural diversity have slowly gained sway in many places. We find this nowadays in Europe and the Americas where Muslims, Christians, Jews, and those of other faiths live alongside each other without strife. Such tolerance belongs to the fundamental principles of Western humanism, which supports ecumenicism and is not threatened by religious varieties. Under those principles no harm comes from dissimilarities among religions and cultures. In the United States, the separation of church and state has further endeavored to insure this (see "A Stranger to Power: On the Separation of Church and State" below). In that light, if moderate, mainstream Islam were to become the majority religion in America, no overall change in American life would result.

However, that benign possibility depends on people embracing those principles and eschewing the tendency to what we might call ideological thinking. By this, I mean a view of life that narrows the range of perceptions and judgments to convictions of absolute certainty inimical to tolerance of difference. Most religions have bred some of this in believers at one time or another, intentionally or unintentionally. Christianity, ostensibly founded on an ethics of love and charity, engendered the Crusades bent of seizing the Christian Holy Land from infidel Muslims, whom crusaders killed indiscriminately in the name of Jesus—and for which radical Islamists continue to seek vengeance. Christianity also sanctioned the creation of the modern slave trade with the promise of saving degraded souls, while tearing inhabitants of Africa from their homes and clapping them into a servitude lasting generations. The examples could go on and on through history and around the world.

Unlike mainstream Islam, radical Islam issues from that tragic heritage of religious fanaticism. And, like much of that heritage, this radicalism is linked to political power. Whether in the form the Taliban, Al Qaeda, ISIS, or, perhaps to a lesser degree, the Revolutionary Guards of Iran or any other, Islamic radicalism derives from a twisted conception of Islam that has fueled a political movement to impose a system of social control on the human beings that would extinguish most qualities of human life and civilization highly valued by Eastern as well as Western societies, and by much of Africa, too, for that matter. Western civilization might prize individuality and political liberty more than do some Eastern cultures (Lee Kuan Yew, the philosophical former longtime leader of Singapore, used to promote the "Asian Values" of authority, community, and tradition against the "Western Values" of political liberty and individualism), but neither West nor East nor Africa nor Islamic countries anywhere could have any civilization if radical Islam had its way. Reasonably enough, some observers have branded this perversion of Islam "Islamofascism" for its resemblance to the totalitarian rule of Nazi Germany.

Consider what radical Islam would do—and did under the Taliban in Afghanistan and under ISIS in Syria and Iraq. For one thing, it would deny half the population, females, the opportunity to develop their minds and learn even to read and write, and this exclusion would prevent them not only from developing their own humanity but from contributing to the full human development of the next generation. Radical Islam would also ban all non-Islamic and secular ideas and confine most learning for males to the recitation of the Qur'an (although its leaders would exploit knowledge of technology and weaponry to help impose ignorance on everyone else). These restrictions on the intellect and imagination would reduce human life to a mindless barbarism devoid of humane values.

Females would suffer the worst. Radical Islam would subject them to an existence isolated from public life and wholly dominated by males, suppressing their social and emotional lives and terrorizing them with threats of horrid punishment for any violation of the professed code of behavior, even if the violation came at the hands of males, as in rape. It would also demand that all males subscribe to this inhumane, misogynistic doctrine or be killed. No one could become truly human under such a regime, or feel safe and secure from a ruthless political power that has no restraints upon it.

In all, radical Islam signals not so much one side in a clash of civilizations as the antithesis of civilization itself. Its systematic dehumanization of people, its totalitarian control of life, and the utter hopelessness it breeds for the future is as bad as anything George Orwell envisioned in the political nightmare of *1984* (see "Orwell.,- Mind Control, and Our Times" above).

That is why radical Islam, like all fanaticism, or rabid ideological thinking, must be resisted. And it must be resisted in the name of some humanistic principles that I would say are about as close to universal as such principles can get. These principles complement but are not quite the same as those prominently espoused by the Western movement for "Human Rights," which is primarily concerned with political rights like making governments accountable for curtailing political liberty and abusing their citizens.

The first of these principles asserts that *human beings possess certain attributes, recognized by both West and East, if in varying measure, fundamental to what we might call humanity.* Chief among these attributes are: *the capacities of mind to think, learn, imagine, and understand the world; the ability to develop and use those capacities to shape a life and contribute beneficially to the lives of others; the need to receive and give human affection, to live amid a supportive community, to have a sense of humane social order and physical security, and to nurture a new generation.*

The second principle follows from the first. It asserts that *the values and practices of any civilization or culture or nation or social movement should be judged according to how well they respect and advance the human attributes enumerated in the first principle.*

If these principles sound like a form of Western humanism, they are, but only in part. For they include Eastern ideals that prize the social being and security in life more than is typical in the West. And they are open to any possibility that benefits humanity as here defined and that, while recognizing other points of view, is ready to defend itself against them. That said, these principles stand firmly opposed to any ideas that claim unequivocal, absolute, undefended truth for themselves and refuse tolerance to any others. If we are to live in a truly human world, we will have to live by principles like those affirmed here.

Now from the heights of those principles we descend to the actual world to look at some real Muslims who have put some of them into practice to the benefit of their Islamic homelands. These are good soldiers in what has been called the "war of ideas" between Islam and the West.

II. On the Political Life

A FEW WORDS ON GOOD SOLDIERS IN THE WAR OF IDEAS

These good soldiers have not thought of themselves that way. And they are far from political ideologues. They are simply thoughtful young people who spent time in the US through international exchange programs and were awakened here to the humane character of democratic culture. They then returned home bent on instilling qualities of this culture there—such as the effusive teacher who exclaimed: "I was back in Turkmenistan! Back in my home country! I made up my mind to do whatever I could to make my country a better place to live" because "America inspired me and showed me what was possible." The brief, anecdotal examples that follow come from reports of individuals who, like that teacher, participated in the American Councils for International Education programs during the late years of the twentieth century and the early years of the twenty-first and live in the predominantly Islamic regions of the former Soviet Union. I might add that in addition to being Islamic, the countries of these regions have no traditions of democracy, as is evident in some of the anecdotes.

"My understanding of the meaning of life has totally changed" since residing in the US, declared a young Azerbaijani woman. In the first place, after experiencing America's freedom of speech and religion and the respect for law, she saw Islam in a new light. Much to her surprise, she explains, "Although I am originally from a Muslim country, I started to read the Qur'an and came to my religion and an understanding of it only in the US, not in my country." That understanding taught her Islam's fundamental humanity. At the same time, she continued, touched by "how the American people can care about and help someone they don't know well"—including herself—she vowed to "do my best to have an open and big heart and help those who need it." She returned home as a Muslim with democratic ideals who has since then thrown herself into securing and defending the rights of children, as well as teaching them, through a widely distributed booklet she wrote and other means, how to protect themselves from physical dangers in their region, particularly frequent earthquakes.

Several young women went back home to Uzbekistan from America carrying similar convictions and aspirations. One of them had studied law and held an internship at the UN. Now she is a prominent law professor in her homeland who has established courses previously unknown there, such as that staple of American law schools "Constitutional Law" and the truly innovative "Women's Rights Under Islam." Another young woman, also newly imbued with concerns about the rights of Muslim women, decided "to improve the status of women," and began by organizing summer camps for girls to "increase their self-esteem by teaching them their basic rights." From that beginning, she intends to expand the cause of women's rights through other educational projects. Yet another young woman, worried that "terrorism is threatening the peace of the world," draws on her American MBA training to promote "democratic and economic reforms" that will "create a true democratic society and build a bridge of friendship between the USA and Uzbekistan."

A young man from Tajikistan says that, after becoming "stronger, more active, free, and responsible" in the US, he set out at home to "study everything related to human rights" and to promote them. He joined the Republic Bureau of Human Rights and the Rule of Law, a human rights protection organization. There he organizes legal clinics for his fellow Tajiks, reports on human rights violations in prisons, and helps a UN agency monitor Tajik laws for their compliance with the International Covenant on Civil and Political Rights.

In Kyrgyzstan, a teacher says she discovered in America that "democracy is not just a beautiful word that allows everyone to do whatever one likes"; instead it means "freedom but responsibility." Adopting the last three words as her motto, she now teaches "what

II. On the Political Life

a democratic state is," and has plans for "a new democratic school" devoted to spreading the principles of democracy throughout "the life of the community and the country." Likewise, a young Kyrgyz man affirms that when he was an exchange student, "the US won an ally in me." And he is acting on that conversion by coordinating a coalition of fifty-five "NGOs for Democratic Civil Society." Next he plans to run for parliament as a vigorous advocate of democratic ideals.

In Kazakhstan, several teachers equally moved by their experience of American freedoms and social equality are now endeavoring within their schools and among adults outside to, as they say, teach the principles of a truly "open civil society" to make their homeland "a real democratic country."

And in Tatarstan (a Russian Republic north of Kazakhstan), a woman struck by America's ethnic tolerance strives to foster this at home by, for one thing, dissuading her countrymen from quarreling over the question "Should Tatar people support their Muslim brothers or be united with their Russian neighbors?" To achieve this she is mounting an ambitious community-wide multicultural educational program.

Although these examples are few and anecdotal, they represent hundreds of people who bring us the good news from the war of ideas that America can indeed nurture open-minded, democratic culture in Islamic and other developing countries without firing a shot. It can do this by (among other things, of course) inviting to our shores, educating, and otherwise exposing to the best in American life ever more of those (many of them women as the examples show) who will help form the futures of those countries. For, again and again, what these people take home with them is not so much a stereotypical image of American prosperity and of boundless opportunities for self-advancement. It is rather a sense that American democratic culture fosters above all such qualities as independent thinking, openness of mind, social equality, respect for others and kindness to them—including regard for the disabled, which came as an eye-opening surprise to many of the exchange participants because neglect and even derision of the disabled is common in most of the home countries—and optimism that with effort one can make the world, or at any rate one's own country, better.

America has its dark sides, to be sure. Perhaps some exchange participants—students, teachers, other professionals—saw these, too. But, by the example of their own lives, they took home with them the better angels of America, not least the hope that they can significantly contribute to imbuing their own countries with the best of democratic culture. And that should give hope to all who desire a fruitful resolution of the war of ideas between the West and Islam. For within this kind of democratic culture—again, at its best—differences of values, beliefs, and ways of life do not need to dissolve or submit to one system of belief or another. They can thrive under the humanistic principles that help human beings fulfill the humanity that they all share.

This essay expands on the original published under the heading "How America Is Earning Respect Abroad," in *The Christian Science Monitor*, May 9, 2006.

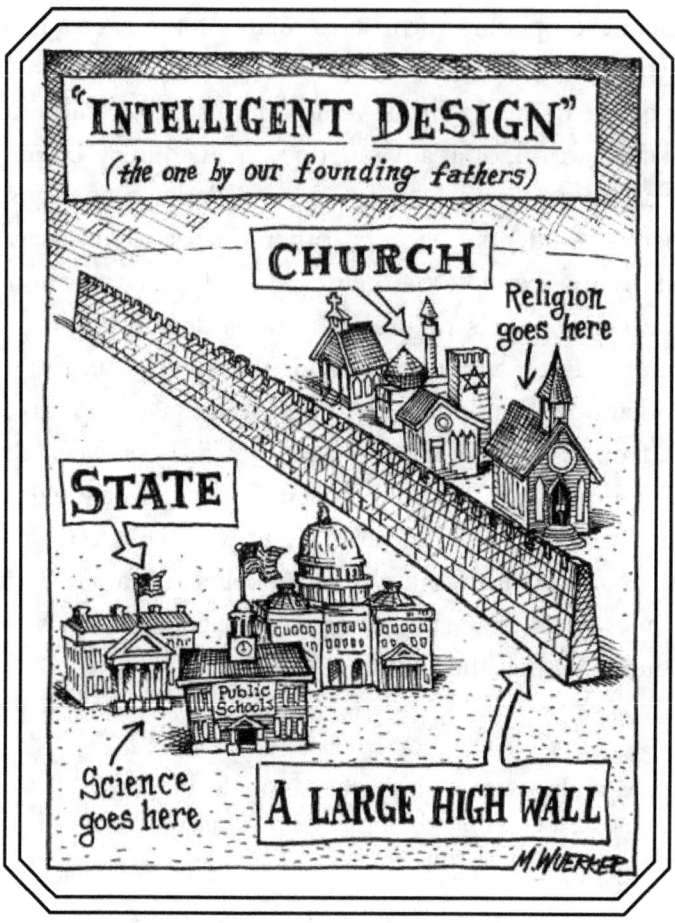

Editorial cartoon by Matt Wuerker.

"*In America, all attributed the peaceful dominion that religion exercises in their country principally to the complete separation of church and state.*"
—ALEXIS DE TOCQUEVILLE

A Stranger to Power

ON THE SEPARATION OF CHURCH AND STATE

When you visit the National Constitution Center in Philadelphia on a school day in May, you can barely reach the exhibits illustrating America's constitutional and political history from its origins into the twenty-first century. Hoards of school children on field trips press the glass of every showcase and surround every free-standing object, reading the legends, listening to the recordings, working the interactive displays, fingering anything they can touch, jotting notes, and chattering inquisitively. Among the exhibits visitors can examine, although hardly the most popular with children, are those that trace important stages in the history of the Supreme Court.

The Center aptly alerts visitors to the role of the Supreme Court in American history first with a presentation on the epochal case of *Marbury v. Madison*. In deciding this case in 1803, Chief Justice John Marshall and his five colleagues elevated the court's original status among the three branches of government from the third rank to virtual equality—the brief Article Three of the Constitution assigned the Supreme Court only the authority of highest appellate court in the land and gave it "original jurisdiction," or authority to act as court of first resort, only in cases involving states or Ambassadors or "other public Ministers." They did this by exercising a judicial power not prescribed in Article Three: the power of "judicial review." That is, the justices decided that the court had the sole authority to interpret the Constitution as the ultimate law of the land above laws passed by Congress (rather than treating the Constitution as merely an administrative document establishing the structure and responsibilities of government) and therefore could overturn acts of Congress if the court ruled that such acts violate the Constitution.

Ironically, the Congressional act overturned in this case was a provision of the Judiciary Act of 1789 that had actually expanded the scope of the court's "original jurisdiction." The case itself dealt with a minor issue that became quite twisty on its way to becoming momentous. It concerned one William Marbury, who had received a low-level appointment in the last days of the departing Adams Administration, but who had then, on a bureaucratic technicality, been denied the position by the new Secretary of State, James Madison, of the incoming Jefferson administration. Outraged, Marbury did what would become a familiar practice in American democracy: he sued. And, under the expanded "original jurisdiction" provision of the Judiciary Act of 1789, he took his case directly to the Supreme Court. Now the twists tighten. Marshall and his colleagues recognized the legitimacy of Marbury's complaint (Marshall had in fact supported Marbury's appointment when he was himself Adams's Secretary of State before becoming Chief Justice), but they ruled that the Supreme Court had no authority to remedy it because that would exercise an "original jurisdiction" in this instance not allowed by Article Three of the Constitution, notwithstanding the Judiciary Act that had granted the court that authority.

Hence, in *Marbury v. Madison*, the Supreme Court claimed an authority for itself not in the Constitution by overturning an act of Congress that had expanded that authority in what the court now judged to be an unconstitutional addition. Maybe a bit of sleight-of-hand there (and probably some political motivation in empowering Marshall and his court against the newly elected opposition Jefferson administration, even while siding with them in denying Marbury redress), but the case stands as the most consequential in American judicial history, delivering to the Supreme Court the preeminent "power of judicial review" not in the text of the Constitution.

14. A STRANGER TO POWER

The Constitution Center proceeds to note that Supreme Court justices have often disagreed over how to use this power. And a wall panel pertinently explains that such disagreements in recent times have often divided the court between "originalists" (or "textualists"), who interpret the Constitution according to their understanding of the original meaning of the text itself, and the "non-originalists" (or "contextualists"), who interpret the Constitution according to their understanding of the historical contexts of both its framers and of the cases that come before the court.

And now we come to the theme of this essay. Although the Center does not dwell on it, few constitutional issues mattered more to the nation's founders, and have more sharply divided "textualists" and "contextualists" on the Supreme Court, than the relation of church to state. In fact, questions about the relation of church and state have animated public debate and inflamed personal passions in America in the past few decades more than at any time since the founding. And that has often brought the Supreme Court an unusual measure of public attention. This might not be the best thing for the court, but it is not a bad thing for American citizens, for it has given us good cause to take interest in constitutional issues. And to think about just what is the proper relation between religion and government in a democracy.

Political and judicial conservatives deserve most of the credit for the latter-day interest in the relationship of church and state. For they have decried court rulings and liberal legislation that, so the zealots among them contend, have delivered America over to a tyranny of secularism amounting to, in the combative words of the former media demagogue Bill O'Reilly, an outright "war on religion"—an oft-repeated phrase seasonally coupled with complaints about a "war on Christmas."

As evidence, they point an accusing finger at the judicial banishment from public schools of official prayers, Bible readings, religious instruction, the teaching of "creationism" and "intelligent

133

design," displays of the Ten Commandments, and so on, along with restrictions of religious symbols on government property. They tag as kindred evils efforts to erase the words "under God" from the Pledge of Allegiance, as well as the legalization of abortion and the expansion of homosexual rights. Such pernicious acts, these conservative critics argue, have divorced church and state beyond anything envisioned by the nation's founders.

As Republican Senator John Cornyn of Texas put it apropos of conservative Samuel Alito's nomination to the Supreme Court, the court's rulings on church and state in recent decades "are way out of step with what the founding fathers intended." In this piously confident spirit, the Texas Republican Party threw down the gauntlet in its platform of 2002 with the fighting words: "Our Party pledges to do everything within its power to dispel the myth of separation of church and state."

Conservatives blame this "myth" on a fallacious interpretation of the First Amendment. And some trace the fallacy to a Supreme Court opinion of 1947. This opinion came in the case of *Everson v. Board of Education of the Township of Ewing*. There a New Jersey man had sued the Board of Education and the state for violating the First Amendment by subsidizing with taxpayer money the transportation of children to parochial schools as well as to public schools. Writing for the majority, Justice Hugo Black surveyed the history of religious persecution and strife that had led to the First Amendment's safeguards on religious liberty, then he stated emphatically: "The First Amendment has erected a wall between church and state. That wall must be kept high and impregnable. We could not approve the slightest breach."

Justice Black was, as he noted, drawing on words of Thomas Jefferson, who as president had written a historic letter in 1802 to the Danbury, Connecticut, Baptist Association assuring them that the First Amendment guaranteed a "wall of separation between church and state." One Supreme Court justice had previously cited Jefferson's metaphor in a decision of 1878, but Black was now adopting it for the first time as a firm constitutional principle broadly and categorically separating religion from government.

In an irony recalling that of John Marshall's epochal ruling in *Marbury*, Black's majority in this case actually ruled for the defense. For, Black concluded, "New Jersey has not breached [the wall of separation] here" since the subsidy merely facilitated the transportation to school of all children in the district, and to deny this subsidy to students of parochial schools would discriminate unfairly against them. The First Amendment, he explained, "requires the state to be neutral in its relations with groups of religious believers and non-believers, it does not require the state to be their adversary."

The liberal dissenters in the case embraced Black's eloquent argument for the separation of church and state but figured it warranted a ruling for the plaintiff instead of for the defense. "This is not," they wrote, "just a little case over bus fares." It was about "public money devoted to payment of religious costs," and that "is the first step" toward "the establishment of religion."

As it turned out, the majority ruling for the defense in the case cast only a faint historical shadow. But Black's dictum declaring that the First Amendment "erected a wall between church and state" that "must be kept high and impregnable," and that this wall "requires the state to be neutral" regarding "religious believers and non-believers," cast a distinct historical shadow. And to some eyes it was a long dark shadow indeed. For Black's words set a precedent (echoed in subsequent rulings beginning the next year with *McCollum v. Board of Education*, which went the other way from *Everson* and removed religious instruction from some Illinois public schools) that many conservatives, especially those on the religious Right, condemn for propagating a spuriously secular and even irreligious reading of the First Amendment's opening lines.

Symbolically reflecting this conservative reaction, the flamboyant fundamentalist preacher and anti-abortion activist Flip Benham, head of Operation Save America, has been known to sport retro wing-tip shoes in homage to pre-1947 America. More substantially, the Christian home schooling movement blossomed in the 1960s and 1970s, and Christian authors set out to rewrite American history to teach the hidden "truth" about it. The essence of this "truth" is, as the journalist Jeff Sharlet summarized in an article on the topic ("Through a Glass Darkly: How the Christian Right is Re-imagining US History," *Harper's Magazine*, December, 2006): "The nation was conceived of as Christian" by the founders, and therefore "the separation of church and state is either a myth altogether . . . or meant only to prevent a single denomination from prevailing." A flood of textbooks and revisionist histories now purvey this "truth" by demonstrating how, contrary to the alleged ignorance and lies of secular historians, Christianity gave birth to this country and has overwhelmingly shaped its character and history. The Internet now delivers these books to homes through hundreds of websites and resources dedicated to, as the website of the American Christian History Institute (founded in 1978) announces, "Restoring America's Biblical Foundations" and "historic Biblical method of reasoning." David Barton's *The Myth of Separation* (1989) has become a standard work for this historical vision, and Barton's high position in the Texas Republican Party surely got the book's title phrase into the Party platform in 2002. The more apocalyptic versions of this Christian American history also warn that since about the mid-twentieth century an evil cult of secularism has ascended— abetted by an overweening government and by adverse court rulings on church and state, abortion, and homosexuality—that may require God's fiery intervention to annihilate.

The late, outspoken Supreme Court Justice Antonin Scalia, moved by a kindred view of what he deemed America's wayward, latter-day judicial history, repeatedly assailed that history and vowed to bring church and state closer together. He told an audience celebrating the nation's second annual Religious Freedom Day in 2003, "the separation of church and state was not our tradition" originally. And he reiterated the charge from the bench at every opportunity.

In a dissenting opinion in *McCreary v. ACLU* (2005), for example,

Justice Scalia proclaimed, "the court's oft-repeated assertion that the government cannot favor religious practice is false" because the principle of "'governmental neutrality between . . . religion and non-religion'" has no source in "the words of the Constitution." He went on to cite a litany of early "governmental invocation[s] of God" and traditional official practices favorable to religion (which other justices have also cited, albeit more often in upholding than denying the separation of church and state). He then accused the justices in the majority of outright "hostility to religion" for ruling in this case against mandatory displays of the Ten Commandments in Kentucky courthouses. He further claimed that the majority's errors not only traduced the Constitution but violated "the interest of the overwhelming majority of religious believers in being able to give God thanks and supplication *as a people*, and with respect to our national endeavors."

Justice Scalia did not stop there. He added a flashy and eccentric coda on his theme. While the First Amendment does allow government to promote "public acknowledgement of religious belief," he wrote, as in displays of the Ten Commandments in courthouses, this government sanction belongs only to devotees of "monotheistic" religions. "It is entirely clear from our Nation's historical practices," he explained, "that the Establishment Clause permits this disregard of polytheists and believers in unconcerned deities, just as it permits the disregard of devout atheists." In Justice Scalia's "originalist" interpretation of the First Amendment, because monotheists wrote the Constitution and often invoked their God, that document implicitly grants wide latitude for the American government to advocate monotheistic religions but *not* other modes of religious belief or disbelief. Secularists worried about the future separation of church and state in America might see in Scalia's peculiar and far-reaching rejection of Justice Black's "neutrality principle" here a curious validation of their concerns.

Writing for the majority in this case, Justice David Souter politely classed Scalia's constitutional claim for monotheism a "surprise."

But in an impassioned concurring majority opinion, Justice Sandra Day O'Connor affirmed that "we do not count heads before we enforce the First Amendment," for "the religion Clauses . . . protect adherents of all religions, as well as those who believe in no religion at all." And, she added resoundingly, given the troubles "around the world" stemming from "the assumption of religious authority by government," anyone who seeks to "renegotiate the boundaries of church and state" in America must "answer a difficult question: Why would we trade a system that has served us so well for one that has served others so poorly?"

The contentions of the religious Right and Justice Scalia—and his conservative Catholic acolyte Justice Alito, who decries how "religious liberty is fast becoming a disfavored right" (speech to the Federalist Society, quoted in Ruth Marcus, "Conservatives Hold Court, but Alito Still Complains," *Honolulu Star-Advertiser*, November 18, 2020)—against the separation of church and state have, of course, found support aplenty among conservative politicians. For instance, moved by his own born-again religious impulses as a man who unabashedly named Jesus Christ his favorite philosopher, President George W. Bush acted to make government more hospitable to religion in a host of ways. To name a few: he lauded Justice Scalia's "originalist" jurisprudence and appointed like-minded justices to the courts; he launched "faith-based initiatives" by executive order; his Department of Education issued new guidelines assisting voluntary prayer in schools; he proclaimed Religious Freedom Day in the aftermath of 9/11 as a rallying call and morale boost for American believers; his Department of Justice, heavily manned by evangelical lawyers, shifted its focus in civil rights from advancing racial equality to fighting "religious discrimination" (which meant undoing constraints on government aid to churches); and he welcomed a constitutional amendment banning gay marriage. I might note that the subsequent Supreme Court ruling recognizing same-sex marriage, thanks to the vote of the moderate Justice Kennedy (since replaced by another conservative Catholic), renewed cries against the so-called "war on religion" and threats to religious liberty.

Such attitudes, ambitions, and actions by those on the political Right opposing the separation of church and state have induced many on the political Left, such as members of Americans United for the Separation of Church and State (created in 1947 to combat government funding of religion after the paradoxical *Everson* decision), to discern here a dangerous deviation from what they view as the truly secular American tradition. Some fear that this deviation could take us down the road to theocracy—a goal unapologetically advocated by fanatical evangelicals. These liberal fears may be no less excessive than much of the right-wing rhetoric about religion in peril. But liberal critics can reasonably argue that the conservative assault on the separation of church and state at least distorts or ignores a lot of history. And they can start at the nation's origins, where conservatives also like to start but from a different perspective.

On looking into this history, we should first see that these divergent perspectives derive from a certain tension between the two religion clauses of the First Amendment. These clauses say: *"Congress shall make no law respecting an establishment of religion, or prohibiting the free exercise thereof."* The first, known as the Establishment Clause, protects the religious freedom of everyone by preventing Congress from endorsing the religion of anyone. The second, the Free Exercise Clause, adds the protection that no federal law can keep people from freely practicing their own religion.

Here is the tension (arising, in no small part, from the vague language): What some people consider "the free exercise" of religion, other people consider an "establishment of religion"—a tension not lost on the Supreme Court, where it was remarked, for example, by Justice Stephen Breyer in *Van Orden v. Perry* (2005). The secular

Left tends to stress the Establishment Clause in order to *curtail* any state-sanctioned role of religion in public life. They say the less religion in public life the better for democratic liberty. The religious Right tends to stress the Free Exercise Clause for the opposite reason: to *expand* the state-sanctioned role of religion in public and private life. They say the more religion in public life the better for religious liberty.

In pursuing their ends, those on the Right assert that the Establishment Clause prohibits only the creation of an official state church but does not restrict other official endorsements of religion. And, like Justice Scalia in *McCreary*, they can cite a litany of historically supportive instances, such as the daily invocation of God by the Supreme Court, morning prayers in Congress, and George Washington's purported addition of the words "so help me God" to the presidential oath of office (although this is historically undocumented and was not reported until the 1850s). Those on the Left acknowledge, and often mention, the same litany but consider its contents more ceremonial than substantive. They contend that the First Amendment prohibits not only an established state church but anything substantively implying or "respecting" government support of religion in intent or effect. And they can support this contention by drawing on the well-documented historical contexts surrounding and succeeding the framing of the First Amendment's religion clauses.

Like the rest of the Bill of Rights, the two religion clauses were added to the Constitution to win the ratification of states demanding more protection from the federal government than they found in the text of the Constitution. And, as the placement of these clauses at the beginning of the First Amendment signals, protections of religious liberty came first in the framers' minds.

Before the Constitutional Convention in 1787, James Madison and Thomas Jefferson had carried out a successful struggle to secure religious liberty in their home state of Virginia. Not long after writing the Declaration of Independence, Jefferson had proposed a bill to the colonial legislature vigorously advocating the freedom of religion against political authority. Nearly ten years later this bill became law, assuring that "all men shall be free to profess, and by argument maintain, their opinion in matters of religion," and that none "shall be compelled to frequent or support any religious worship, place, or ministry whatsoever." This short document, the Virginia Statute for Religious Freedom, expressed Jefferson's deepest convictions and set a standard for religious liberty and the separation of church and state in Virginia that the First Amendment would echo and that other states would eventually follow.

Meanwhile, Madison had penned an influential brief in 1785 arguing that a bill sponsored by Patrick Henry before the Virginia legislature to provide public funding for "Teachers of the Christian Religion" portended "a dangerous abuse of power." In this *Memorial and Remonstrance against Religious Assessments* (later frequently quoted, especially by the liberal-minded) Madison identified that danger in many of the law's probable consequences. But two of these consequences stand out, one political and one religious.

First, Madison wrote, by taxing citizens to get funds for the dissemination of Christianity, even if all sects reaped the proceeds, the bill clearly entailed "the establishment" of the Christian religion. And, he warned, "who does not see that the same authority which can establish Christianity, in exclusion of all other Religions, may establish with the same ease any particular sect of Christians, in exclusion of all other sects?" The political empowerment of religion in any form, he explained, has always caused troubles for "Civil Society," and "in no instance have [official religions] been seen [as] the guardians of the liberties of the people." Hence, Patrick Henry's bill "establishing" Christianity violated the "equal title to the free exercise of Religion" that all citizens of a democracy must possess.

Second, Madison argued in detail, the political empowerment or establishment of religion does religion itself more harm than good. It "is a contradiction to the Christian Religion," he declared, to think it needs government backing to survive. "For it is known that this religion both existed and flourished, not only without the support of human laws, but in spite of every opposition from them." Not only that, Madison went on, "the bill is adverse to the diffusion of the light of Christianity" because "it will destroy that moderation and harmony which the forbearance of our laws to intermeddle with Religion has produced amongst its several sects," unlike the religious oppression and religious rivalries over political power that have spewed "torrents of blood . . . in the old world." What is more, Madison emphasized, "ecclesiastical establishments, instead of maintaining the purity and efficacy of Religion, have had a contrary operation." Just look at what happens "more or less in all places," he said: "pride and indolence in the Clergy; ignorance and servility in the laity; in both, superstition, bigotry, and persecution." By contrast to this sorry fate of established religions, he later proudly wrote in a letter of 1819 referring to Virginia, "the number, the industry, and the morality of the Priesthood, and the devotion of the people have been manifestly increased by the total separation of the church from the state."

Madison's forceful advocacy of that separation derailed Patrick Henry's bill and helped Jefferson's Statute on Religious Freedom become law in Virginia. And, as the separationists expected, both democracy and religion benefited.

Jefferson and Madison were not godless men. Few people in their day were. They often invoked God, even while affirming their secular political principles. But Jefferson and Madison understood that American democracy, with its many religious sects (although only Christian, and almost entirely Protestant at that), could not thrive unless church and state were distinctly separated to head off religious strife. The framers of the Constitution, with Madison in the lead (Jefferson was then in France), honored this separation in several conspicuous ways: they studiously made no reference to God in the text of the Constitution (although the date of its signing was given in the European Christian convention "year of our Lord"); they insured in Article VI that "no religious Test shall ever be required as a qualification to any office"; and they attached the religious restrictions on government in the First Amendment.

But these secular-minded separationists also had surprising allies among many devout religionists, both before the Revolution and after. Just as the secularists saw the political empowerment of any religion as a threat to democratic liberties as well as detrimental to religion, so the religionists, notably Baptists and Presbyterians, feared that the political empowerment of religion would favor only the dominant sect or sects to the detriment of their own religious liberty, a condition they had fled Europe to escape but which persisted to varying degrees in the colonies. Some of these religionists were even more adamant about formally separating church and state than were the secularists. They insisted upon formal constitutional protections of religious liberty, whereas Madison had originally thought this unnecessary because the Constitution gave government no authority in religious matters, and because he believed the very diversity of sects would prevent any of them from gaining dominance. One of the most prominent of these religious separationists was the New England Baptist Reverend Isaac Backus, who had left the dominant Congregational Church for the Evangelical fold during the First Great Awakening in the mid-eighteenth century.

Vexed by discrimination against his own Evangelical Baptist sect and by taxation to sustain the Congregational Church in Massachusetts, Backus nevertheless refused to solicit political privileges for his own flock. Instead, he sought a sharp break between church and state as the only prospect for evangelicals to enjoy religious freedom. He delivered a long sermon to this effect in 1773 entitled "An Appeal to the Public for Religious Liberty, Against the Oppressions of the Present Day." There he ardently argued that "God has appointed two kinds of government in the world," the "civil" and the "ecclesiastical," and they "ought never to be confounded together." For where they "are well distinguished according to the true nature and end of their institution, the effects are happy, and they do not at all interfere with each other: but when they have been confounded together, no tongue nor pen can fully describe the mischiefs that have ensued." He later reiterated some of these opinions at the Constitutional Convention in Philadelphia, where he also remarked that giving political power to religion "may make hypocrites, but cannot create Christians," and that "liberty never flourished perfectly" where religions have held such power.

Similar conflicts and convictions led the Danbury Baptist Association to write to Jefferson in 1801 telling him how they "rejoice" over his election as president because "our sentiments are uniformly on the side of religious liberty." They went on to avow that "religion is at all times a matter between God and individuals," and that "the legitimate authority of civil government extends no further than to punish the man who does ill to his neighbors," leaving "religious opinions" alone. Unfortunately, they added, the state of Connecticut still discriminated against Baptists—and a few other states even had established churches until Massachusetts abandoned the last of them in the 1830s. It was this letter that elicited Jefferson's now-famous words on the First Amendment's "wall of separation between church and state." Jefferson knew this amendment protected religious freedom against only acts of Congress (constitutional protections against acts of the states had to await the Fourteenth Amendment in 1868, and it was not until 1940 that the Supreme Court, in *Cantwell v. Connecticut*, began applying these protections explicitly to matters of religion), but he was thumping the principle. Evangelicals today who debunk that "wall of separation" would do well to recall their forebears who had assiduously helped build it and had even inspired Jefferson to formulate the potent metaphor.

Backus and the Baptists did have some markedly different goals from the secularists. The secularists aimed to shield religious and other liberties from the political power of any religion or "faction"—the evil that Madison had famously inveighed against in *Federalist Paper #10*—that would attempt to impose its will on all people. By contrast, Backus and allied religionists sought to nurture a nation of Christian believers and thought separating church and state would give their faiths the freedom to achieve that end, unconstrained by political privileges for any of them. Despite these differences of purpose, the formative alliance of secularists and religionists delivered the constitutional separation of church and state that most Americans prize in the First Amendment and in the American tradition as well.

Anyone who doubts that this separation took root in the early years of the republic has only to read that most astute observer of American life, Alexis de Tocqueville. A little more than half a century after Jefferson, Madison, Backus, and others joined in their common cause against perilous entanglements of church and state, Tocqueville arrived from France, officially to study prisons and unofficially to examine American democracy. The book he and his traveling companion Gustave de Beaumont later published on the prisons goes largely unread today. But the book Tocqueville published on his other topic is probably the most important ever written about this country: *Democracy in America*.

An aristocrat by birth, Tocqueville had plenty of doubts about democracy, even though he considered it historically inevitable and had modest hopes for it. Wary of its leveling tendencies, he disdained American democracy's egalitarian "individualism" (a word he gave currency), ridiculed its materialistic "hypocrisy of luxury," and rued its general vulgarity. And he suspected that its inclination to let social equality eclipse personal liberty could bring the tyranny of a vast paternalistic government to enforce that equality. These kinds of criticisms later made Tocqueville a mentor to many modern conservatives.

But what Tocqueville found most remarkable, surprising, and

II. On the Political Life

positive in America was the condition of religion. Among the many penetrating observations, arresting analyses, and prescient predictions of *Democracy in America*, none is more significant, thought-provoking, and germane to America today than those on this subject. He deserves to be quoted at length because what he says on religion in America is insufficiently known and should be required reading for participants in any debate over the relation of church and state. And, as a thinker respected by conservatives, and one who considered religion at once necessary to human well-being and indispensable to democracy, he also bears a credibility that should give pause to those who view the separation of church and state in America as a godless, come-lately, liberal idea.

"On my arrival in the United States," Tocqueville writes, "it was the religious aspect of the country that first struck my eye."* Americans were extraordinarily religious. And, even more extraordinary, they identified their religiosity with democratic liberty. "Among us [the French]," he explains, "I had seen the spirit of religion and the spirit of freedom almost always move in contrary directions. Here I found them united intimately with one another: they reigned together on the same soil." He set out "to know the cause of this phenomenon."

"To learn it," he continues, "I interrogated the faithful of all communions." And to his heightened astonishment, everyone told him the same thing: "All attributed the peaceful dominion that religion exercises in their country principally to *the complete separation of church and state* [emphasis added]. I do not fear to affirm that during my stay in America I did not encounter a single man, priest, or layman, who did not come to accord on this point."

Tocqueville could not have been more unequivocal on this. And

---

* I quote from the sections of *Democracy in America* (translated by Harvey C. Mansfield and Delba Winthrop) headed "On the Principal Causes that make Religion Powerful in America" and "Indirect Influence that Religious Beliefs Exert on Political Society in the United States."

the more he probed the topic, the more revealing the facts became to him. The clergy in America, he observes, "seemed to distance themselves from power voluntarily and take a sort of professional pride in remaining strangers to it." And yet, religion was prospering through "an innumerable multitude of sects" that influenced both "mores" and "intelligence." He began to "wonder how it could happen that in diminishing the apparent force of a religion one came to increase its real power." (He seems not to have known Madison's *Remonstrance*.)

This new curiosity led Tocqueville to reflect on how the relation of religion to politics in America differed from that in Europe, and on the consequences of the difference for both religion and liberty. The conclusions he reached are as emphatic as his observations on the separation of church and state in America are unequivocal.

"I know that there are times," Tocqueville says, "when religion can add to the influence that is proper to it the artificial power of the laws and the support of the material powers that direct society." However, "in obtaining a power that is not due to it," he cautions, "it risks its legitimate power." That happens because "when a religion seeks to found its empire only on the desire for immortality that torments the hearts of all men equally it can aim at universality," but "in allying itself with a political power, religion increases its power over some and loses the hope of reigning over all." Consequently, by "uniting with different political powers, religion can therefore contract only an onerous alliance. It does not need their assistance to live, and in serving them it can die."

In short, when religion acquires political power, it loses its soul. At the same time, it rouses hatred among those who suffer at the hands of that power. Tocqueville's older contemporaries had seen this happen dramatically in France as the political power of the Catholic Church had alienated Enlightenment thinkers, stimulated irreligion, and aroused the animus of revolutionaries who echoed Voltaire's anti-Catholic battle cry: *Écraser l'infâme!*—Crush the infamous thing! The effects of allying church and state, as Tocqueville now understood even better than before, were bad for both religion and liberty.

Tocqueville goes on to explain that a wide separation of church and state matters even more in democracies than elsewhere. "Insofar as a nation takes on a democratic social state," he writes, "it becomes more and more dangerous for religion to unite with authority," since democratic leadership changes frequently amid the "ebb and flow of human opinions" and "the parties' struggle" for power. Therefore, "if the Americans . . . had not placed their religion somewhere outside" the political system, religion could not have provided the stabilizing influence that democracy needs. At the same time, if they had subjected religion to the welter of democratic politics, "where would the respect be that is due" to religion? And "what would become of its immortality when everything around it was perishing?"

Tocqueville fervently believed that both religion and liberty were essential to democracy. And he saw them both threatened by entanglements of church and state that could be manipulated by politicians temporarily in power.

He concludes with plaudits for the healthy condition of both religion and liberty in America. "In America," he sums up, "religion is perhaps less powerful than it has been in certain times and among certain peoples, but its influence is more lasting. It is reduced to its own strength, which no one can take away from it; it acts in one sphere only, but covers the whole of it and dominates it without effort." As a result, "religion, which among Americans never mixes directly in the government of society, should therefore be considered as the first of their political institutions; for if it does not give them the taste for freedom, it singularly facilitates their use of it."

In the facts he observed and in the conclusions he drew, Tocqueville provided a compelling testament to the historic benefits of the separation of church and state in America, for the good of both religion and democracy. Why then, we might ask, did

14. A Stranger to Power

American conservatives, who look upon Tocqueville as a forebear, decide that the separation of church and state is an evil modern myth perpetrated mainly by wrongheaded court rulings beginning around the middle of the twentieth century? History tells this story, too.

Start with this. Conservatives just ignore Tocqueville's unequivocal reports and emphatic conclusions on the separation of church and state in America in the early nineteenth century. And they stress that religion held a more central place in American democracy when Tocqueville traveled the country in 1831–32 than it does now. In certain respects they are correct. Some of Tocqueville's own observations on the widespread religiosity of Americans attest to that. After all, the 1830s were a simpler time when God was still routinely invoked in public life, Christianity was pervasive, and few secular schools existed. (It is worth noting though that Sunday mail service, initiated with the US Post Office in 1810, continued in spite of religious objections, thanks to powerful legislators like Kentucky senator, future vice president, and devout Baptist Richard M. Johnson, who was determined to keep church and state separate; Sunday mail service later dwindled as unnecessary and ended officially in 1912.) But the next hundred years would bring social and cultural changes that many religionists would not like, and that pious activists would try to rectify.

These religious activists were responding in part to the secularist bent of state-run public schools. Before the advent of these schools in the mid-nineteenth century as an educational manifestation of American democracy, virtually all schooling was sectarian, and the Bible was the standard instructional text. The rise of state public schools, funded by taxes, thrust the education of the young and the relation of church and state into an unprecedented secular context. This raised inevitable conflicts over the religious content of schooling. To defuse these conflicts, the states permitted nonsectarian Bible readings and prayers (albeit Protestant, not Catholic) in schools for the purpose of moral guidance. But by the end of the nineteenth century only one state, Massachusetts, required Bible reading or prayer in the schools, whereas other states had either voluntarily abandoned such strict practices or courts had banned them for violating state constitutions.

This secular trend, bolstered by the rise of Darwinism, was bound to breed discontent among people who regarded the schools as extensions of churches for teaching Christian principles. Signaling this discontent, some states began in the twentieth century to formally mandate or at least to facilitate public school prayers, Bible readings, religious instruction, the teaching of "creationism" as science, posting the Ten Commandments, and so forth. These actions led to legal challenges under the Establishment Clause and to the court rulings that conservatives would revile as secular extremism and liberal judicial activism. Before the twentieth century, the Supreme Court had addressed cases of religious freedom only a couple of times, and these focused on the Free Exercise Clause as it pertained to the practice of polygamy. Clearly, the increasing promotion in the twentieth century of religion in public schools, sometimes in the guise of secular learning, raised judicial issues of the Establishment Clause as never before.

Justice William Brennan remarked this development in his long concurring majority opinion in *Abington v. Schempf* (1963). The decision in this case banned official Bible reading and recitation of the Lord's Prayer, inaugurated in 1913 and codified in 1949, from a Pennsylvania school district. "What is noteworthy about the panoply of state and local regulations" installing religious activities in public schools, such as had prompted this and similar cases, he wrote, "is the relative recency of the statutory codification of practices which have ancient roots." Religionists would have none of this in their version of American history.

The most celebrated case pitting secularists against a fresh official intrusion of religion into the schools was, of course, the Scopes "monkey" trial of 1925. It followed from an anti-Darwinist

Tennessee law enacted the same year, amidst a wave of religious fundamentalism, that barred teaching in public schools "anything that denies the story of Divine Creation as taught in the Bible" and that teaches "instead that man has descended from lower animals." Secularists persuaded John Scopes to break the law so they could then challenge its constitutionality. As they had expected, Scopes was convicted. But the case did not achieve their anticipated success on appeal. The conviction got overturned on a mere technicality by a state court, and the law remained on the books until 1967—a year before the US Supreme Court, in *Epperson v. Arkansas* found a similar law, enacted in 1928, to be unconstitutional.

The *Epperson* decision foreshadowed future judicial rulings against attempts to slip anti-evolution religious doctrines into the classroom as "scientific creationism" and later "intelligent design." In 2005 the transparency of this strategy provoked a Pennsylvania judge not only to throw out classroom instructions that deceptively presented "intelligent design" (ID) as science. In a lengthy, meticulously detailed, and widely reported decision, he excoriated the "activism of an ill-informed faction on a school board" and their allies for, first, revising with "breathtaking inanity" the "biology curriculum to advance religion" and then trying to "disguise the real purpose behind the ID policy" (*Kitzmiller v. Dover Area School Board*). Here the hubris of religious activists in public schools ran afoul of even a Republican jurist. And to head off critics branding him an "activist judge," he emphasized that the "imprudent and ultimately unconstitutional policy" of a zealous religious "faction" had obligated him to rule as he did "to preserve the separation of church and state mandated by the Establishment Clause of the First Amendment."

Besides conflicts of religion with science, the courts have dealt with a stream of cases from the mid-twentieth century onwards occasioned by other latter-day official insertions of religion into the schools. For instance, the *McCullom* decision of 1948 removed from Illinois schools religious training initiated only in 1940; in *Engel v.*

Vitale (1962) the Supreme Court negated a recent New York state edict requiring the reading in schools of a formal prayer composed for this purpose by the state regents; and in *Stone v. Graham* (1980) the court overturned as unconstitutional a Kentucky law of 1978 demanding that the Ten Commandments be "displayed on a wall in each public elementary and secondary school classroom in the Commonwealth." These are only three of the better-known cases.

Outside the schools, the Supreme Court heard twin cases in 2005 involving twentieth-century displays of the Ten Commandments on government property. In one of these cases, *McCreary v. Kentucky*, the majority disallowed displays that had gone up in Kentucky courthouses in 1999. But in the other, *Van Orden v. Perry*, the majority permitted such a display erected on the Texas statehouse grounds among other historical memorials in the 1960s, and did so partly owing to the display's relative longevity of some forty years. These decisions, by the way, came not long after Alabama's inflammatory Chief Justice Roy Moore was removed from his post for defying a federal court order to remove a two-and-a-half ton monument of the Ten Commandments that he had brazenly installed in his courthouse in 2001. After that, Moore anointed himself a martyr to the crusade against the separation of church and state, convinced that Christianity should dictate public policy, and he fueled his sympathizers' righteous rage with a book characteristically entitled *So Help Me God: The Ten Commandments, Judicial Tyranny, and the Battle for Religious Freedom*. Voters elected him a second time as Chief Justice, and he was a second time removed. He then took his crusade into politics with a run for the US Senate in 2018, but, after winning the Republican nomination, was defeated as too zany—if not wrong about religion—for even the conservative voters of Alabama.

Resistance to modern-day intrusions of religion into public life also motivated the ultimately fruitless legal battle to expunge the words "under God" from the Pledge of Allegiance. These words had made their way into the Pledge only in 1954 to display America's godly anti-communism. There was no long-lived American tradition to defend here, only religious rhetoric coined to serve Cold War political purposes. But that fact did not prevail over what had become for religionists a revered tradition. We might also think of the well-known phrase "In God We Trust." This became the official national motto only in 1956, reaffirming the political insertion of God into the Pledge, and first appeared on paper currency the next year (it had first stamped certain coins during the Civil War and had been added to them all in 1938).

The list of recently invented religious traditions and practices in America could go on. No wonder many secular organizations have arisen, such as Americans United for the Separation of Church and State, Freedom from Religion Foundation, TheocracyWatch.org, and ReligiousTolerance.org, to fend off mounting pressures from the Right to marry church and state. Exemplifying their endeavors, Americans United for the Separation of Church and State led a successful fight to scotch Congressional funding for religious social programs through G. W. Bush's so-called "faith-based initiatives." And when Bush implemented those programs anyway by executive order, the Freedom from Religion Foundation took the case to the Supreme Court charging a violation of the Establishment Clause. In June, 2007, the court dismissed the case on the technical grounds that taxpayers have no legal right, or "standing," to litigate presidential executive acts—despite the court's precedent of *Flast v. Cohen* (1968) ruling that taxpayers can contest acts of Congress explicitly benefiting religion, a precedent that had spawned this suit in the first place and that the self-righteous Justice Scalia blasted as "an inkblot on our jurisprudence."

Liberal critics can therefore legitimately argue that much of what the religious Right regards as a venerable American tradition of government promoting religion in schools and public life is not venerable at all. It is instead the fruit of labors in the twentieth and twenty-first centuries by religious activists to officially, if surreptitiously, ensconce religion in public schools and public life in ways not seen or legalized before.

To be sure, the advocates of closer bonds between church and state (apart from the unapologetic theocrats) insist that they do not seek to "establish" religion. They aim only to correct secular excesses and insure the "free exercise" of religion. Hence, laws protecting prayer in public schools, displays of the Ten Commandments on government property, discrimination against homosexuals, opposing the freedom to have an abortion, and the like do not, they argue, represent the "establishment" of religion at all but only the "free exercise" of it.

This returns us to the tension between the religion clauses of the First Amendment. Reasonable people can disagree over where we should draw the line between the "free exercise" of religion and its "establishment." And with America now the most culturally and religiously pluralistic country in the world—and yet probably the most manifestly religious land among developed nations—reasonableness on this issue is more important than ever.

In the end, Thomas Jefferson, James Madison, Isaac Backus, and Alexis de Tocqueville were surely right. When religion becomes entwined with political power, it might gain some secular power but it loses much spiritual authority. For it then breeds in its followers political assertiveness, moral arrogance, and Pharisaic observances, while arousing enemies who attack its influence and even its very existence. We might well take some of Tocqueville's observations and ideas as a guide to thinking about the proper relation of church and state.

Let us remember above all how Tocqueville admired the clergy for choosing "to distance themselves from power voluntarily and take a sort of professional pride in remaining strangers to it." *To remain a stranger to power.* This could be a wise motto for churches and religious leaders to follow, mindful of Tocqueville's conclusion that "in America religion is perhaps less powerful than it has been in certain times and among certain peoples, but its influence is more lasting."

14. A Stranger to Power

The true home of religion is the church, the family, and the human heart, where its "free exercise" thrives. By the same token, the true home of democratic liberties is politics and the public life. Hence, *both religion and democracy have more to gain by limiting the public role of religion for the sake of democratic liberty than by limiting democratic liberty for the sake of the public role of religion.* In this light, religionists should use restraint in promoting religion and its symbols in politics and the public arena. Just as, I might add, secularists should resist overinterpreting every semblance of religion in public life as an "establishment of religion" and trying to banish it. For no harm will come to democracy from religion, or to religion from democracy for that matter, if reason, responsibility, and the true spirit of democracy reign.

American democracy has gained much from religion, and religion has gained much from American democracy. But let us not forget that we owe this happy history in no small part to religion remaining a stranger to power.

III.

ON MODERNITY & MODERNISM

The essays in this section, all previously published in whole or in part, deal chiefly with some ideas, attitudes, and emblematic figures of the era of Modernism scattered from its origins to its aftermath. By the end of the twentieth century, Modernism had, in the opinion of many critics, run its course and been supplanted by Postmodernism, a reaction against much of the intellectual and artistic earnestness of Modernism.

To be sure, none of the essays attempts to describe Modernism as a whole, only aspects of it. The first is a review-essay that outlines Modernism in general and looks at it from the perspective of three books on the subject. The next two are longer pieces examining characteristics of mind—attitudes toward banality and a corrosive self-consciousness—that underly and display the pessimism or nihilism typical of much modernist thought and literature. Following these come a couple of short review-essays focused on two historic figures who played very different roles in the modernist era: Karl Marx's daughter Eleanor and Sigmund Freud. The last pair of essays dwell on ideas at the end of the twentieth century that reflect a *fin-de-siècle* mood and perceive the twilight of much in Western culture—one of these looks at that *fin de siècle* in relation to the previous one; the other is a review-essay focusing on features of cultural decline in America and the West as the twentieth century came to a close.

Vassily Kandinsky, Cossacks, 1910–11; one of the first modernist abstract paintings.

Many legacies of Modernism—in ways of thinking and perceiving and imagining—will not be left behind soon, nor should they be.

What Was Modernism?

Postmodernism might have brought down the curtain on Modernism, but Modernism shows no signs of losing its attractions for the critical and historical imagination. And no wonder. Looking back from the threshold of the twenty-first century, who could deny that in its many permutations, Modernism dominated much of the intellectual and artistic culture of the century now ending.

From our *fin-de-siècle* promontory we can see Modernism as a historical period, a zeitgeist, an aesthetic doctrine, a constellation of artistic styles, an intellectual orientation, a moral disposition, a condition of life. And we can see how it grew out of the historical circumstances of Europe in the second half of the nineteenth century, which inspired artists and thinkers to assail conventions and embark on groundbreaking adventures under a banner proclaiming the *New* and the *Modern*. These artists and thinkers counted among themselves bohemians and dandies, radicals and reactionaries, spiritualists and technophiles, moralists and borderline psychotics—and a few who crossed that border. It was a widely extended family united by complementary cultural perceptions, an appetite for innovation, and a hunger for elemental things.

This family of modernists began its rise soon after the mid-nineteenth century with the disillusioned romantic idealism of the generation of the 1820s, dealt an emotional blow by the failed revolutions of 1848. It gained ascendancy in the 1880s and held to its adventurous course until the late 1920s, when signs of decline surfaced in waning inventiveness and assimilation of once-shocking modernist ideas and creations into the general culture. We might mark the end of Modernism's revolutionary élan, and the beginning of Modernism's reign as the established dogma and aesthetic, with the founding in 1929 of the Museum of Modern Art in New York, which institutionalized the revolution for the middle class, and with the concurrent appropriation of modernist aesthetics by consumer advertising, as evident in an issue of the prominent magazine for advertisers *Westvaco Inspiration for Printers* devoted in 1930 to "This Dynamic Spirit Which We Call Modern": when "Modernism turns merchandiser," the editors announced, its "spirit of revolt... changes the fashions overnight," and "by boldly challenging the imagination, it opens new avenues" to "the buying public—avenues which keen merchandisers are following apace." If these were triumphs of Modernism's "spirit of revolt" over the philistine culture that many modernists had targeted for reform, such "triumphs" also meant that Modernism had nothing much left to prove amid an emergent commercial culture that pacified, homogenized, and consumed all of Modernism's innovations that it readily could and chucked the rest.

It would take another half century for Modernism to run its artistic course through ephemeral novelties and derivative creativity before the postmodern reaction, bubbling up in the 1960s and 1970s, flooded the landscape in the 1980s. By the late 1990s Postmodernism had itself become the dominant cultural movement, supplanting Modernism's exalted aspirations with its own more populist, eclectic, and quirky artistry, and its snappy intellectual ironies. But despite the long-gone modernist rebellion and Postmodernism's methodical reaction (with a self-consciousness essential to its ethos inherited from the more troubled self-consciousness of Modernism and given a characteristically postmodern stamp—see "Self-Consciousness and the Modernist Temper" below), no one could doubt that Modernism shaped the culture of the twentieth century, nor that it left lasting legacies. We might therefore expect that as the twentieth century drew to a close, intellectuals would be drawn to look back at Modernism's history and take stock of its achievements.

15. What Was Modernism?

Among the retrospective reflections that have issued from the presses in our *fin-de-siècle* days, the pair brought together here agree that if Modernism has passed, it still has much left to teach us. This is because Modernism was not only a historical period or a zeitgeist or mode of artistic and intellectual life. It was also a revelatory of way of thinking and perceiving, an epistemology and a metaphysics. We get this interpretation from a macroscopic perspective in *The First Moderns: Profiles in the Origins of Twentieth-Century Thought* by William R. Everdell, who surveys the wide terrain of early Modernism. And we get it with a narrower focus in *Reconfiguring Modernism: Explorations in the Relationship between Modern Art and Modern Literature* by Daniel R. Schwarz, who dwells on intersections of Modernism's literary and visual aesthetics. A third book, only touched on here, has a related place as a classic work in the early history of interpreting Modernism: *Abstraction and Empathy: A Contribution to the Psychology of Style* by Wilhelm Worringer, recently reprinted with a new introduction by the art critic Hilton Kramer.

William R. Everdell, an intellectual historian of impressively broad learning and a generally limpid style, presents a panorama of Modernism as seen by one convinced of Modernism's conceptual unity and historical import as he searches for its original manifestations in practically every field of human activity. Although he considers his book something of "an elegy for Modernism"—declaring hyperbolically that it was perhaps "the longest-lived cultural movement our civilization has ever experienced"—he believes that in many respects "Modernism is still with us," affecting how we think about almost everything. And yet, he doubts that we really know how to define it. "So what is Modernism?" he asks with a resounding present tense, adding the unexpected assertion, "We had better define Modernism soon or we will lose the use of the term."

That sense of uncertainty and call to urgency will come as a surprise to the legions of critics, historians, and teachers who have been writing and talking about Modernism for decades, and for whom the definition, with all its variations, is pretty clear. They can point to an array of correlated interpretive lines from, say, Baudelaire's "The Painter of Modern Life" (1846) to George Bernard Shaw's "The Sanity of Art" (1895), Ortega y Gasset's "The Dehumanization of Art" (1925), Joseph Wood Krutch's *The Modern Temper* (1929), and Edmund Wilson's *Axel's Castle* (1931), on through Jacques Barzun's *Classic, Romantic, and Modern* (1943), Lionel Trilling's "The Modern Element in Literature" (1960), Harry Levin's "What Was Modernism?" (1960), Irving Howe's "The Culture of Modernism" (!967), and capacious anthologies of original sources and commentaries such as *The Modern Tradition* (1965) edited by Richard Ellmann and Charles L. Feidelson, Jr., and *Modernism* (1976) edited by Malcolm Bradbury and James McFarlane, and historical examinations like Marshall Berman's *All That Is Solid Melts into Air: The Experience of Modernity* (1982), Stephen Kern's *The Culture of Time and Space, 1880–1913* (1883), Frederick R. Karl's *Modern and Modernism: The Sovereignty of the Artist, 1885–1925* (1985). But Everdell does not quite follow these standard lines. Taking his cue from highly technical developments in theoretical mathematics—and allotting more pages to mathematics, natural science, and philosophy than to the arts—he defines Modernism as a particular way of thinking about knowledge and metaphysics first explicitly articulated in the 1870s and later prevalent, explicitly or implicitly, throughout Western culture.

This heady theme could yield a hodgepodge of flaccid generalizations, thin clichés, and spurious analogies building to mere erudite cocktail party conversation. Fortunately, it doesn't. Everdell is a better scholar and writer than that. Although he modestly forswears claims to original scholarship, acknowledging debts to his predecessors in voluminous notes and a lengthy bibliography, this is no secondhand history. It is a remarkable synthesis, rooted in original sources and branching out thick and far.

To keep his sprawling "narrative history of ideas" in hand, Everdell casts it in the form of "biographical profiles of the first great

15. WHAT WAS MODERNISM?

Modernists." Many of these will be new to readers familiar with the general contours of Modernism. Ten of the book's twenty-two chapters focus on mathematicians, scientists, or philosophers; seven concentrate on literary or visual artists; and the remaining four, besides the introduction, view epochal modernist events in several cities. These individual "stories of Modernist creation" converge to tell the larger story of how the modernist way of thinking came to pervade Western culture.

This way of thinking roped in most of the usual modernist intellectual topics, such as subjectivity, reflexivity, relativism, and inductive skepticism. But these boil down for Everdell to a single idea, which he states directly if abstractly: "The heart of Modernism is the postulate of ontological discontinuity." In other words, as modernists saw the world, things fall apart and defy ready grasp because beneath all surface appearances of continuity, there exists a jumble of discrete phenomena that don't fit together. While this idea of discontinuity or fragmentation does not provide a novel clue to Modernism, Everdell tracks it down as never before and into some corners not seen in the same room.

He tells us that this "postulate of ontological discontinuity" began its insinuating career with the German mathematician Richard Dedekind, who "became the West's first Modernist in 1872" when he published a paper identifying irrational numbers, thereby shattering the traditional "continuity" of real numbers. After that, the idea of discontinuity began to crop up all over the place, not so much through a causal sequence as by coincidence and analogy under the zeitgeist. Ludwig Boltzmann, Max Planck, and Albert Einstein perceived it in the atomic structure of physics; Bertrand Russell and Edmund Husserl discovered it in the disjunctions of logic; Santiago Ramón y Cajal and Hugo de Vries found it in the cellular and genetic structure of the brain and body; Edwin Porter applied it in splicing together movies, as did Valeriano Weyler y Nicolau in inventing, of all things, the segregating modern concentration camp; Freud explored it in analyzing the conflicts between consciousness and the unconscious; Seurat, Picasso, and Kandinsky put it to artistic use in breaking up the surfaces of paintings; Walt Whitman (a modernist precursor admired by the French), Arthur Rimbaud, and Jules Laforgue did the same in fragmenting poetic form, along with Strindberg in drama, Joyce in fiction, and Schoenberg in music. These are only some of Everdell's large cast of leading characters. And all are woven into a dense fabric of reference to historical filiations and allied innovators. The result is a liberal education in itself.

But, as with any vigorously argued interpretation of scattered events, creations, and ideas, one senses here a bit of excess in Everdell's determination to fit everything into one room. While the idea of "ontological discontinuity" may underlie, or be consistent with, much of the twentieth century's penchant for subjectivity, relativism, and the rest, Everdell looks for discontinuity so assiduously that he sometimes distorts or dismisses what doesn't altogether reflect it.

Take the idea of "stream of consciousness." Everdell treats it as not truly typical of Modernism. It is instead a vestige of premodernist metaphysics since it smacks of continuity rather than discontinuity. He consequently labels William James, who coined the phrase (originally "stream of thought" expounded upon in *The Principles of Psychology* [1890]), "the last continuitarian." This oddly locks James into a premodernist past, disregarding his influence on a host of modernists, as well as his "radical empiricism" and pragmatism, which could in fact have served Everdell's purposes, and the notable decades-long contention of Jacques Barzun that James was an eminent pioneer of modernist psychology and aesthetics (elaborated in *A Stroll with William James* [1983], unnoted in Everdell's bibliography). By the same token, Everdell relegates Albert Einstein's theoretical explorations of the "space-time continuum"—an analogue in physics to the stream of consciousness in psychology—to Einstein's "dogged efforts to restore a nineteenth-century paradigm" of continuity. Then, switching tactics, Everdell saves Proust, Woolf, and Joyce from the retrograde psychology of stream of consciousness by reading the usual traces of it in their works less as portrayals of psychic flow than as signs of "the puzzling disorientation of experience" caused by subjective "fragments of perception." In Everdell's canon, to be a worthy modernist you have to embrace, or at least openly wrestle with, discontinuity.

Besides slighting partisans of continuity, Everdell passes over other modernist ideas and tendencies that do not, one must suppose, fit snugly enough into his interpretive scheme. You will not learn from *The First Moderns* much of anything about, for instance, the anti-bourgeois social criticism, frustrated idealism, and avant-garde indignation that grew through the second half of the nineteenth century and erupted with nihilistic force toward the end, yielding the "adversary culture" regarded by Lionel Trilling as a defining characteristic of Modernism and feeding an appetite for violence that brought World War I. Such derisive protomodernists as those tormented coevals, Flaubert, Baudelaire, and Dostoevsky, cast scarcely a shadow here; and the emblematic philosopher of modernist rebellion, Friedrich Nietzsche, enters only in passing and without most of his inflammatory rhetoric and supramoral doctrines. Nor, for that matter, is there sustained reference to the widespread revolution in social thought advanced by such figures as Émile Durkheim, Max Weber, and other pathbreaking thinkers whose history H. Stuart Hughes memorably reconstructed in *Consciousness and Society: The Reorientation of European Social Thought, 1890–1930* (1958)—another rare, yet telling absentee from Everdell's large bibliography.

But no book can cover everything. Everdell just elicits the expectation that his will. The omissions do not discredit Everdell's version of Modernism. They rather underscore the fact that, for all of his range, Everdell has defined Modernism very narrowly, equating it with a particular idea or tightly knit set of ideas. This intellectualist slant surely accounts for why Everdell believes Modernism has not been sufficiently understood and adequately defined previously. Perhaps the formative ideas he has culled from permutations of

Modernism, stressing mathematics and science at that, had yet to be fully recognized for their relation to Modernism. At all events, this is clearly a history of modernist *ideas* as Everdell has discerned them; it is not a history of modernist *culture* with the pulse of life that entails. Consequently, one might question some of his intellectualist claims and conclusions. But, however we choose to define Modernism or to chart its history, we can thank Everdell for exploring some unfamiliar regions and detecting some surprising affinities. Our understanding of Modernism is the richer for this.

Tightening the lens from Everdell's panorama (an image that Everdell would probably class premodernist, since the "panorama" was a popular nineteenth-century entertainment providing a captivatingly *continuous* visual array of events) to the more limited perspective of Daniel R. Schwarz's *Reconfiguring Modernism*, we encounter Modernism on a smaller scale. We also get a different causal interpretation of modernist art. And yet many of the features that catch Schwarz's eye are shadings of those that beckoned Everdell.

A professor of English literature who now wears the mantle of "cultural studies," Schwarz set himself a pair of specific aims. The first is programmatic, leaning to the political. Opposing the academic partisans of the "political correctness" that reduces "all cultural effects ... to socioeconomic explanations" or "power relationships," he intends to present a "humanistic version of cultural studies." Above all, he itches to "reclaim the aesthetic" as a legitimate measure of artworks and a source of our response to them. One might think the aesthetic measure of art need not be "reclaimed," but such is the politicized state of cultural studies that Schwarz believes it must be. And he is to be applauded for taking that courageous stand.

From this programmatic position, Schwarz frames his second aim. That is "to isolate essential ingredients of Modernistic culture ... that spill over the borderlands between genres and artforms." He

15. WHAT WAS MODERNISM?

is not after "reductive consistency"; instead he wants "to look at assumptions from a postmodern point of view" in order to see "the world of modern authors and painters from a perspective that understands how they intervene, intersect, transform, and qualify the culture of which they are a part." (Schwarz's writing is not all that one might wish, occasionally marred by carelessness and by the needless strain of hefting artificial intellectual weights with inflated rhetoric.) Schwarz goes on to define Modernism as "an ideology of despair" born of the "difficult circumstance" of "industrialization, urbanization, so-called technological progress, and the Great War of 1914–1918," combined with "an ideology of possibility and hope" that assumed its most efficacious form in art. For these reasons, he explains, "Modernism understands artistic creation as self-discovery" as it seeks "to find an aesthetic order or historic pattern to substitute for the crumbling certainties of the past." But these modernist ideals and efforts met opposition from the "fragmentation" that "undermines the possibility of a unilateral perspective giving shape and coherence to a single vision." This perplexing historical condition left modernists with a persistent, albeit fecund, sense of "irony and disunity."

Schwarz does not make clear how much of this "historical condition" arose from circumstances or from a state of mind. But his apprehension of modernist "fragmentation" and "disunity" plainly jibes with Everdell's notion of "ontological discontinuity." From there they part paths though. For whereas Everdell grounds Modernism in the rational intellectual "choice" of ideas derived by sweet reason and led by theoretical mathematics, Schwarz belongs to those who have long suspected a subterranean psychological disquietude at the heart of Modernism. He treats Modernism not as a chapter in the history of ideas but as a variety of imaginative responses to the woes of a "cultural crisis" or "cultural agon" or "the cosmic loneliness of the modern world" (hinting at a psychological reductionism only subtler and kinder than the pugnacious "politically correct" reductions of culture to power relations that he opposes).

Notwithstanding Schwarz's dark psychology of Modernism, his pairing of writers (chiefly British and American) and painters offers some nice insights into the aesthetic strategies of individual modernists, as well as into some nonaesthetic uses of those strategies in our tenaciously modernist times. In Édouard Manet, Henry James, and Thomas Mann he discovers how the ache of isolation and insignificance, and the absence of a "systematic worldview," could stir a desire for "seeing and being seen" as the preeminently modernist "quest for meaning." Gauguin and Conrad disclose to him the fruitful interaction of Western and non-Western cultural perceptions. He says Cézanne and T. S. Eliot invite us to appreciate a formal order imposed on a disordered existence; Picasso and Matisse challenge us to interpret visual narratives of puzzling and often multicultural compositions; and Picasso (in another vein), Joyce, and Wallace Stevens give us fragmented renderings of existence itself, fraught with masks and mirrors, role-playing and games, to be comprehended from many perspectives at once.

Although Schwarz instructively illustrates these and other affinities among modernist authors and painters, he nevertheless reminds us of an obvious distance separating the two camps of artists, which bears on the psychological character he ascribes to them. That distance arises in part from the inherent dissimilarity in form and content between modernist verbal and visual art. While many modernist authors delved into themselves to depict or invoke self-consciously troubled emotional states and to communicate in evocative words morose cultural judgments, the painters were freer to play with pure aesthetic form in abstract compositions removed from life, and they rarely conveyed messages of "cultural crisis" or "cosmic loneliness." The symptoms of "agon" that Schwarz sees in modernist paintings often therefore seem closer to extrapolations from literature than evidence of the modernist painters' own anguished motives. It is as if Schwarz's "ideology of despair" belonged to the writers and his "ideology of possibility" to the painters.

Even so, Schwarz would get some support for a shared disquietude among modernist painters and writers from the seminal study in the psychology of the visual arts, Wilhelm Worringer's *Abstraction and Empathy: A Contribution to the Psychology of Style*, first published in 1906, reprinted many times, and reissued in 1997. It is curious that Schwarz makes no mention of Worringer or, equally surprising, the renowned Joseph Frank essay "Spatial Form in Modern Literature" (1945), which, as Kramer notes in the introduction to this edition, applied Worringer's ideas to modernist literature.

Observing that the visual arts may be divided historically into styles marked by either "empathy" or "abstraction," Worringer argued that when people feel "confidence between man and the phenomena of the external world," their "empathy" with nature engenders representational art. By contrast, when people feel an "inner unrest" aroused by "the outside world," they experience a "spiritual dread of space," a dread centered on the threatening dimension of depth, and so they turn toward artistic "abstraction" eliminating that dimension. Hence, throughout history, periods tending to abstraction in art have tried to "wrest the object" in art from the "outside world" of dreaded space by attempting to "purify" art of "its dependence upon life," at once "spiritualizing" it and granting it "absolute value."

The idea that abstract art bespeaks psychological discomfiture would play right into Schwarz's hands. Joseph Frank brings this idea even closer to Schwarz's theme when he argues that "Worringer's discussion of the disappearance of depth... in non-naturalistic styles" points to "the complete congruity" of modernist visual and literary art, because, most consequentially, "just as the dimension of depth has vanished from the sphere of visual creation, so the dimension of historical depth has vanished from the content of major works of literature." Afflicted by "insecurity, instability," and "loss of control over the meaning and purpose of life," Frank concludes, modernist writers replaced the disturbing "dimension of historical depth," or historical time, with the secure and stable ahistorical "timeless world of myth."

We might raise an eyebrow at some of Frank's and Worringer's soaring generalizations. But Worringer's little book remains an enduring classic in the ascendancy of Modernism and in the analysis of early twentieth-century painting. And Frank's essay is an epochal, if controversial, synthesis in modernist literary criticism. They will continue to excite debate over modernist visual and literary art, and possibly over the arts of the future, long after other interpretations have been forgotten. Schwarz silently echoes them both.

But, if Worringer, Frank, and Schwarz aptly describe modernist styles of visual and literary art, the underlying psychology they impute to those styles remains highly speculative. Do the conditions of modern life truly afflict artists with "cosmic loneliness" and the like? Or do modern artists—especially writers—self-conscious as they are, just find it gratifying to convey their own self-absorbed perceptions through art? And one wonders just what these critics would say about the restoration of depth, representation, and narrative to the visual and literary arts in the postmodern era. Have "inner unrest" and "cosmic loneliness" faded, and has the comfort of "empathy" returned? Schwarz says he wrote the book "from a postmodern point of view," but he gives us no hint of an answer.

Be that as it may, the books here point to numerous commonalities in Modernism. And although they do not state it, they point to a unifying characteristic of Modernism that may be more fundamental than any other. That characteristic is this: whatever its underlying metaphysics and psychology, and however diverse its intellectual and artistic creations, Modernism was nothing if not consummately serious, aspiring in virtually every arena to nothing less than grasping the elemental nature of things or achieving transcendence. And that is an aspiration to be respected.

15. WHAT WAS MODERNISM?

Now that Postmodernism, with its whimsical winks of eclecticism and its worldly nods of knowing irony, has sent Modernism packing, we would do well to remember that if Modernism was not always easy to love, and may have tried too hard to do too much, it was nevertheless a kind of humanism profoundly invested in the virtues of intrepid inquiry and dauntless imagination, in the verities of science and art, and in a bracing intellectual and artistic integrity. The books here variously make that case for Modernism, if only implicitly, while reminding us that many legacies of Modernism—in ways of thinking and perceiving and imagining—will not be left behind soon, nor should they be.

A previous version of this review-essay was published as "Postmodern Modernism" in *The Sewanee Review*, Winter, 1999.

Photo by Rachel Davis.

"I will show you fear in a handful of dust."

—T. S. ELIOT

Modernity, Modernism, and the Evil of Banality

*E*veryone with a moral sense today knows the "banality of evil." Hannah Arendt coined the now-famous phrase to name the horrifying but seemingly disinterested wickedness of the Nazi Adolf Eichmann. And she meant, as Nietzsche had said before her, that evil had lost its moral transcendence and merged with the commonplace, where it had become mere mundane practice: cruelty has grown passionless, violence has become impersonal, suffering has become dehumanized. Whether or not Hannah Arendt's phrase fits Eichmann's atrocities and his role in the Holocaust, the banality of evil belongs to the very fabric of the circumstances we call modern: the secularity and relativity of moral norms, the impersonality of public life and work, the mechanization of material forces, the omnipresence of technology, and so on. And as long as these circumstances persist, so will the potential for this evil.

But banality and evil have another affinity equally typical of modernity, and it is the mirror image of the first. Not only has evil lost its moral transcendence and become banal, banality has gained moral transcendence and become evil. If this is a paradox, it is not a cheap one, for it expresses the twin fates of the moral imagination in modern culture. As that imagination weakened its overarching demands, evil lost itself in banal actions; at the same time, that imagination discovered a new form of evil in banality itself—the banalities that threaten human autonomy. If the first fate plainly signals a victory of secularism and its allies, the second bespeaks some of the same and more, also giving a telling trait to facets of Modernism. This trait can be found in elaborate theories of the trivial and the commonplace and in the artistic mystification of ordinary things, but it is most conspicuous in fictional and actual selves that view aspects of the ordinary, the trivial, the mundane, the commonplace—all loosely lumped together here in *banality*—as menace.

Banality did not, of course, become evil all at once, any more than evil became banal overnight. These twin transformations of banality grew over time. To be sure, the banal or mundane facts of human existence have been deemed significant in one way or another throughout Western history. In antiquity it was common, for example, to reason by analogy from ordinary properties and processes of the body to unobservable truths or entities, as Plato did in comparing physical health to political justice, and as Saint Augustine did with naïve ingenuity in proving chaste procreation in Paradise. And in the Middle Ages, the sacred meanings of daily affairs—domestic, commercial, hygienic—constantly preoccupied religious minds, as the spiritual daybooks prove. In early modern times, artists directed increasing interest toward the particulars of human beings and everyday life; Montaigne struggled to know himself though his everyday habits and experiences; and Calvinists satisfied their religious callings through devotion to practical affairs. By the time of the Enlightenment, the scientific spirit was turning mundane facts of the entire physical and social world into a laboratory of study to learn how everything worked.

The subsequent ascendancy of political democracy, industrial production, the capitalist economy, and the middle class, along with advances in science, Realism in art, and deepening intellectual explorations of social and psychological reality, put the circumstances of human life at the forefront of consciousness and culture as never before. Effort and merit supplanted aristocratic blood as the road to status, money became the measure of success, work grew more routinized, shopkeepers, bureaucrats, wage laborers, and professionals became the preeminent social types, the railroad at once shortened distances and enhanced the need to keep accurate time, life overall became ever more harnessed to the clock, and the material conditions of life came to rival in importance, if not to transcend, the precepts of religion. These developments made Western society more open, cosmopolitan, innovative, materially productive, and—for most, albeit not all, people—confident in progress. These changes also gave rise to three of the leading intellectual currents of the nineteenth century: the criticism of middle-class life, an intensifying historical and social consciousness, and a keen attentiveness in the arts and social theory to the significance of the commonplace itself. We will look briefly into these three currents, for they foreshadowed, by continuity and contrast with Modernism, the conversion of banality to evil.

The first presents an obvious thread of continuity and, not so obvious, a fundamental contrast.

The leading cultural critics of the nineteenth century saw social and moral life deeply affected by the mundane banality of the modern world—its circumstances, attitudes, and accepted ideas. And they didn't like it. They blamed above all those slaves to respectability and complacency: the middle class, or bourgeoisie, whose tastes were tawdry, emotions false, aspirations misguided, and lives inane. And those critics feared the destruction of all excellence and humanity unless, as the poet/critic Charles Baudelaire said, the true "heroism of modern life" became recognized and cultivated. Baudelaire's modern hero might even wear the bourgeois's standard black coat and suffer some of his humble miseries (like Baudelaire himself), but he would *not* be complacent.

The critics described the enemy in snarling words. The European terms banality, *banalité*, *Banalität*, *banale* came to denote the distastefully vulgar commonplace and triviality typical of middle-class existence. Some critics, like Alexis de Tocqueville, Friedrich Nietzsche, and Paul Bourget, supported their antipathy with rather elitist interpretations of history. They attributed the loss of cultural excellence and high-minded humanity to the decline of aristocratic social hierarchy and the ascending capitalist hegemony of money. Others, artists in the lead, like Baudelaire and Gustave Flaubert, cried out from more personal frustrations over living in the bourgeois world, and they did it with scatological contempt: for them *banalité* was *merde*. The German novelist Theodor Fontane supplied a less abusive but still condemning view of the banal mind when he satirized a bourgeois bureaucrat's longing in *Effi Briest*:

> Happiness, if I am right, lies in two things: in being exactly where one belongs—but what official can say that of himself?—and, especially in performing comfortably the most commonplace functions, that is, getting enough sleep and not having boots that pinch. When the seven hundred twenty minutes of a twelve hour day pass without any special annoyance, that can be called a happy day.

For these critics and the many others who expressed hostility to bourgeois conventions, sometimes through social defiance—e.g., *la vie de bohème*, the pose of the dandy, the artistic avant-garde, and radical politics—banality was obviously more than mere trivia and commonplace. It was a quality of the moral life that approached evil. But this moralistic stance presupposed hope that the evil could be suppressed or surpassed, and this was the purpose of criticism. As Flaubert said in a letter, the loathing of banality is "the beginning of all virtue," so "let us by all possible means stand in the way of the *merde* which envelops us. Let us enlist ourselves in the cause of the ideal."

Flaubert's words make it clear that behind the condemnation of bourgeois banality there could lie a certain idealism and hopes of cultural redemption by means of it. But this kind of affirmation, if not the idealism itself, would decline as the culture of Modernism ascended. As we shall see, modernist writers of the twentieth century would tend less to assail banality and demand its destruction in service of an ideal than to resign themselves to it. It is not that all hope to surmount the despised banality would fail to appear. But an atmosphere of defeat would all but overwhelm that hope. And this defeatist atmosphere would give banality a malevolence not sensed among the cultural critics of banality before. We can see this defeatist atmosphere gathering also in the other two currents of nineteenth-century thought that brought banality to prominence.

The second of these currents, an ascending historical and social consciousness, centered upon the idea that history and society determines, or at any rate profoundly conditions, human life. This idea had sources in the Italian Renaissance and the social sensibility of seventeenth-century France and England, but it properly belongs to the eighteenth century and after.

In the eighteenth century, the material, social, and cultural conditions of history often held primary importance in explanations of human life, with Montesquieu's *Spirit of the Laws* in the lead. Voltaire also stressed these conditions in his principles of cultural history, which recommended studying "how people lived in their family circles and what arts they cultivated" because that is where the history of culture reveals itself. At the end of the Enlightenment, J. G. Herder introduced the idea that nations and cultures are complete organic wholes consisting of distinctive customs, language, and intellectual and moral traditions shaped by history—an idea later elaborated into historicism, captured in the twentieth century by the philosopher Ortega y Gasset in the phrase, "Man, in a word, has no nature; what he has is . . . history."

During the eras of the French and Industrial Revolutions, as every student knows, the awareness of history intensified greatly. History seemed to overwhelm individuals and nations alike. As in fact, so in philosophy, scholarship, and fiction: the likes of Hegel, who saw history as the inevitable unfolding of the Spirit, and Karl Marx, who turned this idealism into deterministic historical materialism, as well as historians like Carlyle, Michelet, Ranke, Buckle, and novelists like Scott and Stendhal, all portrayed history not as a sequence of events only but as the encompassing reality within

III. On Modernity and Modernism

which all persons, ideas, institutions, and events lived and died. Leo Tolstoy wrote *War and Peace* to demonstrate how the will of even so imperious a figure as Napoleon could not defeat the impersonal forces of history. So insistent was this historical consciousness that Nietzsche, writing in the 1870s, found it a burden to the will and wanted to end it. And after the turn of the twentieth century, James Joyce had a character in *Ulysses* bemoan history a nightmare from which he was trying to awaken.

With the weight of historical consciousness came a corresponding social consciousness. This was more than the interest in social role-playing and the nature of sincerity that had arisen in the seventeenth century. It threatened the very will to choose roles. For the rise to preeminence, through the French and Industrial Revolutions, of new social classes with new manners and morals had led observers to see people's purposes, satisfactions, disappointments, and even their images of themselves rooted in social life. Carlyle, for example, whose sense of past and present was, if not unerring, as least never dim, stated the social conception of human nature that was held by both conservative thinkers like Edmund Burke and socialists like Marx: "It is in Society that man first feels what he is; first becomes what he can be." And novelists agreed. Jane Austen, Stendhal, Balzac, Dickens, Trollope, George Eliot, Flaubert, George Sand, and the brothers Goncourt, to name only these, shaped their fictional characters in the light of social reality. The very motives, actions, and effects of these characters were often governed more by that reality than by their own independent wills.

Some of these writers, of course, decried the power of society, like Dickens in *Little Dorrit* with, among other things, the symbol of the prison, and Balzac in *Lost Illusions* with explicit rage: "Society has imperceptibly arrogated to itself so many of the individual's rights that he finds himself obliged to combat Society." The same vexation impelled John Stuart Mill to condemn "the doctrine of the formation of character by circumstances"—by which he meant *social* circumstances—and to articulate a political philosophy in *On*

16. Modernity, Modernism, and the Evil of Banality

Liberty bent on limiting the authority of society over individuals.

But no harsh words or fine ideas could forestall the mounting sense of social determinism. As if to insure this, the philosopher Auguste Comte proposed a science of society to find the laws underlying society's power, followed by Adolphe Quetelet, who devised the science of statistics that reduced the actions of individuals to mere statistical categories. By the end of the nineteenth century the science of sociology came into its own with Émile Durkheim (and others), who showed how all human behavior arises from, and depends on, the preeminence of society, from private suicide to public religion—as Durkheim famously wrote: "God is society, writ large."

When the criticism of bourgeois culture and a rising historical and social consciousness joined the third intellectual current I have mentioned, the commonplace conditions of human life, or banality, could become a true menace.

This last current, attentiveness in the arts and social theory to the significance of the commonplace itself, is closely related, even entangled with, the first two. But I treat it separately to illuminate the gathering interest overall in banal actuality itself.

As noted above, Voltaire gave importance to commonplace facts in the study of cultural history. Later, Romanticists like Keats and especially Wordsworth made conspicuous use of the commonplace. From there, as the nineteenth century moved on, in the words of the historian Siegfried Giedion, "no activity of everyday life was taken for granted."

In the arts, practitioners of both high art and the decorative crafts believed their work had a natural affinity with the commonplace. This is part of what brought the movement known as Realism, with its attention to the particulars of social and material life. No novel of the mid-nineteenth century fails to steep its characters in those particulars. And no one exemplified that more than Balzac. His many novels, which he lumped together under the heading

La Comédie humaine, amounted to a vast landscape of life in France, principally Paris, woven of human emotions, aspirations, and failings amid a complex social order all revealed through commonplace details, like the look of a street, the arrangement of room, the cut of sleeve, the posture of a character. Balzac was the novelist of the commonplace par excellence.

In the visual arts, Gustave Courbet portrayed the world as he saw it—to the disgust of many bourgeois—and urged his fellow artists to put more of the commonplace in their art. About the same time, Henry Cole and William Morris taught manufacturers and craftsmen to put more art into the commonplace. This was not merely a search for novelty. These artists and craftsmen found the trivial and the actual to be a key to the well-lived life. Courbet said he utilized the common "habits, the ideas, the aspects of my epoch" in painting because they enabled him both "to make a living art" and "to be not only a painter, but a Man." And Morris believed "the true secret of happiness lies in the taking a genuine interest in all the details of daily life." These words seem at odds with those of the cultural critics cited earlier, and they are. But Baudelaire, for one, would have said it was just this creative use of modernity that the complacent bourgeois lacked; for that is part of the "heroism of modern life," giving the artist his ability both to portray reality, understand it, and transcend it.

In social thought, besides the growing consciousness of society's power at large, attention to banal appearances in themselves became the stuff of theory. Owing to political and social revolutions that had shredded the age-old fabric of social class and replaced it with a shifting array of appearances that determined social status, banality now had symbolic significance in understanding human beings as well as society.

Alexis de Tocqueville saw this in America, where, without long traditions or learned tastes to guide them—or oppress them—people could acquire social position by displaying the appearances of aristocratic elegance, like the ersatz Georgian mansions on Manhattan's East River constructed of wood, not marble, and whitewashed to complete the disguise. Tocqueville called this use of false appearances the "hypocrisy of luxury." Marx later elaborated on the idea as the "fetishism of commodities." And more analytically and disparagingly than Tocqueville, Marx explained how the "magic of money" causes "a definite social relation between men." And the pattern of appearances that results becomes a "social hieroglyphic" whose commonplace details must be read carefully by those seeking to decipher that hieroglyphic, and must be read constantly by those scrambling for favorable position within it.

This fact lay behind Balzac's lavish attention to appearances, however banal they might be, where a cravat tied just so or a button unbuttoned betokened not only social status but social character. Baudelaire did the same kind of thing in his critical essays as he found secrets of modern life in clothes, gestures, and glances. Carlyle went farther to discern the metaphysics of everyday appearances, eyeing them as "emblems of soul"—especially clothes, about which he wrote extensively in *Sartor Resartus*. These perceptions led the brothers Goncourt, who shared in them, to conclude: "Never have appearances been so despotic, so imperious, and so demoralizing."

In a more theoretical vein, John Stuart Mill outlined a science of the "kind of character" produced "by any set of circumstances, physical or moral." Although he later shed this determinism—and his name for this "science," ethology, now denotes the study of animal behavior—he was describing the logic of a science of personality that would become increasingly common around the turn of the twentieth century as the attention to the revelatory significance of banalities became nearly unbounded. In the newly minted theories of education, for instance, "the sober treatment of every mundane problem," as Richard Hofstadter observed in *Anti-intellectualism in American Life* (1964), bordered on obsession, bestowing the aura of science on such things as the location of school toilets and treatment of the janitor.

Other social sciences put this new attention to the commonplace to better uses. Criminology, for one, born in the spirit of Mill's "ethology" as a study of physical characteristics, established itself through novel techniques of detection and identification. With the invention of fingerprinting, forensic toxicology, and ballistics, the incidental traces of crime became the cipher to its solving. Arthur Conan Doyle's renowned fictional detective pointed toward such techniques as he deciphered traces in "the importance of sleeves, the suggestiveness of thumbnails, or the great issues that may hang from a boot lace." From these kinds of details Sherlock Holmes could deduce not only the identity of a criminal but, as he purportedly wrote in the essay, "Book of Life," the criminal's "inmost thoughts." "Depend upon it," Holmes insisted, "there is nothing so unnatural as the commonplace."

The commonplace enjoyed an ever more expansive career in sociology and anthropology. I have already remarked some origins of sociology, but we could see earlier sources of both of these modern social sciences in eighteenth-century curiosities about social and cultural life—that is, in questions about what would be called social structure, interaction, legitimation, cultural integration, and the like. At all events, sociology and anthropology became "sciences" in the late nineteenth and early twentieth centuries as students of social and cultural life looked into how social and cultural circumstances shape human relations, beliefs, and actions of all kinds. To do this they increasingly focused on what could be revealed by commonplace realities in the lives of human beings. And the closer they scrutinized those realities the more revealing they found them, prompting the scientists to develop what might be called theories of the commonplace, of banality. Do you wish to explain social integration? Learn how infants are suckled and weaned, what phrases they repeat, what foods they eat, what behaviors they develop. Do you wish to discover the source of social action? Scrutinize the practices of child-rearing, determine the rules of facial expression and gesticulation in specific settings, and identify the material interests that actions serve. Do you wish to find the inherent structures of culture and mind? Study table manners, dress habits, and ways of preparing food. No human action or custom is too small, no social relation or material fact or cultural practice too trivial or obscure to contribute to the sociology and anthropology of everyday life.

If there were any doubt that the mundane and the trivial attained unique importance in modern social theory, a glance at psychoanalysis would dispel it. One of Freud's decisive advances beyond previous psychological theory lay in exactly this: he not only explained the workings of the unconscious but did so by analyzing the relation of the unconscious to mundane facts on the surface of life.

Freud's literary forebears, notably the Romanticists and Realists, had often represented social and psychic life quite accurately. But they had not much examined the relations between incidental appearances and deep psychological energies. Balzac, for one, could describe the appearances of social character in impressive detail but declined to go much deeper with them. Or, for a contrary but complementary view, take Balzac's American contemporary Nathaniel Hawthorne. He named his writings "psychological romance," yet he believed psychological insight begins only where appearances are torn away, because "external habits" like "abode . . . casual associates, and other matters entirely upon the surface . . . hide the man, instead of displaying him." Whereas Balzac stayed pretty much on the surface of appearances, Hawthorne dismissed appearances to plumb psychological reality beneath. Neither made much of appearances as the key to the psyche beneath (an attitude belied, however, by Hawthorne's own moral for *The Scarlet Letter*: "Be True! Be True! Show freely to the world, if not your worst, yet some trait whereby the worst may be inferred"). Even Dostoevsky, perhaps the most remarkable pre-Freudian literary psychologist, did not anticipate the psychoanalytic science of banality. Like Hawthorne, Dostoevsky coupled his psychological insights to a limited conception of psychological reality. "The commonness of some occurrences and the conventional view of them," he said, "are not realism in my opinion, but indeed, the very opposite.... What the majority call almost fantastic and exceptional sometimes constitute the very essence of reality for me." And, disavowing the title of psychologist, he concluded: "not true: I am a realist in a higher sense, i.e., I depict the depths of the human soul." Dostoevsky turned from the "commonness" of events—which he associated above all with the writings of Dickens, from which he had learned much—toward only the "oddest facts" to achieve a deeper psychological realism. As a result, his psychology let the trivial remain trivial and psychological conflicts go unilluminated by the banalities that could manifest and reinforce them. Tolstoy, although less probing than Dostoevsky, had the finer sense of the psychological meaning of appearances—what novel better conveys the relation of human character to everyday life than parts of *Anna Karenina*?

Naturalists went farther than the Realists, animated as they were to make literature a science that would, as Émile Zola put it in *The Experimental Novel*, lead from the "facts" and "unexplained phenomena" of the surface to "knowledge of the passionate and intellectual life." The naturalists therefore came closer to Freud. But their literary "experiments" yielded a Darwinian determinism that fell far short of psychoanalysis in their illuminations of the psyche through the commonplace.

Freud thus bridged a gap that literature and the likes of ethology, criminology, and even the expansive psychology of William James largely had not. And he recognized the achievement. "We," he said of psychoanalysis, "have widened the domain of mental phenomena to a very considerable extent and have won for psychology phenomena which were never before accredited to it." Freud believed psychoanalysis to be, for one thing, an unconventional view of the "commonness" of everyday occurrences. This unconventional view unveiled banality, the commonplace—"trifles," as Freud put it—as both a key to interpreting the psychic life and a substantive part of the psyche itself. As a key to interpreting psychic life, these trifles include slips of the tongue and pen, lapses of memory and comprehension, the misplacing of objects, the random images of dreams, and the spontaneous association of ideas—all, Freud said, "commonplace occurrences which have been cast aside by other sciences, the refuse, so to speak, of the phenomenal world." Such incidents provide the "material of psychoanalytic observations" because they signify internal desires or conflicts between desires and the enemy of desire: resistance. Siegfried Kracauer applied this Freudian principle to the psychology of film. "Perhaps the way to . . . the evasive contents of the inner life," he wrote, "leads through the experience of surface reality." And he demonstrated his own ingenuity at interpreting the "surface reality" of life in film to reach its psychological depths in his eminent psychological study of the German cinema, *From Caligari to Hitler* (1947).

But if some trifles provide a way of entering the psyche, others give the psyche its character and content. These latter trifles are the properties and functions of the body. The psychoanalytic interpretation of the body violated tradition not so much by elevating the facts of genital sex, since these possess ritualistic significance in many cultures, but by attributing sexual and therefore psychological significance to all kinds of biological (and related mental) functions. Ingestion and elimination, tactile sensations, discomfort, pain, malfunctions, and neurotic behavior, for instance, are all physical phenomena of a commonplace sort, the kinds of things the naturalists had reported and often imbued with moral meaning in the late nineteenth century. But in Freud's theories, such phenomena belong not just to the body or to a vague morality but to the structure of the psyche: they help define the nature of instincts, object attachments, frustrations, gratifications, regression, repression, defenses, anxiety, etc., the whole catalogue of Freudian psychological reality.

Freud's double use of trivia made psychoanalysis the exemplary science of the commonplace. More dramatically and ingeniously than any other of the social sciences—if a science it is—psychoanalysis replaced the "conventional view" of the banal facts and incidents of human life with an unconventional view. And psychoanalysis kept those facts and incidents always in sight. Like the deductive detection of Sherlock Holmes, psychoanalysis adhered to the maxim: "Depend upon it, there is nothing so unnatural as the commonplace."

The passage of the commonplace from an object of watchful eyes to becoming "unnatural" and then a source of anxiety and malevolence did not have far to go once the three currents of nineteenth century thought outlined here—all strengthened by the widening secularity and banality of modern life, that the sociologist Max Weber called "the disenchantment of the world"—had done their work into the twentieth century.

This is not to say that the evil of banality swept across all of twentieth-century culture, or even Modernism. Many modernist artists and thinkers heeded the commonplace, and even its transcendence, without registering much of a threat by it. For them, rather like the Realists, what Henry James called "the delicate perception of the actual" transformed appearances into a means of understanding human life that, in the words of Walter Benjamin, made "even the most commonplace things have their weight . . . the most insignificant presentations of reality, its scraps, as it were." But more than the Realists, these modernists were drawn to the underlying contents and conflicts of the psyche that appearances might betray. For example, Marcel Proust insatiably scrutinized trivial incidents—the taste of a madeleine dipped in tea, the look of a hawthorn branch, a misstep on the path, etc.—for clues to life's past and inmost secrets; Guillaume Apollinaire proclaimed a "new realism" predicated on the belief that "one can start with an everyday subject: for a poet a falling handkerchief can be the lever with which he will raise a whole universe"; and the surrealists combined Apollinaire's program with Freud's theories to exalt random events and objects. This "transfiguration of the commonplace"—to borrow the title of a book by the philosopher Arthur Danto on developments in the visual arts of the later twentieth century—also fulfilled the hopes of William

Morris and Henry Cole for putting more art into everyday objects (and to more profound purpose than they had imagined), thanks in part to the influential *Bauhaus* of Walter Gropius, who, as the historian Peter Gay remarked, attributed to "mundane objects the unaccustomed stature of a metaphysical problem." To such modernists, banality was the context of life, but it was more insightful than evil.

And yet, notwithstanding the affirmations of the commonplace by some modernists, others more prominently came to view it as a threat to human autonomy. And these are the subject here.

Already among the middle class, or bourgeoisie, of the mid-nineteenth century, as well as their critics, signs had surfaced of a "terror about the imminent," in the words of the sociologist Richard Sennett, because appearances so unmistakably reflected social place and social character. And literary naturalists, like Zola, Hauptmann, Hardy, and Gissing, grew fatalistic over the imperious forces of nature, history, and society. But for all his ill-ease, the bourgeois retained a certain confidence in action and progress, just as artist/critics like Baudelaire and Flaubert retained a measure of hope that the ideal would prevail over banality through art. And for all of their fatalism, naturalists believed in reliable laws of nature. By contrast, numerous prominent modernists tended to question the efficacy of ambitious action, to scoff at ideals, to scorn the idea of progress, and to doubt reliable natural law. Hence, the evil of banality belongs neither to nineteenth-century social anxiety nor to naturalistic fatalism but to a modernist self-conscious sense of impotence. This is the sense of impotence that T. S. Eliot presented in images of a life where we see "fear in a handful of dust," where we "measure out . . . life in coffee spoons," and where we imagine that "This is the way the world ends / Not with a bang but a whimper."

This evil of banality runs through many fields and bogs of twentieth-century culture. Consider first a few attitudes toward an omnipresent commonplace: habit.

III. On Modernity and Modernism

Habit originally signified a trait, manner, or bearing typical of a person formed by behavior, for the better or the worse—Aristotle had put good habits at the heart of character and ethics (habit, character, and ethics being variations of the same Greek word *ethos*). By the mid-nineteenth century habit widely suggested a positive capacity to make oneself into almost anything. The English self-help author Samuel Smiles hyped habit as the means of shaping one's destiny. Flaubert recorded the popular wisdom on habit in his "Dictionary of Accepted Ideas." The bourgeois, he wrote—albeit with satirical intent, as in all of the entries—believed habit to be a "second nature" acquired by regular actions, and so, "given the right habits anyone could play like Paganini." At the end of the nineteenth century, William James reaffirmed this idea in a widely reprinted chapter of his renowned *Principles of Psychology* (1890). By cultivating proper habits, he said, anyone "can with perfect certainty count on waking up some fine morning to find himself one of the competent ones of his generation." Likewise, he said, in morals one should "be systematically ascetic or heroic in little unnecessary points. . . . speaking genially to one's aunt, or giving up one's seat in a horse car, if nothing more heroic offers," because, he concluded with a nod to the mundane sources of virtue, "all goods are disguised by the vulgarity of their concomitants in the work-a-day world."

For James and his readers, as for Smiles and Flaubert's bourgeois, good habits were a source of strength to conquer life. Even so, James acknowledged that good habits could also become ossified routine, the enemy of genius, and should sometimes be broken. And it was this dark side that could render the banality of habit evil.

For habit can be seen as behavior that happens without our willing it, and that can not only overshadow the will but crush human autonomy. This harsh conception could find some justification in behaviorist psychology. The American psychologist, Knight Dunlap, for example, wrote in *Habits: Their Making and Unmaking* (1932) "Habits in their totality make up the character of the individual; that is, they *are* the individual." Which is to say, the habits we acquire, intentionally or unintentionally, more nearly possess us than are possessed. Whatever one might think to the contrary, the will is their servant not their master. Later, the most influential behaviorist, B. F. Skinner, would go farther to argue in *Beyond Freedom and Dignity* (1971) that free will and dignity, or autonomy, are illusions blinding us to the truth that human beings are nothing but a mass of conditioned responses, mere habits.

Samuel Beckett gives a literary version of such a view of habit in *Malone Dies* (1951). Although Malone seeks security in reliable commonplaces, habit holds for him nothing but "a guarantee of dull inviolability"; it is "a great deadness," that enslaves and debases the self like "the ballast that chains the dog to his vomit." Thus the power of habit robs life of its purpose and warrants hopelessness not hope: for just as "Breathing is habit," so "Life is habit," dominating rather than enabling the will.

Years before writing *Malone Dies*, Beckett had found his hostility to habit shared often by Marcel Proust. And several of the denunciations of habit Beckett gave Malone above came from his own book on Proust of 1930. Although, as noted above, Proust used the commonplace to open doors to memory, any reader who makes it through the seven volumes of Proust's *À la Recherche du temps perdu* will run across many a swipe at habit as an enemy of imagination, creativity, mind, and memory. "During the whole course of our life," the narrator cries, "stupefying habit . . . conceals from us almost the whole universe," causing "most of our faculties" to "lie dormant because they can rely upon habit." Not only that, "the force of habit, the oblivion it creates," can be so strong that he rues "the powerlessness of the brain to fight against it." Proust did recognize that sometimes "the anesthetizing influence of habit," which dulls us to "the reality of life," can also yield benefits. But more frequently and vigorously, he stressed habit's evil power to inhibit mind and imagination through the banal routines that anesthetize us to experience.

III. On Modernity and Modernism

We can find a different take on the banal evil of habit in the existentialism of Jean-Paul Sartre. Sartre did not explicitly address the subject of habit, but he obviously viewed it as inherently opposed to existential freedom. As he said, his theory of human existence "recognizes nothing *before* the original upsurge of human freedom." That is, every human choice is spontaneous, with "no excuse behind us, no justification before us." Hence, there is no God to prescribe choices, no human nature to shape them, no unconscious to secretly influence them, and no habits to mindlessly dictate them. The act of existential choice is free in a way that habit could not limit. We could say that Sartre's existentialism is the ultimate modernist adversary of habit.

And yet, even though Sartre's theory of free choice eclipsed the power of habit, Sartre did not deny that we make choices within conditions or, in his term, "situations." And those situations are laden with banalities. Here Sartre takes us from the evils of habit to the evil of banality overall. For Sartre's existentialism is a philosophy of banality as the very context and texture of human existence.

Simone de Beauvoir records the rise of Sartre's intellectual curiosity about banality in her autobiography. First, Sartre reveled in the whimsical disorderings of the ordinary in the surrealist cinema—which he also associated with the madcap Marx brothers, who became his favorite film stars—then he became absorbed in the environmental causes of crime, and he crowned these early interests with a philosophical conversion. This conversion took place after he learned that some German thinkers were philosophizing about champagne glasses. De Beauvoir says Sartre "turned pale with excitement" at the news. Soon he was in Berlin poring over the philosophy of phenomenology. As described by the contemporary phenomenologist Maurice Natanson: "The phenomenologist takes a radical stance with respect to his own involvement in mundane existence. He makes everydayness a theme for examination."

16. Modernity, Modernism, and the Evil of Banality

Sartre embraced this "radical stance" toward "everydayness" because it fed his growing curiosity about how human existence actually works as we find it, without relying on assumptions of metaphysics or psychology. After steeping himself in the writings of Edmund Husserl, the chief proponent of the school, he turned to the more existentialist version developed by Martin Heidegger. Heidegger had adopted phenomenology in the 1920s convinced that philosophy had lost its way in abstractions. He insisted that "thinking must learn again to descend to the poverty of its materials," which are words and the commonplace phenomena of life. Then, drawing also on the influential historicism of Wilhelm Dilthey, Heidegger formulated a philosophy of those commonplace phenomena within the frame of Time. Like Freud, Heidegger believed himself to be retrieving "trifles" from the dust bins of previous thinkers. His greatest work, *Being and Time*, disclosed trifles such as "idle talk," "curiosity," "tools," "work," "care," and "considerateness" as the elements of the "Everydayness" (*Alltäglichkeit*) in which "Human Being" (*Dasein*) has its existence. As Heidegger put it, with characteristic opacity, "'everydayness' is a definite 'how' of existence by which human being is dominated through and through 'for life.'" In other words, the banalities of quotidian reality make human existence what it is.

Heidegger's elaborate phenomenology of the commonplace gave Sartre his true point of departure. Sartre became even more absorbed in prosaic facts, notions, states of mind than his teacher. His solemn theories of such phenomena as sliminess, stickiness, nausea, obscenity, embarrassment, disease, skiing, a comedian's impersonation of Maurice Chevalier, and "certain involuntary waddlings of the rump," surpassed in extravagance all other interpretations of the commonplace, with the possible exception of psychoanalysis.

But Sartre did not confine the commonplace to philosophical ontology, as Heidegger had done. He gave it humanistic and ethical import. He observed that it is the ordinary facts of life that nourish the human self: "it is here that each of us finds himself as well as the others . . ." And it is by living ordinary lives that men become ethical, because moral valor "does not lie in a great romantic rebellion but in daily effort. Our true revolt lies in seeing things clearly, keeping our word and doing our job."

This ethical maxim might sound like an affirmation of banality. And in a way it is. But, in fact, this maxim leaves behind bourgeois aspirations for work to bring achievement and improve the world—unlike, say, George Eliot's similar-sounding ethic at the end of *Middlemarch* (1871) extolling the efficacy of small, "unhistoric acts." It comes closer to that of Albert Camus's Sisyphus, who stoically (existentialistically) resigns himself to the fate of doing "his thing": endlessly, purposelessly rolling a rock up and down a hill. For it says the commonplace realities of existence weigh so heavily upon human beings that they feel impotent to do more that create an ethics of submission rather than opposition. That this submission is willed does not save the will from attenuation.

And therein lies an irony. Sartre devised his existentialism as a philosophy of absolute freedom to make choices within every "situation," irrespective of any influences from outside or in. But he equated that freedom with choosing merely the "daily effort" of rolling our rocks up the hill in the "situation" of everyday banality. It is no wonder this existentialist ethic has been called a morality for slaves. That might not be fair to Sartre's vision. Even so, it is not hard to see a certain submission to the banalities of "everydayness" in existentialist freedom. And a slight nudge could push such submissiveness into hopelessness.

Samuel Beckett's Malone, whom we met bemoaning the crushing power of habit, approaches this hopelessness when appraising his existence at a chophouse. He hopes, above all, "the gravy has not varied," because, he says, "this is the kind of language I can understand . . . the kind of clear and simple" idea "on which it is possible for me to build, I ask for no other spiritual nourishment." Malone can have no higher aspiration in a world of the commonplace than that the gravy at the chophouse not change—Solzhenitsyn's Ivan

16. Modernity, Modernism, and the Evil of Banality

Denisovich would have similarly constrained desires for getting a little grass in his soup, but he was in a concentration camp.

Malone does hope, in his way. As had the existentialists in theirs. But these were hopes limited by the banal conditions of life. Hardly in the spirit of nineteenth-century authors. Now, for an even darker view of the evil of banality, we turn to Franz Kafka.

Walter Benjamin wrote the words quoted earlier—"even the most commonplace things have their weight"—about Kafka. And no writer better than Kafka illustrates how banality became a cause of cringing anxiety.

Kafka said he had modeled his writings on those of Dickens, for it was Dickens who showed him the literary "mastery of the material world" and "the presentation of the interaction between the world and the I." Yet Kafka's realism does not much resemble Dickens's, for Kafka portrays no quite recognizable characters dwelling amid familiar concrete social and material circumstances. Instead, Kafka's realities—social, material, psychological—are somewhat impalpable, abstract, surreal. It is true these insubstantial realities may be found in modern life, and Marxist critics like Georg Lukacs viewed modernist literature with its abstract realism, along with the society it serves, as dual manifestations of decadent capitalism. In any case, by attending to ordinary particulars, however surreal, Kafka sought to reveal the misery and alienation of modern life through them. As Kafka told Gustav Janouch: "In real life the mystery isn't hidden in the background. On the contrary. It stares one in the face. It is what is obvious. Everyday life is the greatest detective story ever written"—echoing the detective Sherlock Holmes's words quoted above: "there is nothing so unnatural as the commonplace." In recording this detective story, Kafka demonstrated the paradox of Modernism mentioned at the outset: although secularization had brought what Max Weber labeled "the disenchantment of the world," the banal realities of that world grew, in a manner of speaking, more enchanted than ever.

Kafka exhibited this enchantment in his renderings of everyday life. And he did it more disturbingly than has anyone else through what T. S. Eliot would deem a singular feature of modernist literature: the "juxtaposition of the matter-of-fact and the fantastic." The opening of Kafka's best-known story, *The Metamorphosis*, strikingly exemplifies this. Gregor Samsa awakens one day to discover that he has become a "giant insect." Yet, instead of screaming alarm, he lets the shocking discovery get immediately lost in thoughts of the banal difficulties this new condition will cause him. His insect's body arouses no terror, only irritation over the increased inconvenience of moving about, opening doors, eating, pleasing his family, keeping his job as a salesman—the "trouble of constant traveling, of worrying about train connections, the bed and irregular meals, casual acquaintances that are always new and never become intimate friends"—and so forth. The entire scene upsets customary proportions of the ordinary and the extraordinary, the trivial and the profound as the bizarre occurrence is enfolded in a life of tedious banalities.

Kafka conveys this disproportion not only by juxtaposing the ordinary and the extraordinary but by recording the former with care and detail and the latter merely in passing, radically distorting the imbalance of trivial and major events (anticipated by Tolstoy in *Anna Karenina* where, as Lionel Trilling noted, the epochal act of Anna's infidelity gets slight mention, whereas pages are devoted to Levin selecting shirts for his wedding). Kafka chose to present the trivial and banal as the more consuming, and the more sinister, because he believed they were. He conveys this belief in the opening scene of *The Trial*. When Joseph K. is arrested at home one day for no stated offense and under no identifiable authority, his wardens ask if this circumstance surprises him. He calmly replies, "Certainly, I am surprised, but I am by no means very much surprised." Because, he explains, "when one has lived for thirty years in this world and had to fight one's way through it as I have had to do, one becomes hardened to surprises." For Joseph K. and Kafka, both anguished bureaucrats, as Kafka's autobiographical writings make clear, their routine, banal, mind-numbing existence was so dispiriting that no event, however bizarre to others, could bring surprise, or make much difference.

Joseph K. and Gregor Samsa are but two of the luckless characters in Kafka's works who experience banality as a power that dehumanizes them and stifles hope. This power haunts all of Kafka's works, in the accounts of family life, business, bureaucracy, the functioning of the law, and the atmosphere of public corridors and city streets. This haunting has given us the noun Kafkaesque, for a menacingly surreal experience of reality that the twentieth century knew well but that nineteenth-century writers could only vaguely foreshadow. Kafka once remarked the difference between his sense of ordinary reality and that of his Realist predecessors. He told his friend and biographer Max Brod that Balzac had carried a walking stick inscribed with the motto: "I break every obstacle." But, he said, "my motto would rather be: 'every obstacle breaks me.'"

Kafka was unusually inclined to labor the insufficiency of the human will, and especially his own. But his melancholy comment here resonates with a more general truth. It is that the "disenchantment of the world," which Shakespeare had long ago feared would make "trifles of terrors," and that Hannah Arendt believed had brought the "banality of evil" in the twentieth century, had the opposite effect on notable modernist writers. It—together with other influences observed here—led them to see trifles *as* terrors and banality as evil. In Eliot's words again, from the great, mournful poem of modernity he named "The Waste Land," they had learned to find "fear in a handful of dust."

That said, it is doubtful that the "disenchantment of the world," through secularization and related developments noted here of the nineteenth and twentieth centuries, wholly accounts for either the banality of evil or the evil of banality. That transvaluation of values, in Nietzsche's term, also certainly arose to some extent from changes in what we might call the temper of the times. That is, in

III. On Modernity and Modernism

new ways of looking at, evaluating, and responding to experience. This temper arose within the circumstances described here, but cannot be reduced to them. Where the evil of banality is concerned, that temper surely involved an intensifying self-consciousness—in addition to the modern historical and social consciousness—that made many people increasingly uncertain of themselves and how to make sense of the world and how to live in it as the commonplace gained sway. This self-consciousness seems to have weakened the will and induced a dehumanizing sense of impotence to master, or to find positive meaning within, the circumstances of life. From there came some pretty bleak visions of life in modernist literature that went beyond the evil of banality. But to enter that dark passage is to depart the evil of banality itself for exploration of modernist self-consciousness, a journey better made elsewhere (see "Self-Consciousness and the Modernist Temper" below).

A previous version of this essay appeared as "Modernity and the Evil of Banality" in *The Centennial Review*, Winter, 1979.

Masaccio, The Expulsion from the Garden of Eden, *c. 1425; with fig leaves added in the 17th century that remained until the late 20th century.*

Suddenly ashamed of their nakedness, Adam and Eve went into the world cursed by their original sin and its punishment: becoming unsettlingly conscious of themselves.

"Oh God comma I abhor self-consciousness."
—JOHN BARTH

Self-Consciousness
and the Modernist Temper

If there is one undisputed attribute of the modernist temper, it is probably self-consciousness. Even critics who debate the merits of that temper and the nature of self-consciousness fall into agreement here. They see self-consciousness—in such guises as multiple selves, psychological probing, self-reflecting thought, manifold simultaneous perspectives, temporal awareness, obsessive guilt, haunting mirrors, bizarre artistic experimentation, and the like—marking virtually every work of thought and imagination during the modernist era.

Critics who find fault with that temper often locate this fault in the caustic effects of self-consciousness. Near the mid-twentieth century, the cultural historian Jacques Barzun observed that "the first striking trait of the modern ego is self-consciousness," and he belabored this trait for subverting the "willingness to take risks," thereby working "to the detriment of happiness . . . and of art." W. H. Auden agreed. Although Auden believed self-awareness could enhance the imagination, he saw modernist writers usually crushed by it; and he concluded that the modernist temper tested itself most with one question alone: "How shall the self-conscious man be saved?" The critic Robert Langbaum, surveying "mysteries of identity" in modern literature, doubted that this salvation was likely. "Modern self-consciousness," he wrote "produces the emotional and moral blankness" that is the modernist's "hell." He cited T. S. Eliot's early poetry as vividly exemplary, and anyone who has read the achingly self-conscious "The Love Song of J. Alfred

Prufrock" could see that. Eliot himself called self-consciousness "the cancer that eats away at the self" and found it to be the besetting malady of the age—just as his Austrian contemporary Robert Musil, author of *The Man without Qualities*, held it largely responsible for the disintegrated "human type that our time has produced." The critic Lionel Trilling was troubled by the response of his students to this malady in the 1950s. For, instead of being disturbed by the torturous "self-consciousness and self-pity" of modernist fiction, as he had been himself a generation earlier, they blithely accepted it all as the normal mood and manner of modern life. John Barth reflected this acceptance a few years later, with an ironic dig at the critics, in his story "Title," where he sighs, "Oh God comma I abhor self-consciousness."

Critics of modernist self-consciousness assail it for weakening the will and imagination. But other thinkers over the years have viewed self-consciousness as a mental quality inherent in understanding experience and apprehending truth. In this light, self-consciousness brings a higher consciousness. We might see something like this implicit in autobiographical writings going back to Saint Augustine. And it is pretty explicit in the essays of Montaigne where he probes his awareness of himself to discover insights into human nature. A century after Montaigne, John Locke and some of his contemporaries even used the term "self-consciousness" to denote functions of a developed mind. Later the philosopher Hegel saw "self-consciousness" (*Selbstbewusstsein*) in the unfolding of the Spirit in history, bringing heightened self-possession and wholeness of being. By Hegel's day, the idea of self-consciousness was very much in the air, and the Romanticists made self-consciousness almost a creed—as we shall see—as they expanded the range of emotional experience and the very concept of humanness. Then, around the turn of the twentieth century, the deepening exploration of reflective consciousness sparked a far-reaching intellectual revolution. The historian of that revolution, H. Stuart Hughes, explained how thinkers and imaginative writers alike "found themselves inserting between the external data and the final intellectual product an immediate stage of reflection on their own awareness of these data. The result was an enormous heightening of intellectual self-consciousness—a wholesale reexamination of the presuppositions of social thought itself." The modern social sciences came from this revolution (we could add methodologies of modern physics as well). And sociologists of modernization would demonstrate that the intellectual self-awareness typical of modern societies—by contrast to the unreflective minds common to traditional societies—breeds confidence in people that they can control their lives instead of thoughtlessly submitting to traditional authority.

This sampling of opinion from philosophy, literature, criticism, and social thought shows that while thinkers have widely recognized the influence of self-consciousness on the modern mind they do not all agree on the effects of that influence. This suggests that they might define self-consciousness differently. And that tells us the idea of self-consciousness itself is a bit cloudy. This cloudiness derives in part from the uncertain history of self-consciousness as a psychological experience or trait, by contrast to the express idea of "self-consciousness," which is easier to track down.

If we try to find the historical origins of that psychological phenomenon, we can identify many. Making a quick survey—passing over for now Romanticism and the two centuries since then—we could see the eighteenth century as the fount of a new self-awareness in the Enlightenment's scrutiny of knowing that dissolved naïve certainties, alongside a near cult of sentimentality that stirred empathy and conscience, and the rise of an aesthetic sensibility that, in W. J. Bate's words, introduced "a self-consciousness unparalleled in degree at any time before"—after all, the very term "aesthetic" was coined at that time. Yet, before that the seventeenth century also has claims to priority in self-consciousness with the birth of modern philosophy in Descartes's self-reflecting mind declaring "I think therefore I am," followed by Locke's affirmation of intellectual "self-consciousness" and the psychologically revelatory writings of La Rochefoucauld and La Bruyère. But then, no student of the sixteenth century could fail to assert that modern self-consciousness had conspicuous origins in the novel subjectivity of that age, evident in artistic Mannerism, Montaigne's self-searching, the Protestant Reformation, the revival of Pyrrhonian skepticism, the development of the mirror and the mechanical clock, the emergence of secular autobiography and the self-portrait, Shakespeare's self-absorbed and often self-doubting characters, and the preoccupation with sincerity and the role-playing self. Of course, earlier still, anyone who knows the Italian Renaissance could place the true source of modern self-consciousness in the fifteenth century with the invention of the Individual and the artist as hero, as well as in the flowering of the arts and letters at the hands of those who self-consciously proclaimed themselves deliverers of a cultural rebirth after an age of darkness.

Yet even before the epochal modernity of the Renaissance, the reforms of Gregory VII had given life to a human type who, as the great historian Marc Bloch put it, was "more self-conscious" than any before him and whose "self-consciousness indeed extended beyond the solitary human being to society," where it stimulated the art and thought of the High Middle Ages. For that matter, Christianity itself may be credited with introducing into Western culture a self-reflectiveness unknown to history through its psychological conception of sin as a state of mind—exemplified in the Sermon on the Mount, Paul's Epistles, spiritual autobiographies, and confessional daybooks. But no sooner had the novelty of Christian self-awareness been noted than late classical antiquity could assert claims to priority through innovative and sometimes scandalous Latin poetry, the metaphysical self-consciousness of Plotinus, and the rise of philosophical skepticism and eccentricity among Hellenistic philosophers and of an educated cosmopolitan personality in multiplying cities. Earlier still the Greeks can make claims with Aristotle's self-contemplating intellect, Plato's analytical idealism,

17. Self-Consciousness and the Modernist Temper

Socrates's irony, and, to be sure, the motto at Delphi echoed by Socrates: "Know thyself." Actually, no search for the historical origins of Western self-consciousness could stop before the awakening of human self-awareness in the Garden of Eden when Adam and Eve lost not only moral purity and hallowed sanctuary but psychological innocence. Suddenly ashamed of their nakedness, they went into the world cursed by their original sin and its punishment: becoming unsettlingly conscious of themselves.

As this little survey demonstrates (echoing Arthur Lovejoy's instructive search for the origins of Romanticism in his well-known essay "On the Discrimination of Romanticisms"), no hunt for the historical origins of self-consciousness can satisfactorily fix the earliest appearance of self-consciousness as a psychological experience. But it is possible to distinguish the self-consciousness characteristic of Modernism from self-consciousness in general. Or, at any rate, to illuminate how it became such a pronounced characteristic of the modernist temper. To do that requires first looking into relations between Modernism and one of its principal cultural forebears, Romanticism.

It is commonly said that at the end of the eighteenth century a new self entered the cultural life in the West. This self had among its attributes a large appetite for feeling and fantasy, abundant energy, and a marked preoccupation with itself. This preoccupation not only heightened the self-awareness already much developed in Western culture but prompted the exploration and exploitation of it. The new self was conscious of its self-consciousness.

This intensely reflexive self emerged first in Germany among Goethe's generation, when many young men withdrew from society into themselves, where, as Goethe's Werther said, they could "find a world" of their own. The German Romanticists who followed Goethe began to depend on self-absorption to satisfy every desire, whether for emotional release, psychological and metaphysical certainty, or artistic expression. Ludwig Tieck wrote plays within plays within plays. Chamisso recorded a man's search for his shadow. E. T. A. Hoffmann told the bizarre adventures of divided selves. Jean Paul Richter (known as Jean Paul) invented the literary *Doppelgänger* after discovering himself to be both the subject and object of consciousness—"Never shall I forget," he wrote, "when I was present at the birth of my own self-consciousness. Suddenly the internal vision 'I am I' passed before me like a lightning flash from heaven . . . my 'I' had seen itself for the first time and forever." Johann Gottlieb Fichte constructed a metaphysics upon a discovery like Jean Paul's, concluding that the objective world depends for its existence on human consciousness. And he taught this theory by telling students to contemplate the wall in front of them and then to contemplate the thing that had contemplated the wall; but, as one student recorded, "It was curious how confusion and embarrassment ensued; many of the listeners seemed not to be able to discover anywhere the thing which had thought of the wall." Hegel skirted these dizzying descents into subjectivity, without diminishing the importance of the theme, in his idea, mentioned above, of growing *Selbstbewusstein* as a manifestation of the objective Spirit unfolding in history.

Outside of Germany, Kierkegaard adopted and modified Hegel's usage in his protoexistentialist version of the human self. "Generally speaking," he said, "consciousness, i.e., consciousness of self, is the decisive criterion of the self. The more consciousness, the more self; the more consciousness, the more will, the more will, the more self. A man who has no will is no self; the more will he has, the more consciousness of self." But unlike Hegel, Kierkegaard was ambivalent toward this kind of self-consciousness, and Kierkegaard's ambivalence, as we shall see, points directly toward the self-consciousness of the modernist temper. I should note that such an ambivalence had already been detected by Friedrich Schiller in his great essay "On Naïve and Sentimental Poetry," which contrasts spontaneous, natural, unreflective poetry with poetry that is halting, subjective, self-aware. Schiller saw virtues in both but believed the modern poet more likely to create the "sentimental" kind, and critics have since agreed—W. J. Bate and Harold Bloom, for example, explained how modern poets, from Romanticism onward, could be nothing but "sentimental" in Schiller's sense, burdened as they are by the daunting awareness of their predecessors and the accumulating expectations of art.

These examples, mainly German, of Romanticist self-consciousness illustrate a deliberate mental exercise intended to advance self-realization or self-discovery. And this exercise, with the ambivalences it could arouse, lay at the source of two of the major strains in European Romanticism. One of them was the play upon psychological and aesthetic ambiguity known as Romantic irony, evident, for instance, in the entanglements of truth and illusion, the ideal and the real in Friedrich Schlegel's *Lucinde*; in the interplay of sublime and ridiculous modes of love in Gautier's *Mademoiselle de Maupin*; and in Stendhal's mockery of social pretense and self-deception from behind a protective front of pseudonyms, masks, and lies. The other strain was not so playful. It brought fear of being consumed by self-consciousness or regressing uncontrollably into the self, expressed by poets like Byron and Keats as the desire to flee from the demon of self-consciousness, and by thinkers such as Thomas Carlyle and John Stuart Mill who embraced an "anti-self-consciousness theory," in Mill's words, to free themselves from burdensome self-reflection (the critic Geoffrey Hartman called it "Romantic anti-self-consciousness" in a widely read essay of that title). It may be that these two strains and styles of Romantic self-consciousness had their homes in different nations—the Germans inclined to psychological and metaphysical explorations, the English Romanticists tending to lyrical self-revelations, and the French to discord between their public and private selves. At all events, no thoughtful European of the early nineteenth could deny that self-consciousness was a condition of the times. As Carlyle observed, "Never since the beginning of Time was there, that we hear or read of, so intensely self-conscious a society."

Romanticist self-consciousness preceded modernist self-consciousness as parent to child, or grandparent to grandchild. And like all passages between generations, this one saw an inheritance enfolded in new needs and appearances. The Romanticists' bold explorations of self-discovery and self-realization, even at the expense of emotional disquiet and intellectual doubt, gave way among modernist authors to a confused longing for such positive ends underpinned by pervasive self-conscious anxiety about experience. This anxiety displayed itself in a variety of moods and manners—e.g., ill ease, affectation, disillusion, resentment, self-criticism, self-dramatization, pessimism, despair—none of them the sign of a willed and exploring self but of a self-awareness that has impaired the will, the ego, and the self.

Upon wondering why the modernist temper lost the strength and adventurous spirit of its Romanticist forebear, we discover, for one thing, that the Romantic occupation with self-awareness, positive and negative, yielded to a mode of critical self-consciousness or self-criticism that became corrosive to the will and imagination. We might detect hints of this in Schiller's idea of self-reflecting "sentimental" poetry and in the anti-self-consciousness of some Romanticists. Half a century or so later, Gautier sensed that critical self-consciousness was now integral to the act of artistic creation itself. And he pointed to Baudelaire as a prime example. "His is a very subtle mind," Gautier wrote, "and one which makes criticism play a part in inspiration." Looking back from the mid-twentieth century, Jacques Barzun said that this statement "could serve as a shorthand definition of our Modernism." The historian Peter Gay put the idea more emphatically: "Modernism is the creature of criticism."

But this kind of criticism was not just a rationally self-conscious appraisal of artistic creation. It could also be an irrational self-criticism debilitating to creativity. To escape this kind of critical self-consciousness, Thomas Mann's Adrian Leverkühn in *Doctor Faustus* traded his soul to the devil for spontaneous "unreflectiveness" in musical composition. Leverkühn escaped self-consciousness but only at the cost of his soul. This debilitating form of self-criticism beyond the critic/artist's control—which could also become an unconscious hostility directed against the self and everything else— helped give modernist self-consciousness its often mocking mood and manners and its bleak world view.

With this critical self-consciousness came a tendency to dramatize the troubled state of mind it instilled. We can see this tendency as early as Goethe's Werther. He steeped himself in subjectivity and self-absorbed aspirations for love, art, and action that transcended objective reality, and when he failed to realize those aspirations that subjectivity turned into hostility toward himself and the world. Then he committed suicide in a melodramatic act of martyred dejection—prefiguring the self-inflicted torment and histrionic exhibition of anguish typical of the modernist temper. We can see a similar attitude among young men in France after Waterloo. They equated the defeat of Napoleon with the death of heroism and the loss of life's meaning, then turned inward and wallowed in feelings of ennui and purposelessness. Alfred de Musset recognized this at the time, remarking that they had translated their own incapacities and ennui into an "affectation of despair" over life itself, when in fact they suffered only from being "idle and tired." The victims of failed idealism and a consequent sense of helplessness and self-contempt, they could only play the woebegoned.

After the abortive revolutions of 1848, this desolate, self-conscious, self-dramatizing temper redoubled, with Baudelaire as its exemplar. In the poem *"Au Lecteur,"* which became the prologue to *Les Fleurs du mal*, he blames ennui itself as the horror of humanity and the curse of the age. Ennui "makes no grand gestures or cries," he says, but it "would willingly reduce the earth to ruin, and swallow the world in one gaping yawn." In the closing lines, he self-consciously takes a taunting swipe at himself and everyone: "You know that fastidious monster—O hypocritical reader—my fellow man—my brother!" (*hypocrite lecteur—mon semblable—mon frère*).

In Baudelaire, the self-conscious modern artist unmistakably steps forward to act out his criticism of himself and others. And there we can see into the soul of modernist self-consciousness. It is a soul, or ego, whose sources, character, and needs reside in the psychological tricks of mind played within everyone by critical or aggressive impulses and by conscious and unconscious defenses against them—resistances, repressions, sublimations, and so on. But that modernist ego also participates in conscious desires for personal identity, self-assurance, self-realization, and the like, of the type that makes self-conscious (and often unconscious) role-players of us all. In this light, all human actions and creations share in the management of impulses and the search for fitting roles to play or a suitable sense of self. And the self-conscious mood and histrionic works of Modernism are complex searches indeed.

Baudelaire illustrates this complexity when he first directs his hostility toward others—*hypocrite lecteur*—in order to exalt himself at the reader's expense, and then turns this hostility on himself—*mon semblable, mon frère*—to convey possession of intimate and unacknowledged truths about everyone. Both gestures grant him superiority while seeming to demean him.

Baudelaire's performances of self-absorbed, impotent ennui, like the symptoms of ennui in Musset's generation, betray a social-psychological malaise of the kind the sociologist Émile Durkheim called "anomie." Anomie is the loss of goals or norms, or the feeling that one is powerless to attain goals or meet norms (Durkheim aptly cited Musset's writings as an illustration). A person suffering anomie aches with a sense of aimlessness and impotence and may disregard accepted behavior, inducing destructive actions against oneself or others. Baudelaire's own life and works played upon this theme continually: failed hopes bred a splenetic sense of incapacity and the injustice of it, which he exhibited in self-denigrating or antisocial actions, ideas, and art. To use his own word, Baudelaire was *L'Héautontimorouménos*, the self-tormentor, who played the role of victim very well:

> I am the wound and the knife!
> I am the slap and the cheek!
> I am the limbs and the rack,
> The victim and the torturer!
> I am the vampire of my own heart
> —One of the great abandoned
> Condemned to eternal laughter,
> Who can never smile again!

A further clue to Baudelaire's and the modernists' anguished and histrionic anomie lies in a commonplace of the sociology of the avant-garde: the economic dependence of the artist on a public he deplores but whose admiration he secretly wishes he could win. Troubled in his relations with both family and public, Baudelaire turned his sense of impotence into that mythology of the modern artist as martyr, the damned, the *poète maudit*. The poet, he wrote, must avoid places where "the rich and joyous congregate" and remain with the "feeble, destitute, and forlorn," for only there can he preserve his inspiration; and yet this requires removing himself from the very society that could sustain him. Baudelaire might have followed this rule only when his improvident expenditures and reckless debts left him no alternative. But this duplicity only intensified his feeling of being an artist who deserves a life he cannot have and resents the failure. To mythologize and embody this conflict was to be Baudelaire's historic role, as Jules Laforgue observed when he attributed to Baudelaire the motto: "I am damned on account of the public—Good—The public is not admitted."

Baudelaire's histrionic defiance and self-pity did not in any way strengthen his will, but they did strengthen his belief that powerlessness and suffering nourished artistic inspiration. Unable to make the public heed even his greatest achievements, which he believed to be his lyrical poems, he cultivated a pose of worldly impotence while pursuing artistic potency in alcohol and opium, his "artificial paradises," crying fatalistically: "It is the devil who pulls the strings that make us dance."

Through these social and artistic performances of despair and self-effacement, Baudelaire established many of the gestures and the mood of modernist self-consciousness. In Laforgue's words again, Baudelaire "is the first who is not triumphant, but who accuses himself, reveals his wounds, his laziness, his bored uselessness in the midst of this hardworking, devoted century." And both the wounds and the uselessness were largely of his own making as a "self-tormentor" in a society whose bourgeois comforts he wanted but not at the cost of wholly submitting to that society.

Baudelaire thus gave the modernist self-consciousness its public face of anxious histrionic criticism of the self and the world. But there is a private face, too, and this is not a mask donned, consciously or unconsciously, and believed in as one's public self. It is rather an anguish more painful and deeply unconscious than the self-conscious discontents Baudelaire performed. This private face is guilt. We might detect elements of guilt in Baudelaire's self-flagellations. But the role of guilt in the self-conscious modernist temper is better illuminated by writers who knew guilt as a secret haunting or even as an open enemy.

There is no written history of guilt. And we might never have one—although social scientists have distinguished between traditional "shame cultures" and modern "guilt cultures," reflecting a passage from social to psychological forms of punishment. For guilt is a psychological drama enacted amid abundant confusions and concealments. The actors in this drama are barely aware of their roles and generally unconscious of those roles' origins; yet what those actors do and say carries such force that guilt is charged with the power to wound. And that power signals the nature of guilt: guilt is an internal injury, a wounding of the heart—or the ego—by a weapon inside the victim not under the victim's control. Little can be known of this drama in ages long past (if it even existed much in traditional "shame cultures") because the effects of intimate human relations that implant and energize the self-criticism of guilt lie hidden. But we can see this kind of self-criticism doing its painful work in plenty of authors of the past two centuries. And possibly none better illustrate this in anticipating Modernism than the lives and works of the two most overtly guilt-ridden writers of the nineteenth century: Nathaniel Hawthorne and Søren Kierkegaard.

These may seem unlikely choices here since they are not usually associated with Modernism and were deeply religious. In fact, their religiosity and their guilt went together. But they demonstrate that while religion may feed guilt, it does not by itself create it, and that guilt can far transcend any of its religious nutrients. They thereby point to how the modernist temper can be at once unencumbered by religion and steeped in guilt. The source of guilt in Hawthorne and Kierkegaard therefore lies not in harsh religious doctrine itself (Hawthorne grew up under New England Puritanism and Kierkegaard under Danish Lutheranism) but in lives—and consequent writings—marked by anxious psychological insecurity, neurotic self-criticism, and a preoccupation with the psychological and philosophical nature of guilt itself.

Hawthorne's guiltily self-critical character was nourished mainly by his reclusive and moralistic mother, who worshiped at the shrine of her deceased husband and fed her memories and devotion to her son throughout the prolonged disability and dependency that confined him to home. "I scarcely had human intercourse outside my own family," he wrote; and his sister remarked that although he had wanted to be among the "multitude," he was too "conscious of being utterly unlike everyone else" and "began to withdraw into himself." He came to depend on that protected life. Just before leaving for Bowdoin College, Hawthorne admitted to his sister: "The happiest days of my life are gone. Why was I not a girl, that I might have been pinned all my life to my mother's apron."

This timid and self-absorbed personality arose in part from the limited activity allowed Hawthorne owing to his physical condition. But his feelings of inadequacy reached deeper than physical weakness, for he was persistently driven to self-contempt by what he considered the overpowering demands of maturity and his own aspirations. And even after achieving some prominence as a writer and establishing a family of his own, he denigrated himself for his uncertain financial circumstances and erratic periods of creativity. Disregarding his accomplishments, he remained haunted by "that same dream of a life hopelessly a failure." This was irrational self-criticism, guilt without religion.

Hawthorne knew little of active sin but much of psychological impairment, and his fiction shows it in many renderings of guilt that concern sins of consciousness—or self-consciousness—not action. He even produced a graphic image of this in the story "Egotism; or, The Bosom Serpent." There he has a character suffer from a serpent inside that unrelentingly "gnaws" him because, as he discovers: "It is my diseased self-contemplation that has engendered and nourished him." Only if he "could for one instant forget myself" would he be able to vanquish the beast. He finally succeeds by heeding the admonition of his neglected wife to "forget yourself in the idea of another." He asks forgiveness for his selfishness and reaffirms his love for her. The snake, real or imagined, slithers away, freeing him from internal self-conscious punishment.

The image of the "bosom serpent" fits guilt very well (even though guilt as such is more implicit than explicit in this tale of self-absorption and self-criticism). In "Fancy's Show Box," the guilty conscience—or consciousness—is explicit. It is "a stain upon the soul" that comes not from actual deeds but from those of mind and contemplations of evil. Hence, "in a church, while the body is kneeling, the soul may pollute itself" through bad thoughts. And as one becomes self-conscious about those thoughts, conscience "strikes a dagger to the heart," like the "bosom serpent," in guilt that inflicts pain with a will of its own. Thus do self-awareness and unconscious self-criticism join to injure the ego independent of both religion and rational judgment.

No one can read Hawthorne's parables of guilt without noting that this guilt gains power from social bonds. Hawthorne tells of individuals inseparably tied to others through shared beliefs and the common conscience that speaks for those beliefs and insinuates itself into the self-consciousness of anyone party to it. So secret and domineering can this guilt of common conscience be that it induces Dr. Grimshawe, in Hawthorne's last, uncompleted tale, "Dr. Grimshawe's Secret," to experience moral self-reproach in an empty room; and it causes Dimmesdale in *The Scarlet Letter* to suffer an agonizing private guilt suggestive of Kierkegaard's "sickness unto death," which leads to his own death for his hidden sin with Hester Prynne, who gets punished instead with the traditional public shame of having to wear the scarlet letter—and she survives. Here Hawthorne's tales of psychological impotence, self-contempt, and consuming guilt depart their Puritan New England settings and enter the more modern world of guilt-ridden Kierkegaardian despair.

Upon turning from Hawthorne to Kierkegaard, it must be said that the "sickness unto death" of Kierkegaard's essay by that name (published in 1848, two years before *The Scarlet Letter*) might not wholly represent Dimmesdale's guilty self-hatred. For Hawthorne let Dimmesdale actually die in an act of repentance, whereas Kierkegaard meant a thoroughgoing "sickness of the self" from which there is no escape. Yet Kierkegaard would have found Dimmesdale's self-lacerating guilt exemplary of the desolate moral and psychological condition he described, because it enabled Dimmesdale to reach a higher stage of pained self-awareness.

I have previously remarked Kierkegaard's belief that the self exists only through self-awareness. Now this self-awareness also discloses itself as guilt. Remove all worldly manners and concerns, Kierkegaard says, and "the only thing remaining is the individual himself, the single individual, placed in his God-relationship under the rubric: Guilty/Not Guilty?" And this means that the highest state of the self and self-consciousness is not, as it was for Hegel, a state of potency and wholeness but one of existential anxiety and despair over that self's insufficiency before God and existence, its conflicts between freedom and sin, and its inescapable, guilt-ridden burden of responsibility.

Although Kierkegaard conceived of guilt more metaphysically than did Hawthorne, there were ample reasons in his life, too, for defining human nature through guilt. Even more than Hawthorne, Kierkegaard as a youth was isolated from the public world and dominated by a morally obsessed parent. His widower father taught a fearsome Christianity, with the crucifixion as its central image. But more important in fostering Kierkegaard's sense of guilt was his father's demand that Kierkegaard, even as a child, accept full responsibility for his actions. Kierkegaard's childhood was therefore more an exercise in self-criticism than in religious devotion. And his earliest memories of school record a nearly compulsive will to do what was expected of him:

> To me it was as if heaven and earth might collapse if I did not learn my lesson; and on the other hand, as though even if heaven and earth were to collapse, this would not exempt me from doing the task assigned to me, from learning my lesson. . . . I had only one duty, that of learning my lesson, and yet I can trace my whole ethical view of life to this impression.

But this compulsion did not come from fear of physical or divine punishment for failure. Kierkegaard's father never so much as threatened him into accepting his obligations. He merely mantled those obligations in the cloak of moral imperative. When he handed his son new books for the next level of the boy's education, for instance, he added these words: "When the month is up you are

17. SELF-CONSCIOUSNESS AND THE MODERNIST TEMPER

the third in your class." No more was said or needed saying. The imperative was adamant. Nor did his father coddle and encourage him. "I was exempted from parental twaddle," Kierkegaard remembered; "he never asked me about my lessons, never heard me recite them, never looked at my exercise book, never reminded me that now it was time to read, now time to leave off. . . . I was left entirely to my own responsibility." And in consequence, Kierkegaard concludes, "I got a thoroughly deep impression of the fact there was something called duty and that it had eternal validity."

Even the rules of Latin grammar assumed for Kierkegaard the authority of moral injunction. Viewing their regular order with "unconditioned respect" and "reverence," he "looked down upon the miserable life the [grammatical] exception led" with "righteous contempt." Understandably, he identified the authority of these regular rules with his father: "When under this influence I regarded my father, he appeared to me the incarnation of the rule; what came from any other source was the exception, insofar as it was not in agreement with his commandment."

Small wonder Kierkegaard developed an acute sense of guilt largely unrelated to religion. Sigmund Freud would have found him an ideal case study on this topic, if Freud had ever read him, which he seems not to have done. For Kierkegaard perfectly demonstrates how a parent's expectations of a child, urged with only the moral authority of the parent, instill in the child the voice of the superego. This internal voice tells the child what to do and chastises the child for failure. The superego is therefore the source of ideals and aspirations and at the same time the agent of self-criticism and guilt. If a parent has done the job well, the child will go forth hearing the voice of the superego instructing and punishing thereafter. And if that voice resounds too loudly, the child will grow up with ideals (or parental expectations) that cannot be sufficiently attained and with the bosom serpent of guilt gnawing and gnawing endlessly. That was Kierkegaard's fate, and that of Hawthorne, as well as of many a sufferer to come. In fact, Freud came to believe that neurotic guilt was the epidemic emotional malaise of the twentieth century.

With Kierkegaard's exalted moral idealism and absorption in guilt, it should have come as no surprise to him that discovering his father's human fallibility devastated him—"the Great Earthquake" he called it, while leaving in doubt whether this had resulted from a lapse of spirit or flesh. But this disillusion did not lead Kierkegaard to abandon either his moral idealism or his sense of guilt. His superego had been too firmly planted for that. Rather he followed that superego by repudiating instead of emulating its source—his father. Relations with his father were never completely restored. But, even though for a time he led a dissolute life which cost him some guilt, he was always wracked by acute guilt for violating any perceived responsibility. And he elevated his private conscience into a cultural and existential superego to judge modern Christianity and the existential conditions and responsibilities of the modern self.

These anecdotal details of Hawthorne's and Kierkegaard's lives and works reveal the private face of modern critical self-consciousness in guilt, just as Baudelaire presented its public face in the histrionic display of self-torment. When the two are joined, modernist self-consciousness blooms in self-critical feelings of worthlessness, anguish, and despair performed in art and ideas often as a nihilistic condemnation of existence itself. The full array of this modernist self-consciousness did not find embodiment in all modernists, but its elements and their pattern are discernible. Here are a few of those who played the role of self-conscious modernist with memorable performances, along with some explanations of what they got out of it.

The modernist who most exemplifies the private sufferings of self-critical guilt and the literary performance of them is Franz Kafka. He knew better than any other, or exhibited more distinctly, as he said, the "pressures of anxiety, of weakness, or self-contempt," and "the boundless sense of guilt" that torments beyond all reason. Kafka was so like Kierkegaard in temperament and childhood experience, if not religion, that they might have been brothers. Both were overwhelmingly dominated by their fathers (although Kafka's father was the more severe); neither could bring himself to marry, after being engaged and seemingly in love; and both suffered from punishing moral idealism, extravagant disillusion, and, to be sure, obsessive guilt.

Kafka's remarkably self-revealing *Letter to His Father*, written when he was thirty-nine, recalls the unhappy formation of his character. His first childhood memory is telling. At about the age of three, Kafka had once complained in the night of thirst and been told by his father to desist. When he continued to complain, his father, without speaking, calmly took him from his bed to the outside of the house and made him stay there for the rest of the night. Kafka interpreted this episode as a primary cause of his feelings of self-contempt: "I dare say I was quite obedient afterwards," he remembered, "but it did me inner harm," for his father's action "meant I was a mere nothing to him," and this seeded the persistent "feeling of nothingness that often overwhelms me."

Kafka goes on to say that such silent, pointedly psychological punishment typified his father's relationship with him. "You hardly ever really hit me," he wrote, rather "you put special trust in bringing up children by means of irony." And that practice of his father's psychological power led Kafka, like Kierkegaard before him, to idealize his father's moral stature: "everything you called out at me was a heavenly commandment, I never forgot it, it remained for me the most important means of forming a judgment of the world." And, also like Kierkegaard, he suffered a shattering disillusionment over an act of his father. But, being the obsessively self-critical youth he was, Kafka turned the disillusionment against himself not his father. The occasion was a seemingly trivial incident that the son never forgot. During adolescence, Kafka had once, in a moment of boyish self-affirmation unusual for him, boasted of his knowledge in the matter of sex. He anticipated words of moral wisdom, but instead his father merely explained "how I could go in for these things without danger." The moral disappointment caused "the whole future world to come tumbling down." For it made Kafka feel that his father "became still purer, rose still higher" and that Kafka himself was more worthless than before: "the purity of the world came to an end with you," he said, "and by virtue of your advice, the filth began with me." Here Kafka turned his moral self-consciousness upon himself rather than his father because he was himself all too completely "seized in my innermost being" by "the weakness, the lack of self-confidence, the sense of guilt" that "your method of upbringing" fostered. In Freudian parlance, the imperious superego cultivated by his father had crushed his ego. And this weakness and guilt inspired his bizarre, self-flagellating, guilt-ridden fiction—like the emblematic novel of amorphous, life-destroying guilt, *The Trial*.

Kafka so thoroughly embodies the private, unconscious sufferings of critical self-consciousness that he is exceptional. But consider the lives of some fellow modernist authors. T. S. Eliot had a childhood not so unlike Kafka's. His mother ruled him insistently, in part because she feared that his congenital physical frailty would worsen if his activities were not limited, and in part because her Unitarian moral teachings demanded self-denial and expected intellectual achievement. Eliot learned the necessity of work and self-control, but also—in the words of his sensitive biographer, Lyndall Gordon—a "self-destructive introspection" and a "self-disgust" that "was in a class of its own" among modernist poets. It was this spirit, Gordon observes, that gave Eliot his "central persona—a performer fixed in his silly role, unable to take command of his real self which is socially unacceptable, outcast, or elusive." Eliot was at home in the company of his characters: such as, Prufrock, Sweeney, the Hollow Men, and Edward Chamberlayne in *The Cocktail Party*, who at once echoes Prufrock's plaint, "I should have been a pair of ragged claws / Scuttling across the floors of silent seas," and speaks for them all: "I am obsessed by the thought of my own insignifi-

17. Self-Consciousness and the Modernist Temper

cance." They are all ruined from within, and self-consciously tell us about it.

Luigi Pirandello is another imbued with the critical self-consciousness that dissolves confidence and yet must be performed. He also came to literature through a highly dependent adolescence and parentally inspired idealism and disillusion. His father, a strong and prominent figure in his part of Sicily, aroused in his son deep admiration for him alongside great expectations for the political unification of Italy through Garibaldi. After those political expectations ran aground and his father failed him both morally and financially, Pirandello felt victimized by the "voice of others within us" that can mislead but cannot be silenced, and that he heard as a kind of wayward conscience. His self-conscious disillusion and uncertainty later gave form to the literature of tangled truths and illusions for which he became famous. And he found the most compelling arena for the performance of his disorienting vision in the theater, where confusions of perceptions and reality made ingenious, even spellbinding drama. With his most celebrated drama, *Six Characters in Search of an Author*, he created a monument to self-conscious performance itself, as well as to the moral ambiguities of existence. There, unannounced to the audience, actors and a director wander onto an open, curtainless stage to rehearse a play by Pirandello but are then interrupted by six strangers searching for an author to put their own life drama into a play. After some peculiar discussion, the director agrees to present the strange story of what is a highly dysfunctional family. From there, through many twists and turns of what is real and what is not, culminating in a couple of apparent deaths, we are never entirely sure what to believe about anything. Finally, the performers drift off the stage, with the director complaining that they have lost a whole day. Here and in his other "Pirandellian" plays, Pirandello was unquestionably *the* playwright of self-consciousness and its disorienting effects on perceptions of reality and on how to grasp its very meaning.

III. ON MODERNITY AND MODERNISM

Jean-Paul Sartre also exemplified this critical self-conscious temper, despite his contention in the autobiography of his youth, *The Words*, that, because he grew up without a father and was much loved by his mother and grandparents, "I have no superego." He might not have known his superego through explicit guilt, but he lived a very inward life as a child and developed a keenly self-conscious image of himself that readily provoked self-reproach, even over so slight an imperfection as catching a cold. The critic Victor Brombert observed that this was in fact a "sense of guilt" that afflicted Sartre's entire generation of middle-class Frenchmen in "an all-pervasive, generic, subjective, largely unaccountable feeling of culpability." Be that as it may, Sartre did not proceed to openly concern himself with guilt. He put his critical self-consciousness to more philosophical use, together with a penchant for intellectual performance. He became *the* philosopher of existentialism, known for his cosmic pronouncements on the inherent meaninglessness of human existence. And he wove that nihilistic vision and self-consciousness together in his first novel *Nausea*. Sartre shows self-awareness overwhelming the hero, Roquentin, to a degree that prevents his mind from spontaneously and objectively organizing experience. The consequence is a kind of existential chaos—sensations become things, words fly about, and the head grows dizzy. This chaos is the brute realm of "existence," bereft of objective meaning. But it arises from Roquentin's almost psychotic self-consciousness. Sartre later wrote in *The Words* that at this time he himself "*was* Roquentin" and had taken pride in revealing through him "the bitter, unjustified existence of my fellow men" while "exonerating my own." An inveterate, self-conscious, intellectual performer, Sartre had gone on from there to find the meaning of his own life in telling others the existentialist truth that life had no meaning. "Fake to the marrow of my bones and hoodwinked," he admitted, "I joyfully wrote about our unhappy state." In all, Sartre plainly demonstrates how critical self-consciousness can bring a pessimistic vision of life that finds a kind of self-gratifying "exoneration" through intellectual performance of it.

It is a theme of this essay that those who suffer from critical self-consciousness are to some extent ignorant of its causes and helpless to effect its cure. It is also a theme that these sufferers choose to dramatize their malaise as substantive, irremediable, and universal. The self-conscious modernists delighted in playing the afflicted and unhealable heart. This desire to act out their pains led modernists to many self-conscious themes, images, and ideas—e.g., debunkery, defensiveness, affectation, inhibition, helplessness, anguish, self-revelation, self-pity, nihilism, and images of insects, puppets, rodents, crustaceans, and the like. But to say these themes, images, and ideas take histrionic forms is not to say they are necessarily false or hypocritical. For the pains of critical self-consciousness that thrust them forward can be genuine. Nevertheless, dramatizing affliction seems to be as important to the modernist temper as the affliction itself—foreshadowed by precursors like Goethe's Werther and Musset's *enfants du siècle*. And that must prompt us to ask if the performance is in fact not *more* important to the performer than the affliction, and if the performance does, after all, honestly represent the affliction.

The answer lies in seeing that the performance of modernist self-consciousness could take on a life of its own, providing a kind of personal identity to the performer—a "fabricated personality," as André Gide termed it. In that light, the modernists' self-conscious performance is a form of self-justification, even idealization and pursuit of authenticity. As such, the performance can be more defensive, anguished, and negative than the actual emotions it purportedly presents. And this can deceive the performer as much as anyone—like the "affectation of despair" Musset diagnosed in his generation. As Pirandello once said, "I think that life is a sad piece of buffoonery; because we have in ourselves, without being able to know why . . . the need to deceive ourselves constantly by creating a reality (one for each and never the same for all) which, from time to time, is discovered to be vain and illusory . . ." That statement might be more typical of Pirandello than of other modernists, but it contains a truth. The modernist's performance is presented for the performer as well as the world. And that performance is never far from the persona of Pierrot, the sad clown—a frequent image in modernist art. In many ways, the self-conscious modernist *is* Pierrot.

Sartre's confession quoted above of his own self-conscious and self-deceptive performance of the sorry human condition tells the tale. As he looked back on his early existential angst, he admitted to being "fake" and "hoodwinked" as he "joyfully wrote about our unhappy state." He had been secretly joyful because the performance gave him a gratifying identity of superior understanding. "The object of my mission, the springboard of my glory," he explained, was to show "that man is impossible" and that Sartre himself "differed from the others only by the mandate to give expression to that impossibility" as "the elect of doubt." "I was," he concluded, "a prisoner of that obvious contradiction, but I did not see it, I saw the world through it" and "regarded anxiety as the guarantee of my security; I was happy."

This remarkable confession is, of course, another performance, as any reader of that artful venture in self-revelation, *The Words*, knows. But it perfectly describes how the modernist self-consciousness, even at its most philosophical in Sartre's early existentialism, is a quest for an identity through performance, a quest made the more urgent by the discomfiture of critical self-consciousness.

Once modernist self-consciousness is seen to be an interplay of acute self-consciousness, unconscious self-criticism, and histrionic self-seeking, many of the appearances of Modernism take on a new character. The debunking tone, revelatory anguish, and vision of an arid and meaningless existence lose their aura of objectivity and become ideological stances. Self-consciously uncertain of themselves, modernists of this stamp dramatize their condition in hopes of gaining security and stature, always perceiving and presenting experience through the lens of their own disorienting self-consciousness. And they are unaware of why they are doing it. No wonder that some, like Sartre—and Goethe long before him—eventually see through their early performances of dejection and embrace artistic, political, moral, or religious commitments.

But I hasten to repeat that notwithstanding the modernists' deceptive performances of their subjective suffering, those sufferings were at least in part real. For a consuming self-consciousness can indeed hamper the will and hinder the imagination. And the critical self-consciousness of guilt—or an overweening superego—can inhibit the formation of a healthy-minded and autonomous identity. We might therefore conclude that the modernist self-consciousness has a pathological quality to it. A cultural pathology at that, born of the circumstances that shaped the lives of many middle-class males from the late nineteenth century well into the twentieth. I have suggested only outlines of those circumstances. But it should be reasonably clear that this gnawing self-consciousness, combined with the performance of the sufferings it causes for the sake of attaining a gratifying personal identity, gave us the self-conscious modernist temper that we have come to know.

A previous version of this essay appeared in *The Georgia Review*, Fall, 1979.

Eleanor Marx c. 1890.

Eleanor Marx lost her love and work in the passage from bourgeois Victorianism and revolutionary socialism to feminist independence and adventurous Modernism, a passage she could not, after all, wholly complete.

More Emma than Nora

A VICTORIAN/MARXIST/MODERNIST MELODRAMA

*E*arly in her forty-fourth year, the youngest daughter of Karl Marx swallowed a dram of prussic acid and died within the hour. Her famous paternity and tragic fate alone assured Eleanor Marx the curiosity of her contemporaries and the interest of later generations. And that curiosity rapidly enfolded her life and death in the atmosphere of Victorian melodrama. For Eleanor Marx, called Tussy by all who knew her—sometime actress, translator of Flaubert and Ibsen, executor of her father's manuscripts and tireless crusader in his cause—took her life in 1898 upon learning that her fellow crusader, author, and common-law husband of fourteen years, Edward Aveling, had taken a legal wife. "The brute has killed her," snapped Keir Hardie (first leader of the Labour Party in Parliament), voicing the opinion made current by socialist Eduard Bernstein's detection—spurious, it turned out—of a murderous plot of Aveling threaded by infidelities, abuses, forged and destroyed letters, and an ill-kept suicide pact. George Bernard Shaw, Eleanor's one-time political and theater companion, set this sad misalliance on the stage in *The Doctor's Dilemma*, altering events and their climax but presenting Eleanor fairly faithfully in the dutiful wife Jennifer Dubedat, and Aveling in her omnivorously selfish artist husband.

Later years turned Tussy's fate into Marxist tragedy, as her suicide got linked to the previous death of her eldest sister, Jenny, victim of overwork and neglect at the hands of her socialist husband Charles Longuet, and then to the double suicide in 1911 of her other sister

Laura and Laura's professed Marxist husband Paul Lafargue. "Had Marx the father somehow mangled the capacity of his children to enjoy the savour of living?" asked the one-time Marxist Lewis Feuer, who concluded that he had, because "the Marxist upbringing" of uncompromising ambitions to change the world had eroded his daughters' ability to live in it and thus nurtured "Marxist Tragedians" (Feuer even wrote an ingenious novel entitled *The Case of the Revolutionist's Daughter* [1983], in which he has Sherlock Holmes and Dr. Watson take on a case revolving around Tussy and her father).

The first full-scale biography of Tussy, by Chushichi Tsuzuki (1967), subtitled *A Socialist Tragedy*, blamed her death on the marriage of her Marxist self-discipline and Aveling's anarchist hedonism, which made "the destruction of the daughter of Karl Marx . . . almost inevitable." As socialist tragedy, Tussy's story also became the subject of BBC series. And the English socialist and author Yvonne Kapp completed a thorough, affectionate, gracefully written, probably definitive life (two volumes, 1972, 1976), dispelling some of the atmosphere of melodrama and attending more to Eleanor's historical importance.

That importance was not small, for although Eleanor was neither a great leader nor intellectual, her life personified many of the aspirations and conflicts of late-nineteenth-century European culture, as well as illuminating the character of Marx and the history of Marxism. And Kapp's biography, although absorbed in socialism and written in the English and Marxist traditions of social history that discount psychological explanations, supplies more reason than ever to conclude that Tussy's fate and importance arose from three salient facts of her life: she was the child of Karl Marx, she belonged to her generation, and she was a woman.

At Eleanor's birth in 1855, the impoverished Marx, now a resident of England, wrote to his friend and benefactor Friedrich Engels: "had it been a male the matter would be more acceptable"—a boy would have cost less to support. Kapp appropriately emphasizes that Marx compounded this burden through his bourgeois sensibilities. For regardless of his poverty and revolutionary ideas, he considered himself of the professional class; and with three daughters to raise with his long-suffering wife (four other children died), Marx believed, as he told Engels, that "certain appearances must be maintained for the children's sake" to provide the "connections and relations which can secure them a future." In other words, Marx concluded, "a pure proletarian arrangement would be unsuitable here." He even confessed to Engels that he would be better off, "if only I could start a business." Karl Marx as capitalist entrepreneur? That would have changed the course of history.

Marx also displayed the Victorian middle-class sentimentality toward children. Although Tussy's childhood was, for Marx, a time of grinding poverty, illness, and the laborious writing of *Capital*, he spent long hours affectionately reading or telling stories to his daughters—often giving the tales a Marxist twist. And Tussy remembered her childhood warmly, happily recalling her father's devotion to her in his pronouncement: "Tussy is me."

This intimacy was heartwarming. But it posed to Eleanor, as it did to many other bourgeois children, the quandary of ambivalent dependency. Eleanor later hinted at this ambivalence in a letter to her friend Olive Schreiner: "If you had ever been in our home, if you had ever seen my father and mother, known what he was to me, you would understand better both my yearning for love, given and received, and my intense need for sympathy." This yearning substantially molded her life, leading her to fervently embrace the causes of the working class and the Jews, as well as to enter the destructive union with the deceptively sympathetic Aveling.

But with that yearning went a desire, shared by a growing number of females of her generation, to free herself from economic and emotional dependency on the bourgeois home (which generally refused girls permission even to hold jobs). "It is time," she said, "that women too may be able to work, and have other occupations than dress." That is, to become what would be known as the New Woman. But Eleanor found the careers open to women to be few, e.g., teaching, hack research, acting, and that novelty of the time, typing. She tried them all, beginning at age eighteen. But her true dream was to live, as Jenny wrote in encouragement, "the only free life a woman can live—the artistic one."

This was not easy to do either. For, besides talent, it required loosening ties to those who expected more of her, notably her fiancé during her early twenties, the revolutionary Prosper-Olivier Lissagaray, and especially her father, from whom she had learned the socialist creed and who was certain to condemn her individualism—despite having also nurtured a measure of that in her along with other bourgeois sensibilities. "How I love him," she wrote of Marx during this time of deep "mental worry," "no one can know—and yet—we must each of us, after all, live our own life. The chance of independence is very sweet." She would abandon fantasies of an acting career at the advice of her teacher, but the theater remained an abiding love and introduced her to a literature that bolstered her identity as a woman and led her toward both socialists and radical individualists who attacked bourgeois conventions. This literature was, above all, the modern drama of Henrik Ibsen.

Eleanor's discovery of Ibsen coincided with lasting changes in the circumstances of her life. Within thirty-nine months she lost her eldest sister, her mother, and her father, and established a household with Aveling, with whom she became known to Engels as the "zealous Ibsenites." Aveling had entered the Marxist circle from secularism, bringing the dogmas of Darwinist science and free thought with him. He had then propagandized the kinship of Marx and Darwin while dabbling in literature and living for his own pleasure. He was the kind of man, said Shaw, who "would have gone to the gallows sooner than recant a syllable" of his convictions, "but he had absolutely no conscience about money or women" (an attitude toward women, it can be said, not uncommon among self-righteous socialist males of the time). Engels, ever the guardian of the Marx family, was more charitable, saying, "I still remember the time I was just such a noodle." And Kapp, who invariably sides with Engels and Eleanor, adds that even with the harm Aveling did her, "from the time her life was joined with his, it became purposeful. She does not doubt where she is going, she goes." Until the end.

With Aveling, Eleanor began promoting the "great teaching" of Ibsen through amateur performances and her own translations. The first recognized reading of *A Doll's House* in England occurred at her invitation, featuring herself as Nora, Aveling as Helmer, and Shaw as Krogstad. She also completed the first English translation of Flaubert's *Madame Bovary*, the story of a heroine, like Nora in *A Doll's House*, with whom she had much in common: "This strong woman," she wrote of Emma Bovary in her introduction, "feels there must be some place for her in the world: there must be something to do—and she dreams."

Unlike Emma, Eleanor was not merely a bourgeois dreamer (the first Marx to live without a maid, she cursed "the fiend that invented housekeeping"). For, besides advancing literature hostile to bourgeois conventions, she and Aveling carried forward her father's work. They labored with Engels over Marx's manuscripts and translated volume one of *Capital*; they took a leading part in Hyndman's Social Democratic Federation, then left it along with William Morris to found the Socialist League; they wrote pamphlets arguing the socialist cause and explaining the oppression of women as another form of economic exploitation; they addressed socialist organizations in the United States during the decisive, strike-ridden year 1886 that gave explosive birth to the American labor movement; they participated in founding the Second International, with Eleanor translating for the often warring parties; Eleanor became an executive of the historic Gas-Workers Union; she was virtually alone among socialist propagandists to enter the ranks of manual workers herself, which she did as a "typewriter" (the name given to operators of the typing machine that appeared commercially in the 1870s); and she was the first to propose a union for typewriting secretaries in a pamphlet, which generations of young women to follow could applaud, on "Sweating in Type-Writing Offices."

III. On Modernity and Modernism

Eleanor's union activities were particularly notable for both English Marxism and the English working-class movement. For in Eleanor Marx, Marxism passed from socialist theory to working-class organization (neither Hyndman nor Morris showed an interest in unions). And the first unions to act on this legacy were the New Unions of *unskilled* workers, most prominently the Gas-Workers Union, the leader in winning the eight-hour day on a large scale and, in E. J. Hobsbawm's words, "the nearest thing to a 'red' body conceivable before the foundation of Communist parties." Amid the Gas-Workers' strike of 1889, Eleanor became the most vocal and beloved sponsor, "speaking every day," she said, "often twice a day in all weather in the open air." These actions made her, so Hobsbawm says, "the most prominent woman socialist militant of her time" (excepting the "brief trajectory through socialism" of Annie Besant).

With all of this activity and achievement, how could Eleanor's life have lost meaning? Kapp provides an answer, but it ignores the cultural significance of Eleanor's mentality, which holds so much of her historical significance. The decline began, Kapp observes, with Eleanor's fears for the Marx manuscripts held by the aging Engels, who showed unrestrained trust in his non-Marxist caretakers. These fears proved unfounded, but they weakened her familial bond with Engels. And after he died in 1895, Eleanor (with Aveling, Eduard Bernstein, and Frederick Lessner) scattered Engels's ashes on the sea knowing the secure life of her past was unrecoverable.

The discontinuity at this time went deeper than personal loss. For Eleanor had left the executive role of the Gas-Workers upon moving outside London and, more consequential, she felt a shift in the winds of socialism away from her father's theories. In the very month of her suicide she wrote plaintively to the still orthodox Marxist, Karl Kautsky, decrying the revisionism of her friend and coexecutor of Marx's manuscripts, Eduard Bernstein. She saw Bernstein drifting toward bourgeois relativism and capitalist apologetics that would strip socialism of its force and virtue and, worst of all, would convince people that "'Marx *must* be played out.'" Hence, Bernstein's ideological defection from Marxist orthodoxy further diminished her confidence in the future, prompting her to implore Kautsky: "Make Ede our old Ede again."

Eleanor here witnessed not only the slipping of Marx's authority among a younger generation of socialists, but the widening retreat from Marxism of what E. P. Thompson would call its "moral self-consciousness or even vocabulary of desire." As Kapp says, Marxism now set foot on the road to becoming a game "played at universities without the smallest application to the life of the people"—even the militant union movement that Eleanor had championed so zealously would become distinctly moderate, stirring Lenin's derision of its comfortable "trade union consciousness." But, as Lenin's words implied, the union movement was almost by nature an alternative to revolution as a strategy for uplifting the working class. Consequently, we might say that Eleanor's promotion of that movement helped plant seeds of a future working class that would see no need for Marxist revolution.

We could also say that Eleanor had exposed the tensions within Marxism of materialist science, political strategy, and moral vision. Kapp remarks that Eleanor "as a genuine Marxist," supported any group exhibiting an "instinctive urge toward socialism." Which is to say that, notwithstanding Marx's scientific determinism, Eleanor lived Marxism as fundamentally a moral vision only loosely allied to science. For her, Marx was always primarily the socialistic moralist whose image became her conscience: "I shall never be good and unselfish as he was," she admitted; "I am not good—and never shall be, though I try." This sensibility reflected Eleanor's bourgeois Victorian moral earnestness and her affinities with the romantic socialism of Morris, whose reply to Engel's dismissal of him as a "sentimental socialist" she might have echoed: "I am a sentimentalist in all the affairs of life, and I am proud of the title." She might have echoed it, that is, if her moral earnestness and guilty

Marxist conscience had not shadowed her through her father's ideals.

These qualities of Eleanor's character bear on another very consequential one. Just as Eleanor shared in the spirit of Victorian moralism and romantic socialism, she displayed the rise among her generation of a new temper marked by an inclination to subjectivity, a tendency to intuition, and an opposition to deterministic materialism. This temper distanced her from the materialistic science of both Marx and Aveling and placed her alongside Bernstein's revisionism (despite her criticism of it) and amid the cultural revolution that brought modernist art and ideas. Not for nothing had she been drawn to *A Doll's House* and championed Ibsen. Eleanor was as much fledgling modernist as congenital Marxist and Victorian sentimentalist. That temper, with its ambivalences, also abetted Aveling's destructive emotional hold on her.

Kapp reasonably concludes that Eleanor killed herself because she had lost the two animating forces in her life: love and work. But more than that, Eleanor Marx had lost her love and work in the passage from bourgeois Victorianism and revolutionary socialism to feminist independence and adventurous Modernism, a passage she could not, after all, wholly complete, leaving her something of a New Woman manqué. In the end, tormented by broken dreams more exalted than those of the ill-fated Emma Bovary, whose story she had put into English, the daughter of Karl Marx, socialist, idealist, laborer, lover, sentimentalist, conflicted woman in *fin-de-siècle* England, proved to be more Emma than Nora: turning her dejection against herself, she could not just walk out the door.

A previous version of this essay appeared in *The Nation*, December, 31, 1977, as a review-essay of *Eleanor Marx* by Yvonne Kapp, volumes one and two.

Freud's consulting room, with couch against the wall and funerary objects on chest in left foreground (photo by Edmund Englmlan).

"*A little world of happiness, of silent friends and emblems of our honorable humanity, to pass our life in calm happiness for ourselves and earnest work for mankind.*"
—FREUD, LETTER, 1882

Sigmund Freud

BOURGEOIS MODERNIST

Freud "is no more a person now," wrote W. H. Auden in a poem commemorating Freud's death in 1939, "but a whole climate of opinion." Yet Freud would be the first to doubt that all who invoke his name have a common understanding of his ideas. For Freud knew that every patient, every curious person, every national culture would encounter those ideas differently, under the sway of diverse defenses against psychological truth. These diverse encounters have given rise to contrasting interpretations of Freud himself as well. One, shared by many historians and nearly all post-Freudian theorists and therapists, views Freud's ideas as creations of turn-of-twentieth-century Vienna and deems them largely unsuited to life in the late twentieth century and after. Another, espoused by the dwindling number of more orthodox Freudians, holds Freud's theories to be true irrespective of their historic origins or direct therapeutic efficacy. We know where Freud would stand. Here we will look briefly at a few books that shed light on Freud's path from his life in Vienna to becoming "a whole climate of opinion."

Alessandra Comini's *The Fantastic Art of Vienna*, like her excellent previous studies of the modernist painters Gustav Klimt and Egon Schiele, explores the strange and self-conscious art that expressed the peculiar Viennese psyche before World War I. But this time Comini goes behind Modernism into the tradition upon which the Viennese modernists drew and which continued through them. "Long before the Viennese dreamt the dreams" interpreted by

Freud, she begins, Vienna was known as the "City of Dreams." And these dreams, even when tinged with laughter, betrayed visions of death and an angst-ridden existential uncertainty incited in part by Vienna's vulnerable place at the crossroads of armies and as the fragile seat of a more fragile empire. From the sixteenth century onward—as Comini shows in a few dozen well-chosen illustrations and a thoughtful, erudite narrative—Viennese art has dealt in escapist fantasies and grotesque imaginings of nature and the self. But at no time did it do so more obsessively and momentously than in the years from the late nineteenth century into the early twentieth.

It is no coincidence that these years also saw the birth of psychoanalysis. In Freud's day the City of Dreams was the decaying heart of Central Europe, its waning Biedermeier propriety yielding to an overripe aestheticism and a rising fascination with eros and psychic aberration. It was the capital city of perverse wishes, morbid anxiety, explosive repression, and a panorama of pathologies, where appearance and reality danced wildly together but never married. That showed up in many places and produced many curiosities, as historians like Carl Schorske and William M. Johnston have detailed. And, as Comini's pages demonstrate, the eerily lush and erotic paintings of Gustav Klimt, the threatening expressionism of Oskar Kokoschka's images, and the deranged, exhibitionistic self-portraits of Egon Schiele could be case studies.

How appropriate that here Freud discovered that psychic disturbances arise not from real but imagined traumas, and that neurotic symptoms are fantastic substitute gratifications of denied desires. And how fitting that here, in the wild dance of fantasy and life, even medicine fell under the spell of aestheticism, giving rise to the doctor of artistic aspirations and tastes, the *Künstlerärzt*. For the *Künstlerärzt* bridges the occupation with pathology that stretched from science to art and life.

Freud may be numbered among those *Künstlerärzt*, for although he derided modernist painters as trivially exhibitionistic, he assiduously collected primitive art (akin to the artifacts that inspired

19. Sigmund Freud

many modernists), with which he cluttered his office and consulting room. He also wrote a fine, quietly elegant prose (for which he was awarded the distinguished Goethe Prize) sprinkled with literary allusions. And he confessed a greater interest in the mysteries of the psyche than in the cure of disease: "I have become a therapist against my will," he wrote to Wilhelm Fliess, because, as he said elsewhere, "the chief aim of psychoanalysis" is not to cure disease but "to contribute to the science of psychology and to the world of literature and life in general."

Yet, Viennese *Künstlerärzt* that he might have been, Freud denounced as "quite exceptionally stupid" the idea that psychoanalysis was simply a Viennese creation. He contended that, whatever its origins, psychoanalysis was a theory of human nature itself. And because he thought this theory threatened the very sinews of established culture, this culture would fiercely resist it. "Precisely for this reason," he concluded in a combative mood, "where the greatest resistance has been displayed must be the scene of the final decisive battle for psychoanalysis."

In the 1970s, Freud's son Ernst painstakingly assembled a collection of pictures, documents, and excerpts from his father's works and letters that traces Freud's life into his efforts to win that battle. Subtitled *A Life in Pictures and Words*, this hefty and informative documentary biography discloses, for example, how Freud, from childhood on, viewed himself as an embattled outsider—which, as a Jew, he was—who welcomed intellectual conflict. Resenting his own father's timid response to anti-Semitic harassments, he took as his earliest hero the Semitic conqueror Hannibal, who, he said, "symbolized the tenacity of Jewry." Later he told his fiancée, in one of many love letters to her, that for him life meant "risking a lot, hoping a lot, working a lot. To average bourgeois common sense I have been lost long ago"—although not lost, as his letters and domestic surroundings make evident, to the comforts and contentments of bourgeois life (pictured more in the Engelman book below). And at the dawn of his fame, he called himself, in a moving phrase oddly missing from this collection, "not an experimenter, not a thinker . . . but an adventurer . . . a conquistador."

Many of Freud's words in the book reflect the hopes and challenges of establishing psychoanalysis as an authoritative, scientific doctrine and method of understanding human beings. Freud promotes and protects his ideas like a proud father or demanding religious leader, insisting upon orthodoxy, creating the International Psychoanalytical Association, warmly embracing devoted followers and sternly rebuking revisionists, even excommunicating heretics for "replacing psychoanalysis." Freud was indeed both an intellectual adventurer and a fervent believer in the truth of his revolutionary ideas—the American psychologist William James remarked after meeting him that Freud struck him as "a man obsessed with fixed ideas," although James also conceded that some of those ideas "can't fail to throw light on human nature." But Freud was also, perhaps in spite of himself, a man of bourgeois sensibilities that he turned to advantage in psychoanalysis.

We can see these bourgeois characteristics in another book of photographs. This one focuses solely on Freud's home and workrooms. And it is enlightening.

When Freud fled Vienna for London in June 1938, he left to the Nazis the residence and consulting room he had occupied at Berggasse 19 for forty-seven years. Here psychoanalysis had its agonizing birth and grew into the preeminent twentieth century theory of human nature and therapy for ministering to psychic wounds. The historic importance of the place prompted one of Freud's associates, August Aichhorn, to "make an exact record" of the rooms shortly before Freud departed so a museum could be created there "when the storm of the years is over"—something not begun until 1969.

For three tense days, Aichhorn's young friend, Edmund Engelman, snapped pictures outside and inside, avoiding the frail and disquieted Freud and denying himself flash and floodlights for fear of provoking the suspicious Nazis who constantly watched the house. When Freud happened upon him, the tension eased a little, and the old "conquistador" even posed for some somber and affecting portraits.

Confined as Engelman was to the normal light of the rooms and to physical arrangements he could not disturb, the pictures display little evidence of a photographer stage-managing shadows, angles, composition, reflections, haze, or even, in some instances, focus. But since he wanted to present "things the way Freud saw them," the restrictions did not defeat his intentions. The result, with the exception of some artful views of Freud's antiquities, is an assembly of ingenuous photographs suited to a family album. But it is also much more than that.

The album contains helpful scholarly notes identifying the objects in each picture and relating them to Freud's life and ideas. It also includes a brief memoir by Engelman recalling the photographic experience and Freud's gentle manner at the end of his Viennese career, just a year before his death in London. And there is a lucid and informative introduction by the historian Peter Gay remarking the interplay of Freud's character, thought, and culture—Gay would later write an authoritative biography of Freud subtitled *A Life for Our Times* and a magisterial five-volume study of Western culture in the nineteenth century with a distinctly Freudian slant: *The Bourgeois Experience: Victoria to Freud*.

But the pictures tell the story to remember. That concerns a bourgeois gentleman who in 1882 had promised his future wife to provide her "a little world of happiness, of silent friends and emblems of our honorable humanity" where they could "pass our life in calm happiness for ourselves and earnest work for mankind." That was a nineteenth-century bourgeois dream for sure. Freud fulfilled this promise with a home and work space that exuded coziness, comfort, and tranquility. This environment might seem at odds with the radical ideas Freud formulated there, but the paradox is not baffling. For, as Peter Gay observes, who but a traditional bourgeois sensitive to rigid emotional restraints would know the force of such restraints and the power of their psychological enemies?

Engelman's photos equally suggest a contrary relation of bourgeois domesticity to psychoanalysis. In an environment where flesh and feelings could relax amid the comforts of physical warmth, familiar faces, and beloved objects, emotions could rise to the surface and seek satisfactions denied them elsewhere. These satisfactions dot the pages of memoirs and fiction of the time—e.g., Walter Benjamin's *Berlin Childhood around 1900* and Hermann Hesse's *Demian*. But since all feelings are not pleasing, this same environment could engender conflict, for it was, as one historian dubbed it, a place of "explosive intimacy." Nineteenth-century bourgeois manners and morals may have demanded public restraint, but the bourgeois home, for good and ill, breathed private release—even while it was also the forge of the very restraints that sought release.

At Berggasse 19, the domestic rooms (of these Engelman photographed only the dining room, the family sitting room, and the sitting room of Freud's sister-in-law) and the consulting room of Freud's daughter Anna displayed conventional comforts touched by feminine refinement with graceful furniture, cheerfully patterned fabrics, and delicate objects. But Freud's own workrooms were more than conventionally comfortable. They were womb-like, especially the consulting room, which physically suggested its purpose as a laboratory of the unrepressed. Carpets lay upon carpets, carpets covered tables, a carpet hung on the wall adjacent to the consulting couch, which lay beneath another carpet, blankets, and cushions. At one end of the couch, where the patient's feet would rest, stood a tile stove equipped with water pipes to supply warmth and moisture. At the head of the couch, occupying the corner of the room and all but hidden under a mountain of pillows, stood the large easy chair where Freud sat to listen—and to analyze.

Along the walls of both the consulting room and the study next door rose bookcases here and there adorned with pictures of people and mythical scenes. And there were antiquities—mainly funerary objects and mythological sculptures from Egypt, Cyprus, Greece, and Italy—everywhere: on tables, in separate cases, atop bookshelves, in front of books. Freud's desk alone held some twenty statues that faced him as he wrote (in an arrangement later exactly reconstructed at Freud's London home, where he had transported all of his possessions possible, including his consulting couch, and which is now a museum).

It seems incongruous at first that no modern art appears in the collection of this quintessentially modern thinker, since artists of his day, none more than in Vienna, were known for expressing unsettled states of mind and emotion. But Freud had only disdain for abstract and expressionistic painting and sculpture, frequently deriding its creators as self-indulgent and affected. This taste further confirms the kinship of Freud's bourgeois way of life to his psychological revolution: Freud sought to understand the psyche by plumbing its depths and to resolve psychological conflicts by liberating authentic feelings (even if born of fantasy), not just to sanction what he judged to be unserious self-dramatization.

Hence Freud's antiquities belonged to his "earnest work." As Gay says, they symbolized Freud's identification with the archaeologist who penetrates layers of the past to unearth hidden realities. But they also illustrated his theories of dreams and the unconscious and an instinctual life beneath the dense manners, restraints, and self-deceptions of modern society. In combination with the enclosed, insistently womb-like rooms that they bedecked, these artifacts therefore represented an emotional freedom Freud idealized as a form of health: "the simplicity of a life free from the almost unbelievable conflicts of civilization, the beauty of an existence almost complete in itself" (words he wrote of animals in 1936).

Nothing in Engelman's photographs is more remarkable than this alliance of bourgeois comfort, mythological and funerary artifacts, and psychoanalysis. For these pictures show that Freud penetrated bourgeois resistances as an archaeologist of the mind to find and liberate repressed emotions with the aid of bourgeois domestic coziness.

Now a few words about the career of psychoanalysis outside the world of Freud's Vienna and the bourgeois life that Freud lived there.

It has become a commonplace of intellectual history to observe that, of all Western societies, America and France responded to psychoanalysis in the most strikingly different ways. The Americans, who, as Freud said, lacked "any deep-rooted scientific tradition" or "stringent rule of official authority" opposed to new ideas, readily welcomed many of Freud's insights and methods. From his visit to America in 1909 at the invitation of the psychologist/president of Clark University, G. Stanley Hall, where he presented lectures later published as *The Origins and Development of Psychoanalysis*, Freud would exercise widening influence, becoming, as W. H. Auden said, "a whole climate of opinion," at least in this country.

American culture, open as it has been to possibilities and differing ways of life, had no rooted reason to resist psychoanalysis as a theory of human nature. But at the same time, American openness seems to have afflicted people with frustrated desires and induced them to seek therapeutic remedies for every discontent. After all, according to the American dream and the cult of individualism, everyone can become anything and be happy. It is just up to everyone to do it for themselves, with no one else to blame for failure. Hence, self-doubt and guilt could come easily to Americans for not measuring up to the expectations inculcated in the individual by family and society. Small wonder that psychoanalysis and other therapies found fertile ground here. In fact, so readily did Americans take to psychoanalysis that Freud doubted they had understood him. And, as he might have predicted, they soon fashioned from his ideas many heresies and un-Freudian therapeutic ideologies revolving more or less around an optimistic Horatio Alger myth of the aspiring ego. In time, the "triumph of the therapeutic," as the sociologist and sympathetic Freudian moralist Philip Rieff put it in the title of a critical book on the subject, America would become a therapeutic culture wherein having a therapist became almost as common as having a dentist, and psychological self-help books would drive many other titles from bookstore shelves. Freud could have lamented all of this with the cautionary words he offered to patients (in paraphrase): "Psychoanalysis will not make you happy; it will only turn neurotic unhappiness into ordinary unhappiness." Politically radical followers like Herbert Marcuse would chastise Americans for refusing to accept that caution in their capitalist quest for a "happy consciousness," which winds up enslaving them to an unsatisfactory life that demands therapy.

By contrast to the singularly receptive, if often misguided, American response to psychoanalysis, the response in France was chilly (elsewhere it was merely tepid). Freud himself remarked that France showed itself to be "the least disposed to welcome psychoanalysis" of any Western country. We might point to several characteristics of French culture that could account for that, such as the deep-seated tradition of rationalism going back to Descartes, the centralization of cultural authority, and an intense pride in French culture itself coupled with zealous efforts to shield that culture from corrupting foreign influences. The sociologist Sherry Turkle duly notes such characteristics in a book entitled *Psychoanalytic Politics: Freud's French Revolution*, remarking that they rendered the French "not ready for psychoanalysis"—until much later.

But even while French culture was poised to resist psychoanalysis, it became home to many of the most artistically radical and psychologically daring creations of Modernism. In fact, strong winds of modernist art and ideas had been lashing against the bulwarks of established culture in France since Baudelaire and Flaubert. For instance, in the year after Freud and Josef Breuer published their pioneering *Studies in Hysteria* (1895), Alfred Jarry sent *Ubu Roi* onto the French stage crying *"Merdre"* (an expletive heard for the first time on any stage, and pronounced with emphasis) at a shocked audience and then zanily acted out unconstrained instincts. And soon after Freud's *Interpretation of Dreams* appeared in 1900, André Gide published *The Immoralist*, a tale of primitive energies and uninhibited willfulness directed explicitly against the repressive bonds of accepted culture and morality. Around the same time, inspired in part by the forms and authenticity of primitive artworks, Picasso invented Cubism in Paris, unleashing the painterly imagination and flummoxing conventional expectations of what painting should be (an artistic rebellion that erupted almost simultaneously elsewhere too, notably Vienna and Munich). World War I then brought the bizarre irrationalism of Dadaism, followed by surrealism, which—substantially inspired by Freud—transformed the subconscious reality of dreams into a "super-reality" of mysterious images and spontaneous expression.

Nor was exploration of the tensions between human irrationality and culture confined in France to the arts. As Freud was plumbing those tensions in Vienna, the groundbreaking sociologist Émile Durkheim detected a spreading opposition to moral constraints throughout modern society. And he saw this opposition rooted in the clash of a restless individualism with the power of society. He regarded that power to be necessary while nonetheless recognizing its costs—what Freud would describe as "civilization and its discontents." The doyen of American sociologists, Talcott Parsons, would conclude that "the convergence of the fundamental insights of Freud and Durkheim" was a "massive phenomenon," yielding insights into the unconscious agency of society's power and punishment, which Freud called the *superego*.

In all, notwithstanding its venerable cultural traditions, France hosted adventurous ideas and innovative Modernism early and yet granted Freud only the surrealists' *coup de chapeau* for his theory of dreams. If there is a mystery in that, some light is shed on it by how French culture moved on from the 1920s into a more uncertain, inward, and insular course of philosophical ruminations and intellectual fashions and celebrities—as the historian H. Stuart Hughes detailed in *The Obstructed Path: French Social Thought in the Years of Desperation, 1930–1960* (1968). Probably the most important of these intellectual celebrities was Jean-Paul Sartre. The theory of human existence he devised in existentialism explicitly rejected Freud (or what Sartre knew of him, which seems not to have be a lot) because existentialism posited a kind of inviolable freedom that denied the very influence of the unconscious, or at any rate its irresistible effect on the act of choice. Where existentialism went, Freud could not follow. Or not a Freud that Freud would recognize. That would also prove true of the French thinker who proclaimed a "return to Freud," Jacques Lacan.

Sherry Turkle is convinced that Lacan did indeed bring psychoanalysis to France for real, if in his own style. And no doubt Lacan thought he was doing that. But a glance at Lacan's career shows as much of France in his version of psychoanalysis as there was of America in the response to psychoanalysis here.

In the first place, Lacan came to psychoanalysis not from a careful reading of Freud's works but from the modernist movement itself in Paris. He fraternized with avant-garde painters and writers, particularly the surrealists, among whom he discovered Freud as an ingenious interpreter of words and dreams. (Incidentally, Sartre, five years younger than Lacan, had also started out as an acolyte of surrealism.) Over time, he studied Freud more closely but derived from him a kind of poetic psychoanalysis steeped in the mysteries of language, contemptuous of tradition, hostile to authority, celebrating desires, and yielding a revolutionary form of self-knowledge. These ideas won him intellectual prominence in France and made him the psychological godfather of the upheavals in Paris of 1968. Under the slogan, "I take my desires for my realities, because I believe in the reality of my desires," those revolutionary Parisian events amounted to, Turkle says, a "projection of Lacanian theory into the social field" as a "revolution of speech and desire."

Yet Lacan's psychoanalytic theories were so typically French (as was his intellectual celebrity)—wrapped as they are in the elusive metaphors and metaphysics of the French language with the motto "the unconscious is structured like a language"—that they must remain for the most part foreign to Americans, much less to any genuine Freudian.

Psychoanalysis might at last have found a home in France, but Freud would not recognize there a triumph of his ideas. For no less than the Americans, the French had found a Freud to their liking, and of their own making. With that happy discovery, sanctioning the liberation of desire, rhapsodizing over language, and theorizing by metaphor (to say nothing of the subsequently fashionable and openly anti-Freudian theories of Gilles Deleuze and Félix Guattari in the two-volume *Capitalism and Schizophrenia* [1972, 1980]), the French further continued their resistance to the sharply observing, searchingly analytical, and cautiously humanistic Freud of early twentieth-century Vienna.

In the end, while Freud might have become "a whole climate of opinion" in the twentieth century, it was not a climate that the earnest Viennese bourgeois thinker could have found very comfortable to live in.

This essay combines revised versions of two review-essays. The first published in *The New Republic*, September 13, 1976: "*Berggasse 19: Sigmund Freud's Home and Offices, Vienna 1938*," photographs by Edmund Engelman. The second published under the title "Freud French-fried" in *The American Scholar*, Fall, 1979: *The Fantastic Art of Vienna*, Alessandra Comini; *Sigmund Freud: His Life in Pictures and Words*, ed. Ernst Freud, trans. Christine Trollope; *Psychoanalytic Politics: Freud's French Revolution*, Sherry Turkle.

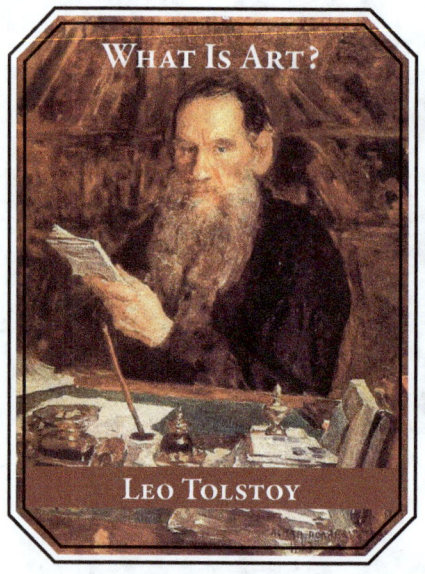 

"*Art is not a pleasure, a solace, an amusement, art is a great matter.*"
—TOLSTOY

"*After I did the thing called 'art' or whatever it's called, I went into 'business art.*'"
—ANDY WARHOL

"*Nothing is more true as art than anything else.*"
—ARTHUR DANTO

Tolstoy's fin de siècle and Ours
FROM DECADENCE TO POSTMODERNISM

As the nineteenth century was packing its bags in 1898, Leo Tolstoy published the most incendiary book ever written on one of the nineteenth century's favorite subjects: art. Approaching his seventieth birthday, Tolstoy distilled in *What Is Art?* the moralistic bile that had been rising in him for two decades and spewed over virtually the entire culture of his times, especially the artistic culture. For he had come to believe that European civilization had gone terribly awry, its society wayward, its morals depraved, its cultural life corrupted, and that a principal cause of those evils lay in the misunderstanding and misuse of art. He set out to save this civilization from itself by awakening it to the errors of its ways and putting it on a healthy course. To do that he prescribed some pretty eccentric remedies. These called for banishing virtually all that western civilization had come to understand and esteem as art, and all that goes with it, in favor of an earthier, emotionally honest, and religiously communal art and culture.

Not surprisingly, the book did not win Tolstoy many friends. George Bernard Shaw, for instance, jabbed that it reflected "the inevitable obsolescence of an old man's taste in art." More sharply, the poet Rainer Maria Rilke dismissed it as "a disgraceful and silly pamphlet." But Tolstoy brushed off the criticisms. After all, he was condemning much of western culture and expected resistance to his searing truths. That those "truths" were oddly singular could only juice the critics.

And yet, notwithstanding the eccentricities of *What Is Art?* and the hostile reactions it provoked, Tolstoy was far from alone in judging European culture of the late nineteenth century deeply troubled and needing help. An international chorus resounded throughout Tolstoy's *fin de siècle* with allegations of cultural decline and cries for rejuvenation. Assailing European culture at large, and its separate national cultures in particular, had in fact become *de rigueur* among artists and intellectuals. These critics included bohemian rebels who reveled in overturning every convention, along with exponents of "decadence" who cultivated bizarre sensibilities, as well as both liberals and conservatives who aimed to purge the gathering menaces and build a better modern order—cast in either progressive or traditional molds. Widespread in their discontents and fervent in their clamor for change, the rebels, decadents, liberals, and conservatives often sounded much the same alarm as they flogged each other and their most common enemies: the self-satisfaction, hypocrisy, materialism, mediocrity, and Philistinism of nineteenth-century bourgeois Europe. Look at some of Tolstoy's vociferous company.

The German Friedrich Nietzsche became the emblematic voice of this rage and its promise of regeneration, sending reverberations far beyond his homeland in the brilliant rhetoric of his aphoristic philosophical style. With heightening intensity through a stream of writings in the 1880s—including *The Gay Science* (1882), *Thus Spoke Zarathustra* (1882–83), *Beyond Good and Evil* (1886), and *On the Genealogy of Morals* (1887)—he excoriated Western culture as "a weak age" that had grown "'decadent" and "sick," typified by Richard Wagner's descent into vulgar theatricality, grotesque nationalism, and gooey Christian mythology. And he prescribed the bracing cure of a "Great Health," to be embodied by a new breed of "preparatory men" and "higher men" recognizing that "God is dead," willing to "live dangerously," and making the way for a new human type, the "Superman," whose courage and strength would "redeem the world."

Nietzsche's inspiriting bravado attracted a swelling international array of followers as diverse as the learned Danish critic Georg

20. Tolstoy's *fin de siècle* and Ours

Brandes, the loquacious Irish playwright George Bernard Shaw, and the flamboyant Italian poet Gabriele D'Annunzio, all answering his call to heroic exertions of will. Other Germans also weighed in with their own scorn for the misdirection of their newly formed nation and of modernity in general. Sometimes drawing on Nietzsche's power-mongering, often yearning for the soulful *gemeinschaftlich* communities of yesteryear, and readily attracted to racist theories of cultural renewal, they gravitated toward political remedies (including the leadership of a mythic *Führer*) for what the historian Fritz Stern denoted their "cultural despair." (Nietzsche's sister, Elisabeth, who cared for her mentally ill brother during his last decade until he died in 1900, was among the racist fanatics, zealously promoting a bastardized version of her brother's books and ideas that Nietzsche would have renounced as thoroughly as he despised her, but that the Nazis later promoted, just as they honored her.) In the same years, as historian Carl Schorske so richly illustrated, analogous eddies of cultural antipathy, racism, and redemptive politics also swirled in that brilliant, turbulent capital of the dying Austro-Hungarian Empire, *fin-de-siècle* Vienna. In France, growing legions of the artistic avant-garde had been battering the conventional culture and plowing a path toward the future since the mid-century. "The artist is truly of the avant-garde," professed an early spokesman, Gabriel-Désiré Laverdant in *De la Mission de l'art et du rôle des artistes* (1845), when art lays bare "all the brutalities, all the filth, at the base of our society" and "fulfills its proper mission" as "forerunner and revealer" of "the destiny of the human race." Reiterating that mission, Gustave Flaubert railed in a letter of 1854, "Our century is a whorish century," therefore "let us by all possible means stand in the way of the excrement [*merde*] that envelops us" and "enlist ourselves in the cause of the ideal"—and he got dragged into court for acting artistically to that end with his "immoral" novel *Madame Bovary* (1857). Trumpeting an equal distaste for conformity and a taste for vice, the poet Charles Baudelaire celebrated "The Heroism of Modern Life" (as he put it in *The Salon of 1846*) with an aesthetic idealism, ravenous sensuousness, and tormented psychology to which he gave shocking expression in *The Flowers of Evil* (1857).

Carrying this campaign forward, the poetic prodigy Arthur Rimbaud threw himself into the life of the "utterly damned," as he told friends, becoming the archetypal modern *poète maudit* with his bohemian antics, ostentatious social alienation, and a pained braggadocio epitomized in the proclamation of *A Season in Hell* (1873): "O damned ones, . . . it is necessary to be absolutely modern." Then, after Rimbaud, "decadence" became the fashion for many artists and art lovers, thanks in no small part to Joris-Karl Huysmans's novel *À rebours* (1884, loosely translated as *Against Nature*) lavishly portraying the dissolute aristocrat Des Esseintes, who lives solely for the luscious sensations of his archly eccentric tastes in a life of narcissistic aestheticism. With a similarly self-absorbed hauteur and self-indulgent passivity, Villiers de l'Isle-Adam had the hero of his wanly decadent drama *Axël* (1894) announce his plan for a life of newly discovered wealth with the withering dismissal: "Live? Our servants will do that for us."

Rejecting fashionable decadence as well as constraining conventions, some French artists accented their cultural estrangement by searching abroad for new lives and inspiration or escape. Rimbaud himself abandoned poetry permanently for adventures and an obscure end in Africa; the painter Paul Gauguin sailed to the South Seas for primitive freedom and native stimulation; and the young novelist André Gide made lengthy sojourns to North Africa and drew on these, along with his reading of Nietzsche, to launch a literary career with works like *Les nourritures terrestres* (1897, translated as *Fruits of the Earth*) and *The Immoralist* (1902), challenging traditional moral and aesthetic restraints. And embodying the whole epidemic of contempt for complacent French culture, Alfred Jarry ignited a notorious scandal with his grotesquely nihilistic play *Ubu Roi* (1896), starting with its inflammatory opening line: *Merdre!* (Psshhiittt). So consuming in its brash deracination from tradition was the cultural rebellion in France that a historian could later describe its gathering tide as less a typical episode in cultural change than a seismic "crisis of humanism" (the title of a two-volume study subtitled "The conflict of the individual and society in modern French Literature," by Micheline Tison-Braun [1958, 1968]), undoing the very premises of humanistic civilization.

In England, *fin-de-siècle* cultural agitation became a lighter affair, visually exemplified by the voluptuous art nouveau illustrations of Aubrey Beardsley that bedecked the stylishly decadent magazine *The Yellow Book* as well as the pages of Oscar Wilde's scandalous *Solomé*. Oscar Wilde himself played the role of decadent dissident with aplomb in his dandified poses, irreverently droll wit, and creation of wicked aesthetes led by Dorian Gray (modeled on Huysmans's Des Esseintes) and Gray's amusing mentor Lord Henry. Wilde's insouciant manner ridiculed everything that Victorian culture esteemed under its stolid code of "respectability" and "earnestness," while exalting aesthetic pleasure as the highest good. Eventually, Wilde's insouciance got the better of him, and he went to jail for brazen homosexuality, having scoffed at one convention too many. A few outright weirdos, like the Satanist Aleister Crowley, added quirkier excesses, and the critic Arthur Symons informed readers in an essay of 1893, "The Decadent Movement in Literature," that the "representative literature of today" was "really a new and beautiful and interesting disease."

By the turn of the century, and the death of Queen Victoria in 1901, apprehensions of impending cultural peril were in the English air, prompting a popular pamphlet called *The Decline of the British Empire* (1905) and worrying General Baden-Powell enough that he established the Boy Scouts and Girl Guides to set things right, warning in *Scouting for Boys* (1908) against "the deterioration of our race," and opening his *Girl Guides* (1909) with the warning: "Decadence is threatening the nation."

In Italy, where the heroic age of the Risorgimento had brought a politically unified nation but left it locked in parliamentary paralysis, idealists lamented, in the words of the poet/critic Giosuè Carducci to an audience in 1886, "Oh radiant days, the freedom and glory of 1860.... What have we become?" Then the aesthete-cum-militarist Gabriele D'Annunzio tried to breathe vitality into his languishing country with Nietzschean effusions like those of his novel *The Innocent* (1892), whose hero asserts he is "superior to the mass of men" and therefore "above all morality." Before long, the Italian Futurists would demand an end to everything from the past—"We will destroy the museums, libraries, academies of every kind," F. T. Marinetti vowed in the *Futurist Manifesto* (1909). And to cap the crusade, Marinetti cried: "Take up your pickaxes ... and wreck, wreck the venerable cities"—especially Venice, since it reeked of history and decline.

Even in seemingly remote Iberian Spain, an accumulating impression of cultural enervation became acute with the loss of the vestigial Spanish empire during the Spanish-American war, persuading intellectuals like the philosopher Miguel de Unamuno that modern Spain had no spine and must be reconstructed. Appeals for national revival—made in philosophy, politics, and the arts—earned these disparate agitators the epithet "the Generation of '98," which supplied the banner for an energized, disciplined Spanish culture carried well into the twentieth century.

Throughout Western Europe as the century turned, there coursed a sense of cultural malaise accompanied by a summons to radical change—complete with the medical rhetoric of "sickness," "disease," and "cure." And this sorry condition fostered a conviction that the best prospects for the "Great Health" might lie in nothing less than violence—enacted here and there by anarchist bomb-throwers, who were lauded, in the irreverent spirit of the times, by their poetic advocate Laurent Tailharde with the line: *Qu'importe les victimes, si le geste est beau?* ("What importance are the victims if the gesture is beautiful?"). That conviction fused with international political and economic competition and insecurity to feed an appetite for the invigorating bloodshed of war. Marinetti spoke not only for Italians but a for a whole European generation when he wrote in the *Futurist Manifesto:* "We will glorify war—the only true hygiene of the world." Amid this atmosphere, what became the desecration of World War I appeared at first like salvation. Even the popular and conventional English poet Rupert Brooke exulted in letters on his way to the front: "I've never been quite so happy in my life, I think. Not quite so pervasively happy. . . . Come and die. It'll be great fun." And he did die, along with the flower of his generation.

Meanwhile, in Tolstoy's Russia, voices of cultural regeneration, spiritual revival, and political reform had been rising through the century from Slavophiles, Nihilists, Populists, Marxists, and a variety of less ideological artist/critics like Alexander Herzen, Fyodor Dostoevsky, and Konstantin Leontiev. Leo Tolstoy had joined them after a religious crisis had awakened him to the depravities of modern civilization in Russia and the West, and he had fixed his vision on spiritual and cultural salvation through a Christian, peasant society. That enlightenment also led Tolstoy to *What Is Art?*, which crowned, without concluding, his labors as a cultural critic.

What Is Art? thus belongs to the panoply of nineteenth-century *fin-de-siècle* critiques of Western culture, diagnosing its ills, prescribing cures, and looking to the next century for renovating change. One of these other critiques has special relevance to *What Is Art?* That is the lengthy volume by the German physician/litterateur Max Nordau entitled *Entartung* (1893), *Degeneration* in English (1895). Nordau's book and *What Is Art?* stand together as probably the two most ambitious, sweeping, and outlandish indictments of the artistic and intellectual culture of late-nineteenth-century Europe. And they go after many of the same enemies. But Nordau includes Tolstoy among them.

Adapting a theory of the founding criminologist Cesare Lombroso, who had recently explained criminal behavior as a manifestation of the psycho-physiological degeneracy visible in certain physical traits, Nordau diagnosed the leading ideas and artistic styles of the late nineteenth century as symptoms of the same thing. Nordau called it *Entartung*, "degeneration," and defined it as a "severe mental epidemic" arising from "an exhausted central nervous system." And he discerned its root cause in the historical circumstances of modernity, namely: "the vertigo and whirl of our frenzied life, the vastly increased number of sense impressions," especially in large cities, and "the excessive organic wear and tear suffered by the nations through the immense demands on their activity" (among the same circumstances that the innovative American psychologist G. Stanley Hall associated with the rise of modern adolescence and its behavioral pathologies in his seminal study, *Adolescence* [1904], and, for that matter, the same kinds of things that William Wordsworth had blamed for the "savage torpor" of modern life in his preface to *Lyrical Ballads* a hundred year earlier). Nordau classed "Tolstoism" as a degenerate "mental aberration" exhibiting a "weakness and despondency" that "assumes the form of pessimism" and inclines to a "mysticism" closely akin to that of Symbolism and Wagnerism, two of Tolstoy's own chief villains.

Nordau wielded the kind of language, jeering the "insanity" and "lunacy" of modern art and ideas, that the Nazis would use to deride modern artworks in the remarkable *Entartete Kunst*, "Degenerate Art," exhibition of 1937. But Nordau was no proto-Nazi. Despite his now quaint biologism, his remedy for "degeneration" was not an idealized Germanic state or a *Führer* but the more liberal causes he had long championed (and which later took him to leadership positions in the Zionist movement), combating "antiquated superstitions," advancing "progress," and promoting "emancipation . . . of the judgment, not of the appetites." But he saw none of these virtues in the degenerate culture of his times—and roused George Bernard Shaw to a vigorous defense in "The Sanity of Art: An Exposure of the Current Nonsense about Artists Being Degenerate" (1895).

Tolstoy never mentions Max Nordau in *What Is Art?* But while he shared Nordau's disquiet over the ascending artistic culture, he would doubtless have dismissed Nordau's theory as pretentious nonsense. Tolstoy needed no psycho-physiological theory to account for the aberrations of the late nineteenth century. He found causes enough in the culture of art itself and in the history behind it.

That history had, he said, severed art—and with it culture at large—since the Renaissance from its legitimate social and religious purposes and unleashed it to drift into the elitism, sensuality, and aestheticism of "false art." Reducing art to supplying "artistic enjoyment" for its own sake, this "false art," he declared, gives that same false purpose to life, with far-reaching economic, social, and psychological effects. Beguiled by "artistic enjoyment," society expends vast resources on the production and dissemination of art and mobilizes "hundreds of thousands" of people to make art possible. This not only misuses economic and human energies, Tolstoy argued, it drives civilization into the ground. For instead of uniting human beings emotionally through their common humanity and brotherhood under God, as Tolstoy believed "true art" does, false art divides people by tastes and pleasures into cliques and claques, desiccating their souls and "stunting" their lives with its life-denying professional demands, its coarse sensuality, its numbing sensationalism, its baffling incomprehensibility, and its pompous intellectualism.

That is where Tolstoy found the art and culture of his times when he joined the plangent chorus of historical decline as the nineteenth century was fading into the dusk. But he did add a coda of hope. For he also wrote *What Is Art?* to restore art to its true purpose. And anticipating the emergence of a populist, global culture in the next century, he confidently predicted that false art would disappear with the elitist ideas and institutions that sustained it, and that a new "art of the future . . . completely distinct, both in subject matter and in form, from what is now called art" would prevail, ushering in a better world and the universal "brotherhood of man." Reading *What Is Art?*, we might wonder whether Tolstoy would find his hopes fulfilled or his fears confirmed in our *fin-de-siècle* times—and after.

Pursuing this curiosity, we can be pretty sure of one thing. Tolstoy would not have admired the career of the cultural movement whose origins he (like Max Nordau) had observed and bewailed and that came to be known as "Modernism." In fact, as Tolstoy was penning his diatribe against the secular artistic tradition that he saw petering out in modernist aestheticism, Modernism was just gaining steam. Over the next half century, Modernism would roll across Western culture, leaving little in the artistic life untouched. The avant-garde would pile novelty upon novelty, shock upon shock, belaboring conventions and assaulting the Philistines. This adversarial spirit, often seeming to turn its wrath on culture itself, would become so prevalent that, in the words of the distinguished critic Lionel Trilling, the "disenchantment with culture," and "hostility to civilization," would become hallmarks of Modernism ("On the Modern Element in Modern Literature," 1961).

That disenchantment and hostility took madcap form in the Dadaism spawned by World War I, deflating every traditional piety of art with an aesthetics of randomness—while nevertheless enhancing the stature of art as a mysterious and transcendent creation. Less anarchistic than the Dadaists, other modernists poured their fervor into exalting art's transcendence—to the detriment of art and humanity, Tolstoy would say. Inspired by aspirations to escape a tawdry world and revitalize human sensibilities, artworks in every genre grew more abstract, esoteric, and inaccessible to common perceptions. The many *isms* that marched under the modernist banner—Impressionism, Symbolism, Expressionism, Cubism, Futurism, Vorticism, Imagism, Dadaism, surrealism, and others—cluttered the artistic landscape and unmistakably removed art from the ordinary life. Then, propelled by a widening cult of the new and riding an accelerating cycle of change, the arcane styles of art became fads among the cognoscenti, the fads became fashions, and keeping up with those fashions became an emblem of elite cultural status. Art became very "interesting" indeed—a term Tolstoy debunked as modern jargon betraying trivial intellectualism and artistic lifelessness—for those emotionally numbed and baffled by it and those willing to explore modern art's mysteries as an intellectual exercise.

When Ortega y Gasset wrote his famed essay "The Dehumanization of Art" in 1925, Modernism was at high tide (although most of its leading innovations were past). Unlike Tolstoy, Ortega had not set out to scold Modernism. He simply wanted to understand why "modern art" was so "unpopular," and he had found the reason in the "explicit act of dehumanization" that banished human content from art. This "dehumanization" had made the "new art" not only unpopular but "antipopular," since "its impulses are not of a generically human kind" and therefore it "is not accessible to everyone." Consequently, "it divides the public into two groups: one very small, formed by those who are favorably inclined towards it; another very large—the hostile majority."

More than a generation after *What Is Art?*, Ortega here plainly confirmed Tolstoy's criticism of modern art, albeit without matching Tolstoy's outrage. And when, another generation later, the eloquent American atonal composer Milton Babbitt published a provocative defense of the inaccessibility of modern music under the editor's title "Who Cares If You Listen?" (1958), Tolstoy was again proven as correct about the intellectual elitism of much in Modernism as he had been wrong about Modernism's limited staying power. It surely would have come as no surprise to Tolstoy—nor should it have to anyone attuned to the career of Modernism—that toward the end of the twentieth century intellectuals like Jacques Derrida and Arthur Danto would proclaim that theories of art had eclipsed in significance the artworks themselves. Here was the crowing intellectualization of art, the antithesis of Tolstoy's "true art."

While the bravura career of Modernism after *What Is Art?* would have given Tolstoy no encouragement, the economic expansion of the artistic culture in general during the same time would have discouraged him no less. For, since Tolstoy's *fin de siècle*, the scale, character, and influence of the artistic culture have changed dramatically. Art, broadly defined, has become ubiquitous—through proliferating arts institutions, artworks sprouting in public places, a myriad of style magazines, the vogue of "good design," the adulation of performers, the omnipresence of entertainment, and much more—until we can safely say that in one form or another, art touches everyone in western society every day. Tolstoy would surely shake his head at how people have become, in his words, so "habituated" to "false art" and "perverted" by it that they are helpless to save themselves from it.

But if the career of Modernism and the expansion of the artistic culture in the twentieth century would obviously have bothered Tolstoy, certain trends that gained prominence in the later years of that century might actually have nourished his hopes—albeit only to dash them. Take three examples: the postmodern reaction against Modernism, the ascendancy of popular culture, and the birth of a truly global culture. Tolstoy optimistically anticipated something like all three.

Tolstoy predicted and would have applauded the reaction against the aesthetics of Modernism that by the 1980s had acquired a title of its own: Postmodernism. Running as an undercurrent to the tide of Modernism, resistance to modernist avant-gardism and the "dehumanization of art" started pulling back that tide like an undertow in the 1960s and 1970s. As critics and artists alike assessed the aesthetic and social consequences of Modernism, many of them found more to fault than to praise. For instance, after the urban historian Jane Jacobs exposed the follies of modernist cityscapes in *The Fall and Rise of Great American Cities* (1961) for placing "rational" planning and abstract form over the needs of human beings with dehumanizing housing projects and desolately empty office plazas, city managers began returning to the humane virtues of traditional, "unplanned" cities. Other architectural critics chimed in with manifestos like Robert Venturi's pathbreaking *Complexity and Contradiction in Architecture* (1966), Brent C. Brolin's bellicose *The Failure of Modern Architecture* (1976), and Tom Wolfe's *From Bauhaus to Our House* (1981), all discrediting the modernist aesthetics that, in the name of "honest" form (so prized by the Bauhaus), had converted office buildings and homes into dehumanizing concrete, glass, and steel monuments to abstract design.

Other critics and artists spread out from there, reproaching esoteric Modernism for ignoring everyone but the cognoscenti and depriving art of its human content, allure, and accessibility by, among other things, rejecting representation in painting, tonality in music, and narrative in literature. In a commonly heard complaint, Modernism had caused much of "high art" to "lose its audience," leaving the arena to the all too accessible vulgarities of popular art. And if high art did not win an audience again with renewed satisfactions of its own, the plaint continued, its world would get smaller and smaller and that of popular art larger and larger until nothing else remained. "We stand on the threshold of an epoch which has put Modernism behind it," announced the born-again postmodern composer George Rochberg in a hortatory essay, "The Marvelous in Art" (1982). "Whatever the art of this new epoch may be capable of," he went on, "we can ask nothing better of it than to reveal once again, in new ways and through new images, the realm of the marvelous"—that is, the realm of compelling aesthetic appeal.

In the 1980s, the passing of Modernism became increasingly familiar news. Seldom did a week go by without magazines and newspapers pronouncing Modernism dead and declaring the peculiar, amorphous creature of Postmodernism its heir (already recognizable to academics, like Ihab Hassan who had groped toward a definition of it in a much-cited article, "POSTmodernISM: A Paracritical Bibliography" [1971]). Headlines blared, to take a sampling from *The New York Times*: "The Postmodern Interior: A Collage of Times Gone By" (1980); "Postmodern Dance Favors Display in Lieu of Definition" (1981); "Modernism to Postmodernism:

A New World Once Again" (1982); "Postmodernists in the Mainstream" (1983); "The Promiscuous Cool of Postmodernism" (1986); "Hip-Deep in Postmodernism" (1988). And books poured from the presses covering the cultural waterfront from *The Postmodern Condition* (1979) and *Postmodern Fiction* (1986) to *Postmodern Law* (1990) and *Postmodern Sexualities* (1997)—at the turn of the century the New York Public Library listed nearly a thousand entries under the heading of Postmodernism. The temper of the times was indisputably changing. But did Postmodernism usher in the "art of the future" and with it the healthy culture that Tolstoy had envisioned?

Not really. For within the postmodernist artistic ideology, which sought to restore the historical, the human, and the accessible to art, came certain attitudes that Tolstoy would not have sanctioned at all. The rejection of Modernism's towering ambitions to transform the world through cultural rebellion, unsettling ideas, and imagination-stretching aesthetics also cast aside a large measure of the very seriousness of purpose that went with those ambitions. "There is a certain weightlessness in Postmodernism," concluded the critic Denis Donoghue in a survey of the subject for *The New York Times Book Review* in 1986, "that makes it possible for an artist to do anything that he chooses, but doesn't suggest that he should try for anything in particular: like a game without rules." In other words, whereas modernist dogma had enjoined artists to "Make It New" (in Ezra Pound's oft-quoted book title of 1934), the postmodern creed said, in effect, "Make It Anything!"

Spurning the modernists' moral and aesthetic pretensions (even Oscar Wilde had made an ethics of aestheticism), the postmodern artistic imagination went the other way. This brought a jaunty eclecticism and unapologetic ornamentation while displaying a disposition to irony at once sportive, cutting, and resigned. The eclecticism traded the vaunted aesthetic "honesty" of Modernism for novel combinations of stylistic elements plucked from history and other cultures, together with the brash shuffling of "high" and "low" art forms. Architecture juxtaposed imitative historical architectural features with modernist lines and even neon signs. Musical compositions freely mingled classical, modernist, non-Western, and pop/rock traditions. Paintings mixed representational and abstract images. Literature cooked up a cornucopia of arcane and pop art ingredients served in narrative and non-narrative forms.

A fondness for decorative and ornamental flourishes, also anathema to the modernists, went with the eclecticism. What used to be scorned as "dishonest" accretions of ornament inimical to authentic form (the architect Adolf Loos had boldly linked "ornament and crime" in an essay of that title in 1908) were used to give art more appeal. Buildings got decorative façades and features long denied them, sometimes attached like a mask to nondescript structures; music got lyrical passages to delight audiences; painting could be "pretty" and fun again; and literature could play games and toy with pop culture.

The eclecticism, ornamentation, and playfulness aimed to tease and please, eliciting smiling appreciation rather than moralistic judgment, and perhaps to provoke amusing questions about the metareality of art and life, asking: What is going on here? And these intentions could not fail to reflect, and likely induce, a penchant for irony. For these eclectic juxtapositions and even mismatches inevitably lent a sly ironic cast to postmodern aesthetics, undercutting the very seriousness of art. To experience that irony was to see art and its history and purposes with a new self-conscious understanding and a kind of cheekiness. That understanding and cheekiness could easily teach one not only to see art anew but to see how all of life has become eclectically entwined, especially with commercialism—and to think, so what? The influential French theorist Jean-François Lyotard described this entanglement when he wrote ruefully in "Answering the Question: What Is Postmodernism?"(1982) that "it is easy to find a public for eclectic works" today because "eclecticism is the degree zero of contemporary general culture" where "anything goes," under the aegis of "purchasing power." Few postmodern artists would disagree with Lyotard's observation, if not his tone. Postmodern irony (successor to the post-Romantic and -modernist irony of disillusioned illusions) is the irony of life in a self-consciously eclectic, not altogether serious, commercialized world.

Where many early modernists had blasted the vulgar commercial world head-on and fled from it into a transcendent aesthetic—or tried to transform it through that aesthetic—postmodernists were more ambivalent, ambiguous, and acquiescent. Because making peace with the undauntable capitalist marketplace had long since earned artistic respectability, and the rewards of that marketplace had grown too great to deny, irony became an appropriate strategy of art and life. The irony made it possible to poke fun at commercial culture, fault it, resist it, succumb to it, and enjoy it, all at the same time. As if "learning from Las Vegas" (the suggestive title of Robert Venturi's postmodern manual of 1972), architects pasted stylized façades on plain box buildings, demonstrating the preeminence of appearance over pure form and thumbing their noses at the canons of "honest" architecture. Painters portrayed imagery of buoyant commerce with artistic techniques muddling relations of art and life—brazenly exemplified by Andy Warhol. Writers traced fictional lives spurred by idealistic aspirations but suffused with consumer sensibilities and the cult of celebrity. Composers wrote music invoking the sounds of old favorites set to the turmoil of contemporary events. And intellectuals in all fields spun theories of how commerce and culture have become inseparably interwoven for good and ill, if one can tell the difference any more.

After a dose of this postmodern irony, it could be hard to greet anything in art or life as before—academicians even found it necessary to coin the vogue verb "to ironize" for postmodern ingenuities. Everything had become entangled with and compromised by everything else. How, then, could one take anything entirely seriously on its own? And therein lies the ultimate postmodern artistic attitude: not just irony but whimsical irony. In a world of irresistible commercialism and savvy ironic perceptions, what grounds exist for continuing the sobering artistic seriousness of the past? Art can aspire to little more than revealing the irony of life in a hodgepodge of cultural fashions and commercial forces that can at once lure and repel. This is an irony that openly invites us, in the title of David Foster Wallace's encyclopedic postmodern novel, to treat all art and life as *Infinite Jest* (1996).

In a nice historical symmetry, this postmodern inclination to whimsical irony recalls that of Oscar Wilde a century earlier. The postmodern artist gave a late-twentieth-century spin to Wilde's own ironic dictum that "the importance of being earnest" (as Wilde told an interviewer when his play of that name opened) is "to treat all trivial things of life very seriously, and all serious things of life with sincere and studied triviality." No one did this more flamboyantly than Andy Warhol. It may not be too much to say that Warhol was the Oscar Wilde of Postmodernism.

With spritely aplomb, Warhol painted portraits of Campbell's soup cans, manufactured multiple images of movie stars and political figures, assembled a museum of trashy mass-consumer products, and made an art form of celebrity. Then he doffed the presumptions of art altogether, reporting in his jocular treatise, *The Philosophy of Andy Warhol* (1975), "After I did the thing called 'art' or whatever it's called, I went into 'business art'" because "good business is the best art." "Why do people think artists are special?" he added. "It's just another job." This marks the end of modernist gravitas for sure. But, Warhol laughed, what of it? His now-clichéd witticism that "in the future everybody will be famous for fifteen minutes" punctuates the point, mocking all aspirations to transcendence with its fine irony of vacuous successes, homogenized celebrity, and pervasive ephemerality. With gestures of jaded, whimsical irony like this, the postmodern artist winks, gives his make-believe top hat a theatrical tip-of-the-cane, and glides offstage to prepare the next act.

Postmodern irony histrionically played with the tangles of art and commerce, and exposed how indifferently tangled up we are. Who can imagine Tolstoy approving such postmodern attitudes and practices any more than he did the aestheticism of Oscar Wilde? Tolstoy was nothing if not earnest to the core—even when humorously satirizing his enemies, as in his parodies of Wagnerian opera in *What Is Art?* "Art is not a pleasure, a solace, or an amusement," he angrily insisted, "art is a great matter . . . indispensable for the life and progress toward well-being of individuals and humanity." That is because "true art" "infects" us with generic feelings that forge a salutary "union among men," whereas "false art" does the opposite. Whimsical irony is therefore about the last attitude Tolstoy would want art to display and instill, for it undermines all transcendent value and deprives people of the capacity to feel anything with spontaneous sincerity or to believe in anything unironically, while tolerating practically everything with a sophisticated, ironic smile.

You could not go much farther from Tolstoy's importunate conception of art than that stated by the eminent philosopher/critic Arthur Danto almost exactly a century after *What Is Art?* in a book entitled *After the End of Art* (1997). Nowadays, Danto says, art "can be anything artists and patrons want it to be" because "nothing is any more true as art than anything else, nothing especially more historically false than anything else." Such anything-goes acquiescence, bespeaking postmodern wisdom, is as alien to Tolstoy as was the iconoclasm of early Modernism.

Tolstoy was looking for God, the good, and ultimate things. He would find none of them in Postmodernism. It is no wonder that as Postmodernism journeyed to the end of the twentieth century it brought with its eclecticism and irony a characteristically *fin-de-siècle*, or *fin-de-millénaire*, mood. This mood intimated that not only was Modernism over but that other Western traditions were passing, too. Jean-François Lyotard rang in early on this theme with *The Postmodern Condition: A Report on Knowledge* (1979), where he argued that the time was now past when an overarching theory of anything could hold. Scores of books played variations on the theme with eschatological titles marking The End: *The End of Law* (1984), *The End of Art Theory* (1986), *The End of Literary Theory* (1987), *The End of the History of Art?* (1987), *The End of the State* (1987), *The End of Nature* (1989), *The End of the Modern World* (1988), *The End of History and the Last Man* (1992), *The End of Science* (1996), *The End of Knowing* (1997), and predictably, *The End of Postmodernism* (1993), as well as a dozen or so headed *The End of the World*. A related outpouring of books remarked the same endings but peered into the void beyond: *After the Great Divide* (1986); *After the Future* (1990); *After the Demise of Tradition* (1991); *After Modernity* (1994); *After Postmodernism* (1994); *After Theory* (1996); *After the End of Art* (1997). And the preeminent postmodern theorist Jean Baudrillard offered a cautionary synthesis of this eschatological *fin-de-siècle* trend in *The Illusion of the End* (1992), chiding those who could believe in the historical "ending" of anything, since that very idea reflects the outdated modern assumption that history was ever going anywhere.

Whereas Tolstoy's *fin de siècle* had diagnosed Western culture as "sick" and prescribed a variety of cures, including the artistic flights of Modernism, the next *fin de siècle* had come full circle, bringing a reaction against those haughty flights and instilling a suspicion that in leaving Modernism behind, Western civilization has also waved goodbye to modernity as a whole, and perhaps to historical culture as such. Tolstoy would recognize this crepuscular *fin-de-siècle* state of mind, and might even take some consolation from it. But it would be small consolation to him for not finding his "art of the future" even a century after *What Is Art?*

Whereas Tolstoy reviled Modernism and would have been disappointed with Postmodernism, he might have taken some encouragement from another cultural trend that gathered alongside Modernism and then flowed on through Postmodernism. This was the ascendancy of popular culture. Tolstoy could have welcomed this ascendancy at least in part because popular culture has many of the attributes that he ascribed to his "art of the future." After all, popular culture is, as he said art should be, "open to everyone"; it is immediately accessible without intellectual or aesthetic pretentions;

it deals in shared emotions; and it seems to have very nearly universal appeal, bringing together millions, sometimes billions, of people around the world watching the same kinds of movies and television shows, listening to the same kinds of music, and living with the same kinds of fantasies.

But looked at closely, modern popular culture would no more please Tolstoy than would Postmodernism. For, unlike the traditional folk art that Tolstoy favored, modern popular culture is driven by commercial, not communal, interests, and it reaches people through technological devices not direct, genuine experience. In both its commercial motives and its technological means of dissemination, popular culture falls short of Tolstoy's ideals on three interrelated counts. First, it allows artists and technicians to stir emotions in others that they do not themselves need to feel since technology does that work for them, amplifying sound, fabricating images, reproducing reality, and so forth, all geared to commercial gain, rendering modern popular culture what Tolstoy would consider emotionally "insincere." Second, and more egregious, this commercially motivated emotional insincerity of the creators and purveyors of popular culture inevitably works to arouse in the people who consume it emotions that are also more artificial than genuine, for when feelings come from artifice, how authentic can those feelings be? Third, in enticing people into its artificial experiences, modern popular culture removes people from actuality and promotes an attitude of diverted unseriousness akin to that of Postmodernism and at odds with the true humanity Tolstoy desired. In short, the art of popular culture molds lives that Tolstoy would deem more false than true.

Tolstoy warned against these consequences when he denounced "amusement art . . . manufactured to ready made, prearranged recipe . . . by armies of professional artists" to produce "artificial effects"—a phenomenon later explored by Walter Benjamin in his epochal essay "The Work of Art in the Age of Mechanical Reproduction" (1936) and by his colleagues of the Frankfort School in their many studies of mass society. Young people throbbing to rock music or thrilling to movieland fantasies would have made Tolstoy cringe at their artificial joys no less than he was repulsed by the depravities of aristocratic art. He would also recoil to see how popular culture can taint even the humane emotions that he extolled, such as mother love, brotherhood, and reverence, by lending them a trite, borrowed, self-indulgent quality elicited by push-button sensations.

This is the very genius of "false art" that Tolstoy execrated: it enables art to seem "sincere," real, and true while merely dealing in "striking effects" and other techniques to make people feel what they do not feel, and to believe what they do not believe, and not to know the difference—or even to care. And worse, by drawing us into its artificially convincing world, which frivolously mimics our own, the art or entertainments of popular culture incline us to carry the mentality of artifice, frivolity, and a casual "suspension of disbelief" into our world, thereby diminishing the emotional honesty, social empathy, and mental seriousness that Tolstoy believed real life requires.

Modern popular culture might be uniting lots of people in shared emotions and fantasies, but Tolstoy would not see fulfillment of his hopes for "the art of the future" in it. By commercializing art and artificially manipulating our responses, by feeding self-indulgent emotions and nurturing the mentality of entertainment, modern popular culture propagates the worst characteristics of Tolstoy's "false art," trivializing the important and ennobling the trivial, even when it seems to do otherwise. No wonder this popular culture found a comrade in postmodern irony. Tolstoy would have to look elsewhere for the "brotherhood of man" to take root. (For more on the depredations of popular culture in the late twentieth century, see "*Fin-de-siècle* America and the Twilight of Culture" below.)

While the ascendancy of popular culture, despite its potential good, would probably strike Tolstoy as another victory of false art, a host of historical developments outside the arts (albeit some in league with popular culture) might still attract his eye as positive prospects for bringing the "brotherhood of man." These have to do with the growth of what came to be known as globalization.

Tolstoy saw some of these arising in his day when he noted optimistically that a universal brotherhood was already being advanced by "means of communication, telegraphs, telephones, the press" and "the ever-increasing attainability of material well-being for everyone." Those globe-encircling technologies of communications and the expansion of "material well-being" certainly became conspicuous traits of the our *fin de siècle*.

The Internet alone proves the technological globalization of culture. Thanks to its technology—and later that of "smartphones"—incalculable quantities of information and millions of conversations flit daily around the earth, knitting mankind together as never before possible. At the same time, the mass media join people everywhere, giving an immediacy and near-simultaneity to events, while jet-age transportation carries travelers the world over, leaving no frozen outpost or jungle village uninvaded by the curious or the commercially enterprising. Owing, in part, to these global technologies, and to the economic growth they reflect, "material well-being for everyone" was much closer at the turn of the twentieth century than it had been a hundred years earlier.

Further advancing that happy end, the rise of globalization saw political power yield a measure of its authority to economic interests, allowing "economic diplomacy" to substantially supplant military force in the international political arena—the annual World Economic Forum in Davos, Switzerland, exemplifies the change, drawing economic and political leaders from around the world to address economic issues and international conflicts. Grasping that baton, multinational corporations took the capitalist ethos of free markets and affluence, as well as consumer products, into every country, installing living monuments to that ethos in shrines of consumerism selling a mounting array of goods, from hamburgers and ice cream to designer clothes and electronics. Eventually every population center on earth would look and feel remarkably alike—as do American towns already—boasting the same rewards of economic enterprise, the same shops and hotels, the same products and services, the same diversions and entertainments. As one free-market enthusiast crowed at a recent conference in New York: "When all markets are free, everyone in the world will be rich—it's no more than a hundred years away."

That could have been a slogan of the twentieth century's *fin de siècle*: after the end of modern and postmodern culture comes a world united in the material abundance of consumer capitalism, facilitated by technology, political pacification, and economic cooperation. Tolstoy, whose own *fin de siècle* had been rent by cultural discontents and rising international discord, might well have seen some possibilities for the "brotherhood of man" in this global unity.

But even this global civilization would not likely bring the brotherhood Tolstoy desired. For he would have found here the same kinds of unfulfilled promises as those of Postmodernism and popular culture. Just as he might have seen some positive prospects in the postmodern reaction against modernist elitism and in popular culture's egalitarianism, he would have condemned the postmodern attitude of antiserious irony and the exploitative commercialism and manipulative artificialities of popular culture. By the same token, Tolstoy might have appreciated the technologies, political pacification, and expanding economic well-being that were bringing the world together in the late twentieth century, but he would have reproved the global capitalist ethos of wealth and acquisitive consumption for missing the communal and spiritual purpose of life. His hopeful dreams would have remained only dreams.

Tolstoy's *fin de siècle* was marked by a widespread sense of cultural malaise and by a spirit of rebellion and renewal. Tolstoy shared that sense and that affirming spirit. *What Is Art?* was therefore both a *cri de coeur* and a *cri de guerre*, born of discontents and nourished by the hope that the future of art and culture would go in the direction he was trying to lead it.

A century after *What Is Art?*, the West was again in the throes of an eschatological *fin-de-siècle* state of mind, but this time marked not so much by cultural malaise and a spirit of renewal as by ironic resignation to a world dominated by consumer commerce, pop culture, and galloping globalization. If the "art of the future" and the "brotherhood of man" could be found there, it would be far from what Tolstoy had imagined. Surveying that terrain, he would probably have blamed the reign of "false art" and "artistic amusement" for "perverting" the culture at large and leading people ever more relentlessly into self-indulgent, insincere, and dehumanizing lives. So our *fin de siècle* would probably have distressed Tolstoy even more than his own.

A previous version of this essay was written by invitation for a centennial edition of *What Is Art?* that was never published. Portions of it appeared in "Tolstoy's Prophecy," *The New Criterion*, December 1998, and with more detail in my book *Worldly Wisdom: Great Books and the Meanings of Life* (2008).

Toward the twilight of culture.

"*The disorientation of culture at its close . . . in a heedless, uncivil world.*"
—JACQUES BARZUN

Fin-de-siècle America and the Twilight of Culture

The waning years of the nineteenth century set a historic standard for diagnosing *fin-de-siècle* cultural decline and urging varieties of renewal. Artists and intellectuals led the way on both fronts. And Modernism ascended on their cries for renewal, becoming the prevailing cultural fashion through most of the twentieth century.

A century after that *fin de siècle*, and at the close of a millennium as well, the cycle has come around with a flood of ruminations on the portentous ending of things. But, while the sense of decline is unmistakable, no resounding calls for renewal with a clear way forward can be heard. Even "Postmodernism," that self-conscious break with Modernism that has become the reigning cultural fashion in the past couple of decades, offers not so much a path into the future as a postscript to the past, declaring the end of culture as we have known it and supplanting it with jaded postmodern perceptions and wry irony. The widely read little book by the French intellectual Jean-François Lyotard, *The Postmodern Condition: A Report on Knowledge* (1979) all but said that in announcing the end of all comprehensive understanding of everything.

Whether openly sharing the postmodern ethos or not, books have poured from the presses in recent years flogging the theme of cultural exhaustion at the close of the twentieth century. A cursory pass through the catalogue of the New York Public Library discloses dozens of titles like *The End of Nature* (1989), *The End of the Modern World* (1988), *The End of Knowing* (1997), and several on *The*

End of the World. Whether or not the times warranted such definitive titles, their eschatological themes now belong to the twentieth-century's *fin de siècle* (for more details, see the previous essay, "Tolstoy's *fin de siècle* and Ours: From Decadence to Postmodernism").

The four books considered here also belong to that *fin-de-siècle* history, if not with such eschatological fervor. Three of them deal specifically with America. Two of these delineate the fateful conquest of this country by mass popular culture, and the third examines the wholesale disintegration of culture itself America. The fourth places *fin-de-siècle* America within the spiraling decadence of modern Western civilization as a whole in the twentieth century.

Michael Kammen, a prolific historian of American society from its origins, turns in *American Culture, American Tastes: Social Change and the 20th Century* (1999) to the hot academic topic of *popular culture*. But he informs us that this "is an inquiry concerning the *problem* of popular culture and its contested meanings rather than a comprehensive history of popular culture." That *problem*, such as it is, consists, he claims, in the misunderstanding by historians, social theorists, and critics of "the historical relationship between popular and mass culture." He intends to solve that *problem*. But this is not merely an academic exercise. He believes that we confuse popular and mass culture at our peril because mass culture threatens to dominate, enervate, and homogenize life more pervasively and perniciously than all varieties of traditional popular culture that preceded it. Whether or not recognizing that distinction will in itself save us is another matter.

This foreboding image of mass culture is not new. We have encountered versions of it at least since the 1920s, when, for example, Ortega y Gasset groused about the advent of the "mass man" in *The Revolt of the Masses*, and the Marxist-oriented thinkers of the Frankfurt Institute for Social Research, particularly Max Horkheimer and Theodor Adorno, began studying what they called the mass "culture industry." For that matter, we could go back to

Alexis de Tocqueville a century earlier and his warning against the cultural homogeneity being wrought in America by democracy. But Kammen does more than recycle familiar theories. He weaves his way through them to grasp the uniqueness of late twentieth-century mass culture and to trace its ascendancy in America.

These tasks first take Kammen back to the late nineteenth century and to what he labels "commercialized popular culture." Introduced by novel technologies and accompanying diversions such as amusement parks, penny arcades, vaudeville, dance halls, cabarets, and team sports, this popular culture had its heyday in the years 1885 to 1935. And Kammen commends it for being "lively... assertive... participatory and interactive," and for encouraging a healthy variety and benign hierarchy of cultural tastes. Those were the good old days. Then, growing out of this hearty "commercialized popular culture" in the 1920s, without wholly eclipsing it, came what Kammen dubs "proto-mass culture." Propelled by newer and farther-reaching communications technologies like movies and radio, as well as by mushrooming enticements to consumerism, proto-mass culture aroused appetites for consumer goods, and it disseminated the entertainments of popular culture more readily and widely than ever. Although the Great Depression of the thirties slowed its growth and limited its social effects, proto-mass culture nonetheless paved the way for the juggernaut of true mass culture.

Meanwhile, with the swelling tides of "commercialized popular culture" and then "proto-mass culture," debates swirled over shifting levels of culture and taste. Discriminating among highbrow, middlebrow, and lowbrow attitudes became a topic of ardent social criticism and something of a parlor game among middle-class Americans seeking the status that "good taste" bestowed. What Kammen regards as the academic *problem* of defining popular culture derives from those debates. But while he thinks that *problem* more pressing than ever, the distinctive levels of taste that provoked it have all but vanished. And that, Kammen says, is a telltale sign that mass culture has triumphed.

Mass culture arrived only after 1950, Kammen contends, owing to World War II, postwar affluence, booming consumerism, and the proliferation of ingenious technologies and techniques of mass persuasion—most obviously television and its trappings. At the same time, a new order of "cultural power" exercised by corporations, communication media, advertising, and public relations was displacing the more traditional "cultural authority" of critics, intellectuals, and institutions as arbiters of taste or value. Unlike those traditional agents of "cultural authority," these "forces of cultural power" acted through intrusive means to shape tastes directly for economic ends, and on a nearly unbounded scale. Wielding seductive promises of "fulfillment" and supplying incessant "entertainment from mass media," those forces insured that mass culture would consume virtually everything in its maw. By the end of the century, Kammen concludes with a critical bite, America was becoming a country of homogenized "cultural populism" and passive pleasures induced by influences whose economic muscle and manipulative ingenuity were seemingly irresistible—and worse would come in the new century.

Kammen credits a range of historical circumstances for the ascent of mass culture, but he does not explore any of them at length. That is not his principal purpose. Still, it would have been helpful to receive more explanatory detail here and there. After asserting, for example, that "The WWII years played an absolutely crucial (and hitherto underestimated) role in accelerating the transition from proto-mass culture to the 'real thing,'" he tosses off only a few anecdotal sentences about wartime America—neglecting, for instance, the substantially unprecedented integration of entertainment into the war effort through adroit propaganda at home and morale-boosting performances among the troops—before moving on to postwar consumerism. Sound as his assertion might be, it wants more evidence from the war years themselves. And Kammen gives only passing reference to World War I, leaving us to guess what he would say about, for instance, the marriage of American

21. FIN-DE-SIÈCLE AMERICA AND THE TWILIGHT OF CULTURE

patriotism and popular culture in the Broadway shows of George M. Cohan and his stirring war anthem sung throughout America, "Over There." Incidentally, by contrast to Kammen on the cultural impact of the World Wars, Jacques Barzun makes WWI the decisive watershed in the decline of the West and skirts WWII (see below). Although Kammen is tracking the rise of American mass culture, whereas Barzun is charting the decline of Western civilization as a whole, these turn out to be complementary perspectives on the same thing.

Kammen might also get a bit rabbinical in slicing his distinctions among types and phases of culture so finely, while wagging an accusing finger at authors he believes have played too loose with nuances and have therefore missed the actual dynamics of American cultural history. But he is surely correct to see that at the end of the twentieth century the power and pervasiveness of mass culture, by whatever name, particularly in America, was something new to history. We can only wish he had shown a way out.

Kammen's history leaves us with a gloomy picture of America at the *fin de siècle*. Neal Gabler records a similar history to a parallel end, if without Kammen's terminological fastidiousness. In *Life: The Movie: How Entertainment Conquered Reality* (1998), Gabler says this history reveals not so much the ascendancy of mass culture in general as the conquest of America by the driving "force" within all popular or mass culture: *entertainment*. Gabler is convinced that the cultural and psychological effects of entertainment reach farther and go deeper than those Kammen attributes to mass culture. Entertainment has become "arguably the most pervasive, powerful, and ineluctable force in our time," he declares; and it has created "the brave and strange new world in which we live—the world of postreality," where life and entertainment are one.

To play out these bold notions, Gabler, the author of two substantial books on the history of publicity and Hollywood, takes his cue from the mid-nineteenth-century clashes in America between defenders of traditional high culture and proponents of an ascending popular culture. The defenders of high culture ("cultural authorities" in Kammen's parlance) championed art forms that served intellect, edification, morality, sophistication, and aesthetics; and they denounced popular culture for abetting the lowly opposites. We could, in fact, trace more or less this same line between high and low culture back through every era of Western history to antiquity where Plato inveighed against any art that appealed to the emotions and the "low parts" of human beings, and we could follow it into every other culture that has separated reverence and revelry, which probably all have, even if they have sometimes let the two flow together in religious rituals. But that long history does not much concern Gabler. He picks it up when popular entertainment in democratic America proudly became all that its detractors condemned it for being—"fun, effortless, sensational, mindlessly formulaic, predictable, and subversive." Entertainment might not consistently exhibit all of the attributes that Gabler names here, but he draws his explanation of "The Entertainment Revolution" from them. That revolution welled up, he tells us, from a universal human "desire for entertainment" rooted in "almost a raw biological urge" for sensory pleasures and "fun" that requires "pains to resist." If this seems like a rather reductionist definition of entertainment by contrast to other pursuits and diversions, it is the most Gabler gives.

He further announces that this "biological urge" for the "fun" sensations of entertainment brought "the single most important cultural transformation in this country in the twentieth century." To be sure, Gabler concedes that this purported "urge" could not alone have carried out the "entertainment revolution." The urge had to be set free from traditional restraints, and to do that it had to get a boost from something. It got both from the usual suspects in the growth of popular culture in America: democracy, consumer commerce, urbanization, technology, publicity, and so on. In addition, Gabler stresses, the "desire for entertainment" was abetted by

21. Fin-de-siècle America and the Twilight of Culture

America's evangelical religions, which sanctioned public displays of unleashed emotion (a merging of reverence and revelry), and by the popular press, which purveyed sensationalism with lurid stories and pseudonews that lastingly blurred distinctions between reality and entertainment. But, again, these only set that desire free. They did not create it.

By the end of the twentieth century, Gabler elaborates, the tentacles of entertainment reached everywhere. And who could have denied it? The litany has become commonplace. Increasingly: television broadcasts the news, churches stage mass meetings, museums present blockbuster exhibitions, businesses advertise products, teachers teach, politicians campaign, etc. as entertainment that will "grab and hold the public's attention." Consequently, entertainment would come to influence practically everything people do, from how they spend their time to how they think and what they value.

Gabler notes that entertainment's influence is nowhere more conspicuous or perverse than in that ubiquitous, latter-day American measure of human worth—*celebrity*, the cult of being publicly known for any reason whatsoever, including for just being known. Because "entertainment is the primary standard of value for virtually everything in modern society," he observes, "celebrity is widely regarded as the most exalted state of human existence." For this reason many people will do virtually anything to become celebrities—if only for fifteen minutes, as Andy Warhol predicted everyone would one day, or even for a moment—or to see a celebrity at a distance. By the same token, Gabler continues, service professionals from fashion designers and interior decorators to fitness instructors and cosmetic surgeons, voguish restaurateurs and stylish hoteliers—many becoming celebrities themselves—all labor to help us live our lives in a world of entertainment as both performers and audiences.

Gabler's catalogue of entertainment's effects leaves out almost nothing in late-twentieth-century American life. And he ticks off the items with a sharply critical eye, remarking along the way (contra

Kammen), that entertainment can hardly be called a passive diversion when it takes over life. But, for all of his criticisms, Gabler chooses in the end not to judge America unequivocally worse off for living under "the tyranny of entertainment." He winds up the book wondering if at the close of the twentieth century "we stood on a precipice" at "the end of traditional human values" or "in a bright new dawn" where "we need never suffer life's hurts again." How could Gabler have not wished for a happy ending to the history of entertainment in America?—although one might detect a note of irony in his words.

And yet, in his zeal to demonstrate that entertainment has conquered life by unleashing and exploiting an elemental appetite for entertaining sensations, Gabler tends to slight, if not ignore, some contrary facts of human life and human nature. Among them are the everyday requisites of survival and the unhappy realities of suffering that entertainment might temporarily palliate as "an opiate of the people," in Gabler's use of Marx's phrase, but cannot eliminate. Another is how the *psychology of fantasy* can, as Freud knew, exert more power over us than does the *biology of sensations* and to more consequential ends. (Whereas Gabler views entertainment as primarily an appeal to sensations not fantasy, twenty years later the even more ambitious social critic, Kurt Anderson, would go the other way, if to much the same end, in a book called *Fantasyland: How America went Haywire: A 500-Year History*, detailing the longtime mounting obsession with fantasy in America, culminating in the "post-truth" culture of the early twenty-first century—which is not unlike Gabler's "postreality.") And another is a bent in human nature that could actually turn out to save us from the "tyranny of entertainment." That is the potential for boredom.

Gabler takes the hunger for pleasurable sensations to be an insatiable human appetite. But, like all appetites, it surely becomes sated, at least for a time. And when it is sated, people get bored—how long can one be "entertained" without growing restless? Once boredom sets in, we might seek a cure in more sensations, more pleasures, more entertainment, but that only stimulates hunger for stronger seasonings, as it were. Inevitably, boredom gathers because its cure is not more entertaining sensations, but fewer.

Long before modern entertainment put its clasp on American life, Aristotle had made a humanistic issue of this truth. In the *Ethics* he separated "amusement" from what he called "civilized pursuits during leisure" (an early distinction between low and high culture). We need amusement, Aristotle said, the way we need rest. It gives us a salutary physical and emotional reprieve from the cares and labors of the day. And this helps us replenish our energies. But it is pointless to fill one's life with amusement any more than to fill it with rest. Neither can satisfy us beyond its natural purpose or make us "happy," as Aristotle liked to say; having too much of either of them deadens us and diminishes our lives. This is where "civilized pursuits" come in. They do not lend us merely the transitory ease of rest and amusement. They stir thought and expand our lives and help us fulfill our natures. And that is how human beings achieve their highest happiness. Or so Aristotle believed. He was probably right. At least he knew something about boredom. As did William Wordsworth, who built his career as a poet on combating it. Wordsworth saw the overstimulation of modern life inducing a "savage torpor" in people that bored and numbed them. He penned his own poetry as an antidote to that torpor, helping people to feel genuine emotions and be alive to life. I might add Jacques Barzun to this company for, as we shall see, he predicts that from the late twentieth century onward boredom will progressively deaden Western culture until a craving rises for a new Renaissance.

Notwithstanding Gabler's neglect of how boredom could eventually render a culture of entertainment, as he defines it, dull if not intolerable, and his related disregard of the psychology of fantasy, as well as his passing over with only a nod the many lives lived not for entertainment but for *real* purposes, Gabler astutely penetrates an undeniable and disturbing trend in America at the century's end. He could even be sadly right about the future if entertainment manages to benumb everyone into the lobotomized bliss of a Huxleyan brave new world inured to boredom. But that would not really be culture at all. It would be the death of culture.

Something quite like that fate presents itself not as a foreboding of the future but as the existing state of affairs in the next book. But here that fate has not come from Kammen's "mass culture" or Gabler's "tyranny of entertainment." Or not from such sources alone. It has befallen from the corrosive character of twentieth-century culture itself. In *Faded Mosaic: The Emergence of Postcultural America* (2000), the literary scholar and critic Christopher Clausen describes that fate as a "post-cultural condition." A genuine *culture*, he argues, provides "an impersonal set of patterns," including "manners, morals, and laws," that bind people together over time and give substance and purpose to their lives. This culture has now faded into a "post-cultural condition," which is analogous to Kammen's "mass culture" and Gabler's "postreality."

This condition has contradictory effects. On the surface, Clausen says, "post-cultural America" makes people and their pursuits more alike, as egalitarianism, technology, and consumerism "break down cultural distinctiveness." In this stew of sameness, even the most traditional forms of cultural identity, such as religion, take on similar hues (just as Gabler notes that many churches ape entertainment). But while these uniformities might appear to constitute a new, more inclusive culture, Clausen contends they could never do that. They are too shallow and amorphous—like the Internet, which, he remarks, is the exemplary post-cultural technology. Beneath those surface uniformities, the sinews of culture have actually disintegrated into a myriad of loose strands, setting people adrift with a "post-cultural vertigo."

Clausen discerns this "vertigo" in longings for the sense of coherence and purpose that a true culture used to grant. The creed of "multiculturalism" bespeaks one such longing to find unity in diversity. And yet, even as the partisans of multiculturalism—like their allies among ethnic groups and restless nationalities around the world—strive to elevate traditional cultural identities, they signal how those identities are threatened by dissolution in a vast post-culture. I might point out that the modish practice of applying the very term *culture* to practically everything and every aggregate of people, from families to corporations to the entire world population, also betrays the same yen to hold fast to what is disappearing—even while unwittingly proving the vacuity that has widely befallen the term *culture* itself. Could a "global culture" ever amount to more than the fatal submersion of all traditional cultures in a cultureless welter of mass humanity?

But nothing represents "post-cultural vertigo" more conspicuously than the "substitution of personality for tradition." In lieu of cultural traditions, Clausen explains, we become preoccupied with "personal feelings and self-gratification," "sentimental narcissism," "emotional exhibitionism," and a spurious "religion of products and celebrities." These aberrations have engendered the oxymoron "mass individualism," denominating the paradoxical conformity that results when "rationality, restraint, and deferred gratifications are out" and "everything becomes a matter of taste" with "nonjudgmental inclusiveness." These aberrations also produce oddities like "the emotional worldwide response to the death of Princess Diana," which "was, in all its shallowness, a deeply post-cultural event" of weepy mass narcissism mingled with misdirected yearnings for loftier cultural ideals.

If some of this criticism sounds familiar to readers of Alexis de Tocqueville, it should. As Clausen acknowledges, he gives us a very Tocquevillian view of late-twentieth-century America. Here, as in Tocqueville's America 170 years earlier, conformity and "individualism" (which Clausen somewhat misleadingly says "originated as a liberal concept," whereas Tocqueville himself coined the term as a conservative insult for a democratic antisocial attitude) rule together as symbiotic evils. Clausen does not mention, however, that Tocqueville, like other Europeans before and since, doubted that democratic America possessed much "culture" worthy of the name, or that it ever would—today some Europeans find that judgment confirmed by the very reign of commercial popular culture in America. In this light, questioning the existence of "culture" in America is an old story.

Clausen does identify a few rewards that the "post-cultural condition" could deliver to the world at large, such as the diminution of brutish prejudices, the lessening of tribal impulses, and the liberation of peoples from local oppressors. And we have seen some of these rewards arising over the last half century or so. But Clausen mainly attends to the worst. Such is the *fin-de-siècle* "condition," to use Clausen's term.

Kammen, Gabler, and Clausen present complementary versions of a late-twentieth-century America in which cultural norms were dissolving into varieties of rapacious narcissism and blind conformity. Jacques Barzun sees much the same historical landscape, but he views it from the perspective of the past five hundred years of Western civilization, and from a long, distinguished career as a cultural historian and critic. This is not the place for a full review of Barzun's voluminous *From Dawn to Decadence: 1500 to the Present: 500 Years of Western Cultural Life* (2000). But the last of its four parts, each of which covers a discrete era in Barzun's scheme of modern history, deserves inclusion here because it deals with the central subject at hand: the state of Western and American culture at the *fin de siècle* and how it got that way.

What Kammen describes as the depredations of mass culture, and Gabler attributes to "the tyranny of entertainment," and Clausen assigns to the disintegration of culture into post-culture, Barzun diagnoses as symptoms of "the culture at its close." And, as symptoms, they are more effects than causes of the sorry state of Western culture as the twentieth century was ending. The causes lie deeper and are more far-reaching. For he finds all of Western culture succumbing to "a failure of nerve" and descending into decadence, especially after World War I. That war tipped the scales from cultural vitality to enervation.

The culture that has now descended into terminal decadence arose with vitality around 1500, Barzun says, with a "revolution" of emancipated individuality. This culture matured in the seventeenth and eighteenth centuries with the formation of nation states, and subsequently flourished in the nineteenth century with the energies of Romanticism and the aspirations of democracy. Then it flowered anew with the innovations of Modernism around the turn of the twentieth century—roughly the first three of Barzun's historical eras—before getting mortally wounded by the Great War. "The impetus born of the Renaissance was exhausted" he declares; and "the reckless expenditure of lives" in the war "was bound to make a postwar world deficient in talents as well as deprived of needful links to prewar culture." After that war, Western culture would never possess its previous vivacity. The loss was too great, and energies flagged under the crushing feeling that "everything had been done" and that life was becoming "absurd."

This plight induced a failure of nerve that turned attenuated energies against Western culture itself—against its past, against authority, against art, against standards of value, against the future. Anti-culture became the order of the day as transitory novelty and jokey ridicule paraded beside incomprehensible artworks and lugubrious pronouncements on the futility of existence. Barzun takes as symbolic of this destructive temper Marcel Duchamp's infamous painting of the Mona Lisa wearing a mustache. It was a sophomoric jape at the expense of culture; but, owing to "the death of the philistine" (an unsung casualty of the war, Barzun notes), few observers could judge such destructive acts with discrimination anymore. From then on it was widely assumed in Western culture that "anything may be done"—a trend one could see jubilantly flaunted in Cole Porter's musical of 1934, *Anything Goes*. The culture began its inexorable decline into the decadence of "the absurd in practice."

III. On Modernity and Modernism

Common sense, coherence, objectivity, concreteness, order, discipline, judgment, authority, respect, and other signposts of a healthy culture, Barzun eloquently argues, yielded to a "demotic," or rampantly populist, culture of "muddled thought" and hapless demands for the "Unconditioned Life" in "a heedless, uncivil world" where "to appear unkempt" would become "the key signature of the whole age." It was a joyless culture to boot. For among its blithe absurdities, it also exalted the false gods of arid abstraction and inflated scientism, which led people into intellectually errant and emotionally vacant lives. "To live amid lax words and dim thoughts," Barzun writes, thumping one of his bruising reproaches, "deadens the joy of life. The man in the street who says 'precipitation probability is twenty percent' is less alive than if he said and felt 'small chance of rain.'"

This "dispiriting catalogue" of "demotic life and times" goes on and on, synthesizing complaints Barzun has hurled for decades at the cult of science, the religion of art, the ruin of education, the degradation of language, and more. And yet, for all of his harsh judgments on "the culture at its close," Barzun holds out a more lively hope for the future than do the other authors here. For if Western culture was succumbing to decadence as the twentieth century folded its tent, another culture was bound to arise sooner or later in its place. And it would likely arise, Barzun speculates, from none other than that aching tendency in human nature mentioned earlier: *boredom*.

Barzun spells out his spry vision of the future with a little fantasy. In another century or two, he imagines, the culture of technological "cybernists," undiscriminating egalitarians, and "overentertained people" will be set upon by the new "blight" of "boredom." Then a "handful of restless men and women from the upper orders" will call for "reform" and return to works of the past, where they will discover the secret of "a fuller life" and "create a new present" neither modeled strictly on the past nor cut off from it. This fresh beginning will launch a vital new culture, igniting "enthusiasm in the young and talented" who will "keep exclaiming what a joy it is to be alive."

We might question this cheery vision of the future, as well as Barzun's use of some historical details to make generalizations about all of Western culture, and his scheme of historical periods, especially the irreparable break he marks at World War I. And couldn't the "failure of nerve" that he sees at the heart of the West's decline into decadence—accentuated by the epochal consequences of the Great War—be viewed as a manifestation of new ways of thinking and feeling wrought by a growing historical consciousness and a deepening psychological self-consciousness, which often engendered attitudes of pessimism? (See "Modernity, Modernism, and the Evil of Banality" and "Self-Consciousness and the Modernist Temper" above.) We might also quarrel with Barzun's scorn for most of the twentieth century, and we might suspect that late-twentieth-century culture was not actually passing through a cyclical phase of decadence but was, as Kammen, Gabler, and Clausen predict, sinking into another, more enduring, wayward current. But, whether the twentieth century's close brought the end of culture or portents of new possibilities, we might thank Barzun for bringing an encompassing historical perspective, rich with luminous particulars, to the *fin-de-siècle* ruminations on how American culture had gone awry, and what would come next.

The predictable outpouring of cultural diagnoses and prognoses at the end of the twentieth century did not make American culture look very good. Narcissistic individualism, numbing conformity, errant intellect, manipulative commerce, intrusive technologies, pervasive entertainment, and other melancholy developments seemed to critics, like the quartet here, to threaten culture and humanity as nothing had in previous times. Such diagnoses could be said to mirror an advanced civilization prone to agonizing over its own ripe discontents, wanton pleasures, and uncertain future. They could also be said to echo a wariness of democratic culture that goes back to Plato. At all events, let them prod us into asking ourselves how we might forge a less ominous path into the future.

One way might be to resist the deceptive blandishments of commerce, technology, entertainment, and so forth—and to keep them out of the schools for sure—even at the cost of some beguiling rewards. Another might be to invest more of our energies in meeting the world's real human needs, rather than being preoccupied with the diversions and divagations of our own "culture." Another yet might be to remember and take to heart the cautionary words that Socrates urged upon his contemporaries 2,400 years ago, and that he reiterated to the court that had put him on trial for subverting the prevailing culture of Athens: "Are you not ashamed of heaping up the largest amount of money and status and reputation [and pursuing pleasure], and caring so little about wisdom and truth and improving your soul?" As the four books here show, the state of American culture at the end of the twentieth century gives ample reason to put Socrates's words, and others like them, high in the American cultural agenda of the twenty-first century.

Postscript: The first two decades of the twenty-first century gave little reason to believe that the *fin-de-siècle* forebodings were off base. The assault on authority, political and cultural, only gathered steam through uncontrollable technologies and ideological zealotry that compromised nation-states, extinguished personal privacy, undermined democracy, and made people feel their lives were less secure. Commerce tightened its rein on humanity across the world, reducing ever more of existence to mere economic value. The "tyranny of entertainment" kept stretching its tentacles into every corner of experience, dissolving truth, seriousness, and the capacity for sustained mental concentration, and undermining respect for traditions and public responsibility with delusional resentments and illusory visions of self-realization. And much more—capped in the year 2020 by a cruel gift of globalization: the coronavirus that closed down much of society and took millions of lives around the world, while nonetheless being denied as "false news" by millions of entertainment-besotted and ideologically blinded people. In all, at this time, the young have yet to find many reasons to exclaim "what a joy it is to be alive." But history never goes anywhere without springing surprises. And

21. FIN-DE-SIÈCLE AMERICA AND THE TWILIGHT OF CULTURE

we can hope that before long the young will heed the lessons of our times and find their own good reasons and creative energies to renew that joy and chart a new path for the betterment of themselves and everyone.

A previous version of this review-essay appeared under the same title in *The Sewanee Review*, Spring, 2001.

IV.

ON HUMANISM, CLASSICS, LAUGHTER, PROUST, & THE MEANING OF LIFE

The essays in this section focus on ideals of humanism as reflected in education, a pair of novels, and life. The first is a short piece chastising academic humanists for betraying humanism. The second follows the same theme but casts the net more widely in looking at complaints about the decline of the humanities and what humanists can do about it. The next two turn to reading and teaching humanistically. The first delves into reading for the purpose of illuminating human existence and the value of the classics for doing that. The second applies some of those ideas to reading the classics as casebooks in how to act, not just how to think.

The last three essays take up humanism more generally. The first reflects on the classic novel *Tristram Shandy* and its author, Laurence Sterne, for insights into human decency and the humanity of laughter. The second delves into Marcel Proust's *In Search of Lost Time*, for its challenges to readers and its life-giving rewards. The third is a friendly dialogue between a humanist and a skeptic on how to think about the meaning of life.

Cartoon illustration by Rachel Davis.

Humanistic education is imperiled not so much by enemies from the outside as it is by betrayal on the inside by the humanists themselves.

How Humanists Have Betrayed Humanism

The annual gatherings of professional humanists, like members of the Modern Language Association (MLA) who met in New York recently, have become occasions not just for fraternizing, sharing scholarship, and job seeking but for lamentations on the state of the humanities. Classes in the humanities dwindle as students turn to the social and physical sciences and other more vocationally practical studies; thousands of aspiring humanists scramble for ever fewer academic jobs; the proficiency of students in reading, writing, and reasoning wanes.

Humanists usually blame their troubles on the hegemony of science and on an economy that measures education only by its "cash value." There is some truth in this blame. But a little time spent among the humanists, attending their conventions, listening to their speeches, reading their books and articles, and interviewing job seekers, discloses another cause of their plight: the humanists have betrayed humanism.

They have done this by converting humanistic education—and most egregiously the teaching of literature—into a pseudoscientific exercise among technical issues set forth in a jargon that baffles common understanding. One does not talk about novels or stories, poems or plays any more. One "decodes" or "deconstructs texts." One does not explore and evaluate an author's thoughts and perceptions for the purpose of awakening the mind and illuminating life; instead, one seeks clues to "performative linguistic acts" for the

IV. On Humanism, Classics, Laughter, Proust, and the Meaning of Life

purpose of achieving "critical enablement." Literature, after all, we are told, is "primarily about language, and not much else."

The infatuation with esoteric academic issues and cant has turned the MLA convention into a circus of professorial hokum. This might be no great loss in itself, but it exhibits how humanistic education is turning into a funhouse mirror's image of science comprehensible only to an initiated elite. And this is a great a loss. For by rendering the study of literature (and of the humanities generally) arcane and exclusive, the humanists deprive us of the education students most need—an education in mental discipline, intellectual autonomy, moral judgment, aesthetic perception, emotional sensitivity, and the like. Worse, they set perverse standards of language and thought that become the norm for ambitious scholars, intimidated educators, and unsuspecting students. This results in the proliferation of misbegotten training in spurious technical skills, ponderous analysis, and pretentious jargon, all of which breed under-education, mask self-doubt, and serve intellectual dishonesty.

This conclusion does not rest on anecdotal impressions alone. Several recent studies confirm it. One group of researchers at the University of Chicago discovered that the grading pattern of English teachers in a number of colleges and secondary schools consistently favored student papers written in a turgid, intellectually inflated style over those written simply and lucidly, even when both contained the same ideas. Why? Because teachers routinely take as their models of writing and intellect the publications of others in their profession. How can students be expected to think and write intelligibly when their teachers, often intellectually unsure of themselves and awed by abstract language, lack the ability or will to teach them how?

A similar failure is evident in the teaching of reading. Base reading scores have been rising lately—after years of decline—but, as thoughtful college teachers could say (and as reported last fall by the Department of Education in its National Assessment of Educational Progress), students read with ever more inactive minds.

They draw few inferences from what they read; they see few relations among ideas; they discern few connections between the written word and life experience; and they balk at having to concentrate for long.

Again, it is easy to blame influences outside academe for this—particularly the entertainment culture that makes a fetish of fantasy and sensations and a habit of passive response. But blame also belongs to educators who, on the one hand, equate reading all the through high school with mechanical "skills development" and who, on the other hand, treat literature in college only as "texts" to be technically deciphered according to abstruse theory.

Rarely are reading, writing, thinking taught with any bearing on the common life anymore—at least in colleges. How very vulgar that would be; how very unprofessional. No wonder young people divorce humanistic learning from their lives and turn to more practical studies And no wonder so many aspiring humanities teachers find no jobs: their profession has ceased to serve anyone but the declining number of professional "humanists." Just try, for example, to find a young PhD capable of teaching courses in writing, classic books, and history in a truly humanistic way. It can hardly be done. Candidates come forward in abundance, and are equipped with up-to-date academic jargon and à la mode theories, but rarely one widely educated and attuned to the uses of humanistic learning in life.

All of this should be enough to convince anyone not already under the sway of The Profession that humanistic education is imperiled not so much by enemies from the outside as it is by betrayal on the inside by the humanists themselves.

Postscript: This essay is a slightly revised version of an op-ed piece originally published in *The Wall Street Journal*, February 2, 1982. Coming before its criticisms were widely recognized, it touched a nerve in many readers who wrote vigorously approving responses to it. Since that time, the then fashionable literary theories of Deconstructionism have given way for the most part to other vogue theories such as those associated with postcolonialism, gender, sexuality, ethnicity, and the current fad of "cancel culture," which assails virtually everything that traditional Western culture represents. The reigning theories might change, but the humanities continue to suffer at the hands of the humanists.

The crisis of the humanities is more a confusion of identity than an agony of impending extinction.

The Humanities and Their Discontents

We have grown used to lamentations over the state of the humanities. Students of literature, languages, philosophy, history, and the arts cry over their unhappy prospects in the desolate academic marketplace and in the fiercely professionalized economy beyond. The Modern Language Association sponsors publications for its forlorn young members under such titles as *Alternative Careers for PhDs in the Humanities* (1982) and *Aside from Teaching, What in the World Can You Do?* (1982). Cultural critics bewail the decline not only of humanistic education and careers in the humanities but of humanistic culture altogether. Humanists organize themselves to foster educational and cultural reform with permanent institutions, public and private, such as the American Association for the Advancement of the Humanities (1977) and the National Humanities Center (1978), and with somber analyses and ambitious proposals like those in *The Humanities in American Life* (1980) by the Rockefeller Commission on the Humanities, and *The Paideia Proposal: An Educational Manifesto* (1982) by Mortimer J. Adler on behalf of the members of the Paideia Group. And through all of these intellectual and institutional endeavors echoes one refrain: there is much cause, as the Rockefeller Commission on the Humanities put it, for "profound disquiet about the state of the humanities in our culture," because "the humanities are in crisis."

The atmosphere of crisis and decline that surrounds the humanities nowadays is not new. [NOTE: that atmosphere might have dissi-

IV. On Humanism, Classics, Laughter, Proust, and the Meaning of Life

pated some since the 1980s but only because the forebodings have proven all too true and resignation has set in, dimming prospects for education in the humanities still more.] Ever since empirical science entered the university curriculum in the nineteenth century, humanistic studies concentrating on general, literary learning have been on the defensive. And before that the emergence of Renaissance humanism, followed by the Battle of the Books, saw various lines of conflict drawn between general and technical learning, bookish and empirical studies, old and new ideas. Even at the birth of the liberal arts curriculum in antiquity with the formation of what became known as the trivium (grammar, rhetoric, logic), tension existed not just between this curriculum and the more quantitative subjects of the quadrivium (geometry, arithmetic, music—which meant the mathematical study of intervals—and astronomy), but within the trivium itself. As historians of ancient education like Werner Jaeger and H. I. Marrou have recorded with regret, this tension issued in the domination in the trivium of rhetoric as a mere technical discipline. But even before the rhetorician Isocrates formed that first humanistic curriculum, Socrates (whose pupil Plato was Isocrates's chief philosophical rival) had foreseen perils to humanistic culture in the very invention that made Western education as we know it possible: writing. Socrates told of a myth warning that writing would cause a decline of memory and, worse, the supplanting of active thought by the passive absorption of inert words, and thus the eclipse of genuine knowledge by a mere shadow or pretense of knowledge. To the idealist Socrates, true humanism could not survive in a culture of writing—and he remained illiterate, while becoming the West's first great philosopher, thanks to the literate Plato.

Plus ça change, plus c'est la même chose. Ideals of humanistic learning and culture have always been challenged by the appeal of technique and specialization. And that is to say, Western culture has held a continuing debate over what constitutes humanism and over what kind of learning and culture best promotes it. Such was the debate between Socrates and the Sophists, between Plato and Isocrates, and so on down to the exponents of the humanities and those of specialized training and vocationalism today. And it is a debate bound to continue for as long as that culture shows any curiosity about human nature and its circumstances. For who can say definitively whether human nature is better served by the spoken or the written word, memory or reading, book learning or experience, abstract or pragmatic truth, science or art, ideals or facts, subjective satisfactions or objective knowledge, imaginative pleasures or professional competence? To be sure, reasonable people would advise a combination of these pursuits. But the debate goes on.

Within this enduring and complicated debate, we might today discern a clue to the current "crisis of the humanities" and to its resolution. It is this: the "crisis" might not be what it seems. Instead of witnessing the twilight of the humanities, we may be just observing a new relationship of the humanities to culture and thus another stage in the quarrel over what that relationship should be. After all, when a society educates as many of its people as ours does, when its museums receive as many visitors, when its publishers produce as many books, when its corporations sponsor as many art exhibits and as much highbrow television fare, and when its intellectual and artistic establishments achieve as much cultural eminence as ours, can that society be said to have altogether rejected the humanities and failed at the tasks of humanism?

This question should set the terms for the debate about the humanities ahead. For it puts the state of the humanities in a new light—the light of late-twentieth-century culture and after. And this light discloses that we live in a largely humanistic culture, but it doesn't feel like one. And it doesn't feel like one because we suffer not from a diminution of the humanities but from a superfluity of them, albeit often in bastardized versions—too many books, too much art, too much schooling, too much self-cultivation, too much culture. Far from having been vanquished, the humanities have become integrated into the mass, technological, consumer culture that thrives on alliances between the hitherto conflicting interests of art and industry, education and entertainment, intellect and management, self-development and consumption, high culture and low. This integration has had two epochal consequences for the humanities and humanism. First, it has woven humanistic experience (of a kind) into the very fabric or conditions of our lives. Second, it has caused that experience to lose some of its power to pose alternatives to those conditions and to enliven and inspire those lives.

The crisis of the humanities is therefore more a confusion of identity than the agony of impending extinction. For the humanities are at once better off than they seem, because they are suffused throughout the culture we inhabit, and worse off, because their appeal has been exploited and their power attenuated by this culture. And this confusion has produced in humanists themselves a faltering sense of the humanities' purpose and promise.

This faltering discloses itself in the tendency of humanistic education to drift toward one of two opposing poles, both intended to affirm the authority of the humanities, but both having the effect of further compromising that authority. I will call these poles sentimentalism and pseudoscience.

By sentimentalism I mean the tendency to identify the humanities and humanistic culture with the subjective pleasures of mind and emotion, or "spirit," aroused by encounters with art and ideas. Most of us have had teachers of this type at one time or another. They summon us to read literature, listen to music, study philosophy, eye the sunset, and so on in order to be moved and elated, to weep and to yearn. And they do so on the grounds that to be so moved is to be awakened to one's elemental and exalted humanness and thereby taught the humanistic meaning of life.

There is certainly some justice in this summons, and some solidity to the grounds beneath it. And many of these teachers can be truly inspiring. The humanities should indeed provide us with transports of mind and feeling that lend value and direction to our lives. And in doing this the humanities should help us cultivate the means, both mental and emotional, of achieving those states. Reading poetry, for example, should teach us not only how to read poetry but how to feel the emotions poetry stirs and how to draw existential instruction from those emotions. Such an encounter with Wordsworth's poetry cured John Stuart Mill of his paralyzing "mental crisis" by opening depths of feeling and heights of aspiration to him that his rational utilitarianism had denied. Here, in full potency, was "the healing power of poetry," as Matthew Arnold regarded it. This power the humanities exercise whenever they give us not only fleeting delights but an affirming will.

But notwithstanding these rewards, there is folly in identifying the humanities chiefly with the subjective satisfactions aroused by art and ideas. That folly is to equate subjective satisfactions with cognitive or moral truth. The teacher who only emotes over poetry and encourages students to do the same does not differ much from the preacher who calls his flock to spiritual devotions or the political demagogue who rouses fervor: all derive their truth from experiences, mental or emotional, that *feel good*, and in so doing all neglect the kind of critical thought that seeks to understand human experience and to determine which experiences should be pursued and when and for what reasons. The history of irrationalism and rapturous self-fulfillment in politics and religion has taught us the worst public consequences of this neglect; the consequence for the humanities is terminal confinement to the emotionally self-indulgent, intellectually vacuous, morally irresponsible regions of psychic need and self-deception.

At the opposite end of the spectrum from such sentimentalism is pseudoscience. Here humanists adopt the trappings of science to wrap themselves in scientific authority. For science provides objective knowledge and curbs the sway of subjectivity. But by embracing science, or rather pseudoscience, humanists undermine the authority of the humanities no less than do those who steep themselves in sentimentalism. While sentimentalism impairs the humanities by reducing them to mere emotional subjectivity, pseudoscience impairs them by supplanting the humanities' unique intellectual role in understanding human existence with inappropriate technical training.

This is not to say that all moves of humanists in the direction of science are misled. Many such moves are necessary with the advance of technical, specialized knowledge in a society that requires this kind of knowledge. We should also bear in mind that the natural and social sciences began as humanistic inquiries into human experience, and then lost their humanistic character only as they became more methodologically exact and empirically verifiable. But whatever the benefits of this historic process, it has put the humanities at a disadvantage. For it has continually nibbled away at their intellectual content and left them intellectually insecure. It is no surprise that humanists would wish to regain some of that intellectual heft.

Yet the loss of intellectual content and authority to science is not the greatest threat posed to the humanities by humanistic pseudoscience. That threat lies in the waning of humanistic purpose in the humanities themselves. The humanists who, for example, make the study of literature an enterprise in abstract theorizing about "texts," or who make the study of history a quantitative pursuit of pseudoscientific explanations and laws, or who turn philosophy into nothing but the analysis of linguistic and logical minutiae, are not really dealing in humanistic issues at all. They are dealing in pseudoscientific researches—aspiring to scientific certainty while lacking the precise methods of physical science—unrelated to genuine humanistic interests. Hence, whatever intellectual ingenuities such humanists come up with, these ingenuities fail to achieve the hard practical knowledge of the natural sciences, and, more regrettably, they deprive us of the distinctive and important services that the humanities alone provide in exploring the nature of human life and the judgments that we might use to guide it and give it purpose. As the familiar adage goes, science can make a bomb or save a life, but it cannot tell us whether we *should* drop a bomb or preserve a life.

23. The Humanities and Their Discontents

When the humanities cease thoughtfully addressing such questions of human value, there is nothing else in our culture that can do it. Then we are left helpless to resist not only the value-free demands of science but the often dehumanizing domination of technology, commerce, and political power, as well as the irrationalist urgings of subjectivity and relativism.

Inhabiting a mass, technological, consumer culture that absorbs and exploits and thus blunts their influence, and torn from within by the contrary ideologies of sentimentalism and pseudoscience, the humanities have ample reasons for their contemporary identity crisis. If there is a way out it can lie in but one direction. That is for the humanities to reaffirm the primary obligations that define their unique and indispensable service to culture: to scrutinize human nature, to identify the experiences and ideas that give value and purpose to human life, and to cultivate in human beings the powers of mind, emotion, imagination, and will to examine their lives and live well.

Many tough-minded humanists have alerted us to the various enemies of humanistic culture that have been gathering over the past half century in commercialism, scientism, narcissistic self-indulgence and so forth, and have sought to put the culture on a more disciplined and beneficial humanistic path. Among the softer-spoken of these critics we can place two figures with long careers in the service of the humanities who have recent books on that subject: Charles Frankel and O. B. Hardison. Both have seen that the humanities are threatened not just by adverse external enemies but by a failure of nerve within that induces humanists to withdraw into arcane research or into consoling communion with an idealist past or with satisfying states of mind, emotion, or imagination. And both have seen, over the course of careers that have led them through the political torrents of Washington, DC, and through the leadership of public institutions dedicated to the humanities, that the humanities can thrive only when given an active public life.

IV. On Humanism, Classics, Laughter, Proust, and the Meaning of Life

Frankel, long a professor of philosophy at Columbia, later US Assistant Secretary of State for Educational and Cultural Affairs, and then founding director of the National Humanities Center, constructed his career around the applications of philosophy to the conduct of life rather than around the technical issues that form the core of professional philosophy nowadays. In the volume of essays recently published in Frankel's honor, *The Humanist as Citizen*, a colleague from Columbia, historian William E. Leuchtenberg, remembers that Frankel was "forever hectoring his colleagues to relate their scholarly endeavors to the everyday concerns of their countrymen." No one lived out that precept better than Frankel himself.

Frankel set forth his perception of the place of the humanities in American life and of their relation to politics in his own contribution to this collection, "Why the Humanities?" He discerned the many tensions in the humanities between objectivity and subjectivity, past and present, criticism and elation. And he knew the satisfactions supplied by the humanities to the hungering heart and the aspiring mind. But he also believed that those satisfactions enhance the vitality and well-being of human life best when put to the public good. Hence, compelled by his ethical conscience, historical learning, and present-mindedness, Frankel promoted the integration of the humanities and political authority. How else could the political institutions that shape the destiny of the nation use their public authority for the welfare of human beings except through an alliance with humanistic intellect and the imagination of value? And how else could a society as enthralled by technique and specialization, commerce and diversion as ours cultivate that humanistic intellect and imagination effectively without the encouragement and support of public authority?

Charles Frankel did not always succeed in making the humanities serve society as he wished—and he departed the State Department over ethical differences with his superiors during the Vietnam War.

23. The Humanities and Their Discontents

Nor did he leave a large body of important writings to persuade us of the truth of his convictions. Instead, Frankel's legacy lay mainly in the existential proof his actions evinced of the power of humanistic understanding to give a vigorous sense of value and direction to human existence. That proof is the subject of Leuchtenberg's solid biographical essay. But that power itself is also the subject of other contributions to the volume that focus on historical figures, like Socrates and Abraham Lincoln, who put the primary obligations of humanistic learning to use in guiding not only their own lives but the course of their societies. The public responsibilities of the humanities also give the theme to essays on the humanities in general, particularly Frankel's own contribution, Jacob L. Talmon's "The Humanist and His Dilemmas," William Bennett's "The Humanities, the Universities, and Public Policy," and John Sitter's biting "The Flight from History in Mid-Eighteenth Century Poetry (and Twentieth-Century Criticism)."

Although several of the sixteen essays here are rather slight meditations, there is a pattern throughout, in both the strong and weak contributions, that reflects the truth that Charles Frankel's career exemplified. That truth is this: the humanities are most potent when embodied in critically minded, ethically motivated, publicly responsible lives or when advocated to advance such lives, and the humanities seldom mean much when simply extolled in lofty statements on their virtues or their plight.

This truth underscores the heedless tragedy of Frankel's death in 1979. How bitterly ironic it is that this man, who dedicated his life not just to enjoying the subjective pleasures of the humanities or to pontificating about them but to promoting a genuinely humanistic society through a life of action, should have had that life cut short by wanton thieves in the night. And yet what more vividly dramatizes the moral and intellectual weakness of the humanities in our society today, and the need to ally the humanities with public authority, than crime—the social malaise that not only took Frankel's life but can rob us of our sense of public well-being, our confidence in public authority, and the very value that society has for us? The murder of Charles Frankel in his suburban home also realized an age-old fear of the humanists: the barbarians are no longer at the gates; they are inside. And the further irony of Frankel's death is that by abandoning the primary obligations of the humanities for either subjective satisfactions or for pseudoscience, or for anything else, the humanists bear some of the blame for letting them in.

Although less publicly active than Frankel, O. B. Hardison has also made a career of trying to keep the barbarians at bay through practical applications of the humanities. As director of the Folger Library in Washington, DC, he has observed close at hand the humanities' growing courtship of government. But, stressing that "the humanities in the academy seem to be as specialized, as remote from the interests of the public, and as opaque as the sciences," he asks, "What do they have to offer our society in general?"

Hardison's answer—ladled out in a potpourri of loosely connected, thought-provoking essays collected under the title *Entering the Maze*, and bearing on such varied topics as the idea of the humanities, the American character, democratic politics, movies, medicine, and Shakespeare—is a subtle concoction that displays a humanist mind agilely and instructively at work—and play.

Hardison's fundamental idea is that the humanities best serve us when they provide the life-giving ideas or "necessary fictions" by which human beings, drawing upon culture, mold perceptions, values, and identities. This notion belongs to a tradition that runs at least from Ibsen's useful "Life Lie," Nietzsche's fabricated "untruths," and the pragmatists' "as if" propositions. But Hardison's chief intellectual allegiance lies with Immanuel Kant, or with a somewhat romanticized reading of Kant's aesthetics. That reading emphasizes the fluidity of the self, forever reshaping itself in response to experience and in accordance with imagination. This "possible self," as Hardison calls it, thrives on beauty, thought, and above all, on imaginative freedom, all of which Hardison lumps together, following Kant's sometime disciple Friedrich Schiller, as "aesthetic education."

With this image of the "aesthetic education" of human character in mind, Hardison urges an "open society," which would encourage the self to grow freely in its shifting passage through time and circumstances, and a school curriculum providing the range of experiences most beneficial to that growth—including a core of common cultural experience embodied in a canon of classics. This "open society" would therefore eschew imposing a fixed system of values upon the self, lest they stunt its powers of adaptation, creation, and satisfaction.

Hardison is indisputably a humanist with his eye on life, not just books. He is to be commended for that. And whatever questions one might raise about his psychology of the "possible self," and about the hints of sentimentalism in his warm references to "spirit" and "aesthetic education," his humanism lends itself to some admirable applications. Hardison's observations on teaching, politics, entertainment, old age, and other particulars exhibit a response to experience that is as broad in reach, sharp in perception, inventive in imagination, resonant in feeling, and sensitive to value in human life as one could wish.

These particular observations disclose the humanistic truth in *Entering the Maze* to be the same as that in *The Humanist as Citizen*: humanism and the humanities are best understood and serve us best when employed in action; in the testing of ideas, not just in the statement of them; in the shaping of experience by thought and feeling, not just in the mere experience of thought and feeling. Socrates hinted at this truth when he cautioned against identifying knowledge and the life of the mind with the written word: thought is most human when it is lived.

So here is the prescription that these books, if unintentionally, give us for curing the humanities of their contemporary ailments: spare us lamentations over the "crisis of the humanities" and pious

IV. On Humanism, Classics, Laughter, Proust, and the Meaning of Life

pronouncements on the importance of the humanities to the human spirit. Give us instead intellectually disciplined, imaginatively fertile, emotionally responsive, and ethically energetic human beings attuned to the ideas and experiences that give value to life and capable of demonstrating how to seize and share those experiences. Give us active humanists.

A previous version of this review-essay originally appeared under the same title in *The Sewanee Review*, Summer, 1983.

A ruminating reader.

To "practice reading as an art" requires "something for which one has almost to be a cow and in any case not a 'modern man': rumination."
—NIETZSCHE

The Existential Reader
READING, RUMINATION, AND THE CLASSICS

In the 1880s the philosopher and cultural critic Friedrich Nietzsche complained, in the preface to *On the Genealogy of Morals*, that people no longer knew how to read. They may be literate, he said, but they had "unlearned most thoroughly" how to "practice reading as an art." This art requires "something for which one has almost to be a cow and in any case not a 'modern man': *rumination*." (A century before Nietzsche, Friedrich Schlegel had placed critics among the ruminants: "A critic is a reader who ruminates. He should therefore have more than one stomach.")

Nietzsche was right—never mind that he was also making a pitch for reading the peculiar books he wrote. And what he said is truer now than then. We have indeed more or less forgotten, or unlearned, how to read in this way. We do read a great deal—printed words are more abundant than ever. We read for technical information. We read for professional advancement. We read for practical advice and, in the current cant, for self-help. We read for diversion. We read for all kinds of purposes on the Internet. But we (with the exception of professional intellectuals and some thoughtful individuals) seldom read with rumination. For this requires chewing and swallowing and chewing again, pondering and repondering the import of a statement, the resonance of a line, the associations of an image, fathoming implications, pursuing insights, following to its utmost consequences the trajectory of an idea. We "modern men" and women want our readings short, quick, and to the point. We don't want to have to puzzle them out. We don't want to have to work at our reading. We don't want to ruminate.

These resistances have many causes. The urgent pace of our daily routine is one. The pressure of vocational expertise is another. The omnipresence of easy entertainments and inviting recreations is still another. Yet the principal cause might well be how we are taught and expected to read in school.

How and why are we taught to read? In the early grades, reading, like the other elementary Rs, 'Riting and 'Rithmetic, is taught as a skill. And skill is needed to do it: we must learn to mentally translate orthographic marks into words that signify meaning—people in oral cultures have often found it puzzling that such visual marks, similar to those they use ornamentally, can possess that kind of symbolic power. But beyond its early stages, reading calls for, or at least invites, much more than skill. For words are the stuff of thought and are our intellectual means of sharing our existence with others, making sense of experience, and understanding life. This has probably never been demonstrated more dramatically than in the life of Helen Keller.

Helen Keller discovered the power of words in a dramatic moment well known through popular versions of her story. Robbed of sight and hearing at the age of eighteen months, she grew into childhood with deepening frustration over her inability to communicate, and in consequence grew intractable, unruly, and inaccessible to instruction. Then one day, when she was seven years old, as she recalls in *The Story of My Life*:

> Someone was drawing water and my teacher placed my hand under the spout. As the cool stream gushed over one hand she spelled into the other the word *water*, first slowly, then rapidly. I stood still, my whole attention fixed upon the motions of her fingers. Suddenly I felt a misty consciousness as of something forgotten—a thrill of returning thought; and somehow the mystery of language was revealed to me. I knew then that "w-a-t-e-r" meant the wonderful cool something that was flowing over my hand.

That living word awakened my soul, gave it light, hope, joy, set it free! There were barriers still, it is true, but barriers that could in time be swept away. I left the house eager to learn. Everything had a name, and each name gave birth to a new thought.

Helen Keller's acquisition of language amounted to much more than learning a skill. It enabled her to envision a common universe, to think as a person, to belong. "The beautiful truth burst upon my mind," she remembered: "I felt that there were invisible lines stretched between my spirit and the spirits of others." Language freed her to live in the human world. And words that continued to be inscribed in her palm, as well as, later, Braille, gave her the language through which she communicated in that world.

Few people discover the power of words as forcefully as this. But discover it they can. And this power need only be tapped to impart an efficacy to reading and writing that far surpasses classroom skill, and that should encourage rumination about what the written word says to us.

The efficacy of the written word does bring risks. And these have caused worriers through the ages to cast a critical eye on books and their uses in the wrong hands. Socrates, who never read or wrote a word, retold in the *Phaedrus* a mythical warning that the very invention of written language would eventually weaken mind and memory by rendering them passive—he confined rumination to pondering the spoken word. And Plato advocated banning all literature except "hymns to the gods and paeans in praise of famous men," because "once you go beyond that and admit the sweet lyric or epic muse, pleasure and pain become your rulers instead of law." This censorious bent also played a notable role in Europe's first novel, Cervantes's *Don Quixote* (a book very much about reading). Condemning the books that had inspired Don Quixote's knightly persona, a cleric cries: "I would pitch them into the fire" for having "the audacity to confuse the minds of intelligent and well-born gentlemen" with lying visions of "new ways of life." Don Quixote's books get burned and his library walled up for just this reason.

There is no denying it: reading can be dangerous. For it can indeed lead to "new ways of life." But that effect is not in itself dangerous. It rather points to the elemental value of reading, especially with rumination: to understand human life and how to live it, and sometimes to find reasons to change it. In Nietzsche's words, rumination prods us to ask: "'What really was that which we have just experienced?' And moreover: 'Who are we really?'" Or, as Cervantes's contemporary Michel de Montaigne wrote in his essays "Of the Education of Children" and "Experience," reading should give us not merely a "bookish competence" but help make us "better and wiser" so we can achieve "our great and glorious masterpiece," which is "to live appropriately."

No readings provoke these ruminative inquiries more insistently than the classics. But what is a classic? Who has the authority to say? Who should read them? How? Why?

These questions are both ancient and modern. The word *classic* originally denoted Roman authors of the highest social class; later the denotation widened to include authors in the two "classical" languages, Greek and Latin. With the decline of these languages in schooling, *classic* became a generic label for all standard authors representing "the best that has been thought and written," as Matthew Arnold had put it with Victorian confidence—embodied, for instance, by the "Harvard Classics" launched in 1909. But in recent times Arnold's confidence has given way to roiling debates over what constitutes a classic, and even over whether any book deserves that old-fashioned status. In short, one of the liveliest issues in higher education today is: what should people read, and how, and why? I will touch on those debates as I consider what defines a classic and how to read them.

24. THE EXISTENTIAL READER

Reading comes first. There are many ways to read a book, and especially the classics, which for the moment we can think of in Arnold's terms. Most of these types of reading can be found scattered through the college curriculum. There is the biographical, which seeks sources of a book in the author's life and illuminates relations between this work and others by the same hand. There is the historical which places a book within the contexts of a tradition and of its own times. There is the philosophical, which analyzes the intellectual framework and content of a book, situating it within the author's oeuvre and identifying its intellectual filiations and philosophical implications. There is the literary-critical, which elucidates and appraises the formal literary properties of a book. There is the social-scientific, which interprets a book within broad patterns of creativity and behavior. There is that of the liberal arts in general, which celebrates the expansiveness of mind that familiarity with the book and the tradition it represents can bring. And there is what might be named the existential, which looks to a book for signs of a common humanity or condition, and for an understanding of how we live now, and how we might live, or how we should live.

All of these and other types of reading are important. They all contribute to a liberal education. But the one that should come first, particularly where classic books are concerned—not in the order of intellectual import but in the order of first things to be done—is the existential.

An existential reading is a practical reading of the kind Nietzsche and Montaigne commended—and Jean-Jacques Rousseau, too, who insisted in his seminal book on education, *Émile*, that we ask of every book and idea: "What is the use of that?" It contrasts with a theoretical reading. Theoretical reading stimulates thinking about the relations of ideas to each other. Existential reading stimulates thinking about the relations of ideas to action. Since living depends on actions—making decisions, managing emotions, exercising will, formulating and following rules, conducting social interactions, and the like—thinking about how we should act is a universal kind of thinking. And reading to these ends is a universal kind of reading. It entails saying to a book: "I will read you not to fathom your intellectual depths, or to discover your author's intentions, or to add to what scholars know of you, but to learn what you can teach me directly about my life." The practical or existential reader herself or himself is therefore the measure of the existential meaning of the book. That is not to say, with the deconstructionists, that the book has no "objective meaning." It is to say that an existential reading draws on lived experience more than on academic learning in framing a response to the book; and it precedes the varieties of reading that search more thoroughly for the meaning of a book historically or on its own terms.

Many people do not think classics can usefully be read this way. Some deem newer books, the fruits of modern learning, to be more informative, accurate, relevant, and beneficial than the classics. This judgment (echoing partisans of modern authors against the ancients in the seventeenth-century Battle of the Books and commonly voiced today by social scientists who labor to advance the scientific understanding of human behavior) misses the point. For an existential reading of the classics does not presume to supplant modern research or the reading of current books. It prepares the ground for them.

Other readers, whose opinions are much in the air these days, judge the classics to be not so much outdated as woefully parochial—historically, culturally, ideologically. Hence, they contest the very principle that an existential reading of the classics could be a suitable foundation for a liberal education. More on this later.

Another argument against reading the classics existentially takes aim from yet another angle. Its exponents prize the classics, but they inveigh against reading them for practical ends, because they judge such a reading guilty of that capital academic crime: superficiality. This contention, which echoes in the corridors of academe and appears regularly in reviews of books and grant proposals, is not only familiar, it has merit. But it can do more harm than good. Hence it warrants extended comment.

To be "superficial," as any dictionary tells us, is to deal in surfaces, not substance, to skirt detail, seize the obvious, overlook subtlety, complexity, genuine significance. Compared to the specialists' expertise, other people's knowledge of a subject can hardly avoid superficiality in being less exacting and extensive. But the charge of superficiality bears scrutiny on several counts. In the first place, that charge often arises not so much from the vantage of professional expertise as from professional ideology and careerist territoriality. It says: we experts alone possess the right to define knowledge in our area of specialization, and others who venture there are interlopers trafficking in the shallow, the incomplete, the obvious, the erroneous. And yet, thanks to a long line of thinkers, including many classic authors, we have learned to see ideological self-interest in even so ostensibly objective a professional judgment as that one (and scholars have demonstrated that not even the pursuit of scientific truth is free of ideological baggage). Indisputably, whatever else it does, the charge of superficiality always serves the interests of those who make it. It protects their conception of what knowledge is and their right to lend that conception professional authority, as well as to admit or deny persons and purported truth to their fold. And it serves those interests whether the results advance knowledge or not.

Professional interests are assuredly not in themselves bad. It was, after all, to legitimize them that professional organizations and schools came into existence (beginning in the late nineteenth century) and continue to proliferate. This legitimacy has made it possible to protect standards of professional training and performance, to license approved practitioners, and to exclude the unworthy. These professional practices have brought many benefits, as has the growth of specialized knowledge in almost every field. Nor should we forget the peril to the culture overall represented by what the great nineteenth-century historian Jacob Burckhardt called the "terrible simplifiers": those who would banish all subtlety and complexity to satisfy the popular desire for easy and self-serving generalizations—they debase all value, and propaganda is their natural idiom.

But for all of the benefits to society of professionalism and specialization, a liability also resides in granting professional insiders the exclusive right to determine what is true and false, what is good and bad, what is genuine knowledge and what is ignorant opinion. This liability inheres in the possibility that someone on the outside, someone not admitted to the circle of specialized knowledge, someone trafficking in the "superficial," might just be right and make a valuable contribution to human enlightenment.

The history of science, for example, is dotted with figures who brought an outsider's perspective to scientific inquiry and gave startling interpretations that changed the course of science—the young Albert Einstein, excluded from academe and toiling in a Swiss patent office, is perhaps the most renowned. But instances occur in every field of learning. For, even though the insider's knowledge is more intimate than the outsider's, it is limited by the insider's close-up perspective, which may encompass too much detail, focus on too many things close at hand, miss the forest for the trees. Participants in any activity will be blind to some facts that only outside observers can see—social scientists, especially anthropologists, combat this impediment all the time. After all, shouldn't an intelligent and reasonably perceptive person without specialized training be able to perceive, say, a psychological truth in the everyday behavior of people, or a key to morals in a novel, or a secret of art in a painting? Superficial though their insights may appear from the professional insider's point of view, they may be as true, as important as the insider's. The history of literature easily demonstrates this.

That the outsider's "superficial" understanding might yield an insight unavailable to the insider points to another fallacy in the charge of superficiality. This has to do with the relativity of the superficial. What is superficial to the specialist, in the sense of being factually incomplete, or intellectually unsubtle, or obvious, or insignificant, may be a sobering truth or a lightning bolt of illumination to someone else. And what is profound judgment or penetrating revelation to the specialist may be a commonplace or an academic pedantry to someone outside. Scholars and journalists often view each other's activities from these contrary perspectives; and we might well remember that no scholar ever turned more savagely against his kind for their pretentiousness and pedantries than that ruminating, revolutionary thinker Nietzsche—read his essay "On Scholars" in *Thus Spake Zarathustra* about those who laboriously "knit the socks of the soul," and smile, even if you are a scholar.

Superficiality is a damning label. Always. And because it is, it can obstruct rather than facilitate learning by intimidating minds and daunting intellectual activity. No one, least of all a student, should be dissuaded by the threat of superficiality from developing the intellectual self-confidence to read and think for himself or herself. But, irony of ironies, as Nietzsche would say, educators themselves all too often undermine this confidence by instilling an intimidating reverence for specialized learning as the only legitimate kind, and by dismissing all other learning as mere vocationalism—or superficiality.

For all of its proper purposes, and they are many, the accusations of superficiality should therefore be but sparingly leveled against general education. And it should be all but shelved where an existential reading of the classics is concerned. For an existential reading is not existentially superficial: it supplies the most thought-provoking and lasting source of useful learning that anyone can have. This is true because of what a classic is. And to define a classic is to return to the venerable debate over the appropriate contents of general education, and to the contemporary controversy over what, if anything, should constitute the "canon" of classics.

Two qualities characterize a classic and distinguish it from other books, even other very good books. One is that it lends itself to the many types of reading noted above. The second is that whatever a classic's rootedness in historical contexts, or its literary properties, or its philosophical insights, it is not confined to them. It rises above—or perhaps we should say, goes outside of—all of these features to communicate to readers who dwell far in time and place from the book's origins, and who may know but little or nothing of history, aesthetic form, or philosophy. The classics can do this because, in addition to everything else we can say about them, they address generic questions of human existence.

This familiar assertion has caused a lot of pother among educators in recent years. The fuss has been highly political, as disputes over education usually are (not for nothing did Plato and Aristotle put education at the heart of their formative political theories). And at their most divisive these controversies have produced two fractious parties loosely identified by their conservative or liberal leanings.

The conservatives tend to defend the classics as a pillar of higher education and indispensable to the "cultural literacy" that has become a shibboleth of conservative educational reform. But to advocate the classics as the source of a cultural identity in this way is to err twice. For one thing, it harnesses the classics too tightly to Western culture and a historical reading. As historical documents charting the course of Western civilization, the classics can seem all too remote from modern readers. For another, and more decisive, it plays into the hands of the liberal critics who, in their fundamental contention, rule the classics irretrievably parochial for a host of reasons. Seizing the opportunity, these critics have won some notable victories in chasing the classics from classrooms with their accusation, in the words of one distinguished and vocal exponent, Henry Louis Gates, Jr., the standard Western classics present a picture of human existence "in which none of the members of the black community, the minority community of color, or the women's community, were ever able to discover the revelation or representation of their images or hear the resonances of their cultural voices." This accusation should be taken very seriously for it holds some truth.

But, if the conservative defense of the classics errs on the side of intellectual and cultural parochialism, this liberal assault often goes farther awry. For, as remarked earlier, it virtually denies the existence of a classic. It claims that no book can address generic human interests because none can be said to arise from common human experience: all merely reflect ideologies born of the author's historical moment, social class, race, culture, sex; and this generally means, as Gates's words indicate, the ideology of privileged white Western males—to say nothing of the "cancel culture" movement that would later assail all established cultural traditions for offending someone or other.

There can be no doubt that differences of time, class, race, culture, and sex are very important indeed in shaping human lives; and it is to grasp this importance that we should read many classic authors. But it is a mistake to believe these differences are definitive, negating common experience, perceptions, understanding, or judgment—even for victims of distinctly trying circumstances, as, for instance, Frederick Douglass and Elie Wiesel illustrate. It is a mistake because it tells us that authors can speak to no readers except those exactly like themselves in time or social class or ethnicity or sex or life experience. And it loses perspective on what makes human beings similar and dissimilar, on what they share and do not share. It also denies the possibility that a classic can issue from any gifted person and from any culture. So, to wisely follow the liberal criticism of the classics, we should not expel the classics from the curriculum and abandon the idea of a classic altogether but rather encourage widening the "canon" of classics, which some colleges have done.

Questions about truth, values, and action, or, in Montaigne's words, about how "to live appropriately," are likely to elicit dissimilar responses from different kinds of people in different times and places. But everyone asks these questions, and everyone gains if the

IV. On Humanism, Classics, Laughter, Proust, and the Meaning of Life

questions are asked and the answers sought collectively. The most remarkable thing about the classics is just this: they enable readers to think and talk together about how to live, despite these readers' dissimilarities.

And this is what a classic, whatever its historical or cultural or human origins, most definitively is: a work of mind and imagination that for all of its historical and authorial particularity is most emphatically *not* parochial. It belongs to no single group. It speaks not with one voice but many. And it says different things to different people and to different ages and individuals, speaking more forcibly to some than to others, ascending and descending in reputation over time. But always, in one way or another, with constant or recurrent force, a classic from any hand continues to speak. Readers have only to listen to it, ruminate, and to hear how the author, with an enduringly resonant voice, is addressing the questions all people ask themselves and their contemporaries almost from the time they themselves begin to speak—and surely from the time they begin to read.

These are the kinds of questions Montaigne had in mind when he listed the things a person most needs to know:

> What you may justly wish; the use and ends of hard-earned coin; our debt to country and to friends; what heaven has ordered us to be, and where our stand amid humanity is fixed by high command; what we now are, what destiny for us is planned; what it is to know and not to know, and what must be the aim of study; what are valor, temperance, and justice; what the difference is between ambition and avarice, servitude and submission, license and liberty; what springs move us, and the cause of different impulses in us; by what signs we may recognize true solid contentment; how much we should fear death, pain, and shame; what hardships to avoid, what to endure, and how.

This is Montaigne (one of the now widely reviled, dead, white, privileged, European males) writing in "Of the Education of Children" nearly five hundred years ago, and drawing on authors who wrote a thousand years and more before him. We all still ask the same questions. We still try to answer them.

The classics do not tell us everything we need to know about these matters. Far from it. But there is no better stimulus to rumination about this skein of queries that entangle our lives than the classics, be they ancient or modern, Western or non-Western—Plato or Confucius, Dante or Murasaki Shikibu, Shakespeare or *The Arabian Nights*, Voltaire or Ghanian folklore, Karl Marx or Frederick Douglass, Sigmund Freud or Virginia Woolf, and many more. For the ruminating existential reader has learned to hear and converse with the voices that speak in the classics across expanses of time and space and the barriers of race, class, culture, and gender about the subject closest to all of us: how to live.

A previous, longer version of this essay originally appeared under the same title in *The Sewanee Review*, Winter, 1991. An expansive elaboration of its subject, with many examples of how to read the classics in the way described here, was published in *Worldly Wisdom: Great Books and the Meanings of Life* (2008).

Classics as Casebooks.

Some things can be learned but cannot, strictly speaking, be taught.

The Classics

CASEBOOKS OF HUMANISTIC EDUCATION

*I*n the Renaissance classic *The Book of the Courtier*, the author, Baldassare Castiglione, has an instructive count point out to his pupil that the secret of a courtier's success is *grace*. Then the count adds: "I am not bound to teach you how to acquire grace or anything else, but only to tell you what a perfect courtier ought to be."

Here Castiglione puts his finger on a troubling truth of teaching: it is one thing to specify the ends of education; it is quite another to prescribe the sure means. This truth points to another, possibly ever more troubling truth: some things can be learned but cannot, strictly speaking, be taught; in other words, they can be learned only through lived experience, not through instruction. Long before Castiglione, Aristotle had identified moral virtue as one of these things. Castiglione's *grace* is a form of unteachable moral virtue. And any parent who has tried to teach virtue to a child knows that Aristotle and Castiglione were onto something.

When we ask why the likes of grace or any virtue can be learned but not taught, we will have to answer that this is because they are not matters of intellectual knowledge or of technical skill but of *right action*. Although the *rules* of right action can—and must—be taught and learned intellectually, right action itself can be learned and mastered only by action itself through repeated practice in experience.

The impossibility—or at any rate the difficulty—of teaching right action does not, to be sure, keep us from trying. Nor should it. And our attempts to do this should alert us to the possibilities and

IV. On Humanism, Classics, Laughter, Proust, and the Meaning of Life

limitations, the successes and failures, of teaching and education, particularly in the humanities.

Within the curriculum of general education, the subjects most closely associated with right action, or the value judgments underlying it, are the humanities—especially philosophy, literature, and history. Yet few who teach or study the humanities nowadays would likely name right action as the end of humanistic education. Among those who do, probably even fewer could say with certainty just how humanistic education is related to action, or how teaching holds the key to making that relationship work.

Here we encounter the uses of humanistic education. Everyone knows that humanistic education has to do with states of mind or feeling, mastering bodies of knowledge, and exercising intellect. But because its very subject matter is the full range of human experience—intellectual, emotional, aesthetic, social, cultural—it also has to do with judging values and determining action. That is, it implicitly addresses the questions of value that underlie action: "How should one act?" "How should one live?"

And this raises anew the issue of to what extent right action can be taught. As noted above, strictly speaking, it cannot be taught because it consists of *willed doing* in active experience, not in *passive knowing*. Only in action can it be mastered. But if we cannot teach right action itself, we can nevertheless lead students toward it. The means of accomplishing this are known to adroit teachers of the humanities and the professions alike—an affinity more teachers of the humanities would do well to notice. For these means are none other than instruction in *how to think about right action* and *how best to translate those thoughts into behavior*.

But how do you teach students to think about right action? Dogmatism is one way. Teach them absolutes, says the dogmatist, then they will know not only *how* to think but *what* to think and *what* to do. Religious fanatics are good at it. George Orwell coined the term "goodthink" for such a way of thinking, and to its exponents in the novel *1984* it meant the official "truth" that must be accepted,

25. THE CLASSICS

rejecting all alternatives (see "Orwell, Mind Control, and Our Times" above).

But dogmatism is not actually thought at all. It is a fixed mentality that precedes experience and tells you how to interpret it, that precludes thinking and substitutes itself for it, that prevents learning by calling it obedience. Voltaire's Pangloss in *Candide* may be the archetypal comic professor of dogmatism in this sense (of which more below).

Thinking about right action is quite the opposite of embracing dogmatism. For such thinking is complicated, not simple; difficult, not easy; active, not passive. It requires the careful examination of facts, ideas, experiences, and choices in the light of value judgments. One must examine, for example, the ideal ends of action, the relative goods in human experience, the costs and rewards of choice and responsibility, the merits of disparate claims to truth and value, the relation of thought to feeling, and the effects of actions on both the actor and others.

Anyone accustomed to asking such questions is thinking about right action. This is not to say that all who ask will agree on the answers. Nor is it to say that anyone who asks will act on the answers reached. Yet, without asking such questions, no one can be counted on to act properly. Thinking about right action is, therefore, a necessary but not a sufficient condition for acting properly: thinking does not by itself cause the action, but the action could not occur without it.

But beyond this training in thinking about value-charged questions, how can teachers lead students from thought to action? If they can, it is only by demonstrating the uses and benefits of such thinking in lived experience. Humanistic education should openly adopt this rootedness in actuality and focus on it. And nowhere is it more appropriate to do that than in reading the classics.

Teachers could even take a cue here from the case study method used in many professional schools. The range of experience addressed by a classic work of philosophy or literature is, of course, far wider than that represented by the specific examples in law school or business school casebooks. But taken as whole books, or by chapters, or even by significant paragraphs, the classics present situations in experience to reflect upon and to rouse debate over how one should act in those situations. That makes studying the classics for right action analogous to how law and business schools study cases for insights into making decisions in the conduct of law or business. Many humanists would recoil at this notion as bastardization. But they would be wrong.

Take, for example, the dialogues of Plato dealing with the trial and death of Socrates, or the *Ethics* of Aristotle. These works are full of high-minded philosophizing, but they also ask the value-charged questions: What is the difference between belief and knowledge, and what difference does this difference make? What are the moral consequences of wrongdoing? To what extent are we responsible for our actions and for our own character? Is there a human nature, and if so, what are its implications for right action? To what ends should one dedicate a life? What is the relative value of material and moral or spiritual well-being? What is the proper connection between self-interest and social obligation? Is it ever right to break a law? And what are the consequences in action of our answers to any of these questions? Such questions directly link education, experience, thought, and action. And the mind attuned to them is both analytically agile and prepared to act with results in mind.

Or take Dante's *Inferno*. As a case study in right action it is an exploration of the moral landscape that we all inhabit. It asks, most generally: What are the nature and consequences of wrong action? In pursuing an answer, Dante takes a journey through Hell where he sees the psychological and cultural effects of wrong action. And this compels us to ask: Why does Dante deem fraud—including flattery, hypocrisy, and theft—worse than murder, and treason the worst evil of all? To answer this question is not simply to become conversant with Dante; it is to see the moral psychology of deception and, above all, the necessity of trust to the social bond. With this knowledge in mind, who could thoughtlessly deceive others, much less betray them? By plumbing the depths of wrong action, Dante sheds a bright light on right action.

Or Machiavelli. Arguably the first political "how-to book," *The Prince* is also much more. For it asks: How do we succeed at anything? Machiavelli presents many historical cases of political success and failure to demonstrate his point that success always requires: (a) clear perception of ends, (b) full understanding of circumstances, and (c) willingness to employ any means within those circumstances to achieve those ends. Although applied by Machiavelli particularly to maintaining power in Renaissance princedoms, Machiavelli's rules can apply to any other pursuit—teaching and living a moral life among them. *The Prince* is, therefore, not just an innovative book in political theory. It is a casebook in how to think about ends and means and how to act on the right means to reach your ends.

Voltaire's *Candide* and Rousseau's *Émile* can also be read as casebooks in right action. They both address the question: How does one learn anything, for good or ill? Candide's misadventures under the tutelage of Dr. Pangloss repeatedly draw the reader, along with Candide, into the gulf between dogmatism and education. The dogmatism of Pangloss, expressed in his unwavering creed "this is the best of all possible worlds," enables him to "explain" every experience, but to understand none. For to understand experience is to be open to what it has to teach us. And thereby to learn from it and be able to judge and master it. Pangloss and Candide can do none of this, as they blindly stumble from one adversity to another, guided, or rather misguided, by Pangloss's dogmatic philosophy. Eventually, Candide discards Pangloss's empty reasoning for practical knowledge grounded in experience—specifically the knowledge that hard work brings greater mastery of experience than does any abstract philosophizing. Experience finally teaches him how to think about right action. And he acts on it.

IV. On Humanism, Classics, Laughter, Proust, and the Meaning of Life

In Rousseau's *Émile*, the barrier to learning from experience is not dogmatism but the mistaken assumptions and misdirected practices of society at large. To reveal those flaws, Rousseau follows Émile from childhood to adulthood under the tutelage of a mentor who examines all customary and conventional practices with the question: What is the difference between the natural and the artificial, the necessary and the accidental, the beneficial and the detrimental, the real and the merely apparently real? No parental practice, schooling requirement, social manners, or mores escape scrutiny under this sobering question. This scrutiny reveals how parents, teachers, and society have repeatedly supplied the wrong answers, with the result that children are usually miseducated to be book-learned but ignorant of life, to be moralistic but dishonest, to be self-indulgent but self-deceived, to be selfish but miserable. We all learn from experience, Rousseau says, but we too often learn the wrong lessons from it, because we fail to examine closely enough exactly how and what we are truly learning. In short, we don't learn how to learn. If we did, we would act more responsibly to the genuine benefit of ourselves and those we influence. No one who reads *Émile* in this way can fail to think a little differently about experience and how we learn from it, and want to act more deliberately as parent, teacher, human being.

The list could go on and on. By treating the classics as something like casebooks in thinking—or ruminating, to use a term of Friedrich Nietzsche (see "The Existential Reader: Reading, Rumination, and the Classics" above)—about right action, teachers can make humanistic education the study of lived experience and a preparation for action that it should be. So, even if we cannot strictly speaking teach right action, we can teach minds to think about how to act and to see the consequences in experience of acting one way rather than another. And there is no more fruitful source for thinking about right action in this way than the classics. When a person can draw on the wisdom of the ages, as the cliché goes, for this purpose, such a person has truly learned how to learn from books *and* experience about right action in life. Humanistic education can have no better end than that.

A previous version of this essay was originally published under the same title in *Teaching and the Case Method*, ed. C. Roland Christensen, Harvard Business School, 1986.

"*Every time a man smiles . . . but much more so when he laughs, it adds something to this Fragment of Life.*"
—LAURENCE STERNE

Let 'em Laugh

TRISTRAM SHANDY AND THE HUMANITY OF LAUGHTER

Everybody likes to laugh. It feels good, and it can turn darkness into light. "Humor is the great thing, the saving thing," said Mark Twain. "The minute it crops up, all our irritations and resentments slip away, and a sunny spirit takes their place." Comedy can even help cure illness, or at least assuage pain. The prominent author Norman Cousins demonstrated this when he successfully combated a debilitating disease with funny films (and vitamin C), as he reported in *Anatomy of an Illness.* Nowadays some hospitals offer a television channel of full-time comedy called the Chuckle Channel to spur health and counter the often disheartening TV fare of daily news and violent entertainment.

No one has known the power—and humanity—of laughter better, or written about it with greater genius and deeper affection, than that genial Anglican cleric and ribald comic novelist of the eighteenth century, Laurence Sterne. His novel *The Life and Opinions of Tristram Shandy, Gentleman* (popularly known as *Tristram Shandy*) remains the quintessential comic novel of all time.

It must be said, though, that many people have found *Tristram Shandy* unreadable. Its frequent breaks and odd punctuation (all preserved in the quotations here), its blank, black, and mottled pages, its fractured chronology, its abundant allusions to other books, and its long, tangled digressions can try patience. But it lives as a true classic that everyone should manage to read for many reasons. No less a reader than Sterne's contemporary Thomas Jefferson said in a letter that "the writings of Sterne form the best course of morality that ever was written." A near contemporary, Johann von Goethe, to whom Sterne became more important with every passing year, declared in *Wilhelm Meister's Wanderjahre* that Sterne was "the first who lifted us above pedantry and philistinism" and "was the most beautiful spirit who ever created; anyone who reads him immediately feels full and beautiful." Later, Friedrich Nietzsche lauded Sterne in *Human, All-Too Human* as "the most liberated spirit of all time," because Sterne broke with conventions about how to write and think with his eccentric prose and lively embrace of life's ambiguities and vicissitudes. That is all high praise, and it has continued on through later authors like James Joyce and Virginia Woolf, who found Sterne's novel inspirationally modern. But in his own modest yet hopeful way, Sterne simply said of it: "I write a careless kind of a civil, nonsensical, good humored *Shandean* book, which will do all your hearts good—And all your heads too—provided you understand it" (349—all quotations from the Modern Library edition).

In short, *Tristram Shandy* is a laughing book to think about—and ruminate on, as Nietzsche would say. I'll briefly—with a few Shandean digressions—take us through some of what Sterne wants us to laugh and think about, down to his laughing and yet highly moral vision of life.

First a few words on comedy. For one thing, comedy is the mirror image of tragedy. Both upset expectations of how life should be. We meet tragedy in literature and life when terrible things happen to noble or good or even merely innocent people, leaving lasting scars and sorrows in their wake. Comedy, manipulating recognizable situations to produce surprising results, turns some of those same upset expectations—about truth, authority, morality, mortality, rationality, and other facts and ideas that affect our lives—into laughter. And we laugh because we are *not* threatened. Whereas tragedy in life engulfs us, comedy detaches us, giving us a pleasurable emotional release

26. Let 'Em Laugh

in laughter, even at things we might fear. It is easy to see why some religions have barred comedy for undermining piety and subverting their power. The novelist Umberto Eco wrote a famous book about this—*The Name of the Rose*, a medieval murder mystery centering on a Catholic abbot's ingeniously lethal tactics for punishing readers of the supposedly sole existing copy of Aristotle's treatise on comedy, which the abbot could not bring himself to destroy.

There are, of course, many kinds of comedy and many kinds of laughter, from loving to cruel. But the kinds that run through *Tristram Shandy* never sink to the cruel or the mean-spirited contrived to boost the laugher's ego at other people's expense. They always lift us up, as they poke gentle fun at our expectations of how life—and literature—work. As Sterne explained in an evocative sermon called "The Levite and the Concubine" (marked by his typical eccentric style and punctuation—but ellipses added):

> There is a difference between [. . .] the malignity and the festivity of wit,—the one is a mere quickness of apprehension, void of humanity,—and is a talent of the devil, [. . .] a setting up trade upon the broken stock of other people's failings—perhaps their misfortunes; [. . .] it is a commerce most illiberal [and] has helped to give wit a bad name [. . . .] The other comes down from the Father of Spirits, so pure and abstracted from persons, that willingly it hurts no man [but helps] sweeten our spirits, that we might live with such kind intercourse in this world, as will fit us to exist together in a better.

Sterne's mirthful, dancing mind skitters from laugh to laugh with this "festivity of wit" and generous reverence for humanity. This makes Sterne's laughter far more than diversion. As he says in his dedication of *Tristram Shandy* to William Pitt, "whenever a man smiles—but much more so when he laughs, he adds something to this Fragment of Life." That is the humanity of laughter.

Sterne well knows that *Tristram Shandy* comes at comedy from a most unusual angle. Although he pays ample homage to his favorite authors—notably Rabelais, Cervantes, Robert Burton, and Swift—he tells us early on (through the voice of Tristram, who narrates the book as its author) that "in writing what I have set about, I shall confine myself neither to" established rules, "nor to any man's rules that ever lived" (4). In that spirit, he advises readers to "laugh with me, or at me," but "let me go on, and tell my story in my own way" (7) in this "civil, nonsensical, good humored *Shandean* book, which will do all your hearts good—And all your heads too—provided you understand it" (349). He adds, "I wish it may have its effect—and that all good people—" will thereby "be taught to think as well as read" (45). To do our hearts and heads good, and teach us how to think and to read—these are high aspirations for a comic novel. At first we wonder what he can mean. In time we learn.

Look at how he begins the story. It is surely one of the strangest beginnings in literature. It has Tristram himself as the narrator commenting on the ill-fated act of his parents' conceiving him one Sunday night when, at the seminal moment, his mother-to-be interrupted his father-to-be by asking if he had wound the clock as he was supposed to do that night. That "very unseasonable question" (2), Tristram says, caused his father's concentration to falter, dispersing the "animal spirits" and planting the seed of an indisputably misbegotten being. This consequence becomes evident at Tristram's birth, portrayed—much later—in a prolonged scene of comic tragedy. But meanwhile, the epochal interruption of Tristram's begetting heralds Sterne's most striking, and often confusing, way of telling his story: interruptions followed by digressions.

Anyone who has read, or even skimmed, *Tristram Shandy* has seen how the story wanders from subject to subject sometimes aimlessly—and finally the book ends almost nowhere, anticlimactically as an admittedly "cock-and-bull story." It takes Sterne nearly a third of the book, for instance, to get from Tristram's account of his own conception to his description of his own birth, while Sterne introduces us to a host of other characters and meanders through their lives and ideas and the events leading up to Tristram finally entering the world with mishaps as bizarre as those of his conception. In fact, we really don't see as much of Tristram himself as we do of other characters. His "life and opinions," as the subtitle promises, run in the background as the tale he narrates wends its twisty way to the much-anticipated love story of Uncle Toby—which actually occurred long before Tristram was conceived—followed by the anticlimactic end.

Sterne is clearly making fun here of our expectations of how stories get told. But, lest the Shandean digressions throw us off, he tells us to appreciate them. For they give us a clue to how to read and think. "Digressions," he says, "incontestably, are the sunshine,—they are the life, the soul of reading" (54). But none can be "a poor creeping digression . . . it must be a good frisky one, and upon a frisky subject too" (497). He even gives us a chart of how his story goes through those frisky digressions in loops and tangents defying straight lines. He also inserts a couple of mottled pages as the "motley emblem of my work" (176). And he says that anyone who wishes to understand human life must travel the same kind of course. "If he is a man of the least spirit, he will have fifty deviations from a straight line" (28) as he looks around and pursues this and that before he gets where he is going.

So, these Shandean digressions do more than complicate the tale. They reflect the way Sterne believes human life unfolds and the mind works. And that is how they teach us how to read and think. The accidental, the incidental, the odd turn here and there lead us from one thing to another without design, accumulating consequences that shape our lives. Sterne traces such a series of accidents and incidents in Tristram's telling of his own birth, awash in thwarted plans, inept doctors, stubborn servants, untieable knots, mishandled forceps, and misunderstood instructions, resulting in the child being born with a crushed nose and receiving the wrong

Christian name. Such is life. A series of misadventures. As Tristram remarks near the end: "We live in a world beset on all sides by mysteries and riddles" (507).

Amidst these mysteries and riddles, the human mind tries to make sense of it all. It does this with ideas that link one experience to another, sometimes by intent, sometimes willy-nilly. These ideas draw our attention to this and that and prompt digressions. Sterne was playing here with John Locke's theory of the Association of Ideas, widely influential at the time, which describes how our minds begin as blank slates, then our experiences write ideas on them, and as these ideas get associated with one another we learn to think and understand the world. I said Sterne *plays* with this theory, and play he does. For he makes as much fun of it as he honors it.

It supplies the comedy that begins the book. Tristram's mother interrupted her husband with the "unseasonable question" asked about the clock because he regularly wound it once a month on the same Sunday that they also shared physical intimacy. That intimacy and the clock went together in her mind—an unfortunate association of ideas at an inopportune moment.

Tristram's uncle Toby becomes the fullest comic embodiment of the association of ideas. A former soldier who had suffered an unspecified groin injury in battle, Toby develops an obsessive "hobby-horse," or enthusiasm, about military matters, especially fortifications, as he reads voluminously while recuperating. With his servant Trim, he constructs a vast fortress and reenacts military operations, and everything he does or thinks or hears or sees now becomes *associated* in his mind with martial doings. Sensations remind him of his military past; conversations take him off to fabled battles; he even embarks on his love affair with the widow Wedman as a military campaign. It all makes for raucous comedy.

Sterne is obviously having fun with Locke's theory here. But Toby's hobby-horse and Tristram's misconception give Sterne occasion to poke fun at more than Locke's theory. They also let him throw an unexpected light on military life and the act and consequences of procreation. In *Tristram Shandy*, Toby's militarism is quite a laughing matter. And for all his sober preoccupation with it, Toby shows himself to be so unwarlike by nature that he will not kill a fly—of which more later. At the same time, Sterne bestows peculiar tragic-comic seriousness on sex, procreation, and childbirth, reversing traditional expectations of what matters most in the movement of history. Tristram's father, Walter, upholds those traditional expectations as he deplores what he views to be the near bestiality of human procreation by contrast to the heroics of war and the "glorious . . . act of killing and destroying a man" with "the weapons by which we do it," which "are honorable" (522). This is all parody for sure.

But throughout *Tristram Shandy* Sterne takes most delight in joking about how sex can wield more importance than anything else. In fact, you can read *Tristram Shandy* as a comedy of sexuality, from the opening scene of Tristram's begetting through the long metaphoric discourse on the historic influence of big noses to Toby's failed love affair with the widow Wedman owing to his impotence, and finally to the inadequate sexual performance of the bull at the very end of the book. But to dwell on that theme can obscure Sterne's higher purposes. That said, one of the erotic incidents does invite some attention because, besides the opening scene, it has won more notice than any other through the years, and it shows us again the sweet innocence of Uncle Toby. It is the vivid account by Trim, told to Toby (and narrated in Trim's voice by Tristram), of his first encounter with the emotion of love, or what he calls love. (Denis Diderot affectionately incorporated this episode almost word for word in his novel inspired by *Tristram Shandy* and modeled on Toby and Trim, *Jacques the Fatalist*).

A corporal wounded in the knee during a battle, Trim was recovering in a peasant household nursed by a virtuous young woman referred to only as Beguine (a charitable lay-sister). One day "'the fair Beguine'" offered to ease the persistent itching of his knee by massaging it. This she does—through a narrative of exquisite detail much abbreviated here—first with one finger, then two, then three, "'till little by little she brought down the fourth, and then rubb'd with her whole hand.'" In time, "'she passed her hand across the flannel, to the part above my knee, which I had equally complained of, and rubb'd it also. I perceived, then, that I was beginning to be in love—As she continued rub-rub-rubbing—I felt it spread from under her hand [. . .] to every part of my frame—'" until "'my passion rose to the highest pitch—I seiz'd her hand—.'" Here Trim reports Toby breaking into his story: "'And then, thou clapp'dst it to thy lips, Trim, said my uncle Toby—and madest a speech.'" Addressing the reader, Tristram professes ignorance of "whether the corporal's amour terminated precisely in the way my uncle Toby described it" but concludes, "it is enough that it contain'd in it the essence of all the love-romances which ever have been wrote since the beginning of the world" (464, 465). Has the erotic comedy of "love" ever been more artfully and amusingly described? After reading Trim's tale, who could fall in love through caresses without remembering Trim's knee and the risible parody of "love" it holds?

Sterne clearly elevates the significance of sex above that of most human pursuits, while getting laughs from them all. Even Walter Shandy, despite his penchant to exalt the likes of warfare and theory, showed himself subject, rather embarrassingly, to the power of sexuality, amidst distraction from it, when misbegetting Tristram.

This returns us to Tristram's own comical conceiving. Sterne treats that and Tristram's birth with a comic seriousness that parodies tragedy. Tristram's misbegetting, his mishandled birth, and his mischristening are nothing less than tragic to Tristram's father. Walter fervently believes large noses go with success in life—Sterne devotes chapters to this belief—as do appropriately dignified Christian names. When his misbegotten child comes into the world with a squashed nose and then, instead of being christened the noble Trismigistis, a thrice godlike name, errantly gets the lowly, sad moniker of Tristram because the priest has received confused instructions, Walter thinks his world has collapsed. Sterne makes comedy of his tragedy.

Walter's consuming attempts to compensate for the tragedy by providing Tristram an ideal education also becomes comedy. The theoretically minded Walter decides to write a detailed child-rearing manual to guide him—an ascending novelty in those days, capped by Rousseau's *Émile*, published in 1764, three years after Sterne's novel—loftily titled with the Greek term for education and most of his son's name, *Tristra-paideia*. But Walter's labors go for naught, because while he devotes himself for three years to writing this book he has no time for Tristram, who consequently matures in those years with no paternal guidance at all. Walter's inclination here, like his scholarly study of noses and many another instance, exhibit his penchant, as Sterne says, "to force every event in nature into an hypothesis by which means never a man crucified TRUTH at the rate he did" (521).

This penchant points to the target of Sterne's ridicule—and morality—more pervasive than any other, even sex. That is: abstract theory, intellectual pretense, pedantry, high seriousness or "gravity," and the hypocritical and inhumane attitudes that often flow from them. Sterne wants us to laugh at life and learn from our laughter (if not only from that) and to shun pretentious philosophizing, Pharisaic self-righteousness, lugubrious theology, and all the nonsense of those he derided as "learned blockheads" (Penguin edition notes, vol. 3 ch. 31).

Consider the scene of Trim and his hat. This does not stir laughter, but it illustrates Sterne's perception of truth and pretense, and his elemental humanity. The scene involves death. Tristram's brother Bobby has just died. And while Walter Shandy pontificates philosophically to Toby about mortality, all but forgetting his deceased son, the servants speak of the loss dolefully downstairs. There Trim comes in to learn the unhappy news and gives his own little discourse on death. But nothing he says speaks as forcefully as a gesture he makes with his hat. "Are we not here now," he says, thumping his walking stick on the floor to signify "health and stability—and are we not—(dropping his hat upon the ground) gone! in a moment!" Responding to Trim's act, Tristram says, "'Twas infinitely striking!" (287). For, although Trim had spoken ordinary words on life and death, "the descent of the hat was as if a heavy lump of clay had been kneaded into the crown of it.—Nothing could have expressed the sentiment of mortality[. . .]like it,—his hand seemed to vanish from under it,—it fell dead,—the corporal's eye fix'd up on it, as upon a corpse. . . ." (288). And Tristram concludes, "Ye who govern this mighty world and its mighty concerns with the *engines* of eloquence,—who heat it, and cool it, and melt it, and mollify it,—and then harden it again to *your purpose*—[. . .]— meditate—meditate, I beseech you, upon *Trim's* hat" (289).

No comedy here, but the simple drama of Trim's act speaks volumes about human mortality and its effects on those who lose someone close. Unvarnished perceptions and honest emotions take us closer to the reality of human existence than any theory or theology. To those whose minds remain mantled in theory and intellectual pretense, Sterne snaps, "I write not for them" (156).

The whole book makes this case in a variety of ways. But Sterne gives us one character who particularly embodies it. This is Parson Yorick, Sterne's alter ego—Sterne published his own sermons under the pen name Yorick, as he did his last book, *A Sentimental Journey*.

Derived from the jester of the same name in *Hamlet*, Yorick is also a jester despite being a cleric (like Sterne himself). A gangly fellow, Yorick rides around his parish on a skinny old horse said to resemble Don Quixote's Rocinante. People laugh at him, and he joins "in the laughter against himself" because "he loved jest in his heart" (13). His jesting heart cannot resist making light of seriousness and the attitude of "gravity" that he finds at once risible and hypocritical.

"Yorick had an invincible dislike and opposition in his nature to gravity," Sterne writes, or rather "to the affectation of it [. . .] as it appeared a cloak for ignorance, or for folly [. . . .] Sometimes, in his wild way of talking, he would say, That gravity was an errant scoundrel; and he would add,—of the most dangerous kind too,—because a sly one" since "the very essence of gravity was design, and consequently deceit;—'twas a taught trick to gain credit of the world for more sense and knowledge than a man was worth" (19).

Fired by this distaste for the affectation of gravity, Yorick skewered every sign of it. And he found plenty of them. Being "a man unhackneyed and unpracticed in the world" (19), he gave free reign to "his wit and humour,—his gibes and jests" (20) at the expense of anyone affecting gravity, especially with self-importance. But, unfortunately, he failed to see that the butt of his jests didn't laugh with him. Eventually, some of these aggrieved "Jestees" attacked him one night and gave him a vicious thrashing. Yorick fought valiantly and survived the assault. Even so, he died soon afterwards, not from his wounds but, "as was generally thought, quite brokenhearted" (22). Mourners marked his grave in the corner of the church yard with a stone and an epitaph in the plaintive words from *Hamlet*: "Alas, poor YORICK!" (24). Sterne follows these words with a full blank black page of grief.

While Yorick embodies Sterne's love of jest and antipathy to affected gravity, he also exemplifies some of the other virtues that Sterne prizes. These include modesty, honesty, and decency. And Tristram warmly observes that Yorick avoided even the appearance of self-righteousness by, for instance, never revealing that he rode a ramshackle horse and endured ridicule for it, rather than riding a better one, just so his parishioners would not ask to borrow the animal and he could therefore continue making his rounds for the old and sick without interruption. He was a pure-hearted fellow, if naïve about some effects of his jests.

But even more than Yorick, the moral comedy of *Tristram Shandy* belongs to Uncle Toby. Toby and Trim ramble about the book like Don Quixote and Sancho. Just as the knight errant sallied forth to right wrongs, Toby performed his faux military expeditions to do good. Both are noble souls, brimming with humanity, if a little daft. And Sterne has Toby say that "the peerless knight of La Mancha . . . with all his follies, I love more and would actually have gone farther to have paid a visit to than the greatest hero of antiquity" (15–16).

Toby possesses a humanity rooted in an innate honesty, simplicity, sincerity, humility, and charity. He is no jester like Yorick, but he disdains affectation, pretentiousness, and hypocrisy—and he whistles a tune whenever he hears highfalutin talk, which happens a lot with his brother Walter. And his humanity shines brightest in his charitable generosity of spirit toward all living things. He is one of the few truly Good persons in literature. That is not an easy type to create, as Plato was the first to observe, noting that the rational and orderly life gives little to portray in literature, whereas conflicts and troubles provide endlessly arresting material. The history of literature, to say nothing of modern entertainment, confirms this, with a few exceptions. We might think of Don Quixote as one of those exceptions, but he wreaks a lot of havoc for all of his good intentions. George Eliot's Dorothea Brooke also brims with good intentions and finally learns to fulfill them, but only after her early overweening moral ideals practically destroy her. Dostoevsky attempted to fashion a Good Man in the character of Myshkin in *The Idiot*, but he had to make him nearly mentally defective to do it. Tolstoy also gave us a morally ideal person in *War and Peace* with Platon Karataev, a spiritually impeccable figure who calmly endures all suffering, but who has to live a rather other-worldly life to make that possible and comes to a sorry, if spiritually uncompromising, end. And W. Somerset

26. Let 'Em Laugh

Maugham thought he had presented a Good Man in the story "Salvatore," whose title character has simple goodness of heart but not much of a life. Toby's goodness has more consistency and depth than any of these and better illuminates the moral life at large.

Toby might be bit of a simpleton, but despite the goofy things he does—like Don Quixote—he teaches Tristram the humanity of moral goodness. He does this first in an offhand incident that no one who reads it will quickly forget. As Tristram recalls it, "one day at dinner" a pesky fly "buzz'd about his [Toby's] nose, and tormented him cruelly." Finally, Toby captured the pest, and "rising from his chair, and going a-cross the room, with the fly in his hand" he said, "I'll not hurt a hair of thy head:—Go, says he, lifting up the sash, and opening his hand as he spoke, to let it escape; go poor Devil, get thee gone, why should I hurt thee?—This world surely is wide enough to hold both thee and me" (87). Yes, Toby literally would not hurt a fly.

Sentimentality? Perhaps. Still, Tristram tells us, "I was but ten years old when this happened," and "the lesson of universal goodwill then taught and imprinted by my uncle *Toby* has never since been worn out of my mind." And he adds: "This is to serve for parents and governors instead of a whole volume on the subject"—like Trim's hat (87). Later, Tristram draws on Toby as his model for how to treat critics (some of whom had scoffed when the first parts of this book were published, prompting Sterne's own reaction): "Never to give the honest gentlemen a worse word or a worse wish, than my uncle *Toby* gave the fly which buzzed about his nose at *dinner time*,—'Go,—go poor devil,' [. . .] '—get thee gone,—why should I hurt thee? This world is surely wide enough to hold both thee and me'" (127).

A second appearance of flies brings another affecting instance of Toby's moral sensibility. On this occasion, Trim tells Toby of his brother once encountering in a shop a "negro girl" who held a bunch of feathers "flapping away flies—not killing them." At this, as Tristram reports: "—'Tis a pretty picture! said my uncle Toby—

IV. On Humanism, Classics, Laughter, Proust, and the Meaning of Life

she had suffered persecution, Trim, and had learnt mercy——." Then Tristram goes on to recount that Toby and Trim began discussing whether all people have a soul. Toby decided that they must, for God would have it no other way, and Trim agreed, otherwise "it would be putting one sadly over the head of another." But then why, Trim asked, "is a black wench to be used worse than a white one?" And they agreed again that it is "because she has no one to stand up for her." So, Toby resolved, this "recommends her to our protection—and her brethren with her," since only "the fortune of war" has "put the whip in our hands *now*," whereas the future might remove it. They then conclude that those who have power must never "use it unkindly" (491).

Sterne heartily opposed slavery in his sermons, and gentle Toby, who could not hurt a fly, speaks for him here. Toby viewed his own martial activities in that light. Not really a path to glory, he believed they provided service to "the good and quiet of the world" by protecting "the lives and fortunes of the *few* from the plundering of the *many*" (494). Sympathy, mercy, generosity, all lived in Toby's heart. To call it sentimentality misses the emotional matrix of morals—a subject of lively interest in Sterne's day, as in Adam Smith's *Theory of the Moral Sentiments* (1759) and Rousseau's *Émile* (1764).

Tristram illustrates these qualities of his uncle's character many times. And he pauses his narrative in one place to list Toby's merits: "—my heart stops me," he says, "to pay to thee, my dear uncle *Toby*, once for all, the tribute I owe thy goodness." And he kneels on the ground to pour "forth the warmest sentiments of love for thee, and veneration for the excellency of thy character":

> —Thou envied'st no man's comforts,—insulted'st no man's opinions.—Thou blackened'st no man's character,—devoured'st no man's bread: gently with faithful *Trim* behind thee, did'st thou amble round the little circle of thy pleasures, jostling no creature in thy way;—for each one's service thou hadst a tear,—for each man's need, thou hadst a shilling (174).

26. Let 'Em Laugh

Who can resist uncle Toby? As loveable as Don Quixote, he surpasses that knight errant in the unwavering sympathy of his soul and the universal generosity of his heart. We root for him to succeed in his Quixotic wooing of the very willing widow Wedman. And we smile at him at the end when he fails for reasons of sexual impotence that he cannot fathom—in a subtly humorous scene the widow delicately questions him about the location of his groin wound, and he naïvely responds by describing the location on the battlefield where it occurred, rather than the place on his body—and then retires from the field of love to itemize the widow's virtues. Tristram tells us that the ever-forgiving Toby has no capacity for suspicion, resentment, or anger. Always he looks for the good and somehow finds it. "I love mankind" (493), he says earnestly, without pretense or the moralizing that can breed an abstract love of mankind alongside indifference to actual human beings. Toby demonstrates his genuine love of real people and other living creatures, again and again, in little acts of humanity.

For all of its wackiness, *Tristram Shandy* gives us a humane vision of life for sure. And this vision is no more simplistic than the book. It is a comic vision born of human experience, wide reading, thoughtful ideas, a moral imagination, and a humane sensibility. Putting its parts together, and adding some of Sterne's elaborations on its themes elsewhere, we might sum up Sterne's Shandean philosophy of life rather like this.

Begin here: We come into this world with whatever our nature and circumstances provide us. And these can be mighty peculiar. We then live our lives "beset on all sides by mysteries and riddles" (507) as experience leads us on a meandering course that defies plans with unpredictable twists and turns and lets seemingly random incidents often yield momentous consequences. At the same time, our minds flit from idea to idea with a logic of association that we do not entirely control as we respond to the rush of experience. This can make for lengthy digressions and a very muddled existence fraught with disappointments and sorrows and warranting a tragic sense of life.

But that is not the conclusion of Sterne's Shandean philosophy. It is only the end of the beginning. The rest follows from it, taking a cue from the epigraph to volumes one and two. This is a line from the Stoic philosopher Epictetus that might be translated from the Greek as: "The troubles of human beings come not from practical reality (*pragmata*) but from doctrines (*dogmata*) about reality." Which is to say: it's not experience itself that causes us the most trouble but how we think about experience (Buddhists have, of course, always known this; and, like Voltaire's Pangloss, Walter Shandy could be a case study in wrongheaded thinking about it). Sterne gave his own variation on the idea in a letter of 1764. "In short," he wrote, "we must be happy within—and then—few things without us make much difference—This is my Shandean Philosophy" (Penguin edition notes vol. 7 ch. 43).

"To be happy within." That may be the core conclusion of Sterne's Shandean philosophy, but there is still more to it. For we must learn *how* "to be happy within." And to do that we must reflect on what Sterne meant by teaching people not only how to read but how to think and act. That turns out to depend on a cluster of related Shandean principles.

Sterne the cleric/novelist wove these principles through both his sermons and his novels. Among them are the virtues he conferred on Parson Yorick and especially the qualities of character he gave to Toby. In a sermon on the deceptions of conscience that he includes almost verbatim in the novel as written by Yorick, Sterne cautions against both religious self-righteousness and irreligious self-importance. He advises uniting humble religious belief with humane secular morality, which can temper each other and guard against those previous errors, while also fostering a generous humanity. We have seen how he embodied all of this in Toby's gentle, compassionate nature and forgiving heart, touched with an innocent religiosity. Who can doubt that Toby was happy within?

26. Let 'Em Laugh

But the more conspicuous Shandean way of thinking flows from Sterne's zest for letting the mind wander happily in "the spirit of Shandeism" (as he wrote in a letter of 1761). Sterne says this spirit saved him from throwing in the towel at bad times because it kept him from dwelling for "two moments on any grave subject," and soon he would always find himself "merry as a monkey—and as mischievous, too" (Penguin edition notes vol. 4 ch. 22). That is a virtue of the digressive mind.

Sterne put this virtue in a nice image in his sermon "The House of Feasting and the House of Mourning." Pondering why "God made us," he writes: "Say we are travellers," who, while mindful of "the main errand we are sent upon [. . .] may surely be allowed to amuse ourselves with the natural or artificial beauties of the country we are passing through," for "it would be a nonsensical piece of saint errantry to shut our eyes." And the traveler Sterne/Yorick adds in *A Sentimental Journey*: "What a large volume of adventures may be grasped within this little span of life by him who interests his heart in everything." The Shandean journey of life wends where it will and gives the mind abundant subjects to think about and to laugh at.

Yes, laugh at. For wit, Sterne insists, holds no less importance in life than judgment, and sometimes more. He even has the intellectually misguided Walter Shandy concede: "Everything in this world is big with jest—and has wit in it, and instruction too—if we can but find it out" (312). Sterne found humor everywhere. And he thought we all need to do that to fend off troubles, learn humility, and live well. As he says, if *Tristram Shandy* "'tis wrote against anything,—'tis wrote [. . .] against the spleen;—in order" through "laughter, to drive the *gall* and other *bitter juices*" from the body (237). Sterne believed laughter is good medicine.

Sterne dedicated the book, as we have seen, to William Pitt with a testimonial to laughter as an antidote to life's trials. "I live in a constant endeavor," he says there, "to fence against the infirmities of ill health, and other evils of life, by mirth; being firmly persuaded that every time a man smiles,—but much more so, when he laughs, that it adds something to this Fragment of Life." Is there a more humane prescription for humor than that? In the same vein, he begins the sermon quoted just above by saying that to think "sorrow is better than laughter" might do for "a crack'd-brained order of Carthusian monks, I grant, but not for men of the world." After all, he continues, "the Author of our being" does not wish us to "go on our way sorrowing," and for this reason has given us ways "to charm away the sense of pain, to cheer up the dejected heart under poverty and sickness, and make it go and remember its miseries no more." Sterne makes God as good-natured and good-humored as he is—and in another sermon he says God must have bestowed on human beings a great capacity for good, because otherwise God could not expect them to become good. Stern's generosity of spirit—like Toby's—knew no bounds.

Sterne draws these themes together in a celebratory conclusion at the end of volume four. "True Shandeism," he says, "opens the heart and lungs" and "makes the wheel of life run long and cheerfully around." And he has Tristram fantasize there that if he could, like Sancho Panza, choose a kingdom to rule, it would be "a kingdom of hearty laughing subjects" who are "as WISE as they [are] MERRY" and therefore "the happiest people under heaven." (Incidentally, that great admirer of Sterne, Friedrich Nietzsche, echoed this idea in celebrating the laughter, good cheer, and joy that he believed come with true wisdom.)

Here Sterne's Shandean philosophy concludes in a kind of utopia: a place where everyone embraces the wandering journey of life with a cheerfully digressive mind; where laughter turns darkness to light, assuages pains and sorrows, and nurtures a generous humanity; where wit and merriment aid judgment and wisdom, and where, in return, judgment and wisdom encourage wit and merriment. And where all agree that *every time a man smiles,—but much more so, when he laughs, it adds something to the Fragment of Life*. Again, that is the humanity of laughter.

Marcel Proust; Salvador Dalí's 1931 painting The Persistence of Memory.

"*Existence is of little interest save on days when the dust of realities is mingled with magic sand, when some trivial incident of life becomes the springboard for romance.*"

—WITHIN A BUDDING GROVE

"*We possess only what is really present to us, and many of our memories, our moods, our ideas voyage away until they are lost to sight.*"

—THE FUGITIVE

"*The discovery of our true life, of reality as we have felt it to be.*"

—THE PAST REGAINED

As Time Goes By

ON READING PROUST AND FINDING THE MAGIC SAND

BEGINNING AT THE END

On the day that brings Marcel Proust's epically long novel, *À la Recherche du temps perdu*,† to a close (more or less—the book invites such qualifiers), the narrator, presumably now in his fifties, finally discovers the meaning of his life. That meaning is to write a book about that life (or at least based on it). And to write about it as he had lived it—from inside himself. But it will not be merely an exercise in self-revelation. He says he wants his book to be "useful for other people, . . . those for whom it was

---

† Note on translations. I have used the translation by C. K. Scott Moncrieff and Terence Kilmartin, with the last book translated by Andreas Mayor, published in three volumes under the English title *Remembrance of Things Past* (New York: Vintage, 1982). The English titles in this edition of the seven books that constitute the novel are *Swann's Way*, *Within a Budding Grove*, *The Guermantes Way*, *Cities of the Plain*, *The Captive*, *The Fugitive*, and *Time Regained*. In this essay I identify the sources of quotations from those books parenthetically by volume number in that edition, a key word from the individual book's title, and the page number. I have compared all of the English quotations to the original French to ensure no misinterpretations, and in a few instances have made slight changes in the SM/K/M translation for accuracy or clarity. But I have not included in the notes the page numbers in the French versions I consulted because those versions come from diverse publishers, which was acceptable for my purposes. I have also included the French wording in some instances to underscore the original where the words particularly matter or where my translation differs from that of SM/K/M.

intended" (III, *Regained*, 1093), by giving them "the means of reading inside themselves" and learning if "'it really is like that'" (III, *Regained*, 1089). A nice ambition, but one that would probably surprise readers who find the novel that the narrator wrote, which is now ending, so inward and rambling, so meditative and convoluted that parts of it can read almost like a solipsistic dream.

Taking a cue from the narrator here, we might ask, "Is it really like that?"—life, that is, as he describes, explores, reveals it? Another question crowds upon this one. Does the novel tell us things that are truly "useful" and that will enhance our lives, making them fuller, more vital, more worth living? It might be invidious to split these two questions, yet I cannot help but answer the first with a waffling *Yes and No*, whereas to the second I would give a confident *Yes*.

But before delving into those questions, we must first see the kind of novel this is and how we might best proceed through its complex, sprawling, seven-volume, three-thousand-plus-page narrative. To do that, we will start where Proust starts—or rather where he ends the last book, *Le temps retrouvé*, *Time Regained*, on the day his narrator decides to write the novel we have now read as *À la Recherche du temps perdu*—in English as *Remembrance of Things Past*, or, more accurately, *In Search of Lost Time*.

Although this narrator had long yearned to write a novel, how to do it in his own way had eluded him, and his confidence had foundered again and again. Now it comes to him, in the library of an aristocrat's stately mansion in Paris while awaiting the end of a musical performance before entering the drawing room for an afternoon party, or *matinée*, where he will see people he knows, but most of whom he has not seen for many years because he had been away in a sanatorium for his health. There in the library, he ponders an incident that had occurred outside the mansion.

After getting out of a cab, he had tripped on an uneven paving stone, and suddenly a wave of elation had rushed over him, just as it had on several other occasions of distinctive sensations, like the taste of tea with a madeleine dipped into it provided by his mother one cold day in Paris many years ago. And there on the street he had recalled how the elation had always made him lose "all anxiety about the future" (III, *Regained*, 899) and doubts about himself. "At once," as he had said of the tea and madeleine, "the vicissitudes of life had become indifferent to me, its disasters innocuous, its brevity illusory." Wondering where that elation had come from, he had tracked down its source that first time in a memory of the same taste of tea and madeleine while visiting his aunt Léonie in the village of Combray during his childhood. But he still could not figure out "whence came this powerful joy?" (I, *Swann*, 48). This time on the street he was determined to figure it out. He had tried the uneven stones again with his foot, and a memory had taken form from years before of stumbling on the steps of Saint Mark's Cathedral in Venice, bringing with it a whole vision of his visit to that peerless city, just as the taste of tea and madeleine had brought back his childhood days in Combray, and similar incidents had had similar effects. But he still did not know why such occurrences should arouse joy. What was the "riddle of happiness" (*l'énigme de bonheur*) that lay in those moments? (III, *Regained*, 899). He had taken this question with him into the library.

There two more remarkable incidents occur. A servant clinks a spoon against a plate, sending the narrator back to a time on a train when he had heard the clank of a railwayman's hammer against a wheel while the train was stopped near a small wood. Shortly after this memory, the butler brings him a snack with a starched napkin, and when he puts the napkin to his lips he instantly returns to the sensation of a starched towel pressed against his face many years before while he had looked out the window at the majestic sea on his first visit in youth to the seaside town of Balbec. As he thinks about these peculiar occurrences, he speculates that they "derive probably from the following cause: the slightest word that we have said, the most insignificant action that we have performed at any one epoch of our life was surrounded by, and colored by the reflections of, things which logically had no connection with it" and so had been dismissed "by our intellect which could make nothing of them for its own rational purposes" (III, *Regained*, 902). But these incidents revive when something reminds us of them. Recasting the idea, he thinks, "the simplest act or gesture remains immured" in us "as within a thousand sealed vessels [*vases*], each one of them filled with things of a color, a scent, a temperature that is absolutely different one from another" (III, *Regained*, 903). These vessels hold remnants of the past, and they are suddenly thrown open by an unexpected experience, usually a sensation, like tripping on the paving stones, that awakens a deep memory.

These thoughts lead to an epiphany. It strikes him that the moments of joy that accompany the unbidden memories all signify one thing: the *felicité* of uniting past and present, of existing in both at once, which makes him feel "outside of time." And there he becomes, however briefly, an "extratemporal being" attuned to "the essence of things" (III, *Regained*, 904) in a kind of mystical union with the universe. In that "extratemporal" mystical state, he has nothing to fear from the future, not even death. Naturally, he had felt joy. At last, he had solved "the riddle of happiness" in those moments. Or thought he had. But he does not stop there.

He goes on musing about such things in the library for scores of the pages we read. And the effort pays off. For he discovers nothing less than "the whole purpose of my life and perhaps of art itself" (*le but de ma vie et peut-être de l'art*; III, *Regained*, 923). But these discoveries do not come to him all at once. They come in several stages, and, like much in the novel, he gets to them after some false starts and wrong turns.

First, he thinks he can "rediscover days that were long past, the Time that was Lost" (III, *Regained*, 904) by engaging in "contemplation of the essence of things" (III, *Regained*, 909) outside of time. He will soon learn that going outside of time will not take him where he wants to go. But his ruminations have put him in a heady mood.

Carrying on, he also decides to proceed by turning away from the "real world," where things exist physically, to "what lay deep within myself" (III, *Regained*, 910). There he finds those "vessels" of the past, whose disparate contents he thinks of as "impressions." But how do these "impressions" get there? Trying "to understand what actually happens at the moment when a thing makes some particular impression upon one" (III, *Regained*, 925), he concludes that in those moments, "sensations" and "memories" come together, jointly *impressing* experiences deep into our hearts and minds, or our consciousness (and unconscious), whether we know it or not. And therein he detects the clue to "reality." For "what we call reality," he says, is just "a certain connection [*rapport*] between the immediate sensations and the memories that envelop [or surround, *entourent*] us simultaneously with them" (III, *Regained*, 924). That is, our very "reality" consists of the "impressions" deposited within us through the union of "sensations" and "memories."

But here the narrator leaves a silent question unanswered. If "impressions" are created by sensations enveloped in memories, wouldn't every sensation or experience have to have a remembered past in order to make some kind of an "impression"? Proust cannot have intended that. After all, how did the original sensation of tasting the tea and madeleine make a sufficient "impression" on the narrator, without itself being enveloped in memories of the past, that he could later have a compelling "involuntary" memory of that sensation when he tasted tea and madeleine again at home with his mother (and could then remember this instance of "involuntary memory" with his "voluntary memory" well enough to write about it years afterwards)? The answer lies in Proust's ideas of time and memory, consciousness and attention, which we will meet more fully later. For now, let us just say that time, memory, consciousness, and attention infuse everything in human life as Proust sees it. Our every experience comes to us through consciousness and attention in the dimension of time with its tracks of memory. Therefore, even the narrator's original sensation of the tea and madeleine, like tripping on the steps of Saint Mark's and all other such original sensations, happened *in time and consciousness with attention*, however slight that attention might have been. Memories of the past can surely intensify attention, but attention to sensations does not need direct memories of the past in order to occur. And even when the original attention to sensations carries no memories of the past, it plants seeds of future memories (we might even think of these as memories beginning to envelop, or surround, sensations here) that are borne along in the stream of consciousness through time and flower when we experience similar sensations. In other words, whereas the original sensations do not depend on memories, they make future memories possible, providing a bridge of memory from the past to the future. The "impressions" that Proust's narrator considered "reality" implicitly entail all of this.

The narrator goes on to explain that it is the role of "the writer" to plumb these "impressions" for their essential meaning, or "spirit" (*dégager l'esprit*; III, Regained, 924, 912). This meaning, this "spirit," is none other than "the discovery of our true life, of reality as we have felt it to be" (III, Regained, 915). *Our true life, reality as we have felt it to be* (*notre vraie vie, la réalité telle que nous l'avons sentie*). If there is one phrase that holds the nub of the narrator's subjective world view, this could be it.

In this light, he sees that the "materials for a work of literature were simply my past life," (III, Regained, 935) accumulated from experience and stored within as "impressions"—"reality as he had felt it to be." Now he had found the true nature of art and his "Vocation" as a novelist (III, Regained, 936). For he believes that interpreting these "impressions," this "inner book of unknown symbols," (III, Regained, 913) and converting them into their "spiritual equivalent" (*équivalent spirituel*) is the very "method" or means (*moyen*) used "to create a work of art" (III, Regained, 912). As he sums it up later: his novel would be "the re-creation by memory of impressions [*la recréation par la mémoire d'impressions*] which had then to be deepened, illumined, transformed into equivalents of understanding," and, he asks rhetorically, "was not this . . . almost the very essence of the work of art?" (III, Regained, 1102). At least "the essence of an art worthy of the name," which he judges so-called Realist art not to be because it is "content to 'describe things,' giving of them only a miserable abstract [*relevé*] of lines and surfaces" (III, *Regained*, 921). For true art goes beneath the surface to translate the artist's unique internal impressions into artistic creations that reveal the inner life to others. "Through art alone," he declares, "we are able to emerge from ourselves, to know what another person sees of a universe which is not the same as our own and of which, without art, the landscapes would remain as unknown to us as those that may exist in the moon." And so, "thanks to art, instead of seeing one world only, our own, we see that world multiply itself and we have at our disposal as many worlds as there are original artists" (III, *Regained*, 932). With such artists, he had earlier exulted (having in mind particularly the painter Elstir and the composer Vinteuil), "we truly do fly from star to star" (III, *Captive*, 260).

He is steeped in these revelations when the butler informs him that the musical performance in the drawing room is over and he could now go into the party. In the library, his epiphanies had indeed showed him "the whole purpose of my life and perhaps of art itself." A fruitful time spent there without reading a book.

Then shortly after entering the drawing room, another epiphany descends upon him. But it conflicts with his previous vision in the library of how memory can take him outside of time. As he looks at the guests, he fails to recognize them because they appear to be wearing masks at a masquerade. After a while, he sees that they are not wearing masks at all. They are people he knows, as he had expected, but they have grown old almost beyond recognition (never mind the many years he would have had to be away for them to age that much; that is one of Proust's chronological sleights-of-hand, of which more to come). Therefore, he thinks, they actually embody the passage of time, demonstrating that life is lived *within* time not *outside* of it.

This realization causes him some distress because discovering the "destructive action of Time" (Proust often capitalizes the word) in the faces of these old people clashed with his just-hatched, if not yet fully articulated, "ambition to make visible, to intellectualize in a work of art, extratemporal realities" (*des réalitiés extra-temporelles;* III, *Regained*, 971). Now he knows that his book "could not consist uniquely of the truly full impressions that were outside of time" (*les impressions véritablement pleines, celles qui sont en dehors du temps;* III, *Regained*, 974). For going "outside of time" through those incidents of spontaneous or "involuntary" memory that unite past and present, thrilling as it might be, does not lead to finding Lost Time. "Memory by itself," he explains, "when it introduces the past, unmodified, into the present . . . suppresses the grand dimension of Time, according to which life is lived" (*cette grand dimension du Temps suivant laquelle la vie se réalise;* III, *Regained*, 1087). In that sense, memory is the enemy of Time. By taking us outside of Time in the union of past and present, memory would eliminate life as it is lived, with all the transformations that passing Time entails.

Consequently, the narrator decides his book will treat Time as "some sort of transforming fluid" in which "men and societies and nations are immersed," changing them all (III, *Regained*, 974). And those changes are not only external but internal, since Time also alters how people think and feel, and their very "selves." His novel must therefore display many changes, even reversals, in his characters' perceptions, emotions, and judgments—preeminently his own, just as he had changed his mind about Time since leaving the library. And yet, he muses, even while Time alters people as it passes, it leaves them in some ways who they were—we are not ourselves, and yet we are. This suggests that, like the memories that unite our past and present seemingly *outside of Time*, the passing of Time also brings the past and present together *within Time* as we age. This insight shows him more clearly how he must tell his story. It will be "the recreation by the memory of impressions" from his past set in "the grand dimension of Time." "This notion of time embodied," he thinks, "of years past but not separated from us, it was now my intention to emphasize as strongly as possible in my work" (III, *Regained*, 1105). He had found the secret of "Lost Time." But his epiphanies were not over.

27. As Time Goes By

While pondering these thoughts and mingling with the disturbingly old guests, he faintly hears the sound of footsteps then the jangle of a bell. Not from outside but inside. He covers his ears to listen, and he identifies the footsteps as those of his parents escorting their neighbor Charles Swann out of his grandparents' house in Combray, where his family had often stayed when he was a child and Swann would come to dinner (Swann's father had been a friend of the narrator's grandfather, who had remained friendly with Swann). The sound of the bell came from the gate signaling that Swann had departed and that now his mother would be free to come upstairs and give him the goodnight kiss denied him earlier in the dining room, and that he had plotted in his bedroom to win from her no matter how late the hour or firm her resistance. That plot had more than succeeded when he had confronted his mother outside his room with a flood of anxious tears that had won him the surprising sympathy of his normally cold father, who had just arrived on the scene and had told his mother to spend the night in their son's room to comfort him, a cherished prize, but one that also afflicted the boy with a feeling of guilty triumph over his mother's will, prompting more tears. This Pyrrhic victory the narrator would not forget. As he now listens to the bell in his mind, he senses that it has been inside of him ever since that night, an emblem of his existence in Time. "From that moment onwards . . . there must have been no break in continuity, no single second at which I had ceased or rested from existing, from thinking, from being conscious of myself" (*conscience de moi*; III, *Regained*, 1105–06). This means to him that "all this length of Time" had "been lived, experienced, secreted by me, that it was my life, was in fact me." And that "I . . . could retrace my steps" to that time in the past "merely by descending to a greater depth within myself" (III, *Regained*, 1106). As he absorbs these thoughts, it dawns on him that "the date on which I had heard the garden bell at Combray—that far-distant noise which nevertheless was within me—was a point of reference in this vast dimension [of time] that I did not know I had" (*un point de repére*

IV. On Humanism, Classics, Laughter, Proust, and the Meaning of Life

dans cette dimension énorme que je ne savais pas avoir; III, *Regained*, 1106). And there, in that time long ago, lost but not irretrievable, is where he would begin his novel, his own work of art, telling the story of Lost Time in his life, demonstrating, as he says at the end of the novel he proceeds to write, how we all "occupy a place, a very considerable place . . . —in Time" (—*dans le Temps*; III, *Regained*, 1107).

So it is that the end of Proust's novel is where the story actually begins. And with this précis of that ending, we are now ready to start reading the book from its first page. Fervent Proustians contend that only after reading the entire novel are we adequately prepared to read it, and so we should start over. Upon completing it, most readers can probably see why they say that, although few follow the advice. To their loss.

Turning now from the end of the novel to where Proust opens the story, we read the first line: "For a long time I used to go to bed early"—to toss and turn and think and fantasize and dream and remember people and places, like Combray, where the narrator had first heard that garden gate bell, and where he had first sipped tea with the madeleine, the memory of which launches the story of his days in Combray and of his remembered and reimagined life thereafter.

The story the narrator tells of his life from his childhood memories of Combray to the *matinée* at the end gives us a novel like no other. It defies adequate summary or even truly comprehensive explication—just look at the shelves of publications it has spawned. No essay can, of course, treat it more than rather, well, impressionistically. Here I will touch only on what seems to me the most striking challenges of reading the novel and the rewards of reading it to the end.

The challenges take several forms. In the first place, not only does the 1.2-million-word novel span roughly fifty years from the early 1870s to the 1920s (with a few anticipations of future events) in the life of its narrator and of the social world around him, but it does this primarily, as we have seen the narrator promise, from inside his mind, depicting "reality as [he had] felt it to be." It weaves together past and present, events and meditations, history and memories, emotions and ideas, specificities and uncertainties, concreteness and amorphousness, perceptions and misperceptions, actualities and errors, consistencies and contradictions. What happens on one page—or seems to happen—might prove illusory or erroneous or reversed on another page. Just when you think you have got hold of the beast, it slips away. But instead of growing exasperated, we would do better to conclude that this inconstancy or fluidity of things is no flaw but betokens Proust's, or his narrator's, very sense of life, especially the inner life, as lived in the dimension of Time.

WHO IS TELLING THE STORY?

The challenges to comprehending this inconstancy start with the narrator himself. To say Proust tells the story in a complex narrative style understates his literary acrobatics. Some readers find the narration to be an impossible tangle. And, in truth, it might be just as well not to try too hard to untangle it. To oversimplify, we could say that Proust wrote a novel within a novel. For, at the end, we see a man in middle age deciding to write a novel based on his life. That will be *this* novel. He is therefore the Author of the novel we have read (as created by Proust). But this Author tells his story substantially in the voice of a narrator he has invented, who speaks in the first person as he gives us an intimate account of his life. This is what literary critics call a framed story—a story within a story (and the "Swann in Love" section of *Swann's Way* is a story within that, reported by the narrator as told to him by another person). It should come as no surprise, incidentally, that Proust refers many times in the novel to *The Thousand and One Nights*. For, among other reasons Proust alludes to it (such as the thousand nights the narrator says it will take him to write the novel, and the genie-like quality he sees in involuntary memory), that is a classic tale of stories told within stories, beginning with the frame of an anonymous narrator who introduces the internal framing story of Shahrazad, who then tells a new story every night to dissuade her grotesquely misogynistic husband from killing her in the morning, as he had killed his other wives to avenge an unfaithful one, and some of her stories have still more stories in them. But Proust gives us only half the frame for his novel within a novel, and only at the end where we finally learn that an Author has been telling the story mainly through another narrator.

I say "mainly" because here Proust further muddles the narrative. He has the Author weave his own narrative, observations, and commentary into the story along the way, usually without distinguishing his voice from that of the "narrator" telling the rest of it. So the novel actually has two intermingling narrators, whom some astute readers distinguish as the "young narrator" and the "old narrator"—whom I call the "Author," as he does himself. These vying narrators often make it difficult to identify who is speaking or from what perspective in time, especially since we don't meet the Author until the end.

And it gets worse. The Author occasionally steps up to address the reader in an authorial voice. Some of these instances simply foreshadow things to come like, "We shall see, in due course...." (I, *Swann*, 173). But others engage the reader more directly. Such as: "The Author would like to say how grieved he would be if the reader were to be offended by his strange portrayals" of certain aristocrats, although he also says he would not be surprised if the reader "finds that the aristocracy seems accused of degeneracy more than other social classes" (III, *Captive*, 40); and "'I forgot whether I've told you' I might ask the reader, as one might ask a friend with regard to whom one has forgotten, after so many conversations, whether one has remembered or had the chance to tell him something"—in this instance something about the Dreyfus Affair (III, *Captive*, 236); and again: "In this book... there is not a single fact that is not fictional, not a single character who is a real person in disguise," for "everything has been invented by me according to the needs of my purposes"‡ (*selon des besoins de ma démonstration*; III, *Regained*, 876)—even though he has said the book will come from his own life.

The Author even occasionally toys with the reader's uncertainty over who the narrator is. In one place, referring to a forgotten name, he says, "The reader will remark . . . 'Allow me, dear Author'" to tell "'you that it is a great pity that, young as you were (or as your hero was, if he be not yourself), you had already so feeble a memory that you could not remember the name of a lady whom you knew quite well" (II, *Cities*, 675). Later, he further teases the reader about his relation to the narrator when he wryly confides: "if we give the narrator the same name as the Author of this book," it "would be . . . Marcel" (III, *Captive*, 69). This is an obvious bit of sport on Proust's part as his fictional Author considers letting his narrator share his own name, which is, of course, that of Proust himself, the original of the three Marcels. (For convenience and in an attempt at clarity, I will from now on follow the Author's lead and call his fictional narrator Marcel, just as I follow his lead in referring to him as the Author). Finally, in the last volume of the novel Marcel and the Author inconspicuously merge into one, and the Author tells of the book he will write. He even implies very near the end that we have already read it and done so with a critical eye, remarking, "one has seen" in "various episodes of this story . . . errors of our senses" that "proved to me" how "our senses falsify for us the actual appearance of the world" (*l'aspect réel de ce monde*; III, *Regained*, 1103). The Author's candor here might raise eyebrows, but it confirms what most readers have sensed all along.

While the Author's self-conscious intrusions might take us aback, readers who get through the novel should be used to such oddities. For there are Pirandellian twists like these throughout the narrative,

---

‡ He says this to stress the exception of two very minor characters with the last name of Larivière, whom the narrator respects for aiding relatives of his housekeeper, Françoise, during World War I, a tip of the hat by Proust himself, so scholars say, to a family of that name who did the same kind of thing for his own housekeeper's family.

inducing readers to ask: What is going on here? Who is speaking? Who is who? Sometimes it is impossible to tell for sure—as noted at the outset, much in Proust can be known only "more or less." After all, only in the novel's last pages do we learn who has been telling the story, pulling the strings.

Adding to the perplexity of the knotty narrative style, both the Author and Marcel are notoriously undependable in what they say about events, emotions, and people. The Author admits as much when he speaks of his own memory lapses and the fallibilities of perception and memory that beset him and everyone. For that matter, whoever in the novel is speaking, what is said might turn out to be false, or at least inaccurate. But then, once again, that must be counted among Proust's intentions: to show how unreliable and changeable we are in our perceptions, judgments, emotions, memories, even our very selves, as we pass through the vicissitudes of life lived "in the dimension of Time." As the Author says, "Truth and life are very difficult to fathom"§ (III, *Fugitive*, 637).

TIME WILL TELL

Then there is the idea of Time itself. For a book whose Author promises it will be about life lived "in the dimension of Time," it treats chronological time in a manner that readers can find careless and confusing. In fact, chronological or historical Time mean little here, except, perhaps, for signs of the evident decline of the French aristocracy from the 1870s to the 1920s, which provides the social context of the story, and for a few historical events—notably the Dreyfus Affair, which affects many of the characters, and World War I, prominent in the last volume. I might add to these few indications of chronology the dates of Marcel's treatment in

---

§ Proust's line is: *La vérité et la vie sont bien ardues.* Scott Moncrieff and Kilmartin added "to fathom," which seems to complete the thought and makes more sense, and so I keep it.

27. As Time Goes By

two sanatoria, which we will examine shortly. Most other references to chronology appear indistinctly and in passing, tucked into long stretches of narrative, descriptions, conversations, reflections, and so on. When Proust chooses to be elusive about when things happen or to simply leap over Time, he does it at will.

Take Marcel's time in the sanatoria. The Author mentions that Marcel will likely be going to a sanatorium (*maison santé*) for his health, but we never learn when he does go there, and only after he returns in "August, 1914," do we learn that he had been there for "long years" (*les longes années*). We are also told that, after remaining in Paris for a couple of months, he had gone back to the sanatorium then returned again to Paris at "the beginning of 1916" owing to the sanatorium's shortage of medical staff during the war. Following this "second return in 1916" (these chronological details all come on a single page, as if an afterthought; III, *Regained*, 743), we get a hundred and fifty pages on Marcel's life in wartime Paris. Then we learn of a "new sanatorium to which I withdrew" for "many years" (*beaucoup d'années*), which "was no more successful in curing me than the first one" (III, *Regained*, 885), although we get no hint of when he went there. A little later he tells us that "on my return" after "my long absence from Paris" (III, *Regained*, 887)—presumably at that sanatorium—he found an invitation to the climactic Guermantes's *matinée* to be held the next day. When was that? The *matinée* follows the war, to be sure, but certainly not by the purported "many years" of Marcel's last sanatorium stay, which had to begin sometime after his "second return" in 1916. And at the party the Author remarks it was "now scarcely a year after [his friend] Robert was killed" in the war (III, *Regained*, 1029), indicating the *matinée* took place in 1919, although we can't count on it. Be that as it may, it is simply impossible to match the passing of time in the narrative here with the passing of actual time. But Proust did not seem to care. He just needed Marcel to be away from Paris long enough to set up a baffled reaction to the agedness of the guests at the party. To do that, Proust contrived a passage of time for Marcel at the sanatoria to fit his own fictional needs. Likewise, near the end of the book, amidst the Author's epiphany at the *matinée* about how to write his novel, Proust has him jump into the future and tell of actually beginning to write the book and even letting companions read "a few sketches," which, however, "no one understood" (III, *Regained*, 1098–99).

Proust goes back and forth in time, just as he switches from one narrator to the other, seemingly without hesitation and typically without signals, to the perplexity of readers. He often handles time rather like many movies do, with leaps in chronology and logic to suit their way of telling the story, following what some aficionados dub "movie logic." Proust has the Author allude to something like this in the library when he observes that the vital link—the deep "impressions" of experience—between sensations and memories normally gets "suppressed in a simple cinematographic vision" of life that splices sensations and memories together in our minds, and "the writer has to rediscover" (III, *Regained*, 924) that link of "impressions" in order to properly portray human existence. Proust might be said to ignore this injunction when he splices time together. But he has his Author recognize that doing this is frequently necessary in literature, for in dealing with Time "novelists are obliged, by wildly accelerating the beat of the pendulum, to transport the reader in a couple of minutes over ten, or twenty, or even thirty years" to make the "flight" of Time over long distances "perceptible" (*sensible*), as it ordinarily is not "in one's life" from day to day (I, *Grove*, 520). Proust clearly does that with the sanatorium episodes in the last volume. What is more, he also seems convinced that chronological tricks and the like typify not only cinema and literature; they are part of life. Early on in the story, he has the Author concede that, "our life being so careless of chronology, interpolating many anachronisms into the sequence of our day, I found myself living in those" (I, *Grove*, 691). Reading the Author's story, we often find ourselves there with him.

So do not expect fastidious chronological, historical, and clock Time. In Proust, Time is almost metaphysical. For Time here belongs to the very nature of human existence; it suggests part of what Martin Heidegger (in his philosophical classic *Being and Time*, published the same year, 1927, as Proust's last volume, *Le temps retrouvé*) called human *being-in-the-world*, the existential reality of Time, melding past-present-future, in human life. But more than metaphysics, Time in Proust is psychological and metaphorical. Psychologically, Time is a component of human consciousness loaded with accumulating associations in memory. We might even say that, in some respects, Time and consciousness are one, flowing together in a stream, where the passing of Time is commonly invisible to us but occasionally can seem to vary as the stream flows—like the startling attenuation of Time Marcel senses when traveling rapidly by train or car. At any rate, that is how we experience Time and our lives psychologically (of which more to come). Metaphorically, Time in Proust is "more or less" a metaphor for the mysteries of change, the effects of experience, and our travels down the winding trail of understanding in human life. As the Author says to himself while in the library, "An hour is not merely an hour, it is a vase full of scents and sounds and projects and climates" (III, *Regained*, 924). That is, Time signifies much more than anything clocks can measure. It represents the unfolding of experience from incomplete, uncertain, and frequently faulty first perceptions, laden with expectations, memories, "scents and sounds," "projects and climates," and forgetfulness, toward fuller understanding, as we take on and shuffle off what Proust's Author thinks of as our many "selves" in passing through the vicissitudes of life—which we see happening to Marcel again and again, and which we see happening to ourselves as we read the novel from our early uncertainties and even confusion to ultimate enlightenment.

This complex sense of Time had hit the Author at the *matinée* amid the aged guests, whom he had at first misperceived. But his discovery of Time there had actually been foreshadowed in his youth when, as Marcel reports, his father had told his mother that their son was "quite capable of deciding for himself what will make him happy in life" because "he's no longer a child" and "knows pretty well now what he likes" and "it's very unlikely that he will change," (I, *Grove*, 519). The words had jarred Marcel out of his naïve sense that he was "situated somewhere outside Time" and not "subject to its laws"—namely, the necessity of growing up and getting old. And "so it is with Time in one's life," the Author had explained: from day to day we are not aware of Time's passing any more than we are "aware that the earth revolves"; but the earth revolves, and Time passes, all the same. "My father," Marcel exclaimed, "had suddenly made me appear to myself in Time" (*apparaître à moi-même dans le Temps*; I, *Grove*, 520).

That incident had foreshadowed both of Marcel's/the Author's epiphanies about Time at the end: the misleading one in the library about memory taking him "outside of Time" and the corrective discovery in the party that life is "lived in the dimension of Time." But Marcel seems to have forgotten this early incident by the end of the novel that the Author wrote about him to demonstrate this very discovery. In fact, however, such forgetting belongs to life lived *in Time*. For life in Time, as the Author came to understand it, evolves for us all as a skein of fragmentary experiences engulfed in ambiguities, uncertainties, misperceptions, forgettings, and our groping to put it all together and understand what is going on. As Proust surely intended, that is how most readers make their way through the novel. And it takes them a long Time to do it.

I include one more observation that bears on the experience of Time in Proust. That has to do with error itself—or with errors of perception and judgment. We have seen instances of Marcel and the Author misperceiving and misremembering, and we have heard the Author acknowledging inevitable "errors of our senses." But here we get a somewhat new take on the subject. While life lived in Time is shot through with human fallibilities in grasping reality, and those fallibilities change with Time, they might not go away because they are rooted in the deepest parts of us. Marcel and the Author admit to misremembering names, for example, but in one place Marcel (or the Author) says the fault lay not so much in his errant memory as in the common mistake of "believing that things usually present themselves as they are in reality," whereas "in fact this is not at all what we ordinarily perceive" because "we see, we hear, we conceive the world all wrong" (*tout de travers*; III, *Fugitive*, 585). Therefore, we "have of the universe only inchoate, fragmentary visions" (III, *Fugitive*, 586). This pertains not only to "the visible and audible universe" but to "the social universe, the sentimental universe, the historical universe, and so forth." And it can induce "perpetual error[s]." But such errors, he says, are "precisely 'life'" (III, *Fugitive*, 585) as shaped by experience and by our assumptions about reality—like lovers blinded by romanticized images of the beloved, or ideologues wrapped in "dangerous illusions," such as the Germans convinced that "the French are thinking only of revenge" (III, *Fugitive*, 585–86). In the end, our assumptions, the preconceptions in our minds, tend to rule. For, as the Author says, "the testimony [*témoignage*] of the senses is also an operation of the mind in which conviction creates the evidence" (III, *Captive*, 188). Or, as he puts it bluntly early in the novel, "Facts do not penetrate the world where our beliefs live; they did not give birth to those beliefs; they do not destroy them" (*Les faits ne pénètrent pas dans le monde où vivent nos croyances, ils n'ont pas fait naître celles-ci, ils ne les détruisent pas*; I, *Swann*, 162).

Our inherent subjectivity and proclivity to misperception and self-justification may go through Time with us, but they nonetheless adapt to our lives as we live. So, in one way or another, Time has its way with us all. Therein, we might say, lies the crux of Proust's metaphor of Time.

IT'S PRETTY VAGUE

To read Proust it is therefore best to banish common expectations of chronological, narrative, or strict psychological coherence, or perhaps consistency would be more fair. Keep in mind also

IV. On Humanism, Classics, Laughter, Proust, and the Meaning of Life

what the Author says at the end about the kind of novel this will be: *a novel of impressions inscribed in the Author's mind by experience, summoned by memory, and placed in the dimension of passing time.* That can pose challenges to the reader for sure. And it makes for a portion of what William James (an older contemporary of Proust, who had much in common with him) had said he aspired to achieve in the science of psychology: "the reinstatement of the vague and the inarticulate to its proper place in our mental life" (*BC*, 164).¶ For a certain vagueness of the "mental life" pervades the atmosphere of the novel, thanks especially to the narrative inwardness and ambiguities, with their Pirandellian twists, and to the hazy rendering of Time, along with the depiction of some characters—albeit not most of the rhetoric itself, which rolls eloquently through even the prolix sentences with notable clarity, punctuated by many lively descriptive passages.

Vagueness, or uncertainty, enshrouds much of Marcel himself, who remains nameless until volume five where the Author offhandedly, and in the conditional mood, thinks of naming him Marcel, like himself. We do know he is the only child of a prosperous bourgeois couple who live in Paris and spend time in the village of Combray, where, during his youth, they all stayed with his maternal grandparents and often visited his aunt Léonie and her mother. He is physically sickly and complains of suffering from "vagaries of my nerves" (*caprices des mes nerfs*; I, Grove, 697), although he evidently grows to be fairly tall and thin, sporting black hair and a mustache, which is how he describes his appearance at the *matinée*. But his age throughout can only be approximated, and his character, along with reasons for his acceptance into aristocratic society, are a bit nebulous.

¶ This and other quotations from William James come from *Psychology: Briefer Course*, James's somewhat condensed version of his classic *The Principles of Psychology* (1890). I used the edition in the Library of America volume, *William James; Writings 1878–1899* (New York: Literary Classics of the United States, 1992). In the page references I abbreviate the title: *BC*.

27. As Time Goes By

His parents, important as they are to him, are also portrayed imprecisely. Neither of them has a name. His father is identified here and there chiefly as a man of some influence, possessing an arbitrary will, intimidating authority, a coldly calm manner (although someone once told Marcel that "beneath his icy exterior [*froideur glaciale*] he conceals an extraordinary sensibility" because "what he has above all is fear of his sensibility" [*a pudeur de sa sensibilité*; III, *Fugitive*, 104]), and a critical view of Marcel's childhood attachment to his mother. But he can also be sympathetic to Marcel's physical condition and sometimes displays "unexpected kindnesses," as when he tells Marcel's mother to stay with the boy overnight, and when he later tells her they should not pressure Marcel into a career because "he's no longer a child" and is "quite capable of deciding for himself what will make him happy in life." Such kindnesses always sparked in Marcel a wish to "kiss his glowing cheeks above his beard," but the boy never acted on that wish "because I was afraid of annoying him" (I, *Grove*, 519). And the father silently leaves the narrative after Marcel's formative years. As for Marcel's mother, she remains a physical and emotional presence in his life from childhood on, but we know her almost entirely through her relationship with him, in the likes of her doting care, her willingness to discipline him with days of silence, her indulgence of his relations with Albertine, her dismissing his wish to remain in Venice, and their long conversation on the train back to Paris from Venice in volume six, after which she vanishes from the narrative with nary an *adieu*—except for a parenthetical note saying she would be going to a tea party while her son attends the final *matinée*, implying that he continued living with her to the end, other than his time in the sanatoria.

Outside Marcel's family (which also includes his Combray relatives to whom he is devoted), the most important attachment and preeminent love of Marcel's life, Albertine, is so elusively rendered that she leaves us mystified. We are told she was a poor orphan, kind of plump, dark, and rather plain at first but attractive later.

She can be quite flirtatious and willful, and she appears to have lesbian tendencies, as well as a taste for Marcel's caresses. He says she is intelligent, but we don't see that amidst her compliance to his wishes and submission with hardly a murmur to her "captivity" and to his emotional abuse in jealous suspicions, selfish demands, and heartless rejection. Marcel was originally attracted to her and to the "little band" of girls he had seen her with at Balbec by the alluring "nuances" and "vagueness" (*nuances* and *vague*) they had conveyed to his imagination (I, *Grove*, 854). But even as he pursues her and wins her affection, he despairs of ever understanding her. For "out of that tangled mass of real details and deceptive facts" (*détails réels et des faits mensongers*), he sighs, "I should never unravel the truth" (II, *Cities*, 760) or "the enigma of her intentions" (II, *Cities*, 1053). She seemed to live "behind five or six lines of defense . . . organized like field fortifications [*fortifications de campagne*] that, for greater security, were of the kind that at a later period we learned to call camouflage" (II, *Cities*, 759–60; camouflage was invented in World War I). But finally she leaves him, convinced he no longer loves her. Subsequently, he learns by letter that she has died in a fall from a horse. A suitably anticlimactic end for a peculiar antiheroine. "When I think of it," Marcel says looking back, "I cannot say how densely Albertine's life was covered by alternating, fugitive, often contradicting desires" and "lies" (III, *Captive*, 414). She was inaccessible, truly a "daughter of the mists outside" (*fille de la brume du dehors*), as he had once thought of her (II, *Guermantes*, 367). Enigma that she is, Albertine seems to be largely a foil for Marcel's self-absorbed raptures and melodramatic jealousy. Almost a figment of his inner life, where, after all, most of the book, and all of his loves, transpire.

The drifts of uncertainty and air of vagueness in the novel make many details difficult if not impossible to nail down. Trying to comprehend exactly what is going on or the relations of one event to another or of the Author to Marcel can be like trying to grasp a cloud—although, again, that does not apply to most of Proust's rhetoric itself (unlike, say, that of the late works of Henry James, composed not long after Proust started writing, which can be rhetorically opaque beyond deciphering). The haze no doubt thins out some with every reading of the novel. Still, the cloudy atmosphere surely belongs, in part, to Proust's desire to explore the inner life as he understood it, allowing, like William James, "the vague its proper place in our mental life."

All that said, we should also be aware that Proust should not be blamed for everything that we might find careless or confusing in the book. Scholars tell us that he wrote most of the first and last volumes before the other five, but, because he was inclined to revise extensively, he augmented and reworked the complicated tale as it grew under his hand and through his imagination. He would paste inserts and write variations on variations as he went back and forth through the sprawling creation, piling it up and fitting it together. A learned Proustian designates this practice "incrustation," an illuminating interpretation akin to what Henry James, another lavish reviser, called the "accretions" that he would keep inserting into his late works. Proust's Author puts it this way: "I should construct my book, I dare not say ambitiously like a cathedral, but"—taking as a model his housekeeper Françoise, who had been with his family since his childhood days and often made dresses—"quite simply like a dress . . . pinning here and there an extra page." (III, *Regained*, 1090). He would be the artist as seamstress. A modest aspiration for the Author of what would become one of the world's longest and greatest novels. But Proust died before he could finish his task—particularly, so scholars say, revision of volumes five and six, which revolve around Marcel's troubled love affair with Albertine—leaving parts disordered and stacks of material that he would have integrated. That has kept many a scholar occupied sorting papers and recasting even parts of what was originally published. That makes for a somewhat amorphous novel. But never mind that. It is a great novel, however far it might fall short of what Proust intended to put into our hands.

SOCIETY AND THE HUMAN COMEDY

Before we move on to the heart of the novel and the principal rewards of reading it, a few words on Marcel's social world and the two "Ways" that early characterize it in his mind—and on the comedy of the novel overall. Here we see through the narrative and temporal haze to a couple of the characters and some of the manners the Author sharply describes.

For a glimpse of Marcel's social world, we return to Combray, where the Author's memories take him as the novel opens, and where Marcel meets the two "Ways" that will mark his life. There Marcel's parents and grandparents socialize occasionally with their neighbor Swann—as they did on the night of the garden gate bell—another prosperous bourgeois, who is Jewish, married to a former courtesan named Odette, and who becomes lastingly important to Marcel. They also know of, but do not presume to socialize with, the Duke and Duchess de Guermantes, aristocrats of high status who have an estate in the opposite direction from Swann's. Marcel comes to contrast the households of Swann and the Guermantes, and the worlds they represent, by the two Ways (*Côtés*) or paths that take him past them. Swann's "Way" (or the "Méséglise Way," for the town in that direction) is short, easy, and friendly, although often taken on rainy days for convenience, and it is associated for him with the familiar bourgeoisie; whereas the Guermantes "Way" is longer and pleasant, running beside a river, reserved for sunny days, and associated for him with the remoteness and mysteries of the aristocracy. Marcel will meet the Guermantes and enter their world, which he rather idealizes, through a nephew of the Duchess, Robert de Saint-Loup, whom he meets and befriends at Balbec during youth. Marcel's affluence (conveniently boosted by an

27. As Time Goes By

inheritance from his aunt Léonie's mother), amiable manner, and tact in society—if not in romance—seem to earn him sufficient entrée there that he eventually socializes with aristocrats almost as though he is one of them, albeit it remains unclear just why he is so fully accepted. The two "Ways" influence Marcel's life to the end of the novel, where he muses at the party given by the Princess de Guermantes (a cousin of the Duchess, second wife of the Prince, and previously seen often in the book, prior to her first husband's death, as the music-loving, social climbing, often ridiculous Mme. Verdurin), on how those "Ways" have at last come together through Saint-Loup's marriage to Swann's daughter, Gilberte, and in the daughter they bear. Along the way, as it were, Marcel and the Author have witnessed, with ambivalence, the deepening decline of the aristocracy itself, through marriage—including that of the nonconformist aristocrat Saint-Loup to the undistinguished commoner Gilberte—and other concessions to Time, displayed in the aged faces at the party sometime after the end of World War I.

Now to the comedy. One cannot read Marcel's story amidst that social world, along with his urgent devotion to his mother, his overwrought emotions for Gilberte, and especially his overbearing and erratic love of Albertine, without smiling. Or chuckling. A lot of this is funny stuff. In a deadpan comic style, along with swaths of broad satire woven into the tapestry of the rich and circuitous prose, Proust sends up many of his characters. Marcel's aunt Léonie, for instance, is an ailing hypochondriac who eventually won't get out of bed, where she talks to herself incessantly but "never spoke save in low tones, because she believed that there was something broken inside her head and floating loose there, which she might displace by talking too loud" (I, *Swann*, 54)—although she did manage to serve Marcel tea and madeleines at her bedside. Among the aristocrats, Baron de Charlus, brother of the Duke de Guermantes, stands out for his comical self-regard and extravagant affectations. He parades through the book with a mercurial temperament, the antics of a Vaudeville villain, and the gaudy condescension of the eccentric aristocrat he is, as in this culmination of his ripe, 1,200-word response to Marcel's hesitant apology for a possible affront: "An olive-hued, bilious juice seemed ready to start from the corners of his malevolent mouth . . . 'Who says that I am offended?' he furiously screamed . . . 'Do you think it is within your power to offend me? You are evidently unaware to whom you are speaking? Do you imagine that the envenomed spittle of five hundred little gentlemen of your type, heaped one upon another, would succeed in slobbering so much as the tips of my august shoes?" Marcel reacts to this piquant performance with his own melodramatic rage, shredding Charlus's "new top hat," stomping on it, and "heedless of the continuing vociferations," fleeing the room (II, *Guermantes*, 577, 580). His social tact had been no match for the imperious Charlus—who nonetheless whimsically summons him back, and he returns.

The aristocracy itself frequently gets satirized for its manners, hauteur, and folly as it sinks into decline. The Guermantes, for instance, are said to regard the "surface" of social appearances to be more "profound" than any internal qualities could be, and to believe that observing the "worldly politeness" (*politesse mondaine*) of courtly manners is "a duty more essential and more inflexible than those . . . of charity, chastity, pity, and justice" (II, *Guermantes*, 442). Here is a description of that etiquette at work:

> All those who were genuine Guermantes, when you were introduced to them, proceeded to perform a sort of ceremony almost as though the fact that they held out their hands to you were as significant as if they had been dubbing you a knight. At the moment when a Guermantes, were he no more than twenty, but treading already in the footsteps of his ancestors, heard your name uttered by the person who introduced you, he let fall on you, as though he had by no means made up his mind to say "How d'ye

do" to you, a gaze generally blue and always of the coldness of a steel blade which he seemed ready to plunge into the deepest recesses of your heart.... When a Guermantes, after a rapid tour round the innermost recesses of your soul to establish your credentials, had deemed you worthy to consort with him thereafter, his hand, directed towards you at the end of an arm stretched out to its fullest extent, appeared to be presenting a rapier to you for a single combat, and that hand was on the whole placed so far in advance of the Guermantes himself that at the moment when he proceeded to bow his head it was difficult to distinguish whether it was yourself or his own hand that he was saluting. (II, *Guermantes*, 460–61)

Those manners could intimidate, but Marcel adapts to them. He tells, for instance, of entering an aristocratic social gathering given one afternoon for the visiting Queen of England, and seeing the monarch with the Duke de Guermantes, who, "from a distance of nearly fifty yards" gestured toward Marcel with "countless signs of friendly welcome." And, "becoming word-perfect in the language of the court," Marcel knew exactly how to acknowledge the gesture properly. "Instead of going even one step nearer, [I] made a deep bow from where I was, without smiling, the sort of bow I should have made to someone I scarcely knew, then proceeded in the opposite direction." To which he proudly adds: "Had I written a masterpiece, the Guermantes, would have given me less credit for it than I earned by that bow." (II, *Cities*, 687).

Proust's satiric wit turned on the aristocracy might remind us of Molière's *Misanthrope* or *Tartuffe*. Proust could certainly vie for comic stature with the best of French satirists for both his deft touches and piercing hits. It should, however, also be acknowledged that he has Marcel and the Author display appreciation of aristocratic virtues, like the gracious generosity of *noblesse oblige*, which the bourgeoisie does not possess for lack of secure social status, and to register a certain regret that the aristocratic world is vanishing altogether. Still, one would have to be tone deaf to miss the cutting comedy in Proust's portrait of Marcel's social world. And there is nothing vague about it.

When it comes to Marcel's quirky personal life, Proust takes him so far over the top, with the disproportion of his reactions to their causes in his distraught emotions, self-absorbed loves, and paranoid jealousies, that readers have to laugh. Otherwise, they will find Marcel unbelievable and sometimes intolerable. Take a few examples. Proust devotes some fifteen pages—six thousand words—to the childhood incident of Marcel's agonized plotting, with the "cunning of the condemned" (*ruse de condamné*; I, *Swann*, 30), to get his mother's good-night kiss after his father had sent him to bed from dinner without it, scoffing, "These exhibitions are absurd" (I, *Swann*, 29). Marcel had trudged up "the hateful staircase," which "gave out the smell" it had "absorbed and held of the special quality of sorrow that I felt each evening" (I, *Swann*, 29–30), and he had resolved to win the kiss even at the cost of punishment—like his mother's refusal to speak to him for days. As we have seen, his plot prevailed, and then some, when she stayed with him for the night, but he suffered anew over his very success, along with thoughts that "tomorrow night my anguish would return" because "Mamma would not stay by my side again" (I, *Swann*, 46). Proust treats Marcel's getting his mother's good-night kiss as an intense psychological drama, complete with desperate strategies of confrontation, the alliance of a sympathetic staircase redolent of his sorrows, and calculated, copious tears. It is all as amusing as it is a telling self-portrait.

Later Marcel's romantic life exhibits the same kind of excess. We will shortly see his visceral overreaction when he first sees—and instantly falls in love with—Gilberte. As to Albertine, let one instance speak for hundreds of pages laced with them. While still pursuing her, he waits on one occasion for her to call on "Dr. Bell's invention." Typically, he is "tortured by the incessant recurrence of my longing, evermore anxious and never gratified for the sound of a call." Finally, "having arrived at the culminating point of a torturous ascent through the coils of my lonely anguish . . . I suddenly heard, mechanical and sublime, like the fluttering scarf or the shepherd's torch [*le chalumeau du pâtre*] in *Tristan*, the top-like whirr of the telephone. It was Albertine" (II, *Cities*, 757). Has ever a teenager awaited a romantic phone call with more white-knuckled anxiety and received it with a more exalted thrill?

A final example of Marcel's comic excess. Near the end of the novel, when he runs across a party invitation he had cast aside reminding him of a social obligation he could not face, he cries: "I fell back exhausted and closed my eyes, not to emerge from a purely vegetal existence before a week had elapsed" (*ne devant plus que végéter pour huit jours*; III, *Regained*, 1098). Like a vegetable? For a week? Really? Poor Marcel. He has referred to "the vagaries of my nervous system" (I, *Grove*, 697), and even confessed that, owing to "total egotism . . . I have found myself obsessed by mental worry or merely by nervous anxieties [*inquiétude nerveuses*], sometimes so puerile that I would not dare to reveal them" (I, *Grove*, 912). Quite so—although one wonders what could be more puerile than some of the anxieties he does reveal. Reading of Marcel's exaggerated feelings and zany antics could easily put one in mind of Holden Caulfield, who tells his own bizarre and funny story in *Catcher in the Rye*, climaxing in the disclosure that he had told it all from an asylum. One might well imagine that Marcel goes to the sanatorium for his mental as well as his physical health, returning at last to become the Author of the book we are reading. We might also imagine that, given Marcel's often overwrought attitudes and sometimes outrageous actions, Proust was likely having some fun with him, and maybe with some memories of his own youth, just as he was taking delight in satirizing his own social world.

At all events, one should not read Proust without hearing the comic tone that resounds throughout, and enjoying the satiric humor of it all. Among the many things to be said about *À la Recherche*, none is more inviting than this: it is a funny book.

CUPID'S ARROW, OR THE ELECTRIC SHOCK OF LOVE

Now we get to the heart, or perhaps I should say the romantic heart, of the novel, and then to what I would say are the highest rewards of reading it.

That romantic heart belongs chiefly to Marcel, with Swann as his mentor, and it throbs through most of the first six volumes as the sagas of love roil on practically every page. Love in Proust is often a disease that possesses, disorients, and nearly destroys. Yet, it must be said right off that we see it almost exclusively from the male first-person point of view. We could chalk this up to the story being told primarily in the first-person voices of Marcel and the Author. Even so, all of Marcel's accounts of love—along with the Author's observations—from love of his mother to his adolescent flirtations and lusts (he is not shy about his sexual appetites) to his adult obsessions, as well as the homosexual behavior, whether male or female, that arrests his curiosity and enflames his jealousy, smack of male attitudes, influenced, no doubt, by the historical and cultural context of Marcel's times. We never really get to know much of what a female character feels about love or anything else, except perhaps about other people and her place in society (and Mme. Verdurin's comically inflated response to music), although Marcel occasionally attributes to females, rather unconvincingly, feelings he presumes they have. He even proclaims indifference to Albertine's intelligence, since, he boasts, a "female companion's superiorities of mind having always so little interested me" (*les supérioritiés d'esprit d'une compagne m'ayant toujours si peu intéréssé que*; III *Captive*, 10). Love as he felt it appears to be about all Marcel could associate with females.

27. As Time Goes By

We see love first when, as a child, Marcel demands his mother's good-night kiss as though his life depended on it—a melodramatic incident he recalls again and again. And well into his twenties (an age we can only estimate) he behaves toward her much like a child, as when, late in volume six after Albertine has left him, they travel together to Venice, where he petulantly refuses to leave when she wants to—so he can ogle Venetian girls—but then races after her because he can't bear being without her. Marcel's love of his mother is almost creepy.

Marcel's romantic life is, if anything, more excessive than his love of his mother, and more consuming. "As by an electric current that jolts us," he says, "I have been shaken by my loves, I have lived them, I have felt them; never have I succeeded in seeing or thinking them" (II, *Cities*, 1165). That love life starts when Marcel sees the young Gilberte among the hawthorn blossoms while walking along Swann's "Way." She could not be more than about ten years old and he not much older in early adolescence—again, such details are impossible to know. His reaction is as immoderate—and amusing—as the excess that typifies much of his sensibility and behavior. "Suddenly I stood still," he says as if breathlessly, "unable to move," seized by the "kind of perception" that "takes possession of the whole of our being." For "a reddish blond little girl, who appeared to be returning from a walk, and held a trowel in her hand, was looking at me" (I, *Swann*, 153). He gazes at her, and she, while keeping an eye on him, turns aside and, with a "concealed smile" that he judges a sign of "outrageous contempt," makes an "indelicate gesture" with her hand that he thinks has an "insolent intention," (but will later reinterpret as coquettishly flirtatious). Then her mother calls her away, and "there was wafted to my ears the name of Gilberte, bestowed on me like a talisman" (I, *Swann*, 154). He says to himself, "I loved her." But immediately he wishes that before she had left he had had "the inspiration to insult her, to hurt her," to "shout, 'I find you ugly, grotesque, repugnant'" in order "to compel her to keep some memory of me" (I, *Swann*, 155).

IV. On Humanism, Classics, Laughter, Proust, and the Meaning of Life

A peculiar turn of mind. Such does Marcel fall in love for the first time—and with traces of his tendency to negatively overinterpret his beloved's behavior and his inclination to couple "love" with psychological domination and emotional abuse.

He manages to win Gilberte's youthful interest sufficiently that at one point they engage in a playfully titillating wrestling match that culminates in Marcel's sexual release. Marcel is a lusty lad. And he will go on loving Gilberte for years, finally giving up when she definitively rejects him, even though he will continue to harbor intermittent desire for her. Meanwhile, he repeats this kind of attraction many times whenever he sees "pretty girls," whatever his age, as he notably does early at Balbec and much later in Venice. Love, or what he calls love (*amour*) comes easily, even irresistibly, to him, as does jealousy. And these become full-fledged obsessions with Albertine. But before getting to that we must pause for a glance at the section entitled "Swann in Love," for Marcel takes Swann as kind of a model in matters of love. Or, at any rate, he finds a kinship between their tormented lives of love.

Marcel tells us that "Swann's great love affair" with Odette began "about the time of my birth" (I, *Swann*, 211)—although a few pages earlier he had said the "love affair" had occurred "before I was born" (I, *Swann*, 203)—and so he reports it as told to him much later by someone else. Swann's slavish love, with its bouts of jealousy sparked by imagined wanderings of Odette's eye, goes from irresistible attraction to obsessive passion to obsession for its own sake, with many ups and downs. He lusts for her and distrusts her and despises her and craves her and disdains her and hopelessly loves her all over again. "Swann's love" Marcel reports, became a "malady ... so closely interwoven with all his habits, with all his actions, with his thoughts, his health, his sleep, his life" that "it would have been impossible to eradicate it without entirely destroying him" (I, *Swann*, 336). Is that really love? A malady indeed. And at serious cost to Swann's social standing, since Odette was a woman of questionable and shady reputation. But Swann had gone beyond caring about such things. His case is hopeless. "To think," he says at the end of "Swann in Love," "that I've wasted years of my life, that I've longed to die, that I've experienced my greatest love, for a woman I didn't like [*ne me plaisait pas*], who wasn't even my type" (I, *Swann*, 415). Then he marries her.

Marcel's intense feelings for Gilberte put him on the path toward a love not unlike Swann's for Odette. Enter Albertine. Marcel first sees Albertine among a "little band" of other girls in Balbec, where he had gone for a vacation in his adolescence with his grandmother, inspired by Swann, who had told him of Balbec's remarkable Gothic cathedral (which he then finds disappointing, as he does with many expectations). He is enraptured by the "nuances" and "vagueness" of all the girls, but especially by Albertine. And he meets her through a new acquaintance there, the "more or less" postimpressionist painter Elstir, whose studio he visits—if having the girls, more than art, in mind—and who becomes a figure in Marcel's life, teaching Marcel how to see the world with new eyes through art. Marcel quickly falls in love with Albertine, and gets her to spend time with him, but she does not fully reciprocate his feelings—if she ever does—until they meet again later in Paris when she is a young woman and he must be in his early twenties. There he falls madly in love with her and becomes recurrently just as mad with jealousy over what he convinces himself are her affairs with other young women. Perhaps these affairs did happen, but, just like his intimate relationship with her, Proust is vague or coy about how far it goes physically—although on one occasion they caress each other, while clothed, to the point that he ejaculates, and on another he embraces her naked body in bed, a brief scene that becomes more comic than erotic when the housekeeper, Françoise, walks into the room. And given Marcel's persistent self-absorption, we cannot be quite sure of anything he says about people and events—he even grants, in a confessional moment, that his love for Albertine, "being a mental state . . . was less a love for her than a love in myself" (*mon amour était moins un amour pour elle qu'un amour en moi*; III, *Fugitive*, 568).

IV. ON HUMANISM, CLASSICS, LAUGHTER, PROUST, AND THE MEANING OF LIFE

In any case, Marcel's love for Albertine and his jealousy over doubts of her loyalty preoccupy him (as similar doubts had wracked Swann over Odette) to the extent of perversion, and say more about him than about love or jealousy. His love is all a hunger to possess. "The complete possession of Albertine," he declares, "had been my goal and my dream ever since the day when I had first set eyes on her" (III, *Fugitive*, 506). And he does not mean merely physical possession. He wants to possess her being, to make her part of him—as he says, "we exist only by virtue of what we possess" (III, *Fugitive*, 497). (We will see a more substantive variation on this idea later.) He even persuades her to stay in the Parisian residence he shares with his parents while they are away. For an entire volume of the novel, he holds her "captive" there (or thinks he does, and for only several months) in an attempt to keep her from enflaming his jealousy. But whenever he feels that he does possess her completely, his passions wane and he announces that he no longer loves her. Then the cycle repeats itself. Love and jealousy and possession and faded love and love regained and jealousy and possession and faded love again—the cycle even spins on after Albertine's death, as Marcel purses clues to the secret life he believes she had led.

He generalizes his experience with such claims as: "we love only what we do not wholly possess" (III, *Captive*, 102), for when we do possess the beloved, our love inevitably dies, but when we do not possess the beloved, jealousy brings love back because "the revolving searchlights of jealousy" always fall upon new threats (III, *Captive*, 98). Switching metaphors, he accents the idea: "jealousy is also a demon that cannot be exorcized, but constantly reappears in a new form" (III, *Captive*, 98–99). And he concludes that the sufferings of jealousy are inherent in love. "Suffering," he says, "when we are in love, ceases from time to time but only to resume in a different way" (III, Captive, 98). Not only that, he comes to believe that suffering serves life itself rather than impairs it. He implies this in saying, "It is often simply from a lack of the creative spirit [*par manque l'esprit créateur*] that we do not go far enough in suffering" (II,

Cities, 1153), as though we should suffer as much as possible. He probably had love life in mind there, but later the Author says to himself in the library, "the whole art of living [*l'art de vivre*] is to use the people who make us suffer as a step" toward the "divinity or Idea" that they "reflect" and that "gives us joy instead of pain" (III, *Regained*, 935). Whatever exactly that notion means, it exalts suffering. And I must say, Marcel's view of love and suffering strikes me as not only honoring the venerable tradition of love as a painful passion inflicted by Cupid's arrow, but as perverse.

I say Marcel's idea of love is perverse because it swings so violently between domination and an almost masochistic yen for suffering. In fact, I would go so far as to say Marcel has a sado-masochistic streak in him. Not sexual but psychological. For besides that yen to suffer, he displays traits of sadism, a topic that openly interested him. We can see hints of this as early as the night long ago in Combray when his histrionic sobs had induced his parents to submit to his will and grant his wish for his mother's good-night kiss and all-night care—then he had sunk into suffering over his success. We also saw a suggestion of it in his first reaction to Gilberte with his desire to insult and hurt her so she would remember him. And, of course, tracks of psychological sado-masochism appear all over his tempestuous relationship with Albertine. It is not surprising that he can say: "jealousy is often only an anxious need to be tyrannical applied to matters of love" (III, *Captive*, 86), and "In life it is generally sadism that gives rise to melodramatic effects" (*l'esthétique du mélodrame*; I, *Swann*, 178)—like the hypocritically virtuous daughter of the kindly composer Vinteuil, who despises her father and abuses his memory, and about whom Marcel says: "A sadist of her kind is an artist in evil" (I, *Swann*, 179); but the words could also describe his own penchant for "melodramatic effects." And when, after Albertine has fled her captivity and then died, Marcel resists his mother's wish to leave Venice but then submits to her, he says he felt "that defiant spirit [*volonté de lutte*] which drove me in the past to impose my will brutally upon the people I love best in the world, though finally conforming to theirs after I had succeeded in making them yield" (III, *Fugitive*, 666). That "defiant spirit" and its sequel in humiliating submission might not rise to true sado-masochism, but they betoken something close to it. Marcel even identifies a source of it, or of the sadistic side, in his father. "I had doubtless inherited from my father," he says, "this abrupt, arbitrary desire to threaten the people I loved the most" (III, *Captive*, 86). If Marcel inherited a degree of psychological sadism from his father, he seems to have acquired the yen for suffering on his own.

Be that as it may, love and jealousy as Marcel experiences them, from his attachment to his mother through his infatuation with pretty girls and his tortured, jealousy-ridden affair with Albertine, tell us as much or more about Marcel's neurotic character than about love or jealousy as most people experience them, except perhaps episodically. It is true that Cupid's arrow can incite lust and passion, possessiveness and anguish, as well as blind idealization of the beloved and odd behavior, especially in the early days of romantic love—Stendhal wrote a whole book on that theme entitled *De l'amour* (1822), in which he described the stages of love centering on the "crystallization" that exalts the beloved in the lover's mind and causes the lover to go a little nuts. As Shakespeare said in *A Midsummer Night's Dream*: "The course of true love never did run smooth." But if romantic love is to endure, the urgent emotions of its early phase must yield to deeper and more appreciative affection for the beloved, anchored in respect, admiration, and genuine caring for a person. For all of Marcel's vaunted love of Albertine, he does not even seem to *like* her—any more than Swann *liked* Odette.

In Proust, then, love is mostly a drama of attraction, passion, possessiveness, jealousy, waning affection, reviving desire, and all over again. He calls this drama "intermittences of the heart"—his original title for the whole novel. These can indeed be the caprices of love, but Proust treats them as though they are pretty much all there is to love. And, again, he does it primarily from the male point of view. Not of all males, mind you, but stereotypical males. I dare say the portrayal of love would have been quite different if Proust had revealed more of the inner lives of his female characters, letting them speak for themselves: less animal lust and egocentric psychological domination and more enveloping empathy and genuine affection, as well as ambivalent resignation to male domination. One wonders why Proust did not do that, being the perceptive observer and sensitive, voluminous writer about people that he was. Perhaps the omission arose from the fact, contended by critics, that his model was male homosexual love more than heterosexuality—an inspiration for Albertine is said by some critics to have been a particular male companion of Proust's named Alfred Agostenilli, who served for a time as his chauffeur and secretary, and, like Albertine, died in an accident far away. In fact, "inversion" in both sexes is almost as prominent in the book as heterosexual love, and is the stated theme of volume four, entitled by Proust, *Sodom and Gomorrah* (*Cities of the Plain* in Scott Moncrieff's translation). But, whatever its origins, a narrow version of love it is, ringing false to the tender, deep, and enduring reciprocal affection known to homosexual and heterosexual couples alike. If Proust knew of this kind of love, he does not show it.

PROUST'S PROSE

This brings us back to the questions posed at the outset and takes us to the rewards of reading the book. Does Proust show us human life, in the words of the Author, "as it really is," and, beyond that, enhance our living of it? As should be clear above, I do not think he gives us a complete enough picture of love and jealousy as most people know them. But, love and jealousy aside, he does, for one thing, artfully throw light into many corners of human experience with the Author's meditations and *aperçus* scattered through the book. They are worth reading for themselves, and Proust devotees have compiled lists of them. Several of these *aperçus* have shown up, or will, in these pages, but here are a few nice, relatively aphoristic lines: "It is not only by dint of lying to other people but also by lying to oneself that one ceases to be aware that one is lying" (II, *Cities*, 938); "The indifference to the suffering one causes, whatever other names one gives it, is the most terrible and lasting form of cruelty" (I, *Swann*, 180); "We do not receive wisdom, we must discover it for ourselves, after a journey which no one else can make for us, which no one can spare us, for our wisdom is the point of view from which we come at last to regard the world" (I, *Grove*, 923–24); "It is life that, little by little, case by case, enables us to observe that what is most important to our hearts or to our minds is taught us not by reasoning but by other powers" (III, *Fugitive*, 429–30). Such pithy thoughts—and there are many—put Proust in the great tradition of French moralists going back to La Bruyère, La Rochefoucauld, and Montaigne. But Proust sets them within the context of a world and a time where they also have their own resonance.

I might add—what should be obvious—that the artfulness of Proust's prose is also itself worth reading for its own sake. Notwithstanding the long-winded sentences and the unbroken paragraphs, and sometimes precisely because of these, the rhetorical sweep can be symphonic and the lines poetic. For the symphony, one must, of course, read at length, but shorter lyrical pieces abound. And many can be found in these pages. But a couple of my favorites are memorable lines that conclude parts of *Swann's Way*. The very moving section "Combray," ends with a long, flowing description of Marcel awakening from a night of dreaming and memories and seeing the first dim light of day peeking into his room, while images of those dreams and memories linger "in the whirlpool of my awakening" until gradually "put to flight by that pale sign traced above my window-curtains by the uplifted forefinger of dawn" (I, *Swann*, 204). And there are the poignant, well-known closing words of that volume: "the memory of a particular image is but regret for a particular moment; and houses, roads, avenues are as fugitive, alas, as the years."** Let these two quite familiar instances, along with others in this essay, suffice as a tiny sample of the evocative beauties to be encountered in Proust's writing, within the difficulties of following the narrative.

But insightful as the *aperçus*, and as elegant as the prose, I would say the greatest value of reading Proust lies in what his novel as a whole tells us about *what makes life most worth living*. For, unlike much of the depiction of love and jealousy, here we do see life as "it really is," and, better, we see how to find a vitality in it all too easily lost to the ordinary routine of our days. And this takes us first to the idea of consciousness. For what Proust says about how we experience our lives through consciousness, makes *À la Recherche du temps perdu* a book to ponder, absorb, and learn from for sure.

ON CONSCIOUSNESS AND ATTENTION

I might almost venture that whatever else Proust's novel may be, it is a book about consciousness. That might seem pretentious or forbidding, but it isn't. After all, consciousness is the principal sign of our being alive. Without it we are nothing. The question here is: does Proust tell us anything about consciousness beyond what common sense tells us? I think he does. For he shows us some uses of consciousness that most of us don't think about or use as fully as we might. And those uses can awaken us to life in new and inspiriting ways.

We begin with the idea of consciousness itself, or rather with a couple of seminal philosophical/psychological conceptions of it

---

** Actually, Scott Moncrieff, sometimes prone to lyrical embellishments (which I have pared down in a few of the quotations) in what is one of the great literary translations, deserves some credit for the artistry in the first quotation here, since the original line concludes with the slightly more prosaic, *le doigt levé du jour*. But he translates the last lines of *Swann's Way* quite literally.

395

from Proust's own times that fit this novel illuminatingly. I mean those of Henri Bergson and William James.

Although Bergson was seventeen years younger than James, the two thinkers had many intellectual affinities and would become close colleagues at a distance. What united them was opposition to the monistic, materialistic, mechanistic worldview—with its insistence on scientific observation and rigid rationality as the only paths to truth—then dominant in science and philosophy. James had been inveighing against this in articles since the 1870s, several of which he would incorporate into his classic *Principles of Psychology* published in 1890, when Proust was just under twenty years old. Both James and Bergson opposed the idea that the universe consists only of material stuff governed by absolute, mechanistic laws. They thought of reality as more of a fluid process. It is constantly in flux, incompatible with mechanistic laws, and it does not readily lend itself to understanding by intellect alone. They agreed that intuition can come closer. For intuition can better probe variety, change, and fluid relations (Proust's Author echoes the idea when he says, "our intelligence is not the most subtle, the most powerful, the most appropriate instruments for grasping the truth" because that depends on "other powers," including "unconscious intuition" [III, Fugitive, 429–30]). Their notions of consciousness went with these judgments. For them, consciousness was the fluctuating essence of human nature. And, particularly for Bergson, consciousness was a temporal phenomenon. In his first book, *Time and Free Will*, published in 1889, Bergson spoke of consciousness and time as "pure duration." This, he said "is the form which the succession of our conscious states assume when our ego lets itself *live*, when it refrains from separating its present state from its former states." In other words, consciousness is the psychological duration of life from past to present. This has obvious implications for memory. In "recalling these states," Bergson writes, consciousness "forms both past and present states into an organic whole" like "notes of a tune, melting, so to speak, into one another" (*Time and Free Will*, Gutenberg online, 100).

27. As Time Goes By

Bergson would soon go on to write *Matter and Memory* (1896) and other books on this process of consciousness and time and the flux of existence. It is easy enough to see Bergsonian notions in *À la Recherche*. Probably too easy. In fact, Bergson and Proust were cousins by marriage and knew each other reasonably well—Bergson's name even pops up in Proust's novel, on whether or not sleeping pills can affect memory: he doubts it (II, *Cities*, 1016). But Proust was not putting Bergson's ideas into fiction. He did not need to. Explorations of the inner life of consciousness and its ramifications were becoming widespread by the time Proust wrote. He probably contributed more to those explorations than he borrowed from them. But none of these explorations came closer to Proust and better illustrate the consequential character of consciousness in his novel than some of those by William James—who nonetheless seems to have remained unknown to Proust.

Assailing theorists who considered mind or consciousness to be a mechanical apparatus that passively receives disconnected sensations and joins them piecemeal through acts of thought, James asserted that consciousness is not "chopped up in bits" but is more like "a 'river' or 'stream'." In this "stream of thought, or consciousness, or of subjective life" (*BC*, 159), or "time-stream of our thinking" (*BC*, 270), our thoughts and feelings, sensations and memories, fantasies and knowledge, and everything else, flow together through a process of "duration" (*BC*, 266) and "constant change" (*BC*, 154). But that is not all that happens. The "wonderful stream of our consciousness" (*BC*, 159; James's coinage, which would become a cliché of literary criticism) contains the faculty of *attention*, usually in league with *will*. Sometimes *attention* occurs involuntarily, as in a surprise or with something barely noticed. But more often it functions voluntarily through an act of *will*, as in "paying attention" to something (*BC*, 213). Either way, "the whole drama . . . the whole sting and excitement . . . of our voluntary life hinges on the amount of attention, slightly more or slightly less" that we bestow on experience (*BC*, 228). For, James says, while we swim in the stream of consciousness, "what is called our 'experience' is almost entirely determined by our habits of attention" (*BC*, 170).

Taking a few liberties, I would say that Proust's novel is awash in that "stream of consciousness" and the moments of "attention"—"slightly more or slightly less"—that shape experience within that stream. I say this not to characterize the book's literary style as "stream of consciousness" (although many critics do) but to accentuate the conceptions of *consciousness* and *attention* that flow together through the book. Marcel reflects these ideas when he observes on one occasion that, to prevent an experience from sinking into the stream of his consciousness out of sight and mind, he had mustered, "an exercise of will and attention" (*un exercise de ma volonté et de mon attention*) that "heightened the acuteness of my inward vision" (II, *Cities*, 675) so he was able to hold onto what would otherwise have been lost (in this case, a name). Later the Author punches the value of attending to experience rather than letting it go as he invokes the idea of psychological possession (more substantive than the romantic possession seen earlier): "It is only in one's mind that one possesses things," he says. For example, "one does not possess a picture because it hangs in one's dining room if one is incapable of understanding it, or a landscape because one lives in it without even looking at it" (III, *Fugitive*, 563), any more than "to possess a thing materially, to take up residence in a town, is the equivalent of possessing it spiritually" (*équivalait à la posséder spirituellement*; II, *Guermantes*, 364). We must consciously attend to such things and make them part of us inside. If we do not do that, if we do not "exercise will and attention" to possess those experiences in our minds, our consciousness, they merely flow over us to be lost in the stream. As he says, "we possess only what is really present to us, and many of our memories, our moods, our ideas"—and we could add our perceptions—"take voyages far away where we lose sight of them" (III, *Fugitive*, 497).

The exercise of attention, he also remarks, is crucial to the literary artist, who must attend even to "trivialities" like "the tone of a voice," a "facial expression," and "the movement of the shoulders" (III, *Regained*, 937). The prolific Henry James had offered similar advice to novelists when he said, "Try to be one of those on whom nothing is lost." But for Proust, "attention" should not be equated merely with the "powers of observation" that Marcel associated with the art of Realism and had thought he lacked—to the detriment of his art, until he saw the light and turned against the superficialities of Realism. True attention goes deeper than that. It draws from experience the makings of "impressions" that get deposited within us, and that are the "reality" of human life the imaginative writer should explore. I should note, however (as indicated earlier—p. 361), that attention can be, as Willliam James said, "slightly more or slightly less," or we might say more active or more passive. This is how some experiences, or sensations, and the "impressions" derived from them, enter our consciousness through more attention and remain available to our voluntary memory, while others sink deeper into vessels of our unconscious through less attention, where they remain as latent memories to be released only by new and unexpected incidents of more attention prompted by sudden involuntary memories of past experiences. In short, if we have no attention, however slight, we have no experience and no memories, past, present, or future. We are not all artists, but sharpening our attention to experience in the stream of our consciousness, is, I would say, probably the highest reward of reading Proust. For it is, in Proust's lyrical words, how "the dust of realities is mingled with magic sand" and then even "some trivial incident of life becomes a springboard to romance" (I, *Grove*, 925). We will return to this idea below.

Most of *À la Recherche* is a story told from within Marcel's (or the Author's) consciousness as he attends to this or that. It is true that his subjectivity makes Marcel sometimes seem almost solipsistic. He lives in the world, but he doesn't. As he (now the Author) says to himself in the library, "really everything is in the mind" (*tout est dans l'esprit*; III, *Regained*, 950). In a similar vein he had asserted earlier that "the bonds between ourselves and another person exist only in our minds," for "we exist alone" (III, *Fugitive*, 459). Marcel had also confessed, "it was my fate to pursue only phantoms [*fantômes*], creatures whose reality existed to a great extent in my imagination" (II, *Cities*, 1045). The "phantoms" he was referring to were mostly his loves—and he says Swann "had been a lover of phantoms," too (I, *Grove*, 1046)—but they are also the impressions that experience has inscribed inside him. Such are the phantoms of memory: what his mind's eye sees and remembers but that he cannot find in the external world, to his recurring disappointment—as when he returns to Combray and Balbec and to the Paris he wistfully finds at the end of *Swann's Way*.

Reading Proust, we therefore read of a character swimming in the stream of his own consciousness where he is captivated by sensations, animated by emotions, besieged by fantasies, bewitched by memories, and haunted by dreams from childhood to adulthood. Dreams, I should point out, had always meant a lot to Marcel and the Author. Marcel thinks of dreams as he falls asleep and awakens from them to find they are not outside his life but belong to it, rendering many of his waking perceptions rather dreamlike. The Author even says just before he leaves the library, "dreams . . . had done most to convince me of the purely mental character of reality" (*caractère purement mental de la réalité*; III, *Regained*, 953). Dreams are a fount of his sense of reality. As are memories, which give *consciousness* and *attention* the dimension of Time. And it is through the dreamlike awakening of memories that Marcel eventually becomes the Author who will write the story of his life—his inner life—showing the value of attending to experience inside us no less than outside.

ON MEMORY

Anyone who knows anything of Proust knows that memory plays a central role in *À la Recherche du temps perdu*. The title implies as much. We have followed Proust's Author through enough meditations on memory that here I will do little more than briefly summarize.

We have seen how near the end of the novel the Author discovers that memory is the key to unlocking the door to Lost Time and to the impressions inside him that have shaped his life. As he said in the library, "what we call reality" comes down to "a certain connection between . . . sensations and the memories which envelop us simultaneously with them." That "connection," that "reality," is the "impressions" formed by sensations and memories and deposited within us. For everyone, he says, "carries within himself an awareness, linking him to the past, of the continuity of his life" (III, *Regained*, 1011), because we are "a product of memory, and our memory of a moment . . . endures still, and lives still" (III, *Fugitive*, 487). It is the task of "the writer" to explore those memories to find the vital impressions (III, *Regained*, 924)—this is what the Author vows to do when he says his novel will be "the re-creation through memory of the impressions" born deeply within him of life experience.

A century before Proust, William Wordsworth had made a similar discovery. He wrote in the long autobiographical poem *The Prelude* how he had looked back over his life in search of its meaning, and how he had found that meaning in what he called "spots of time." These were moments that glowed in his memory for the joyous feeling they had brought him originally and that he felt again when recalling them. When those feelings merged with thoughts, he saw "what is most important" to him in life. And what he found to be most important was none other than these intense feelings themselves, along with a desire to rouse them in others through poetry that makes us excited to be alive instead of succumbing to what he had earlier derided as "the savage torpor" of modern life (and that was modern life around 1800!). Anticipating Proust's Author, Wordsworth had discovered through memory the meaning of his life—and art.

Proust's Author seems to have first learned the power and mysteries of memory when sipping tea with the madeleine at home in his youth. The taste had triggered in him a peculiar joy. And he had discovered that the joy came from an unexpected memory of a related sensation in his past. He did not yet understand why that should be, but he would come to think of this as an "involuntary memory" and find that it takes him more deeply into himself and his past than can the "voluntary memory" of intellect, because "the efforts of our intellect are useless" in searching for the past, which lies "hidden outside the realm and beyond the reach" of thought itself (I, *Swann*, 47–48). He has said: "our intelligence is not the most subtle, the most powerful, the most appropriate instrument for grasping the truth." But he will also say intellect could become "the collaborator and servant" of "other powers" that could lead to the past and to truth (III, *Fugitive*, 429-30). Hence, he would have to depend on that "collaborator and servant" in using "voluntary memory" to search out the sources of his "involuntary memories," as well as to knit them together in the novel he writes.††

We have also seen how memories of the impressions in his mind, his consciousness, would become more real to him than the world outside. That would be the gist of the lyrical ending of *Swann's Way* quoted in part earlier. There the Author tells of returning to the Bois de Boulogne in Paris, where in his youth he had enjoyed many

---

†† I might note a third type of memory that Marcel and the Author experience. These are the memories that come from neither involuntary sparks nor voluntary effort but simply linger in mind, not to be forgotten but recalled from time to time whether one wishes it or not. And, unlike "involuntary memories," they do not bring joy but often regrets. We could call these "haunting" or "nagging" memories. And Marcel's memory of the good-night kiss, with his Pyrrhic victory over his parents' will, is one of them. Incidentally, Freudian memories of incidents or fantasies too painful to endure, so they get repressed into the unconscious, do not seem to have much place in Proust. Forgetfulness in Proust is generally not caused by anxious repression but by the continuing flow of consciousness that carries everything with it, letting most things sink beneath the surface (some through the anesthesia of habit, of which more below) until some are retrieved, while others disappear permanently, and still others swim on the surface with persistent attention.

happy moments, and where he now thinks, "I wanted to find them again as I remembered them" (I, *Swann*, 461). But he couldn't. Not only had things changed over Time. He had learned "how contradictory it is to seek in reality for the pictures that are stored in one's memory, which must inevitably lose the charm that comes to them from memory itself." For "the places we have known" were "never more than a thin slice, held between the contiguous impressions that composed our life at that time; the memory of a particular image is but regret for a particular moment; and houses, roads, avenues are as fugitive, alas, as the years" (I, *Swann*, 462).

Marcel's and the Author's inner life of memories, impressions, dreams, "phantoms" always eclipses the external world. And exploring that inner life along the paths and byways of memory would give the Author the purpose of his life in the novel he will write, which he hopes will help readers to see themselves better, too, and to live more fully—in the dimension of Time.

THE MAGIC SAND

Here we reach the highest rewards of reading Proust. Which should be evident by now. Drawing together clues found along the way, we can confidently say that *À la Recherche du temps perdu* lives up to the vision of art that the Author sees at the end of the novel before starting to write it. It is a commonplace of literary history to say that the novel he, or rather Proust, wrote marked the passage of Western literature from portraying the external world to portraying consciousness within, which is to say, from varieties of Realism to the spirit of Modernism—Proust's novel wowed Virginia Woolf, for instance, who adapted it's subjective "method" to her more lapidary style. But this was not art for art's sake. Proust wanted none of that. As Proust's Author says, he believed that, by plumbing the inner life, art can disclose things about ourselves and human existence that we might not otherwise be able to see without art, and that we can share with other people. For "through art alone are we able to emerge from ourselves, to know what another person sees of a universe which is not the same as our own" (III, *Regained*, 932). Marcel had first beheld this vision of art under the tutelage of the painter Elstir, who had shown him how to find aesthetic beauty anywhere, from the misty seashore to a nondescript Gothic cathedral to domestic scenes at home. "Since I had seen such things depicted in water-colors by Elstir," Marcel says, "I tried to find beauty where I had never figured that it was, in the most ordinary things," even at the dinner table "in the profound life of 'Still Life'" (*dans les chose les plus usuelles, dans la vie profound des "natures mortes"*; I, *Grove*, 929). Decades after that, as the Author, he has made this transformative vision of art his own. And he will share it through his novel by demonstrating that art can educate the senses to be more aware, the emotions to feel more intensely, the imagination to soar farther, and the intellect to attain new enlightenment.

Reading Proust the artist, we can gain all of that. But, the powers of art aside, Proust also shows us that perhaps nothing is more valuable to anyone than learning to pay attention to the stream that is our own consciousness and to the kinds of experiences that we can bring into that stream to expand our lives.

This is why, by the way, Proust has Marcel and the Author repeatedly denigrate habit. Habits may be necessary to organize our days and even to shield us from a measure of pain and trouble, but the "anesthetic effect of habit" (I, *Swann*, 11) also dulls the attention that should animate our experience. "Stupefying habit," Marcel rues, "during the whole course of our life conceals from us almost the whole universe" (III, *Fugitive*, 554), because it is "an annihilating force that suppresses the originality and even the awareness of one's perceptions" (III, *Fugitive*, 426). As a result, "most of our faculties lie dormant because they can rest on habit" (I, *Grove*, 706). But at the same time, habit can become "so riveted to one's being, its insignificant face so incrusted in one's heart, that if it detaches itself," or gets unintentionally broken, it "inflicts on one sufferings more terrible than any other and is then as cruel as death itself" (III, *Fugitive*, 426)—as happened to Marcel when he suddenly lost Albertine, and with her the habit of having her with him. To head off both kinds of peril, we should seek experiences that "awaken forgotten selves, counteract the torpor of habit" (III, *Fugitive*, 500), free us from "the cocoon of habit" (I, *Grove*, 897) and enable us to fly. I might note that William James, who famously judged habit integral to the mental life, and for good if harnessed to productive ends, also warned against its detrimental effects and urged breaking old habits in order to revitalize experience and remake life in the spirit of *genius*. "Genius, in truth," he wrote, "means little more than the faculty of perceiving in an unhabitual way" (*BC*, 309).

No author more than Proust shows us how the secret of life is to perceive the world and to meet experience *in an unhabitual way*. Or, in another of James's phrases, to develop "habits of attention" that enliven our experience rather than dull us to it. Marcel affirms this when he remarks, "It is our attention that puts objects in a room, and habit that removes them" (*C'est notre attention qui met des objets dans une chambre, et l'habitude qui les en retire*; I, *Grove*, 717). Noticing things, paying attention, perceiving them far and near, outside and inside, "possessing" them mentally, are essential to the vision of both art and life in *À la Recherche*—accounting for the many references to visual perception and optical devices in the book, e.g., microscope, telescope, binoculars, kaleidoscope, stereopticon, X-ray. And, when we include a dose of imagination, we have the makings of a truly artful life. The Author captures this idea in an eloquently metaphorical line: "Existence is of little interest save on days when the dust of realities is mingled with magic sand, when some trivial incident of life becomes a springboard for romance" (*L'existence n'a guère d'intérêt que dans les journées où la poussière des réalité est mêlée de sable magique, ou quelque vulgaire incident de la vie deviant un ressort romanesque*; I, *Grove*, 925). For then "everything is fertile," and "we can make discoveries no less precious than in Pascal's *Pensées* in an advertisement for soap" (III, *Fugitive*, 553–54). That might be a bit

IV. On Humanism, Classics, Laughter, Proust, and the Meaning of Life

of a stretch, but we get the point: shake off the habitual "dust of realities" whenever we can and sprinkle them with "magic sand," alerting us to the bountiful varieties of experience and spurring us to discover new worlds anywhere.

Something like that happens with the involuntary memories that burst upon Marcel and the Author from time to time, awakening them to a forgotten past that suddenly resurfaces in the stream of consciousness. Forgotten but not lost because the experiences, or the impressions of them, like the garden gate bell the Author hears at the end and decides will launch the novel, have always been there within. Put in the stream by moments of attention to experience, however slight, in the past and still flowing to be retrieved by the "magic sand" of renewed attention—with both involuntary and voluntary memory.

The more attention we give to experience, then, the more impressions and seeds of memories flow in the stream of our consciousness, bringing greater understanding of ourselves and a keener feeling for life. It is in this light that Proust urges us to be aware of the inner world even more than of the outer world of experience at large. And to use art to explore both worlds with powers of perception, emotion, and imagination that art alone can provide. And to see how all lived experience flows together in our consciousness through attention, turning sensations into enduring impressions along with memories of them, and containing telling clues to our lives as we pass through Time into the future.

In sum, Proust tells us to be as alert to everything as we can, especially to our inner lives, always seeking "magic sand" and any "springboard to romance" for widening and deepening the stream of our consciousness, enlarging our selves, and enhancing the joy of being alive. Literature gives us no higher rewards than that.

Acknowledgment. I must give a grateful *coup de chapeau* to my friend Stan Burnett, Proust scholar, capacious intellectual, and *personne extraordinaire*, for his inspiration, guidance, and friendly criticism in the writing of this essay. He enlightened me more about Proust than I can say or will remember. He is also gentleman enough to keep the criticism coming in good-natured banter over my obstinacy on a few points. I cannot thank him enough for his encouragement and advice, in this and other things, and I can blame him for nothing.

The Thinker (Le Penseur), *Auguste Rodin; meaning of life Daily Toon by Mark Lynch.*

The meaning of life is not some cosmic truth out there waiting to be discovered. It's more ordinary and interesting than that. The fundamental meaning of life is the feeling that our own lives have meaning.

Thinking about the Meaning of Life

A DIALOGUE

Humanist: Ah. My genially skeptical friend. I am pleased to see you. I suppose you have been pulling rugs from under many claims to truth since I last saw you. I've heard sounds of wreckage. Now, even though you don't believe anyone can know anything for sure, I've been thinking about some things I'd like to discuss with you. And you might not wholly reject what I have to say.

Skeptic: My friendly and loquacious humanist. It is always a pleasure to talk to you. You're such a good-natured optimist. Full of ideas about life and how to make it better. Faulty as they might be. But I would never wholly reject anything you say. Question your claims to truth, yes, but that's about it. I'm a modest skeptic, not an arrogant cynic.

H   Modest, not arrogant, to be sure. That's what makes you so congenial. But there is a fine line between a skeptic and a cynic. And if I'm an optimist, does that make you a pessimist?

S   As a skeptic I'm neither cynical nor pessimistic. I don't claim to know enough to be either. And I don't scoff at everything people think. All I do is try to keep them intellectually honest and not to think they know more than they do.

H   Very Socratic of you. But to your credit you are not as condescending as he was. Although you do like to play the Devil's advocate.

S   Of course I do. But not only that. And I don't work for the Devil, whatever some people might say. So, my friend, let's get on with it. I suppose you want, as usual, "to talk of many

IV. On Humanism, Classics, Laughter, Proust, and the Meaning of Life

things . . . of shoes and ships and sealing wax, cabbages and kings"?

H   Aha. You know your Lewis Carroll. Well, to continue your line, what I have in mind is something like "why the sea is boiling hot, and whether pigs have wings." The meaning of life. I think I've figured it out. At least how to think about it.

S   Oh, my. That old chestnut. The phrase is such a cliché it has no real "meaning" at all..

H   A cliché, yes. But not an empty one. It does have a meaning. It's kind of a name, a label, a bit of shorthand, almost a metaphor.

S   What?

H   Let's just make it shorthand for what matters most to us, for what makes life most worth living—if we could narrow that down to one thing, but never mind this complication. That's all. But if you want more, and I'm sure you will, I'd say the phrase "meaning of life" signifies both the ends and means of our lives. That is, the purposes we give our lives as a result of what matters most to us, and the strategies we use to achieve those purposes. Here's a simplistic example. Say the love of music matters to you more than anything else, and that this love is what makes your life most worth living. So, you make satisfying that love the overriding purpose of your life. And to achieve that purpose you decide to become a performing musician, with all that entails. Consequently, you live a life in music as a performing musician. There you have the "meaning of life" for such a musician—shorthand for what makes a musician's life most worth living, and therefore gives a musician purpose in life and strategies for achieving that purpose.

S   But that doesn't . . .

H   Wait. Before you criticize, I have to add that this is a mere definition of the phrase "meaning of life," but it doesn't tell

28. Thinking about the Meaning of Life

us what "the meaning of life" actually is. For it doesn't tell us what a person for whom—sticking with the same example—music is the "meaning of life," as I have defined it, has in common with another person for whom, say, sports is the "meaning of life." If people's different "meanings of life" don't share a common quality, then the phrase "meaning of life" only signifies the diverse things people care most about and the disparate purposes and strategies that they choose to live out those "meanings." That is why we have to go beyond a simple definition of the phrase and think about what one person's "meaning of life" shares with everyone else's. In other words, what is the fundamental or universal "meaning of life" that all individual "meanings of life" share. And that's what I think I've figured out. Or, as I said, at least how to think about it.

S Wow. That's a pretty dense thicket of "meanings." But I won't carp about your definition, as I could. I'd rather talk about your claim that you've figured out the "universal meaning of life." Ha! That *is* a laugh. You'll forgive my chuckles and my doubts. Still, since you say this with a wry smile, as you should, I'll contain my laughter. For now. And because I have to admit you've stirred my curiosity, and you are always interesting and often amusing, I'll sportingly hear you out. Just don't presume to know too much.

H I would never do that. Certainly not with a dedicated skeptic like you. And I welcome your doubts. Naturally I smile when I say I've figured out "universal the meaning of life." Who wouldn't? To deflate the seeming pretentiousness of it. But you're such a good sport, I thought you'd be game. And you might even go for my ideas.

S You *are* amusing. I might not be able to contain my laughter.

H I'll try to entertain you. So, I'll start with this teaser: I'm not sure that everybody thinks about the meaning of life, but I'm

IV. On Humanism, Classics, Laughter, Proust, and the Meaning of Life

pretty sure everybody knows what that meaning is even without thinking about it.

S   What? At least you got my attention. With nonsense. I don't know if many people think about the meaning of life. But, it doesn't matter because I don't think anybody will ever know what that meaning is, if there is such a thing.

H   I expected you to react that way. Doubting everything. But once I explain my ideas, you might not dismiss them all as nonsense. I say everybody knows the meaning of life simply because we live it out every day. We might not know we know, but we do.

S   You're being perverse. How can we know the meaning of life without knowing we know, or live it out if we don't know what it is, or don't know we know?—or rather, *think* that we know, not that we can ever *know* anything for sure.

H   Easily. Because the fundamental meaning of life isn't a kind of knowledge. It's a feeling—the feeling that our own lives have meaning. Plain as that. We might not think about that feeling, but it's what gets us up in the morning, and we have to have it or we stop living.

S   What? You think the meaning of life is just a feeling, an emotion?

H   Not *just* a feeling. But the meaning of life is not some big cosmic truth out there waiting to be discovered like a new galaxy in the heavens, or something suddenly revealed to us as if we were Paul on the road to Damascus—at least not for most people. It's more ordinary and interesting than that. Virginia Woolf, perhaps an unlikely source of wisdom on this subject, got it right, or partly right, when she had a character ask in *To the Lighthouse*: "What is the meaning of life?" And answer: "The great revelation had never come. The great revelation perhaps never did come. Instead there were little daily miracles, illuminations, matches struck unexpectedly in the dark." I'd say the great revelation doesn't come because the meaning of life isn't outside of us but inside, in the everyday feeling that our own lives have meaning. Those "matches struck unexpectedly in the dark" show us that feeling and perhaps help us see how we can get it.

S   Wait a minute. Whatever the meaning of life might be, it's surely not a mere emotion. Emotions are unreliable. They come and go with our moods. They vary from moment to moment. They don't tell us about anything but themselves and our susceptibility to them. They can't tell us anything about the meaning of life itself.

H   I'm not talking about the meaning of life *itself*, as you put it, but I'll come back to that. You are wrong about emotions. Emotions tell us a great deal about ourselves and our lives. Read Romanticism. Read Freud. We might not want to govern our lives entirely by emotions, since we also need rationality to understand the world and to make good judgments. And one of the things rationality can teach us is to recognize the value of emotions, including how *the fundamental meaning of life lies in feeling that our own lives have meaning*. For if you really think about it, nothing is more important to us than that feeling. This might not be the same as discovering the "meaning of life *itself*," but it's the essence of it all and the best we can get.

S   My good humanist. I'm afraid you are trivializing the subject. The meaning of life, if there is one, has to be much more than a feeling.

H   Triviality is not a sin. It can puncture inflated pieties, as Oscar Wilde showed so cleverly. But I'm not trivializing anything here. If we look for the meaning of life *itself* as some absolute truth about reality out there, we'll never find it—you would surely agree, with your skeptical modesty. Of course, people have claimed to find that meaning in many different "truths" about reality, and this has caused no end of conflict. But if people were to look for the meaning of life not as absolute, universal truth outside of themselves but as a feeling inside that everyone shares and acts on every day, then we could all agree on what the meaning of life basically is. We might disagree over how to get it, but not over what it is. Religion is an obvious example of people sharing that feeling but failing to see it for what it is, and so they quarrel over conflicting "truths" when, in fact, they differ only in their opinions of what gives them that common feeling.

S   Religion is not simply a feeling. It is a set of beliefs and precepts about human existence and the universe. Those beliefs assert truths that I think can't stand up to scrutiny, but they can't be reduced to feelings either.

H   I'm not reducing religious beliefs to feelings. I'm just saying that all such beliefs deliver the same feeling of meaning. So, whereas conflicting religious beliefs about God and the universe cannot all be true, all religious beliefs *are* true in the sense that they give believers effectively the same feeling that their lives have meaning. The feelings of meaning we get from religion prove only that religion can give us those feelings. That is all. But that's not nothing.

S   Hold on. When you say the truth of religion comes down to a feeling you not only slight religious belief but also spirituality. You think spiritual life is only emotion?

H   I challenge anyone to prove that spirituality is not an emotion. Or, to put it another way, one person's spirituality is another person's emotion or imagination, or even, as Ebenezer Scrooge said of his ghosts, perhaps a bit of underdone potato. But let's not get into that. The inner life lies in shadows. I'm not trying to denigrate religion or the spirit or the soul. I only question how we can distinguish our religious or spiritual experience from a kind of emotion. I would expect you to share that doubt. Believers in one religion declare that believers in other religions cannot possibly have the same spiritual experience—which is to say the same feeling—as they themselves do. But since we can't very well compare these spiritual lives, there is

28. Thinking about the Meaning of Life

no way to distinguish the "truth" of one religious experience from another. And from that we must conclude that it is not the so-called "truth" of a religious belief that really matters, it's the feeling of meaning believers get from it. And, as history proves, some people will kill for that feeling, convinced that it belongs to them and fellow believers in their "truth" alone.

S   It's obvious that people often deceive themselves into thinking they have religious truth when they don't. But that's because they confuse knowledge with faith. Faith is a substitute for knowledge. If we could *know* something to be true we wouldn't need to have *faith* that it is true. Honest thinkers acknowledge the difference. Some skeptics, like Montaigne, have openly embraced religious faith for that very reason, honestly doubting that religious *truth* can ever be known. But, skeptics or not, many people crave some kind of *truth* about the meaning of life, whether they get it from faith or purported knowledge, and they can't be satisfied with a mere feeling.

H   Yes they can. Although they might not admit it. They just want to wrap their arms around a believable *truth* that will give them the feeling that their lives have meaning. Whether they find a verifiable truth or rely on faith is ultimately less important to them than getting that feeling. In the end, people simply want to feel that their lives have meaning, no matter how they get that feeling.

S   So, in effect, you're saying there is no objective meaning of life itself beyond our subjective feelings?

H   Well, yes and no.

S   That's not helpful. My friend, do you even know what you're talking about?

H   Of course I do. And it is growing clear that you, my dear skeptic, don't yet understand how to think about the meaning of life. It's good we're having this little chat. Let me clarify some distinctions.

S   All right. But don't be flippant or condescend. You accused

IV. On Humanism, Classics, Laughter, Proust, and the Meaning of Life

Socrates of that. Your humanism should be generous and smiling.

H   Quite so. Like your skepticism. Just trying to keep the conversation lighthearted. But enthusiasm can get the better of me. Feel free to chide me if I slip.

S   Oh, I will.

TWO MEANINGS OF LIFE

H   All right. I'll start with this. When I say that the meaning of life is the feeling that our lives have meaning, I'm simply describing an elemental fact of human life. A psychological fact. I'll call it the *psychological meaning of life*. Namely, the subjective psychological experience, or feeling, that our own lives have meaning. When we have that experience, our lives *do* have meaning for us, because the meaning resides in the feeling itself. And we can get that feeling in any number ways, from religion to love, from art to classic books, from serving others to professional accomplishment, and so on. Anything that, as William Wordsworth put it, reveals "what is most important to us." OK. Now, there is also another meaning of life, and this is closer to what you've been driving at. I'll call it the *philosophical meaning of life*. It comes from more or less rational judgments we make about reality. These are judgments that deem certain ideas, beliefs, facts, etc. to be objectively true independent of us, and therefore they provide the meaning of life *itself*. We generally embrace both of these meanings of life in one way or another because we couple the feeling that our lives have meaning with judgments we make about what is objectively true of reality itself.

S   So, you concede that feelings are not enough, and that you think there is an *objective* meaning of life itself. But, here's one problem with your version of it. By reducing the objective,

28. Thinking about the Meaning of Life

or, as you say, the philosophical meaning of life, to a personal value judgment, you make this about as subjective and relative to us as our feelings. If life has an *objective* meaning, surely it should be independent of feelings and personal value judgments. I say it *should* be. But, as you are aware, I doubt that we can ever know anything for certain because all our alleged "truths" dissolve into subjective judgments about *how* we know "truth," and none of these judgments has solid ground to stand on once we analyze them closely.

H Yes, that's the quicksand of your Pyrrhonian skepticism. It can consume everything in a spiral of asking *Why?* But it sounds like you're edging toward my side.

S Not at all. I just acknowledge the problem of subjectivity in knowing anything. That's the intellectual integrity of skepticism. But I reject your solipsistic celebration of subjectivity.

H I don't celebrate subjectivity. But, instead of viewing it as a stumbling block to knowledge, I make the most of it in understanding the meaning of life. We can't live for an idea or a purportedly objective *truth* about reality if it doesn't somehow give us the feeling that our lives have meaning. However, we *can* live for that feeling without asserting any objective truth about reality.

S I'll reserve a verdict on that.

H Naturally. Well, what I say holds whether the feeling of meaning gives rise to a judgment about the philosophical meaning of life or follows from it. For instance, you might have a spiritual experience that immediately makes you *feel* that your life has meaning, and then you adopt a religious belief that supports this feeling with theological claims about objective reality and the philosophical meaning of life. Or you could start the other way by adopting—perhaps from childhood—a religious belief with its judgments about objective reality and the philosophical meaning of life, and then that belief gives you the feeling that your life has meaning. Either way, the feeling is the

S most essential thing. Not only that. There's a kind of paradox here.

S I think you've been playing with paradoxes from the beginning.

H This is a nice one. Although the *philosophical meaning of life* depends upon a quite rational judgment about objective truth and reality, it turns out, as you complained, to be relative to subjective personal opinions. That is, we all make our own value judgments about what the philosophical meaning of life is. Therefore, *there are many philosophical meanings of life* in the variety of judgments people make about reality. By contrast, *there is only one psychological meaning of life* in the universal feeling of meaning that we can get from various sources. That makes the *philosophical meaning of life* more relative to individuals than is the *psychological meaning of life*. What do you think of that?

S You're not only playing with paradoxes but with semantics. And you're probably getting lost.

H Not at all. Remember Kant said that beauty gives us a "disinterested pleasure" that is both subjective and universal because, although it's a feeling, everybody feels it. That's my point. But setting Kant aside, let's move on.

S Wait a minute. You seem to be saying that it doesn't matter what people think the meaning of life is, because while their thoughts about it may differ the feeling is the same for everyone. That's absurd and sounds like a formula for moral chaos.

H I didn't say it doesn't matter. It does matter, and morally. And no ultimate relativism or moral chaos either. We'll deal with moral questions later. For now I want to punch a different point.

S All right. Go on.

SURVIVAL AND HAPPINESS

H Thanks. The new point is this: although the feeling of meaning is essentially the same for everyone, it can not only come from various sources but vary in intensity. It can be exhilarating, like "the oceanic feeling" that Freud said is the sensation of being at one with the universe and God. Or it can be as lowly as the elemental desire to get through another day rather than perish. Think of Solzhenitsyn's Ivan Denisovich. Locked in a prison camp where he had nothing much to live for, he nonetheless found the feeling of life's meaning in sheer survival and in little things like occasionally getting a taste of grass in his watery soup. So the feeling that our lives have meaning only has to be strong enough to keep us going, otherwise we get depressed and eventually either change our lives or stop living.

S   Now you're reducing the meaning of life to the mere will to live. Forgive me, but that's either silly or a tautology, as if to say the meaning of life is life itself.

H   Didn't Goethe say something like that? Anyway, it can be true. Not a truism. I don't want to lean on this. But you're right. The fact is, the most elemental feeling that our lives have meaning comes from no more than the will to live. Most people who live for survival alone—as, I'm sorry to say, many people do in this cruel world—surely don't think about the meaning of life as philosophy or feeling. They just get up in the morning and struggle on. Thinking about the meaning of life is more or less a luxury of people for whom survival itself is not a challenge. Look at aristocratic Pierre in Tolstoy's *War and Peace*. He keeps wondering about the *Why?* of life, as he says, in part because he doesn't have to worry about the *How?* But once he faces death and must struggle to survive he learns that the meaning of life lies more in the *How* to live than the *Why*—the *Why* takes care of itself.

S   So it's better to just live without thinking than to think about living?

H   That could be right. We can learn a lot about the meaning of life from people who never think about it. Socrates, of course, would not agree. He launched a philosophical tradition based

IV. On Humanism, Classics, Laughter, Proust, and the Meaning of Life

on thinking about the *Why?* Survival itself evidently was easy for him, since he whiled away his days in the sunny agora of Athens badgering everyone about the philosophical meaning of life, and cultivating his soul. Maybe that's why he could conclude that the philosophical meaning of life is not just to live but to live well. He lived up to this, too. After annoying people with his endless questions and getting convicted of religious heresy and corrupting the young, he chose not to live at all if he couldn't live well as he defined it, namely, searching for the True and the Good. So he drank the hemlock. It was a suicide over the philosophical meaning of life.

S Yes, which proved Socrates defined the meaning of life philosophically, not psychologically or emotionally. Feeling had nothing to do with it.

H I agree that Socrates defined the meaning of life philosophically. But I think living out that meaning by pursuing truth and cultivating his soul gave him the feeling that his life had meaning. And he knew he wouldn't have that feeling if he couldn't live that life. So, he lived and died for the psychological, no less than the philosophical, meaning of life after all.

S Socrates was too philosophical to be guided by his feelings. He even warned people against emotions for readily leading us astray. That was his complaint about poetry.

H Yes, he distrusted emotions, or at least Plato did as he mingled his own ideas with those of Socrates in writing the dialogues. But they both also prized love and beauty and goodness. Surely Plato and Socrates recognized that emotions can serve truth. At all events, I think every sensible person understands that thoughts and feelings often work together to teach us many things. Wordsworth contended that only when they converge do we find what is most important to us in life. Aristotle went almost as far.

S Aren't you straying from the subject?

H How could I? Our subject encompasses all others. Aristotle saw that emotions play an important role in finding the meaning of life and living it out. You see this, for instance, in his idea of happiness—a subject that didn't matter much to the morally idealistic Socrates and Plato, although they assumed happiness would come with wisdom and living well. Aristotle said happiness is the meaning or goal of human life because that's what people say they want most. He wasn't talking about ideals, just everyday facts of life.

S So what? Just because people say they want happiness doesn't make that the actual goal or the meaning of life.

H Aristotle explained what he meant in the *Ethics*, which is, so to speak, a book of philosophy on happiness and how to get it. But I wouldn't equate the feeling of meaning in life with happiness. As I've said, we can feel that our lives have meaning when we are just struggling to survive, and happiness has nothing to do with it. I might add that Freud's whole career revolved around the human quest for happiness—or rather, avoiding unhappiness. Which brings us to Buddhism.

S Buddhism? You *are* meandering. And rather shamelessly, if I may say so, even for you. It's all cabbages and kings.

H Actually, it only seems like that. And Buddhism is pertinent. It sheds light on how we can find both the psychological and philosophical meanings of life *without* happiness. Remember, Siddhartha Gautama became the Buddha by claiming to have discovered the philosophical meaning of life in the Four Noble Truths: life is full of suffering; suffering comes from desire; to end suffering we must extinguish, or at least control, desire; and to control desire we must follow the Eightfold Path toward the mastery of mind. Buddha said, in effect, the philosophical meaning of life is an objective truth about the psychology of human nature and managing the emotions.

S And that gives Buddhists your vaunted feeling that life has meaning? How can control of mind and emotions to avoid suffering do that?

H   Easy. Good Buddhists feel that their lives have meaning in grasping the Fourfold Truth about suffering and following the Eightfold Path to end suffering. Everything they do goes from that truth toward that end, giving them the feeling that their lives have meaning all the time. That's kind of a model for how anyone can find meaning in their lives.

S   It still seems to me you are exalting feeling and subjectivity, like the modern narcissism that treats the individual psyche as the measure of all things.

H   Not really. I said the feeling that our own lives have meaning is a fact of human existence that we must recognize. This is not the same thing as lauding navel-gazing narcissism. I also said that we can get this feeling from various sources, including religion, humanistic ideas, the pleasure of beauty, the love of family, sheer survival, and so on. And most of us find that feeling without consciously looking—it just happens through experience—while others get it from a philosophical truth they discover. Still others take another track.

S   There are others? What, if I dare ask?

H   They *create* it.

S   Create it?

CREATING A MEANING OF LIFE

H   Yes. Instead of finding the feeling of life's meaning through immediate experience, or searching for some truth to give us that feeling, we can simply choose or invent a belief or set of ideas or a way of life to do that for us as our philosophical meaning of life. And then with an exercise of will we can make it work.

S   Now you've taken your relativism and irrationalism too far. How can anyone accept as the meaning of life something that they know they have just made up?

28. Thinking about the Meaning of Life

H   Ah, human beings are more resourceful than you might think. Our perceptions of life are a fabric woven of both fantasy and fact. And often more of fantasy than fact. Freud thought so. In any case, it is not so strange a thing to invent or choose a philosophical meaning of life to try out in order to get the feeling of meaning. We do it all the time. And if it works, it becomes true for us.

S   That's garden variety pragmatism or existentialism.

H   It is indeed. But that's no strike against it. Pragmatism and existentialism go hand in hand here. Pragmatists like William James said the test of ideas is whether they work for us in the whole context of our lives. The existentialists went farther. Jean-Paul Sartre said that we all have to invent a meaning of life that works for us because no such meaning exists until we do that. There is no God to give us purpose, and no fixed human nature to follow. We make it all up as we decide how to live. Those decisions give a feeling of meaning to our lives. I wouldn't go as far as Sartre in throwing out human nature, but I think the act of creating a philosophical meaning of life is much as he described it. As he said of ethics, "You're free. Invent. Create." And make it work.

S   No one is that free.

H   You're not enough of an existentialist. Or you don't think you are. The fact is, people invent meanings of life for themselves through experience and ideas, whether they do it deliberately or not. The only thing that matters to any of us is that these inventions give us the feeling that our own lives have meaning.

S   I don't think invented meanings could work for long. They're mere fictions. A fiction is not a truth or even an animating belief. We probably can't find the absolute truth of anything, but fiction can't take its place.

H   Don't count on it. Fiction can become truth. Or an animating belief, as you put it. For a skeptic, you seem to have a touching confidence in human beings to know the difference. Consider idealism. Ideals are fictions that become true when we live them out. William James made a point of that as the pragmatic truth of religious belief, and long before him Socrates and Don Quixote proved it in their actual and fictional lives.

S   You live in a very vaporous world my friend. It's all feelings and fictions and subjective value judgments.

H   I wouldn't say that. But I do think that the world of feelings is where we find the elemental meanings of our lives. And to satisfy your skeptical turn of mind, I do not assert this as an absolute truth but only as a provisional pragmatic "truth" of experience. To return to existentialism, Sartre also said that when we create the meaning of our lives through the choices we make about how to live, we must take full responsibility for every choice we make. We can't hide behind the excuse that someone else or some circumstance or even our emotions made us do anything. That responsibility is a burden, but it contributes to the feeling that life has meaning as we invent our lives and ourselves. That is the existentialist ethic. And it's a good one.

S   But isn't existentialism like the very religion Sartre chased away? Both depend on unverifiable claims of objective truth about the universe. Religion says the universe is loaded with meaning, thanks to God, and existentialism says the universe has no meaning without God. And they both derive their ethics or morality from those arbitrary claims.

H   I salute your astuteness. But I don't want to quarrel with you or Sartre about this. I'd just class the existentialist assertion of a godless, meaningless universe, and of the absolute existential freedom that goes with it, among the philosophical meanings of life that can give people the *feeling* of meaning in their lives. It's a judgment about reality. The important thing is that this particular judgment can help us find that feeling in the free invention of our lives. That is enough.

S   I still say that arbitrarily inventing a meaning of life is a precarious maneuver at best.

28. Thinking about the Meaning of Life

H   Well, we have to get the feeling that our lives have meaning from somewhere. If it doesn't come from the lives we live—which I think it usually does—or from a "truth" we discover, we have to invent something to provide it. Don Quixote did that. He consciously invented a philosophical meaning of life with his new identity as a knight errant, and he had the will to make it work, so he felt his life had meaning every day—until the end.

S   Don Quixote an existentialist? That's rich. Delusional people might invent philosophical meanings of life for themselves and feel that their lives have meaning as a result, but you surely wouldn't say they confirm your theory.

H   No, I wouldn't. But that is because the meanings of life invented by delusional people don't really work for them. Don Quixote invented a philosophical meaning of life that actually worked for him, until he lost it and died because of the loss. And that shows how much we need to feel that our lives have meaning, regardless of how we get that feeling. If we lose that feeling we have to change our lives, or worse. Besides Don Quixote, I could point to other literary characters who followed similar courses, like George Eliot's Dorothea Brooke and Tolstoy's Anna Karenina.

S   More fiction? I hesitate to ask, why them? They seem unlikely companions to Don Quixote.

H   Because they illustrate what I've been talking about and point to where I now want to go.

S   Oh dear. Another tangent? You digress about as much as Tristram Shandy.

H   I like the pedigree. It's true that I might be a bit Shandean, but I do have a focus. You'll see very soon. OK. Dorothea, whom I mentioned earlier as a "good" but partially misled person, decided early in her life that the philosophical meaning of life is to do noble deeds as a kind of secular "saint." This idea was at least partly invention. And to live it out, she married the high-minded scholar Casaubon, convinced that assisting him with his great work of writing *The Key to All Mythologies* would be a noble deed and give her the feeling that her life had meaning. She succeeded at first. But in time she learned that he was an intellectual fraud just compiling notes and writing nothing, and then her feeling of meaning slipped away. She went into a funk. But after Casaubon died, she eventually found a new life, lowering her expectations from becoming a "saint" to advancing the "growing good of the world" through "unhistoric acts," like being kind to people and furthering lives. She had adapted her philosophical meaning of life to new circumstances so she could feel that her life had meaning again. Don Quixote couldn't do that. Neither could Anna Karenina.

S Don Quixote was delusional. And Dorothea Brooke was as obsessive as she was admirable. They could both have used some salutary skepticism.

H Perhaps they could have, but I disagree with your opinion of them. Anyway, Anna Karenina is a much sadder case. At first, she thought the meaning of her life was to become a wife, mother, and socialite. She became those things, and they seem to have made her feel that her life had meaning, despite her loveless marriage to a dull husband. Then she fell in love with the dashing Vronsky. This love gave her an intense new feeling of meaning, for which she abandoned her marriage, her child, and her social status. But later, the love affair went bad, and she lost all feeling of meaning in her life. So she threw herself under the wheels of a train.

S Yes. A sad story and pathetic ending. What's your point?

H Her story is about the feeling of meaning in her life passing from low to high and then collapsing, leading to her suicide. But hers was no philosophical suicide, like Socrates's. It was more like anomie. And that's where we now need to go.

S Anomie? You are Shandean.

28. Thinking about the Meaning of Life

H   And with a purpose. You'll see.
S   I hope so.

ANOMIE AND THE MEANING OF LIFE

H   You know anomie. It's a feeling of emptiness, or lack of direction and purpose in our lives. That makes it more or less the opposite of feeling that life has meaning. Anna Karenina had anomie in her despondent way—just as Don Quixote did in his terminal melancholy at the end. But she shows us not only the worst that can happen when we lose the feeling that our lives have meaning, she also gives us a surprising clue to how the feeling of meaning can arise in the first place. That has to do with the remedy for anomie. We could see this in any number of literary characters.
S   We could talk about literature all day. Much as we might enjoy it, let's not. On with anomie.
H   Fair enough. But we should be having a good time. I am. Well, here is that clue. Before Anna fell in love with Vronsky, she had managed to feel that her life had sufficient meaning even in a joyless marriage. How was this possible? It was possible for the same reason that anyone in unhappy circumstances can nonetheless come to feel that his or her life has meaning. It is by heading off anomie. I'm sure you are familiar with this, but bear with me while I play it out.
S   Don't wander from the subject.
H   I won't. It's important.
S   Isn't everything you say?
H   A charming concession. As you know, the word anomie comes from the Greek for being without law or without constraint. Émile Durkheim wrote about this in his classic book on suicide. We feel anomie, he said, when we lack constraints on our lives. These constraints are at least half of what having a pur-

IV. On Humanism, Classics, Laughter, Proust, and the Meaning of Life

pose in life gives us. It works like this . . . and please forgive me for sounding pedagogical; sometimes I can't help it. Our ideals and purposes play two contrasting roles for us. On the one hand they give us some goal to pursue. On the other hand, they constrain us, limiting what we believe to be possible, and this constraint or limitation actually helps us have the confidence that we can achieve our goals. I'll put it in a formula: *Having limited goals to pursue gives us confidence that we can achieve them, and then we feel that our lives have meaning.* This is why Anna's life had a meaning in her unhappy marriage that it did not when her love affair died. She had the constraints of limited goals in her marriage that she could live within—family life does this for most people—but then she gave up those constraints for the thrills of a passionate love affair. When that affair ended she had no goals left to live for, or constraints to live within. She had lost all feeling that her life had meaning, and the fatal train came down the track. That's anomie *in extremis*. A profoundly revealing and paradoxical phenomenon. Durkheim learned it from Rousseau. He could have learned it from Buddhism too.

S   You're not wrong, but you're oversimplifying again. Back to Buddhism? And now Rousseau?

H   They share a psychology. Like Buddhism, Rousseau saw that our discontents come mainly from unsatisfied desires. He didn't tell us to extinguish desires, as many Buddhists do, but he pointed out that whenever our desires outstrip our powers to fulfill them, we feel impotent, frustrated, hopeless, and unhappy. That's what Rousseau thought modern society does to people. And that's where Durkheim got the idea of anomie. Our goals, desires, and expectations have to be close enough to our lives and to our powers of attaining them—whether they are high aspirations or just striving to survive—to make us feel that our lives have meaning. Otherwise, we lose that feeling and sink into the frustrations and unhappiness that

28. THINKING ABOUT THE MEANING OF LIFE

Buddhists and Rousseau and Durkheim thought come with unconstrained desires, which feels pretty much the same as having no desires or purpose at all. That's all anomie—a way of understanding why some lives lose the feeling of meaning.

S   You're lumping these things together rather casually. And you seem to discourage people from dreaming and hoping for the best. Aren't the young supposed to believe anything is possible? Teachers encourage them to do that all the time. Do the young feel anomie because of it?

H   As a matter of fact, a lot of them do. They expect too much too soon and succumb to feelings of powerlessness and dejection. And some commit suicide because of it. It is one thing to say hopefully that "anything is possible" in life, but it is another to decide what is possible today and tomorrow and how to achieve it. That requires translating aspirations into limited goals and expectations that fit everyday reality—as well as coming up with new limited goals and expectations when we have reached the ones we have met. And that is why everybody feels anomie now and then—such as after we have accomplished something we've worked toward for a long time and then feel adrift afterwards. The postpartum depression that some mothers feel after childbirth is like that because they have reached a very definite goal that has shaped their lives for nine months and now they have nothing that purposeful and constraining to replace it. Or think of the many professionals who look forward to retiring after long years of labor but who then feel at loose ends in retirement and wish they could go back to work. The same kind of thing happens to many soldiers after wartime and to prisoners when released from jail; hard as their lives were in war or prison, they found a feeling of meaning in surviving (soldiers with the benefit of comrades) to the end, but lost that feeling after the end arrived. Anomie can also secretly creep into even the most seemingly satisfying lives. We should know it's here when we gradually feel adrift, unfocused, dissatisfied, and a little depressed for no clear reason. That's anomie. A feeling that our lives have lost some of their previous meaning.

S Yes, anomie is a familiar experience. But you are exploiting it to support your questionable idea about the meaning of life.

H Exploiting it, sure. Because it's revealing. Especially what anomie tells us about how to avoid or remedy it to assure that we feel life has meaning for us. That remedy is: to give our lives constraints—limited goals that will get us out of bed in the morning with something to achieve that day, something positive to live for. Ivan Denisovich did that with his hopes for grassy soup and survival. Twelve-step programs systematically follow this same principle. They tell us that to shake an addiction, you can't expect to change your life forever all at once. Forever is too far away and too amorphous to work as a goal. You have to limit your goals to things you can accomplish from hour to hour and day to day. When you can do this, you feel that your life has meaning because you are conquering your addiction and gaining control of your life every day. That might not give you a buoyant feeling of meaning, but it is enough.

S That's a mouthful. But I think you overstate the danger of desires and unrealizable ideals. What about Socrates and Plato? They declared ideals like Truth and Goodness to be beyond this world and never attainable here. But they kept pursuing those ideals and urged everyone to do the same. They didn't have anomie or lose meaning in their lives. Why not?

H A good question. But I have already answered it. They did say that such ideals are too perfect for us to ever achieve them in this imperfect world. And this would seem to be a prescription for anomie. But Socrates and Plato knew better. They understood that even though we cannot achieve these ideals in this world, we can strive toward them through specific, purposeful activities every day, particularly philosophical inquiry and moral discipline, and possibly teaching these things to others. That's why, idealists that they were, Socrates and Plato never suffered anomie—they had serious work to do. Lofty as our ideals might be, we have to keep our daily lives focused on what can be done today before looking toward tomorrow, much less to eternity.

S Sounds like we're getting back to the prison camp mentality and the meaning of life amounting to not much more than getting through the day.

H Call it that if you wish. But don't knock it. It's more powerful and common than you might think. And, as I've said, however high or low our goals, and good or bad our circumstances, the feeling of meaning that we get is basically the same, differing more in the degree than in kind.

S Do you mean that Ivan Denisovich eating his soup and a religious enthusiast celebrating God have the same feeling that their lives have meaning, except for a possible difference in the intensity of that feeling?

H Yes. The feeling can be as exalted as the religious oceanic feeling or as minimal as the will to survive. But I think it is more similar than different—not counting the delusions of the deranged.

S Well, we can't settle this unless we can measure feelings, which we can't. But there is a more important issue here that you ignore. Morality. By equating the meaning of life with a feeling that you say is largely the same for everyone, you neglect morality. You can't reasonably say that all feelings of meaning in life are morally equal. As I indicated before, that would justify the worst moral relativism and bring moral anarchy. I don't care what you say, feelings are not morals.

IV. ON HUMANISM, CLASSICS, LAUGHTER, PROUST, AND THE MEANING OF LIFE

MORALITY AND THE FEELING OF MEANING IN LIFE

H   I told you we'd get to morality. And I hinted at this in talking about addiction.

S   So, how do you fit your notion of life's meaning into a reasonable morality?

H   Like this. You just said that feelings are not morals and that saying the meaning of life is a feeling similar for everyone amounts to moral anarchy. You are right on the first count, wrong on the second. Here's why. I grant that feelings in themselves are neither moral nor immoral. They are just feelings. Morality—or we could say ethics, but for convenience let's use morality because the terms can be interchangeable—deals not with feelings but with actions. We judge people morally by what they do, not by what they feel. The same can be said of ideas. It is true that we might judge some people's ideas to be morally wrong, but we don't judge people themselves morally by their ideas alone; we judge them by the actions that flow from their ideas. Of course, expressing ideas and feelings can itself become an action if doing that influences others to act. Demagogues, propagandists, and preachers often tread that line, and some of them cross it. But most of us probably have friends whose political or religious ideas we abhor but whom we still like because their actions don't reflect those ideas in ways consequential to us.

S   Yes. We agree so far. And the second count of my charge?

H   OK. Here's why you are wrong to equate with moral anarchy my idea that the meaning of life is a feeling similar for everyone. I've already said we don't judge feelings morally, we judge actions. But we can judge feelings by the consequences they have in action. Take religion, for instance. I suggested earlier that the oceanic feeling is perhaps the most intense and exalted feeling of meaning in life and therefore probably the

28. Thinking about the Meaning of Life

most emotionally satisfying psychological meaning of life. But this would not necessarily make it the morally *best* psychological meaning of life for us, or make the religious beliefs that arouse or support it the morally best philosophical meaning of life. That's because this feeling and those beliefs might have consequences in actions that are not good. After all, such an intense feeling of meaning can inspire people to do terrible things to serve that feeling and the beliefs behind it. Islamic suicide bombers dramatized that horrendously on September 11, 2001. Surely we can to some extent judge their feelings by the actions those feelings produce. Or take an example outside religion.

S   Hold on. You assume that your own definition of good and bad consequences go without scrutiny. How do you *know* what is good and bad?

H   Ah. I knew you'd hit me on that sooner or later. Can you be patient a bit longer for me to get to that?

S   I guess I have no choice since I'm playing your foil.

H   Such a gracious skeptic and supportive friend. Back to my nonreligious example of a morally faulty feeling of meaning. It is rather offbeat. John Marcher in Henry James's story *The Beast in the Jungle*. Marcher is not religious, but he lives for a fervent belief. It is the belief that his own life is marked for something unique that will make him unlike anyone else. And he lives in wait for this "beast in the jungle" of his life to spring. Finally, after watching all his life—and inducing a young woman to watch with him—he comes to the realization that he is indeed unique, but not because of anything special that was to happen to him. He is unique because he is the one person to whom nothing would happen because he had done nothing in his life except wait for something unique to happen. There are a couple of fine ironies here. One is the obvious irony that although he was right about being unique, he was wrong about what was uniquely in store for him. The deeper irony, though, is that even while his certainty of being marked for something singular deprived him of living a real life, it nevertheless gave him a strong feeling that his life had meaning every day. He eagerly got up in the morning—to watch and wait. John Marcher is the model of those who feel intensely that their own lives have meaning, but who fail to judge that feeling and see its adverse consequences in their lives and those of others. That is where morality comes in. *Living for the feeling that our lives have meaning has effects in the real world. We must morally judge those effects as well as the feelings and ideas that caused them.* John Marcher got the feeling that his life had meaning from an idea that led him to misspend his life, and to consume the life of a woman who loves him. In other words, both his feeling of meaning and how he got it turned out to do him harm.

S   At last you're admitting that there is much more to the meaning of life than a feeling and that feelings can lead to folly.

H   Once again, I never denied that there is more to the meaning of life than a feeling. I have said that feelings are at its core. Morality is another matter.

S   But now you seem to imply that morality actually eclipses the feeling you've been exalting.

H   I don't exalt feelings. I merely recognize their importance in the meaning of our lives. And when we feel that our lives have meaning we should judge that feeling not only by the satisfactions it gives us but by its consequences in the lives we live. John Marcher may be an unusual case. But consider serial killers. They are obsessed individuals who, I assume, get up in the morning and go through the day thinking about the thrill they will get from committing their next crime. Those thrills and the thoughts about them give these people the feeling, perverse though it may be, that their lives have meaning. And yet, exciting as this feeling may be to them, it is tainted by obsession and self-destruction. I suspect that serial killers suffer conflicts over this, aware that their lives are running off the rails, but they are unable to stop because of the thrills. Like addicts of any kind. Being out of control is hardly a good way to feel that your life has meaning. To tell you the truth, I would like to think that a person can't fully feel that life has meaning if the consequences of living for that feeling are bad for himself or others. But that's my bias.

S A fine sentiment. But are you serious? History roils with evils perpetrated by people who seem to have felt fine about doing harm to others. Look at those suicide bombers you mentioned. They feel that their lives have meaning, and they judge that feeling to be good. They exhibit the moral flaw in your entire argument about the meaning of life being a feeling. You can't trust feelings as a guide to life, and surely not to morality.

H But feelings and morality have a very intimate and complex relationship. As I said, emotions can give birth to morals. Empathy, for instance—an emotion Rousseau and the Romanticists praised for precisely that reason. And Nietzsche dwelled on how emotions and morality are always tangled in our lives. That aside, I readily concede that there are people who don't feel bad about doing bad things—I wish they did. But I think they protect themselves through moral rationalizations. They define "bad" and "good" in their own self-serving way. And those rationalizations—often delusions—are exactly what enables them to feel that their lives have meaning. Islamic suicide bombers have a strong feeling that their lives have meaning because they possess transcendent religious truth and are acting for God. This truth tells them to hate life in this world and to leave the world by murderous suicide. But to feel that your life has meaning only because you are going to kill people and yourself so you can go to a better world is not the same thing as feeling that your life has meaning *in this world*. It's a perversion. And a kind of madness.

IV. On Humanism, Classics, Laughter, Proust, and the Meaning of Life

S   You keep dismissing inconvenient cases as madness. But what about the leaders? They're not suicidal. They just persuade others to be or to do other violent things.

H   I'd say that the leaders here, like all tyrants throughout history, feel that their own lives have meaning mainly because they like having power over other people, whether or not they enfold themselves in some higher moral purpose. And the harm tyrants do to others probably causes them no qualms. But they always make the world worse and usually come to bad ends themselves. Their feeling of meaning might be intense, but it is misguided because it leads to unhappy ends they hadn't wished for. They are curiously akin to John Marcher.

S   Those are questionable and naïve claims about history's tyrants, but I'm not going to belabor the point. It still sounds like you admit that morality eclipses feelings, as it must. And it amounts to a kind of fuzzy humanism.

H   Humanism, yes. What else would you expect? But not fuzzy. I'll have to make it clearer. First, let me sum up my case like this: although we can't very well judge the morality of feelings in themselves, we can judge actions: therefore, *if a person's feeling of meaning in life leads to actions that harm that person or others, then those actions and their effects are morally wrong.*

S   You are a conventional moralist after all. You judge as "bad" the actions of people that "harm" others or themselves, and you judge the feelings that prompted those actions the same way. And you judge the feelings and actions that don't "harm" anyone to be "good." But now you can't put it off any longer: how do you know what "harm" and "bad" and "wrong" mean? Aren't your definitions of moral good and bad just conventional and self-serving value judgments of your own?

H   Now who's the relativist? Not me. But, to answer your question, I'll have to talk more about how the meaning of life is both psychological and philosophical, a feeling and a rational judgment, and delve further into human nature and morality.

28. Thinking about the Meaning of Life

S   Are we starting over yet again?

H   No. I just have to explain more things. And we have to go back to Aristotle's *Ethics*.

S   We can always go back to Aristotle. But let's move on and not go in circles. I may be a friendly skeptic, but I can lose patience. Remember, you are supposed to be a warmhearted humanist.

H   Yes. Yes. I understand. I don't know about warmhearted, but I'll try to be efficient and not tax your friendship beyond endurance.

S   I'll hold you to it . . . in my friendly way.

H   You are a warmhearted skeptic to be sure.

S   Just a modest one.

HUMAN NATURE, MORALITY, AND THE MEANING OF LIFE

H   All right. As you know, Aristotle said a lot about the meaning of life. But we only touched on his idea of happiness. Now we have to go to his definition of *good*, which precedes his idea of happiness and brings his conception of human nature. Then everything I've been saying will come together and convince you I'm right.

S   I doubt that.

H   Of course you do. But give me the chance.

S   I can't very well walk away now.

H   OK. Drawing on a common sense Greek definition, Aristotle said "good" . . . his word here was *agathon*, with the superlative *aristos* for best; isn't that neat? . . . means simply the end toward which anything aims, or how it fulfills its nature by doing what it is supposed to do. When it does that it attains *virtue* and *excellence* . . . as you probably know, both are *areté* in Greek. Sorry about the pedantry. So, a *good*, *virtuous*, or *excellent* horse is one that fulfills its nature by doing well what a horse should do:

run fast, carry riders, and so forth. A *good, virtuous,* or *excellent* road is one that fulfills its nature by doing well what a road should do: efficiently and safely take travelers where they want to go. By the same token, a *good, virtuous,* or *excellent* human being is one who fulfills human nature by doing well what a human being should do. But human nature is more complicated than the nature of a horse or of a road, or of anything else. For instance, human beings are social creatures with an inherent need for other people, and they are emotional beings with an inherent need for emotional gratification—I would also say they are existential beings who have an inherent need to feel that their lives have meaning. But, above all, Aristotle says, human beings are uniquely endowed with rationality. This rationality enables them to choose wisely how to live well. And living well entails satisfying all of their human needs in the *best* ways. Therefore, they must cultivate their rationality in order to make the choices that will achieve that. When people learn to use their rationality to this end they can fulfill their natures and become truly *good, virtuous, excellent,* and happy human beings.

S   Thank you, professor. You do have a penchant for lecturing. If at an elementary level. But you're not really talking about morality. Or if you are, you're relying on the questionable premise that moral good derives from nature. You know the Marquis de Sade did that. He decided that because physical cruelty is common in nature, and can even bring a kind of pleasure, it is *natural* and therefore *good.*

H   The Marquis de Sade confused wild nature with human nature. Nature as you find it in the wilds is not the same as human nature. That was Aristotle's very point about human beings. They have a distinctively rational nature and ability to choose how to live their lives. In any case, I'd say all thinkers have based their moral ideas on some assumptions about human nature. Those who think human nature is irrational and bestial want to restrain it with authority, distrusting freedom, whereas those who think human nature is more rational and benign give freedom more leeway than authority. Political conservatives and liberals have historically divided pretty much along these lines. But politics aside, I think Aristotle, and later Rousseau—both leaning to the liberal side—gave perhaps the most persuasive arguments for how we should follow human nature to define morality as well as the meaning of life.

S   Rousseau once more? You do go in circles.

H   Just circling around to the conclusion, and tipping my hat to some of the thinkers who tell us most about how to think about the meaning of life. When Aristotle says that we become good human beings by satisfying our human needs in the best ways, he means we do it by choosing the right amount of everything we need—not too much or too little of anything. This calculation can vary with individuals because some people have greater needs for some things than other people do. Aristotle distinguished here between *needs* and *wants*. *Needs* are essential, and satisfying them in the right amount is *good* for us as human beings. *Wants* go beyond *needs*. A person might *want* more of something than he or she *needs*. And if the person acts on that *want* instead of *needs*, the true *needs* will suffer and the person will fail to be a *good* human being. Like a musician who has a great natural *need* for music, but who *wants* to live for music alone, neglecting other needs and consequently failing to live a *good* life as a *good* human being. That's not Christian morality, but it's Aristotle's, and it makes sense.

S   As psychology maybe, but morality is different. Psychology is not morality, except for narcissists.

H   True. But there is more. Give me a minute and I'll put it together as I promised. First a necessary word on Rousseau.

S   If you must.

H   I appreciate your gentlemanly patience. Rousseau agreed with Aristotle that we must fulfill our natures as human beings in order to be good and happy. He called that happy condition *autonomy*, by which he meant thinking freely and honestly, learning from experience, and managing our own lives instead of being dominated by others or society. But he also thought this autonomy difficult to achieve in modern society because this society miseducates minds and induces people to live for false values. So instead of leading them to a meaning of life that fulfills their true natures as autonomous, *good*, and happy human beings, society misleads them to find the meaning of life in ways of thinking and acting that breed dependency and insecurity, selfishness and dishonesty, moral blindness and discontent. Like Aristotle, Rousseau was probably more right than wrong about what is naturally *good* for human beings.

S Anyone can define human nature. And history is littered with damage wrought by arrogant people who claimed they knew human nature and derived a self-serving morality and politics from it. All political and religious fanatics do this. The debacle of Communism is a classic case of political tyranny born of a faulty idea of human nature. It's dangerous to assert what human nature is and then construe policies and practices from it.

H True enough. I share your skeptical concern about the perils of declaring certainty about human nature—or anything else, especially in politics and religion. But I still say that Aristotle and Rousseau were on to something about how morality and the meaning of life are rooted in human nature. I don't call this an absolute truth. It's just a useful idea. And now I'll put it all together for you.

S It's about time.

H I've suggested this already, but now that we're dealing directly with human nature and morality, I'll spell it out. We base our moral judgments not so much on abstract principles as on what we find to be good and bad *for us*—Nietzsche made a big deal of this. And I'd say that what we think is good *for us* has to do with our need to feel that our lives have meaning. We

28. Thinking about the Meaning of Life

implicitly judge having this feeling to be *good for us*. By extension, we also judge *the way we got this feeling* and *how we act on it to be good for us*. Our value judgments about what is morally good and bad will therefore always reflect and serve our need to *feel* that our own lives have meaning. So, in a manner of speaking, psychology trumps morality.

S   Now we're back to those damn feelings. I thought you were going explain in more detail how you would judge the moral consequences of anyone's meaning of life. Specifically, what are the *good* and *bad* actions that help us fulfill our natures, as you vaguely put it? In short: how *should* we feel that our lives have meaning and why? And how do you apply this to yourself?

H   I was coming to that. And I'll wrap everything up with a neat finale.

S   I'm not asking for entertainment. Just make it short and sweet.

H   You've become very demanding. Are you getting bored?

S   Let's say I'm ready for the climax, if there is one.

H   Fair enough. There is. And it's sweet.

HOW *SHOULD* WE FEEL THAT OUR LIVES HAVE MEANING?

H   I'll be as plain as I can. Start with my premise: The meaning of life is fundamentally a feeling... this is *the psychological meaning of life*. Add to this the ideas that: (a) we can get this feeling in many ways, from life experience to lofty ideals; (b) however we get it, and whether it is strong or weak, it is necessary to us and is essentially the same for everyone. Now, here are the moral or normative judgments that follow: (1) However we get it, the feeling that our lives have meaning *should* be strong and life-enhancing, for then it is at its *best*. (2) That feeling *should* promote actions that enable us to satisfy our natural human needs—crowned by those of mind—in the *best* ways and therefore fulfill us as human beings and as individuals. (3) Acting on that feeling to fulfill ourselves *should* also lead us to help other human beings fulfill themselves too. Or to put the moral principle in two general statements: *The feeling that our lives have meaning <u>ought</u> to be good for us as individuals and as human beings, leading us to actions that help us fulfill our natures and help other people do the same. If that feeling leads to actions that harm us or others as human beings, then that feeling and the actions that follow from it are not morally good but bad.* That should be clear enough.

S   There is something suspiciously circular about all of this. But the fog might be lifting some. However, I want to know how you would bring this down to the lives we actually live and tell me what specifically gives *you* the feeling that your own life has meaning as you describe it, and how you act on it in morally good ways to, as you say, fulfill yourself and help others do the same?

H   I thought you would see that by now. But, to satisfy your curiosity, I will start with this: I discovered through experience that the fundamental meaning of life is none other than the feeling of meaning, and this discovery opened my eyes to the *psychological meaning of life*. From here, I developed the principles I enumerated above, which gave me in general, *my philosophical meaning of life*. Now, to answer your question with more personal detail, here is a trio of concise statements, with a coda, and you're going to love it: (1) Experience has taught me that I have an intellectual nature and therefore an *indispensable need* to think and talk about things. (2) I get the feeling of meaning, or the *psychological meaning of my life*, from many sources, as does everyone, but none is higher for me than thinking and talking about such things as human nature and the meaning of life. (3) From this feeling comes my judgment, or the *philosophical meaning of my life*, that acting on that feeling by talking about such things will help me fulfill my nature and possibly

28. Thinking about the Meaning of Life

help others do it too in their own ways. There you are. Now, here's the coda: I have keenly felt that my life has had meaning throughout our conversation, talking as we have been doing about human nature and the meaning of life; and acting on that feeling with you has not only aided me in fulfilling myself, it has also made it possible for me to help you do the same. So, you see my friend, you are a beneficiary of my acting on the feeling that my life has meaning. Touché. How about that?

S Ha! Ingenious. Still, kind of circular, but with your incorrigible humanistic confidence and good cheer, you almost pull it off.

H I didn't expect to convert you. As a good skeptic you wouldn't let that happen. I only wanted to share these ideas and get your reaction and maybe your agreement here and there. Your good-natured patience and skeptical curiosity proves, as you said, you're no cynic. My ideas might take time to work on you. Not that this would change you. It would only show you more clearly how you do in fact live out your own feeling of meaning in life.

S Pray tell, what would you say that is?

H This, too, should be obvious by now. In a nutshell, I would say it is this: You are a person with an intellectual nature and a skeptical mind, so, you have an *indispensable need* to use that mind and question everything. Consequently, you feel your life has most meaning—which is the *psychological meaning of your life*—when you are doing exactly what you have been doing today—skeptically questioning someone else's way of thinking. And you judge this feeling to be good for you, and that acting on it is good both for you and for the people you question, which gives you *the philosophical meaning of your life*. So there it is, the meaning of your life, psychologically and philosophically. I applaud you for it. I always benefit from talking to you. So, after all, the meaning of your life, psychologically and philosophically, is much the same as mine. And we both gain from acting on them together. I suspect you haven't been aware of it until now.

S   Ingenious again. Quite a theory. I'll keep questioning it.

H   As a good skeptic, you could do no less. I respect that. But I don't really have a theory. It's just a set of useful ideas on how human life works and on how to think about the meaning of life. And you might even find that you think about the meaning of your life a little differently as a result of our chat. Anyhow, I've jotted down a tidy list that puts it all together. You can question it all you like. Or you can throw it away. Maybe somebody else will find it and make the most of it.

S   How industrious of you. I can hardly wait.

H   Don't get too cynical on me now.

S   Never

H   Well, here it is.

1. To think clearly about the meaning of life, we have to start by recognizing the necessity for human beings to feel that their own lives have meaning.
2. If we do not have this feeling, our lives don't have meaning for us and we will either change our lives to get that feeling or stop living.
3. This feeling is a psychological fact of human life and is basically the same for everyone, but it can vary in intensity from uplifting exhilaration down to the gritty will to live. This feeling is the *psychological meaning of life*.
4. We can get this feeling in many different ways, from an experience—such as love, or beauty, or spirituality, or achievement, or even from struggling to survive—or we can get it from ideas such as those we encounter in politics, religion, and books, or we can get it in several ways together. And we can have this feeling without being entirely aware of how we got it.
5. Whatever gives us this feeling, we implicitly or explicitly

28. Thinking about the Meaning of Life

judge it to be good, and this judgment, however implicit, gives us our *philosophical meaning of life*.

6. The *philosophical meaning of life* is a judgment about reality that can come from a purported truth we *embrace*, as in religious revelation or adopting a moral creed, or it can come from an ideal we *invent*, as in imagining the life we want to live, or it can arise almost unconsciously from the lives we live from day to day and the feeling of meaning that those lives give us.

7. The *psychological meaning of life* is therefore universal to all people in the feeling that our lives have meaning. The *philosophical meaning of life* is relative to individuals in their diverse ideas or judgments about reality.

8. The psychological and philosophical meanings of our lives are therefore closely related.

9. We might not be able to judge the moral quality of a person's feeling that his or her life has meaning—the *psychological meaning of life*—or the ideas that usually go with it—the *philosophical meaning of life*—in themselves, but we can morally judge the effects of acting on that feeling and those ideas.

10. Those effects are morally good if they help us fulfill ourselves as human beings and individuals—satisfying our inherent needs—and they are even better if they also enable us to help others do the same. Those effects are bad if they diminish our ability to pursue those ends.

11. Consequently, the best feelings that our lives have meaning, as well as the ideas that usually go with them, are those that are strong and affirming, inspiring us to fulfill ourselves as human beings and as individuals and to help others do the same.

S   You call that tidy? But I'll take it in the spirit of amiable skepticism.

IV. On Humanism, Classics, Laughter, Proust, and the Meaning of Life

H   Just as I meant it in the spirit of genial humanism. It's a reasonable inference from experience. And it's the best I can do, at least until something better comes to mind, which I doubt will happen.
S   On that skeptical note, I *feel* like having a drink. Join me?
H   Ha! I *feel* the same way. A beautiful friendship. And we can continue "to talk of many things—of shoes and ships and sealing wax, . . ."
S   "And cabbages and kings."
H   I'll drink to that.

Index

A

Adams, [John]: and *Marbury v. Madison*, 132
Adorno, Theodor: on mass culture, 276
advertising: and irrationality, 92–93
Aichhorn, August: and Freud, 238
Alexander II and III, Tsars: and Dinner of Three Emperors, 24
Anderson, Kurt: on American culture, 282
anomie: and meaning of life, 427–31; Durkheim on, 428–29
Apollinaire, Guillaume: and commonplace, 186
Arendt, Hannah: and banality of evil, 173, 195
Aristotle: on rationality, 87–88; on habit, 188; and self-consciousness, 202; on high and low culture, 283; and education, 324, 329, 332; on morality and good, 329; 437–40 *passim*; and comedy, 339; and meaning of life, 420–21, 437
Arnold, Matthew: on poetry, 305; on classics, 318
Arrington, Leonard: and Topaz, 118
art [arts; artist, artworks]: and style, 1–83 *passim*; *Mrs. Dalloway* and, 62; and *sprezzatura*, 61–62; Nietzsche on, 62, 75–76; Wilde on, 74–75, 77–82; and ethics, Wilde on, 77–83; Tolstoy on, 249–72 *passim*; and Modernism and Tolstoy, 258–59; and Postmodernism, 261–63; Proust on, 360–63, 403–04. *See also* Art Deco, Modernism, Realism, Postmodernism
Art Deco: description and Essex House, 28–33, 36; at Four Seasons Hotel, 36
Auden, W. H.: on self-consciousness, 199; on Freud, 235, 242
Augustine, Saint: and banality, 174; and self-consciousness, 200
Aveling, Edward: and Eleanor Marx, 225–32 *passim*

B

Babbitt, Milton: on modern music, 259
Backus, Reverend Isaac: on church and state, 143–45, 154
Baden-Powell, General: and decadence, 253
Balzac, Honoré de: and La Tour d'Argent, 24; on society, 178; and Realism, 179–80, 181; and appearances, 183; and Kafka, 195

Barth, John: on self-consciousness, 198, 200
Barton, David: and church and state, 136
Barzun, Jacques: and Modernism, 162; on William James, 164; on self-consciousness, 199, 206; on decline of Western culture, 174, 283, 286–89; on WWI and WWII, 279
Baudelaire, Charles: and La Tour d'Argent, 24; and Modernism, 162, 165, 243; as social critic, 175, 176, 187, 251–52; on modernity, 175, 180, 181; and banality, 187; and self-consciousness, 206, 207–10
Baudrillard, Jean: on Postmodernism, 267
Bate, W. J.: and self-consciousness, 201, 205
Bauhaus: and Modernism, 261
Beardsley, Aubrey: and decadence, 253
Beckett, Samuel: on habit, 189; and commonplace, 192
Beckwith, Jane: and Topaz, 110, 114–19
Benham, Flip: and church and state, 135
Benjamin, Walter: and commonplace, 186; and Kafka, 193; and memoir, 240; and art, 268
Bennett, William: on humanities, 309
Bergson, Henri: anti-materialism of, 396; and William James, 396; on consciousness, memory, time, 396–97; and Proust, 396–97
Bernstein, Eduard: and Eleanor Marx, 225, 230–31, 232; and Marxist revisionism, 230–31

Besant, Annie: and socialism, 230
Beauvoir, Simone de: and Sartre, 190
Biddle, Francis: and Japanese internment, 111
Bismarck, Otto von: and Dinner of Three Emperors, 24
Black, Justice Hugo: on church and state, 134–35
Bloch, Marc: on medieval self-consciousness, 202
Bloom, Harold: and self-consciousness, 205
Bourget, Paul: as cultural critic, 175
Brandes, Georg: and Nietzsche, 250–51
Brennan, Justice William: on church and state, 150
Breuer, Josef: and Freud, 243
Breyer, Justice Stephen: on church and state, 139
Brod, Max: and Kafka, 195
Brolin, Brent C.: and Postmodernism, 261
Brombert, Victor: and Sartre, 220
Brooke, Rupert: and WWI, 255
Buddhism: and meaning of life, 421–22, 428–29
Buffon, Georges-Louis Leclerc, Comte de: on style, 5, 76
Burke, Edmund: on manners and society, 13, 86, 98–99; on human nature, 90–91, 178; and conservatism, 90, 95; and liberalism, 96
Burckhardt, Jacob: on simplifiers, 322
Burton, Robert: and Sterne, 340
Bush, George W.: and church and state, 138, 153

Byron, [George Gordon, Lord]: and self-consciousness, 205

C

Café Anglais: and Dinner of Three Emperors, 23, 24
Camus, Albert: and commonplace, 192
Carducci, Giosuè: and cultural decadence, 254
Carlyle, Thomas: and history, 177, 178; and social consciousness, 178; and appearances, 181
Carroll, Lewis: quoted, vii, 409–10
Carter, Stephen L.: and civil society, 60
Castiglione, Baldassare: on courtier, 12; on *sprezzatura*, 61; on teaching, 329
Cervantes, [Miguel de]: and Don Quixote, 317; and Sterne, 339. *See also* Don Quixote
Chamisso, [Adelbert von]: and self-consciousness, 204
Christianity: Nietzsche on, 69; and Islam, 122; and ideological thinking, 123; and self-consciousness, 202; and Kierkegaard, 214, 216. *See also* church and state
church and state: history of in America, 131–55 *passim*
civility: and dining, 12–13, 19; *Mrs. Dalloway* and ethics of, 51–65 *passim*; and civil society, 60; rights of, 96–99
classics: and reading, 315–27 *passim*; definition of, 318, 323–27; as casebooks, 331–34 *passim*
Clausen, Christopher: on American culture, 284–86
Cohan, George M.: and WWI, 279
Cole, Henry: and commonplace in art, 180, 187
comedy: of manners, 13; Wilde and, 73; idea of, 338–39; Laurence Sterne and, 337–56 *passim*; and *The Name of the Rose*, 339; in Proust, 380–86. *See also* laughter
Comini, Alessandra: on Viennese art, 235–36
Comte, Auguste: on society, 179
Confucius: as classic, 327
consciousness: stream of, 53, 164–65, 398; William James on, 53, 396–98; and self-consciousness, 199–223 *passim*, 289; Proust and, 361–62, 373, 395–400, 406; Bergson on, 396–97
conservatism: and human nature, 89–99; and church and state, 131–55 *passim*; and Tocqueville, 145, 149
Cornyn, Senator John: and church and state, 134
Courbet, Gustave: and commonplace, 180
Cousins, Norman: and laughter, 337
Crowley, Aleister: and decadence, 253
Cunningham, Michael: and *The Hours*, 52

D

Dali, Salvador: and Felix restaurant, 43; and *The Persistence of Memory*, 356
D'Annunzio, Gabriele: and Nietzsche, 70, 251; and cultural revival, 254
Dante [Alighieri]: as classic, 327; and *Inferno* and education, 332–33

Danto, Arthur: and commonplace, 186; and art, 259; and end of art, 266
decadence: in Western culture, 250, 252–56; Barzun on, 286–89
Dedekind, Richard: and Modernism, 163
Deleuze, Gilles: and Freud, 246
della Casa, Giovanni: on manners, 12, 17
Derrida, Jacques: and art, 259
de Sade, Marquis: on morality, 435
Descartes, [René]: and self-consciousness, 201
Delouvrier, Christian: and restaurant design, 32
DeWitt, John L.: and Japanese internment, 112
Dick, Philip K.: and Starck, 42
Dickens, Charles: and society, 178; and Dostoevsky, 184; and Kafka, 193
Diderot, Denis: and *restaurant*, 22; and *Tristram Shandy*, 343
Dilthey, Wilhelm: and Heidegger, 191
Donoghue, Denis: on Postmodernism, 262
Don Quixote: and power of reading, 317; and Sterne, 349; and *Tristram Shandy*, 346–48, 349, 351; and meaning of life, 424–27 *passim*
Dostoevsky, Fyodor: and Grand Inquisitor, 107; and Modernism, 165; and psychic life, 183–84; and cultural criticism, 255; and Myshkin, 348
Douglass, Frederick: and commonplace, 325; as classic, 327
Doyle, Arthur Conan: and Sherlock Holmes on commonplace, 182
Duchamp, Marcel: and Modernism, 287
Dunlap, Knight: on habit, 188–89
Durkheim, Émile: and social theory, 165; on society, 179; and anomie, 208, 428–29; and Modernism, 244; and Freud, 244; and Rousseau, 428–29

E

Eco, Umberto: and comedy, 339
Eichmann, Adolf: and banality of evil, 173
Einstein, Albert: and Modernism, 163, 164; as outsider, 322
Eliot, George: and *Middlemarch*, 54, 348, 422–23; and Realism, 178; and banality, 192
Eliot, T. S.: and London in *The Waste Land*, 59; and Modernism, 168; and banality, 173, 187, 194; and self-consciousness, 199, 200, 218–19
Engelman, Edmund: and Freud, 237–41
Engels, Friedrich: and Karl Marx, 226–27, 229, 230; and Eleanor Marx, 228, 230; and William Morris, 231
Enlightenment: and *restaurants*, 22; and "civil society," 60; and rationality, 93; and church, 147; and commonplace, 174; and historicism, 177; and self-consciousness, 201
Epictetus: and *Tristram Shandy*, 352
Essex House Hotel, NY: design of, 28–33
ethics: and humanism, 56; of civility,

58–63; of style, 68, 70, 75–83 *passim*; Wilde on 72–74, 77–82; Aristotle on, 87–88, 188, 283, 420–21, 437–41 *passim*; existentialism and, 191–92, 423–24; and morality and meaning of life, 432–41

Everdell, William R.: on Modernism, 161–66, 167

existentialism: and Clarissa Dalloway, 56; and Sartre, 190–92, 220, 222, 245; and meaning of life, 423–25

F

feminism: and Virginia Woolf, 51, 62; and liberals, 96; and Eleanor Marx, 227–29

feng shui: and dining room, 18; at Felix, 44

Feuer, Lewis: and Eleanor Marx, 226

Fichte, Johann Gottlieb: and self-consciousness, 204

Flaubert, Gustave: and Modernism, 165, 243; as cultural critic, 176, 251; and banality, 178, 187; on habit, 188; and Eleanor Marx, 225, 229; and *Madame Bovary*, 229

Fontane, Theodor: and banality, 176

Four Seasons Hotel, NY: design of, 35–38

Frank, Joseph: on Modernism, 169–70

Frankel, Charles: and humanism/humanities, 307–10

Freud, Ernst: and Freud, 237–38

Freud, Sigmund: and *Civilization and Its Discontents*, 54; and Virginia Woolf, 56; on human nature, 92; and Modernism, 163, 241; and appearances, 183; and naturalists, 184; and commonplace, 184–85, 186; and Heidegger, 191; and guilt, 216; and Kafka, 218; life and works of, 235–46; and Vienna, 235–37; as bourgeois, 238–42; and fantasy, 282, 421; and Lacan, 245; and Proust on memory, 402n; and emotions, 413; and oceanic feeling, 419; and happiness, 421

Fromm, Erich: and escape from freedom, 107

G

Gabler, Neal: on American culture, 279–84, 286

Garibaldi, [Giuseppi]: Pirandello and, 219

Gates, Henry Louis, Jr.: on classics, 324–25

Gauguin, Paul: and cultural alienation, 168, 252

Gautama, Siddhartha: as Buddha, 418

Gautier, Théophile: and Wilde, 77; and irony, 205; and self-consciousness, 206

Gay, Peter: on Gropius, 187; on Modernism, 206; on Freud, 239–40, 241

Gide, André: and Wilde, 67; and *The Immoralist*, 67, 244; and self-consciousness, 221; and cultural alienation, 252

Giedion, Sigfried: and commonplace, 179

Goethe, Johann von: and self-consciousness, 203, 207, 221–23; on *Tristram Shandy*, 338; and meaning of life, 419

Goffman, Erving: on role-playing, 60–61
Goncourt, [brothers]: and Realism, 198; on appearances, 181
Gordon, Lyndall: on T. S. Eliot, 218
Gray, Rose: and River Café, 47, 49
Gregory VII, Pope: and self-consciousness, 202
Greenspan, Alan: and rational markets, 94
Gropius, Walter: and commonplace, 187
Guattari, Félix: and Freud, 246
guilt: and self-consciousness, 199, 210–20, 223; nature of, 210–11; Hawthorne and, 211–13, 216; Kierkegaard and, 211, 213–16, 217; Kafka and, 216–18; Sartre and, 220; in America, 242

H

habit: and banality, 187–90; history of, 188; Proust on, 189, 404–05; William James on, 397–98, 404–05
Hall, G. Stanley: and Freud, 242; and adolescence, 256
Hardie, Keir: and Eleanor Marx, 225
Hardison, O. B.: and humanism, 307, 310–11
Hartley, Florence: on table manners, 13–14
Hartman, Geoffrey: on self-consciousness, 205
Hassan, Ihab: on Postmodernism, 261
Hawthorne, Nathaniel: and psychic life, 183; and self-consciousness and guilt, 211–14, 216
Hegel, [Georg Wilhelm Friedrich]: and history, 177; and self-consciousness, 200, 204, 214
Heidegger, Martin: philosophy of, 191; and Sartre, 191; and Proust, 373
Henry III, King: and La Tour d'Argent, 21; and fork, 21, 23
Henry IV, King: and La Tour d'Argent, 21
Henry, Patrick: and church and state, 141, 142
Herder, J. G.: and history, 177
Herzen, Alexander: and cultural criticism, 255
Hesse, Hermann: and *Demian*, 240
Hinduism: and Islam in India, 122
Hitler, Adolf: and Nietzsche, 70
Hobbes, Thomas: and conservatism, 90
Hobsbawm, E. J.: on Eleanor Marx, 230
Hoffmann, E. T. A.: and self-consciousness, 204
Hofstadter, Richard: on educational theory, 181
Holmes, Sherlock: and commonplace, 182, 186; and Kafka, 193; and Eleanor Marx, 226
Homer: and *Iliad*, 54
Horkheimer, Max: and mass culture, 276
Hughes, H. Stuart: on social theory, 165; and self-consciousness, 200–01; on France, 245
humanism (humanities): and *Mrs. Dalloway* and *Iliad*, 54; and ethics, 56; and Aristotle, 88; principles of, 122, 125, 129; and radical Islam, 123–24; and human rights, 125; and cultural studies, 166; and Modernism, 171; and French

culture, 253; and humanists, 295–97; and education, 295–335 *passim*; and humanities, 301–12; uses of, 301–12 *passim*; and modern culture, 302–07; and meaning of life, 409–46 *passim*

human rights. *See* rights

Huntington, Samuel P.: and clash of civilizations, 121

Husserl, Edmund: and Modernism, 163; and phenomenology, 191

Huxley, Aldous: and *Brave New World*, 108, 284

Huysmans, Joris-Karl: and decadence, 252; and Wilde, 253

Hyndman, [H. M.]: and socialism, 229, 230

I

Ibsen, Henrik: Eleanor Marx and, 225, 228–29, 232; and "Life Lie," 310

irony: Romantic, 205; Postmodern, 171, 262–66, 271, 275

Islam: in India, 122; and West, 121–29 *passim*; radical, 123–24; and human rights, 125, 127

Isocrates: and education, 302–03

J

Jacobs, Jane: on city planning, 260

Jaeger, Werner: on ancient education, 302

James, Henry: and Clarissa Dalloway, 56; and Modernism, 168; and appearances, 186; style of and Proust, 379; and attention, 399; and *The Beast in the Jungle*, 433

James, William: and stream of consciousness, 53, 396–97; and Modernism, 164; and Freud, 184, 238; on habit, 188, 404–05; on vagueness, 376, 379; anti-materialism of, 396; and Bergson, 396; on consciousness and attention, 396–98; and Proust, 397–98; and pragmatism, existentialism, meaning of life, 423–24

Janouch, Gustav: and Kafka, 193

Jarry, Alfred: and *Ubu Roi*, 243–44, 252

Jefferson, Thomas: on rationality and rights, 88; and equality, 97; and *Marbury v. Madison*, 132; on church and state, 134, 140–42, 144, 145, 154; on *Tristram Shandy*, 338

Johnston, William M.: on Vienna, 236

Joyce, James: and Modernism, 164, 165, 168; on history, 178; and *Tristram Shandy*, 338

K

Kadoorie, Michael: and Starck at Peninsula Hotel, 41–42

Kafka, Franz: and banality, 193–95; and self-consciousness of guilt, 216–18; and Kierkegaard, 217

Kammen, Michael: on popular/mass culture, 276–79, 280, 282, 284, 286, 289

Kandinsky, Vassily: painting by, 158; and Modernism, 164

Kant, Immanuel: and aesthetic education, 310–11; and beauty, 418

Kapp, Yvonne: on Eleanor Marx, 226, 228, 230, 231, 232; on Marxism, 231

Kautsky, Karl: and Eleanor Marx, 230, 231

Keats, John: and commonplace, 179; and self-consciousness, 205
Keller, Helen: on words, 316–17
Kennedy, Justice Anthony: and same-sex marriage, 138
Kierkegaard, [Soren]: and self-consciousness, 204; and guilt, 211, 213–16; and Kafka, 217
Klimt, Gustav: and Vienna, 235, 236
Kokoschka, Oskar: and Vienna, 236
Kracauer, Siegfried: and psychic life in film, 185
Kramer, Hilton: and Modernism, 161, 169

L

La Bruyère, [Jean de]: and self-consciousness, 202
Lacan, Jacques: and Freud and psychoanalysis, 245–46
Lafargue, Paul: and Laura Marx, 225–26
Laforgue, Jules: on Baudelaire, 209, 210
Lakoff, George: on framing, 93
Langbaum, Robert: on self-consciousness, 199
La Rochefoucauld, [François de]: and self-consciousness, 202
La Tour d'Argent: in history, 21–26 *passim*
Lalique, René: and Art Deco, 29
Laverdant, Gabriel-Désiré: on avant-garde, 251
laughter: and courtier, 12; and Wilde, 74, 77, 82–83; Nietzsche on, 77, 83; humanity of, 337–54 *passim*; and *Tristram Shandy*, 337–54; and comedy, 338–40; and sex in *Tristram Shandy*, 343–44; and pretense in *Tristram Shandy*, 345–47; Sterne on, 353–54; and comedy in Proust, 380–86
Lenin, [Vladimir]: against labor unions, 231
Leontiev, Konstantin: and cultural criticism, 255
Leuchtenberg, William E.: on Charles Frankel, 308, 309
liberalism: and conservatism, 87–99 *passim*, 135–53 *passim*; and church and state, 133–53 *passim*
Lincoln, Abraham: and humanism, 309
Lissagaray, Prosper-Olivier: and Eleanor Marx, 228
Locke, John: quotation, 86; and liberalism on rationality, 88; and self-consciousness, 200, 201; and association of ideas, 342; and Sterne, 342
Lombroso, Cesare: and criminology, 255
Longuet, Charles: and Jenny Marx, 225
Loos, Adolf: and Modernism, 263
Lovejoy, Arthur: and Romanticism, 203
Lukacs, Georg: on Modernism, 193
Lyotard, Jean-François: on Postmodernism, 263, 266, 275

M

Machiavelli, [Niccolò]: and human nature, 90, 96; and education, 333
Madison, James: on human nature and

Index

politics, 91–92; and conservatives, 95; and liberals, 96; and civility, 98; and *Marbury v. Madison*, 131–32; and church and state, 140–43, 145, 147, 154; and faction, 145

Maistre, Joseph de: on conservative view of human nature, 91

Mann, Thomas: and *Death in Venice*, 78; and Modernism, 168; and *Doctor Faustus*, 207

manners: and style, 3–5; and democracy, 6, 178; history of, and dining room, 11–14, 17, 19; dining, George Washington on, 13; Molière and ridicule of, 13; and new restaurant etiquette, 22–23; and *Mrs. Dalloway*, 53, 58–59, 63; and Rights of Civility, 98; Burke on, 98–99; bourgeois, 240; Freud and, 241; Proust and, 382–83

Marbury, William: and *Marbury v. Madison*, 132

Marcuse, Herbert: and Freud, 243

Marinetti, F. T.: and Futurism, 254–55

Marrou, H. I.: on ancient education, 302

Marshall, Chief Justice John: and *Marbury v. Madison*, 131–32, 135

Marx, Eleanor: life and work, 225–32; and feminism, 227–28, 229; and Ibsen and Flaubert, 228–29; as socialist, 228–31; and Marxism, 230–32; and Modernism, 232

Marx, Karl: on human nature and communism, 89, 178; and Eleanor, 225–32 *passim*; and history, 177; and appearances, 181; bourgeois sensibility of, 227

Marxism: and revisionism, 230–31

Masaccio: painting, *The Expulsion from the Garden of Eden*, 198

Maugham, W. Somerset: and "Salvatore," 349

Mill, John Stuart: on rationality and individualism, 88–89; and society, 178–79; and appearances, 181; and self-consciousness, 205; and Wordsworth, 305

Modernism: and Virginia Woolf, 52, 53, 59, 62, 403; and cultural rebellion, 83; in Western culture, 157–292 *passim*; and Postmodernism, 157, 171, 260–67, 275; origins, character, and history of, 159–71, 258–61, 275; and humanism, 171; and banality, 173–76 *passim*; and Realism, 186; and self-consciousness, 196, 199–225 *passim*; Eleanor Marx and, 232; and Vienna, 235–37; Freud and, 236, 241; in France, 243–44; Barzun on, 287; Proust and, 403–04

Molière: and manners, 13, 282

Montaigne, Michel de: and banality, 174; and self-consciousness, 200, 202; on reading and education, 318, 319, 325, 326; and Proust, 394; as skeptic, 415

Montesquieu: *Spirit of the Laws*, 177

Morris, William: and commonplace in art, 180, 187; and Eleanor Marx, 229–31; and trade unions, 230

Moore, Judge Roy: and church and state, 152

Museum of Modern Art: and history of Modernism, 160

INDEX

Musil, Robert: and self-consciousness, 200

Musset, Alfred de: and self-consciousness, 207, 208, 221

N

Natanson, Maurice: on phenomenology, 190

naturalism: and commonplace, 184, 185; and Modernism, 187

Nazis: and Freud, 238–39; and Nietzsche, 251; and Degenerate Art, 256

Nietzsche, Elisabeth: and brother, 251

Nietzsche, Friedrich: on style, 5, 75–77; on art and artists, 62, 75; life and death of, 65, 68–70 *passim*; and Wilde, 65–81; Nordau on, 66–67; and Gide, 67, 252; as cultural critic, 68–70, 83, 175–76, 250; on resentment, 69; and morality, 69–70, 75–77, 83, 195–96, 437; and Modernism, 83, 165; and banality, 173, 175; and history, 178; and Nazis, 251; and untruth, 310; on reading, 315, 318, 319, 334, 338; on pedantry, 323; on *Tristram Shandy*, 338; on laughter, 354; and emotions, 435

Nordau, Max: on Nietzsche and Wilde, 66–67; as cultural critic, 255–57; and *Degeneration*, 255–56; and Tolstoy, 255–58

O

Obama, Barack: and liberal rationality, 87, 89

O'Connor, Justice Sandra Day: on church and state, 138

Okubo, Miné: and Japanese internment, 113, 114

Ortega y Gasset, [José]: and Nietzsche, 70; and Modernism, 162, 259; and historicism, 177; on mass culture, 276

Orwell, George: and *1984*, 93, 101–08, 115; on language and politics, 93, 101–02, 103, 105–06; and liberals, 96; and freedom, 101; and "goodthink," 102, 330–31; and radical Islam, 124

P

Parsons, Talcott: on Freud and Durkheim, 244

Pater, Walter: and Virginia Woolf, 53; and Wilde, 77

Pei, I. M.: and Four Seasons Hotel, 35, 36, 37

Peninsula Hotel, Hong Kong: and Felix design, 41–44

phenomenology: and commonplace, philosophy of, 190–91

Piano, Renzo: as architect, 48

Picasso, [Pablo]: and Modernism, 164, 168

Pirandello, Luigi: and self-consciousness, 219, 221–22; childhood of, 219; and Proust, 369, 376

Pitt, William: and *Tristram Shandy*, 339, 353

Plato: and irrationality, 89–90; and banality, 174; and self-consciousness, 202; on low art, 280; and democracy, 290; and education,

302–03, 317, 324, 327, 332; and goodness in literature, 348; and Socrates, 420, 430; and idealism, 430

Plotinus: and self-consciousness, 202

Popper, Karl: *The Open Society and Its Enemies*, 90

popular culture: characteristics of, 267–69, 276–84; and Tolstoy, 268–69, 271; Plato on, 280; Aristotle on, 283

Porter, Cole: "Anything Goes," 287

Postmodernism: as design, Four Seasons Hotel, 35, 36, 37–38; and Starck, 42; and Richard Rogers, 47; and Modernism, 42, 83, 160, 167, 170–71; origins and character of, 160, 260–67, 275; and Tolstoy, 266–68, 271

Pound, Ezra: and Modernism, 262

Proust, Marcel: and Modernism, 164–65, 403; and commonplace, 186; on habit, 189, 405–06; and *À la Recherche du temps perdu*, 357–406; on memory, 359–64, 400–03, 406; on art, 360–63, 389, 403–04; on time, 360, 363–67, 370–75; and *The Thousand and One Nights*, 367; and WWI, 369n, 370; and Dreyfus Affair, 370–71; on consciousness, 373, 395–400, 402n; and William James, 376, 396–98, 404–05; and comedy, 380–86; on love, 385–92; and Bergson, 396–97; Virginia Woolf and, 403

Q

Quetelet, Adolphe: and statistics, 179

R

Rabelais: and Sterne, 340

Realism: and commonplace, 179–80; and psychic life, 183; Dostoevsky on, 183–84; Apollinaire on, 186; and Modernism, 186, 402; and Kafka, 193; Proust on, 362, 398

Redgrave, Vanessa: and *Mrs. Dalloway*, 52

Renaissance: and dining room, 11; and Castiglione, 61, 329; and historical consciousness, 177; and self-consciousness, 202; Tolstoy on, 257; Barzun on, 287; and humanism, 302; and Machiavelli, 333

resentment: and culture, 7; Nietzsche on, 69, 72; and right-wing politics, 95; and entertainment, 290; Mark Twain on, 337

restaurant: origins and history of, 13, 21–26

Richelieu, Cardinal: and La Tour d'Argent, 21

Richter, Jean Paul: and self-consciousness, 204

rights: Equal, Amendment, 87; natural, 88, 91; of Man, 90; of Civility, 96–99; and Fourth Amendment, 111; human, and humanism, 121, 125; and women and Islam, 127; homosexual, 134; civil, 138; Bill of, 140; John Stuart Mill on, 178

Rilke, Rainer Maria: on Tolstoy, 249

Rimbaud, Arthur: and Modernism, 164; as *poète maudit*, 252

Rochberg, George: and Postmodernism, 261

INDEX

Rochon, Pierre Yves: and Art Deco design at Essex House, 29, 31, 32–33

Rogers, Richard: as architect and River Café, 47–49

Romanticism (Romanticists): and commonplace, 179; and psychic life, 183; and self-consciousness, 200, 203–06; Lovejoy on, 203; and Modernism, 202–07; Barzun on, 287; and empathy, 435

Rose, Phyllis: on Clarissa Dalloway, 54–55; and Virginia Woolf, 62

Roze de Chantoiseau, Mathurin: as first *restaurateur*, 22

Roosevelt, Franklin D.: and Japanese internment, 112

Rousseau, Jean-Jacques: on education, 319, 333, 334, 345; and morality, 350; and Durkheim and anomie, 428–29; and Buddhism, 428–29, 439–40; and empathy, 435

Ruhlmann, Émile-Jacques: and Art Deco, 28, 29, 31–32

Ruskin, John: and Wilde, 78

Russell, Bertrand: and Modernism, 163

S

Sartre, Jean-Paul: and habit, 190; and commonplace, 190–92; philosophy of, 190–92; and Surrealism, 190, 245; and self-consciousness, 220–21, 222, 223; and Freud, 245; and existentialism and meaning of life, 423–24

Scalia, Justice Antonin: and church and state, 136–38, 140, 153

Schiele, Egon: and Vienna, 235, 236

Schiller, Friedrich: and self-consciousness, 204–05, 206; and aesthetic education, 311

Schlegel, Friedrich: and irony, 205; on rumination, 315

Schorske, Carl: on Vienna, 236, 251

Schreiner, Olive: and Eleanor Marx, 227

Schwarz, Daniel R.: on Modernism, 161, 166–70

Scopes, John: and monkey trial, 150–51

Scott, [Sir Walter]: and history, 177

Sennett, Richard: and appearances, 187

Shakespeare, William: and trifles, 195; and self-consciousness, 202

Sharlet, Jeff: on church and state, 136

Shaw, George Bernard: and Nietzsche, 70, 251; and Modernism, 162; and Eleanor Marx, 225, 228–29; on Tolstoy, 249; on Nordau, 256

Shikibu, Murasaki: as classic, 327

Sitter, John: on humanities, 309

skepticism: and self-consciousness, 202; and humanism, 407–42 *passim*

Skinner, B. F.: on habit, 189

Smiles, Samuel: on habit, 188

Smith, Adam: on rationality and economics, 88; on free market, 94; and moral sentiments, 350

Smith, Page: and Japanese internment, 111

Socrates: and self-consciousness, 203; on culture, 290; and education, 302–03, 332; and humanism, 309, 311; on writing, 302, 311, 317; and

meaning of life, 416–17, 420, 423; and idealism, 420, 427
Solzhenitsyn, [Aleksandr]: and Ivan Denisovich, 192–93, 415
Sommer, Elke: and Essex House, 33
Sorel, Georges: on human nature and politics, 92; and liberalism, 96
Souter, Justice David: and church and state, 137
Starck, Philippe: and design of Felix, 41–44; and Postmodernism, 42; and River Café, 49
Stendhal: and history, 177
Stern, Fritz: on cultural despair, 251
Sterne, Laurence: and laughter, 337–54 *passim*; and *Tristram Shandy*, 337–54; praise of, 338; on wit, 339–40; and association of ideas, 342; and humor of sex, 343–44; against pretense, 345–50; and vision of life, 351–54
Strachey, James and Lytton: and Virginia Woolf, 56
style: import and varieties of, 1–83 *passim*; in life and culture, 3–8, 33; and dining room, 11, 16–19; and restaurants, 22–49 *passim*; of life, and Essex House, 29–33; and Art Deco, 29–33, 36; of life, and Starck, 43; of life, and Richard Rogers, 48, 49; literary, and Virginia Woolf, 52–53; and Clarissa Dalloway, 55, 58–59, 61, 62; ethics of, Nietzsche and Wilde on, 68, 70, 75–83; and truth, Wilde on, 74, 79; artistic, Worringer on, 169; artistic, Nordau on, 255–56; and Postmodernism, 260–66; literary,

and Proust, 366, 393–94, 397
Surrealism: and Starck, 41; and commonplace, 186; and Freud, 186; and Sartre, 190, 245; and France, 244–45; and Lacan, 245
superficiality: uses and misuses of, 320–23
Swift, Jonathan: and Sterne, 340
Symons, Arthur: and decadence, 253

T

Tailharde, Laurent: and anarchism, 254
Takei, George: and Japanese internment, 114
Talmon, Jacob L.: on humanities, 309
Terrail, Claude: and La Tour d'Argent, 21
Thompson, E. P.: and Marxism, 231
Thousand and One Nights, The: as framed story, 367; Proust and, 367
Tieck, Ludwig: and self-consciousness, 204
Tison-Braun, Micheline: on French culture, 253
Tocqueville, Alexis de: and manners, 58–59; and conservatism, 95, 145–46, 149; on church and state, 145–49, 155; as cultural critic, 175, 180–81, 285–86; and mass culture, 277
Tolstoy, Leo: and history, 178; and *War and Peace*, 178, 348, 419; and appearances, 184; and *Anna Karenina*, 194, 425–28; and *What Is Art?*, 249–72 *passim*; as cultural critic, 255–60; and meaning of life, 419, 422, 426–28
Trilling, Lionel: and Modernism, 162,

165, 200, 258; and *Anna Karenina*, 194
Tsuzuki, Chushichi: and Eleanor Marx, 226
Turkle, Sherry: on psychoanalysis in France, 243–45
Twain, Mark: on humor, 337
Tzu, Chuang: Wilde and, 74

U

Unamuno, Miguel de: and Spanish cultural revival, 254

V

Verdoia, Ken: and Topaz, 114, 117
Venturi, Robert: and Postmodernism, 261, 264
Victorianism: as design, 14, 29; moral values of, Wilde on, 71, 73–74, 78, 253; and Karl Marx, 227; and Eleanor Marx, 225, 231, 232; Matthew Arnold on classics and, 318
Villiers de l'Isle-Adam, [Auguste]: and decadence, 252
Voltaire: against church, 147; and cultural history, 177; and commonplace, 179; and Pangloss on education, 331, 333; and Pangloss and *Tristram Shandy*, 352

W

Wagner, Richard: Nietzsche on, 75, 250; Nordau and Tolstoy on, 256
Wallace, David Foster: and Postmodernism, 265
Walter, Wolf: and Essex House, 33
Warhol, Andy: and Postmodernism, 264–65; and celebrity, 281
Washington, George: on manners, 13; and church and state, 140
Weber, Max: and social theory, 165; and disenchantment, 186, 193
Wiesel, Elie: and commonplace, 325
Wilde, Oscar: on triviality, 55, 413; and Nietzsche, 65–83 *passim*; Nordau on, 66–67; as cultural rebel, 70–75; on earnestness, 73–75; on art, 77–81; and ethics of style, 80–83; and decadence, 253; and Modernism, 262; and Postmodernism, 265; and Tolstoy, 266
Wilhelm I, Kaiser: and Dinner of Three Emperors, 24
Woolf, Virginia: and *Mrs. Dalloway*, 51–63; career of, 51–55; and feminism, 51, 53; on writing *Mrs. Dalloway*, 53–54; and Modernism, 164; and Sterne, 338; and Proust, 403; and *To the Lighthouse* on meaning of life, 412–13
Wordsworth, William: and commonplace, 179; and "savage torpor," 256, 283; and, J. S. Mill, 305; and memory and Proust, 401; and meaning of life, 416, 420
World War I: in *Mrs. Dalloway*, 56; and Modernism, 165, 167, 244, 258; and cultural revival, 255; and Dadaism, 258; and popular culture, 278–79; Barzun on, 287, 289; and Proust, 369n, 370–71, 378, 381
World War II: and Orwell on language, 93; and Japanese internment, 111–19 *passim*; and mass culture, 278; Barzun and, 279

Worringer, Wilhelm: and Modernism, 161, 169–70
Wright, Frank Lloyd: and Richard Rogers, 48

Y

Yew, Lee Kuan: and Asian values, 123

Z

Zola, Émile: and appearances, 184; and fatalism, 187

www.ingramcontent.com/pod-product-compliance
Lightning Source LLC
Chambersburg PA
CBHW071226070526
44583CB00017B/2071